THE LUSIADS
OF
LUIZ DE CAMÕES

Much have I voyaged in the realms of gold.

> . . . *nor could his eye not ken*
> *The empire of Negus to his utmost port,*
> *Ercoco, and the less maritim kings,*
> *Mombaza, and Quiloa, and Melind,*
> *And Sofala, thought Ophir, to the realm*
> *Of Congo, and Angola farthest south.*

PARADISE LOST, BOOK XI, 396–401

> . . . *As when to them who sail*
> *Beyond the Cape of Hope, and now are past*
> *Mozambic, off at sea north-east winds blow*
> *Sabéan odors from the spicy shore*
> *Of Araby the blest; with such delay*
> *Well pleas'd they slack their course, and many a league*
> *Chear'd with the grateful smell old Ocean smiles.*

PARADISE LOST, BOOK IV, 159–165

THE LUSIADS
OF
LUIZ DE CAMÕES

TRANSLATED BY

LEONARD BACON

WITH AN INTRODUCTION
AND NOTES

THE HISPANIC SOCIETY OF AMERICA
NEW YORK / 1950

TO
CONSTANCE AND ALICE
BIDDLE

CONTENTS

PREFACE

NO APOLOGY is necessary for a new translation of a poem, concerning which it was known from the first that "its destiny was to wander everlastingly through the hearts of men." The task has been absorbing, however it may have tried or baffled the spirit. But the translator hopes that he has brought some vestiges of original splendor across the oceanic gap that separates Languages and Times, and that the work may help the English or American reader to a better understanding of the race that carried on the great explorations and founded the gigantic Commonwealth of Brazil. The author of the Books of the Maccabees knew the proper thing to say at such a juncture: "If I have done well, and as is fitting the story, it is that which I desired; but if meanly and slenderly, it is that which I could attain unto."

No one ever had more vigorous and delightful assistance than the translator. All ages and both sexes have leaped to his aid, as if he were drowning, which was not infrequently the case. It is pleasant to be specific.

Professors W. T. Brewster, R. Selden Rose, and Raymond T. Hill have read the manuscript entire, and their marginal comments, though often wormwood in the cup, have been invaluable. The same may be said of the observations of Mr. Harold M. Landon, Mr. William Rose Benét, and Mr. Ferris Greenslet. Mr Harry Lydenberg, Director Emeritus of the New York Public Library, his successor, Mr. Ralph A. Beals (quondam discipulus meus), Mr. James T. Babb of the Yale University Library, and Mr. Lawrence C. Wroth of the John Carter Brown Library have helped me over many places where the going was rough. I am specially indebted to Professor Francis M. Rogers of Harvard College, who not only sent me much hard-won information beyond my ken, but tore my notes to pieces, aided and abetted by some brilliant students, to my infinite advantage. Two of these young men, in particular, I must mention with real appreciation, Mr. Edward Glaser and Mr. J. R. Fonseca. Professors Alfred L. Kroeber, David G. Mandelbaum, T. Harper Goodspeed, Andrew C. Lawson, Robert P. Blake, Ivan M. Linforth, Clarence W. Mendell, and Franklin Edgerton have given me the benefit of their special knowledge of such fields as Anthropology, Botany, Geology, Greek and Latin Literature, and Religion in Ancient India. Nor should I forget Dr. John K. Wright of the American Geographic Society, or Dr. Robert Cushman Murphy of the American Museum of Natural History, for the unfailing kindness with which they endeavored to diminish my ignorance. For various aid and comfort I must thank Mr. Henry Clapp Smith, Dr. Lewis Hanke, Mrs. Alexander Knox, Mrs. Henry R. Hilliard, Jr., Professor C. B. Tinker, Mr. Wilmarth S. Lewis, Dr. Karl Vogel, Professor Henry Roberts, Professor C. R. Boxer, Dr. Harold V. Livermore, Mr. John T. Westlake, Mr. Alfred Noyes, Professor Jacques Le Clercq, Mrs. Mae Y. Ellis, Professor William Howel Williams, Mrs. Willard H. Durham, and the Misses Constance and Alice Biddle. My Secretary, Mrs. Dorothy Browning, has copied the text five stricken times and the notes twice, nor can I be sufficiently grateful for her patient and painstaking thoroughness. And my wife and my three daughters have not only borne with me during five years of monomania, but have criticized, suggested, and given me good counsel generally.

The publication of such a work in times like these is a matter of difficulty. Professor J. D. M. Ford of Harvard College, one of our most distinguished Camonians, has from the first taken an interest in this enterprise. In the kindness of his heart, he suggested that I approach the Hispanic Society of America. To that Society and to its founder, Mr. Archer M. Huntington, who has labored in the Iberian vineyard for a lifetime, I express such thanks as may be permitted to real gratitude, always at a disadvantage when confronted by real generosity.

INTRODUCTION

I.
LUIZ VAZ DE CAMÕES

HOWEVER good the guesses, however elaborate the researches, it must be admitted in all honesty that very little is known about Camões. The diarist and the memoir writer were rare birds in the 16th Century and contemporary biographies of men of letters had not yet become an endemic pest. Accordingly, exact information about a poet who has been the object of loving admiration for eleven generations in his own country and all over the world is as limited as exact information about his younger contemporary, Shakespeare, and for the same reasons. We may put it in a nutshell. Fifty-six years, which was his life span, add up to some 20,000 days. Not counting at least one term in prison, we can say with some certainty where he was, or what he was doing, or that something momentous for him happened, on perhaps thirty of those allotted days. Some things we perhaps have the right to infer, but always with caution. And above all it is necessary to beware of that strange tissue of intuition, picturesque gossip, and actual invention founded on the second-hand, the nonexistent, or the impossible, which is the Camonian myth.

From an entry in a register of enlistments for the Indies, which, if it be genuine, is properly considered equivalent to a birth certificate, because (as is alleged) the poet's father was there to vouch for his son, it appears that he was born sometime in 1524, but whether in Lisbon or elsewhere conflicting traditions do not help us to decide. He was descended from a noble Galician family which fled to Portugal in 1369, having taken the wrong side in a quarrel which was duly decided when Bertrand Duguesclin barred the tent door while Henry of Trastamare was engaged in the congenial task of murdering his half-brother, Peter the Cruel. The founder of the Portuguese House of Camões appears to have been unlucky in his political guesswork, for, as Juromenha remarks, he managed to lose everything for the second time when he had the bad taste to fight for the Spanish party at Aljubarrota, in 1385, against the great John I. But there is a tradition that he was a poet of parts and perhaps wrote several Galician sonnets often included among the works of his more celebrated descendant. The family was sufficiently distinguished, though never powerful. And its fortunes did not increase. The poet's father, Simon Vaz de Camões, was a poor gentleman entitled to a coat-of-arms, of whom nothing of importance is known except that he resided at Coimbra for some time and later at Lisbon. Oddly enough he appears to have been related to Vasco da Gama. The story that he too went to the Indies requires more proof. The name of the poet's mother was Anna de Sa de Macedo and that is nearly all that we can say of her. If recollection and information are correct, there is not one direct allusion to either of his parents in any of Camões' works. But nothing can be inferred from this. The 16th Century seldom played up such matters.

Did he spend his childhood in Coimbra? Even the most assured ask the question. And when did he attend the University? Professor Prestage thinks it was from 1539 to 1542, but it could be pushed back a year or two without much difficulty, though it could hardly be brought forward. We know nothing much, except that Camões cannot mention the town or the meadows of the Mondego, already legendary because of the tragedy of Ignes de Castro nearly two centuries before, without bursts of infectious excitement. It has been supposed that an uncle of the poet, Dom Bento de Camões, was a figure in the University, and that the poet addressed to him a sonnet and a precocious prototype of his elegies. But it has been thought more likely that Bento de Camões, although a relative, was a mere fellow student. The biographers do not hesitate to provide him with several friends, the brothers Gonçalo and Alvaro de Silveira, and, with less probability, Jorge de Montemayor, the author of the celebrated "Diana." The Martyrdom of Gonçalo de Silveira in East Africa is mentioned explicitly in the Lusiads, and Sonnet XXXIX evidently concerns him.

The University of Coimbra, founded more than two centuries before Camões matriculated by the most attractive of kings, Dinis "o Lavrador," was a remarkable institution. At the moment John III, the Peaceable, took a great interest in it for religious rather than intellectual reasons, and men of the first reputation were attracted to its various faculties from every part of Europe. But Camões did not sit at the feet of George Buchanan, the humanist, who could not have arrived till after the poet had departed. The editors repeat with gusto that the standard of excellence was such that it was discreditable to an undergraduate if he conversed except in Latin or Greek, in spite of which it would seem to be a sound opinion that Camões was not expert in the latter tongue. This last statement is of course tentative. But a fairly diligent search has failed to reveal in any work, certainly his, any allusion to classic literature, which can be proved to be derived directly from the Greek, whereas the echoes of Ovid, of Virgil, of Horace, of Catullus, are so numerous that it is hardly worth a man's while to indicate them.

If, as seems likely, Camões left the University and went to Lisbon in 1543 to make his fortune, he arrived at an exciting moment. Acute statesmen might be vaguely aware that Portugal had passed her peak. But there was little to show it. The empire founded by Manuel the Fortunate still kept up the appearance of expanding, as empires must. If they fail to, as has been frequently pointed out, they begin to wane. But the flag of the Algarve Castles and the Thirty Pence flew in the Moluccas, in Brazil, along both coasts of Africa and the west coast of India, in Ceylon, Sumatra, Malaya, and Indonesia generally. It had reached Japan the year before, and it would be natural if there was some buzzing on the Chiado about a presumably easy future conquest. The sciences and arts were initiating chain reactions all over Europe. But Portugal like Spain stood aloof from the intellectual and religious convulsions. And the young bachelor of arts from Coimbra would know nothing of a shadowy figure from the Low Countries who was robbing the gallows with a view to advancing the science of anatomy beyond anything Galen knew. Nor could he possibly have heard of an obscure Pole who died that year, but not before seeing the first copy of his book, in time destined to destroy the Ptolemaic system, which Camões was to expound with such magnificence. Calvin and Luther, rival antichrists in the sight of the young Portuguese, had been at war with Rome and with each other for a long time. Henry VIII in England had scandalized Europe by his divorces and his schisms, "which were intimately connected." In France, Francis I had created a similar sensation by allying himself with the Grand Turk against the Emperor. And that Emperor, the remarkable Charles V, who had sacked Rome and besieged a Pope seventeen years before, was vainly endeavoring to sweep back the heretic tide. Rabelais was satirizing what Saint Ignatius and Saint Teresa were passionately endeavoring to restore. Incidentally, the great humorist amused himself by making fun of Portuguese discovery. Titian and Michelangelo were still painting, and Vasari was writing the lives of great masters, many of them only recently dead, whom he could admire but not emulate. New poetry was in the air. Garcilaso de la Vega and Boscan, for whom Camões, explicitly or implicitly, expresses his admiration, were published this very year. And Portugal had her poets too, who were feeling, for good or for evil, the pressure of Italian influence. But the native poetry was still strong. It may be guessed that to a young poet, who came to Lisbon at the very height of her brilliance and perhaps with powerful patronage behind him, the world did not look unpromising.

What was done for him, or what he did for himself, is hidden from us, though he appears to have been much about the Court of John III. And it seems certain that on Good Friday, 1544, he saw a lady in church. A violent controversy now rages as to her identity. Many still believe that her name was Caterina de Ataide and that she died while Camões was in India. But there is a whole school devoted to the thesis that the one real love of Camões' life was the Infanta Maria, whose personal qualities have been equated with various passages in Camões' love poems. It has been reasonably held that Camões had at least four great passions. But the whole subject seems a mare's-nest of conjecture and intuition. This much may perhaps be said, that the Tenth Canzone, "By the Rivers of Babylon," and a number of the finest sonnets ever written by man could be to the address of one uncertainly identified Beatrice. At any rate, the glorious verses fly at Dante's pitch. And Camões had gone through some similar experience, for human passion had led him to the divine, as he himself states explicitly.

Be that as it may, it is probable that between his last years in Coimbra and 1550 or thereabouts he wrote three plays of some interest, but which was written first, second, or last, this translator will not pretend to decide, in the absence of any real evidence. El-Rei Seleuco (King Seleucus) is based on a story in Plutarch (Life of Demetrius) according to whom, Seleucus gave up his young wife Stratonice to his son Antiochus. It is not too exciting, but some of the commentators believe that it irritated John III, whose destined bride had been pre-empted by his father, Manuel the Fortunate. Camões seems to have been in trouble shortly after we believe, or fancy, it was played in 1545. His other two plays, we may guess, are near in time. Os Amfitrões (The Amphitryons), an imitation of Plautus, has real humor, and Portuguese admiration for Camões has not hesitated to compare his play favorably with Molière's variation on the same wellworn theme, the seduction of Alcmena by Jupiter in the form of her husband. Of Filodemo, there will be something to say a little later in this paper.

As stated above, Camões seems to have got into trouble with the Court some time around 1546. And upon a foundation of shadows a fabric of the imagination, as enormous, as unconvincing, and as self-contradictory as the Baconian theory, has been created. Camões had boasted too publicly of his amorous success. He had made love to a princess of the blood. He had hurt the King's feelings or violated the taboos imposed by a strait-laced Queen. Points of view are legion. And out of the laboring mountain comes a mouse. A young man in difficulties, concerning which we have no information, was rusticated to some point up the Tagus. It is a fair guess that he was visited by the Muse in his exile.

It seems probable that about this time the idea of the Lusiads began to possess him. If the Fourth Eclogue, as has been thought, on the strength of some nearly contemporary editorial tradition, was written in early youth, Camões was thinking of a poem, "which from hour to hour should increase the glory of Portugal and make Smyrna envious in spite of her being the birthplace of Homer." In support of this notion, Stanzas 5, 6, and 7 of the Seventh Book of the Lusiads may be adduced. In these stanzas he makes a vitriolic attack on the Kings of England and France. Now the phrase "duro Ingrês" would suit Henry VIII very well. It would be impossible to apply the expression to the child Edward VI, nor would it fit his sisters Mary and Elizabeth. If this reasoning is correct, then this stanza was written in the brutal Henry's lifetime. The King of France is excoriated in the remainder of the passage for not crusading against the Turk. And Francis I had actually made an alliance with Solyman the Magnificent, and in consequence was almost as popular as a Protestant in Portugal. Both kings died in 1547. And these stanzas would appear to have been written before that date and not later than Camões' twenty-third year.

Perhaps in 1547, the year of the birth of Cervantes, who would one day pay Camões the noblest of compliments, and who was to have plenty of trouble himself, the powers that were came to the conclusion that rustication on the Tagus was not a sufficient penalty, and he was sent to Ceuta on the African Coast across from Gibraltar. That fortress, since its capture by John I and his sons more than a century before, had been the Portuguese place d'armes in Morocco. But the invaders never got the Moors wholly down, and the wild horsemen raided "to the very walls." Service there, as I have gathered, was so hard that in Northern Portugal able-bodied men paid a tax which exempted them from being drafted across the Strait. In a vivid verse letter, attributed to Camões, we can still feel a man's tense loneliness and catch sight of barbaric cavalry. And it would seem that the simile of the lion of Ceuta in the Lusiads goes back to some real experience when horsemen in "the Tetuan country" surrounded and speared one of the great creatures. The lioness robbed of her whelps, and bellowing till all the echoes of the Mountain of the Seven Brothers are wakened, is evidently out of the same chapter of hardship and peril. In addition to his other misfortunes, Camões lost an eye in some fight by sea or land (there are two traditions) during this interlude.

xvi

In 1549 his exile, or term of service, was up, and according to Prestage, the poet returned to Lisbon in the train of Afonso da Noronha who had just been appointed Viceroy of India. The house of Noronha seems always to have been friendly to him, and he speaks highly of an earlier ruler of the name in his epic. But for some reason which we do not know he did not at the time embrace what would appear to have been an opportunity at the time. And it was not till 1550 that he enlisted for service in India in the presence of the official who recorded his age, as we have mentioned, and who added the detail that Camões had a red beard. This document as above stated is to some suspect. Yet still he did not go, and we know nothing definite about him till Corpus Christi Day, 1552, when a sharp, authentic, and terrifying light suddenly focuses on him. The religious feast had its carnival side, and a couple of maskers who were friends of Camões got into a brawl with a court official named Gonçalo Borges. The poet, who seems to have been accidentally drawn in and who, on his own say so, was a proper fellow of his hands, drew his weapon and stabbed the courtier, for which act he was promptly cast into prison. There he remained for eight months. Borges did not die, and, whether out of Christian charity or for other reason, not only did not prosecute but after receiving an apology on February 13, 1553, forgave the poet altogether. The King's pardon followed on March 7, and on March 23 Camões sailed for India on the "São Bento," the flagship of Fernão Alvares Cabral. Things had moved rapidly, and it was unlikely that he would see the visionary lady again. Whether he was exiled to India or went of his own accord is a point which we need not raise.

At any rate he was six months on the voyage from Lisbon to Goa. And it is a legitimate inference that the account of the storm off the Cape in the Third Elegy and the gigantic myth of Adamastor in the Lusiads are the results of that perilous sea-faring. In this connection it may be mentioned that the name of Adamastor seems to have been invented by Rabelais who died almost as Camões sailed. Table Mountain with its crown of cloud might have impressed itself on a far less imaginative mind. And one of the most wonderful of European eyes was viewing novel if less splendid stars as well as observing the waterspout swelling like a leech on the lip of a steer. The first great artist had crossed the Equator. But perhaps Camões did not at this time visit Mombassa and Quiloa and Melinde, all of them of interest to Gama, for it has been thought that Cabral, after weathering the Cape, pushed right across the Indian Ocean for Goa, where the "São Bento" arrived in September.

Something ought to be said about Goa dourada, "not golden but gilded," if only at second hand. The town was on an island at the mouth of a river, the Mandavi, about two hundred and fifty miles south of Bombay. Barros says that the Mandavi had been "stocked with crocodiles on purpose," an interesting method of defence. But, in spite of the crocodiles, Albuquerque took Goa from its Moselm prince permanently in 1510, after being ejected once. In forty-three years it had become the metropolis of the Portuguese Orient and perhaps had a population of 100,000, many of them Eurasians. The government and trade of the East were concentrated there, and it was the seat of the viceroys, who had to be fidalgos, or the governors, who might be of lower degree. These rulers, if they did not die of dysentery, usually made their fortunes in the normal term of three years. And most of them were able as well as avaricious. The place was full of palaces and great churches. There was enormous wealth, and vice to correspond. A 19th Century Portuguese frankly calls it Sodom. And Camões, who repeatedly expresses his hatred for the place, in a sonnet bitterly contrasts the monstrous boom town with the Sion of Lisbon. The Portuguese took up with native manners and customs, even "veiling their women." But in spite of intrigue and corruption, one thing ought to be noticed: Goa still belongs to Portugal, where other empires alter. Easy-going régimes may have a lot of staying power. Goa was the first European outpost in Asia and perhaps will be the last.

Camões, a few weeks after arriving in the huge, beautiful, and outrageous city, which he called "the mother of knaves and stepmother of honest men," went on an expedition against the King of Pimenta far south on the Malabar Coast. The force recaptured an island in favor of the King of Cochim, a steady ally of Portugal, and returned victorious, with some loss of life, as appears from the Third Elegy. After that he seems to have lived pleasantly in Goa for some time. The picturesque and much quoted statement, which illustrates the number of his quarrels at home—that in Lisbon he had seen the soles of the feet of many, but that none had ever seen the soles of his—may be exaggeration. But in Goa he was "more respected than a Merceana bull and quieter than a monk's cell."

It seems probable that in 1554, or early in 1555, he went on an expedition to Ormuz under the command of a young member of the great house of Meneses, a family which he mentions with respect several times in the Lusiads, as also in a sonnet. If we had no direct evidence that he had gone on such an expedition, we could still infer it from the minute account in the Lusiads of the Coast of the Persian Gulf, which is almost as meticulous as an Admiralty chart, though even here he could have found many a detail in Barros. Near this time the famous first Eclogue seems to have been written, which he considered to be better than his other performances till then. But poets, good or bad, are apt to feel that the latest is also the best. The poem is concerned with the death of his friend, Antonio de Noronha, of whom he speaks with a pathos well beyond the pastoral convention, as also with a death whose consequences he probably did not foresee, for the Infante John died at the same time, the father of the luckless and feckless Dom Sebastião.

In February, 1555, Camões can be located with some precision in what used to be Italian Somaliland, on the unpleasant shores of the Aromatic Cape, now called Guardafui, which is the easternmost point of Africa. It lies south of Arabia Felix, and southeast of Aden, where Albuquerque's imperial plans for taking Mecca had been foiled some forty years before Camões' arrival. And in general, except for a few irritating raids, the Portuguese had little success in the Red Sea regions. The naked, drab coast is powerfully described in the splendid Tenth Canzone, though with less vividness in the Lusiads, and a line in the lyric is the last line of the First Book of the epic. No one but an idiot can fail to feel the fire in his cry to the lost lady, whether she was Caterina or the Infanta Maria, from the uttermost parts of the sea. If she were

Caterina, he was never to be nearer to her again in space than when he watched the westward migrating birds on that disconsolate shore. But even a foreigner must notice at once the splendor of lines which remind one of Milton towering in his pride of place.

In the same year he returned from that abomination of desolation to Goa (apparently by way of Mombassa) in time for the inauguration of Francisco Barreto as Governor. Barreto appears to have been a just man, and, oddly enough, popular. Camões would presently get in his bad books, or so it is believed. But at the time all went well, and the poet's comedy Filodemo was performed for the first time, as part of the celebration. The play has a sort of Winter's Tale motif. A lovely peasant girl and her brother turn out to be of the blood royal. There are bright gleams of poetry in the comedy, but one may say farewell to Camões as a dramatist with no unbearable sense of discomfort, for he never got much above the level of, let us say, Love's Labor Lost.

In connection with the Barreto festivities Camões is supposed to have written two satiric pieces, one in prose and one in verse. The first, Satyra do Torneio (Satire on the Tourney), has lost most of its point (as most satires do), with the disappearance of its unimportant victims, who were local drunkards, gamesters, and such small deer. The legend is that it made Camões enemies. If so they were easily made, and to no purpose. But the Disparates na India (The Follies of India), which might well have made him enemies, is quite a different affair, and will make a man laugh today. The fire is much more accurate. And one sees that Joseph Sedley had come to India long before John Company. The peculiarities and personalities of Goa are dealt with unsparingly. And there is genuine contempt in the piece for the favorite local pastime, which was graft.

In 1556 it appears that he was sent to Macão, and perhaps to the Moluccas, though as always there is room for doubt. Some have supposed that this was exile in the second degree. To which it has been rejoined that it is a strange kind of exile which provides the victim with a chance to make a fortune. Camões seems to have had a big responsible job. He was the government official in charge of the effects of all persons dead or absent, and accountable for those properties. He probably arrived in Macão some two years after the Portuguese took it over peaceably from the Chinese. The history is a little obscure, but this resumé may clear it up somewhat. Earlier in the century the Portuguese had got a foothold on the south coast of China, where they did not behave well, and whence they were expelled after a general massacre conducted by the indignant natives. More enlightened proconsuls came along, and a punitive expedition destroyed a nest of river pirates who had defied the Chinese government. As a reward, the Son of Heaven granted his new allies the district of Macão across the big bay from Hongkong. Thenceforward, with some vicissitudes, the relations of East and West were scrupulously correct. And Macão is still a Portuguese possession. It is also said to be the wickedest city on earth, and the largest gambling hell. All this may have its interest, but it remained for the Senhora Vasconcelos to point out that nowhere in his works does Camões explicitly refer to a city in which he is supposed to have resided for two or three years. And it is odd that in the Lusiads, in his description of the Coasts of Asia, he passes from Cochin China and the Island of Hainan to a description of the Celestial Empire, without any mention of the Portuguese colony. However, to this day the so-called "Grotto of Camões" is exhibited to tourists who have never read a line of his poetry and don't intend to.

It is believed that at this time he may have visited the Island of Ternate. In the Lusiads he shows some read knowledge of the place. But, in his account of the birds of Paradise, he repeats the legend that the creatures lived on the wing till they died. Given his habitual veracity, if he had seen the birds alive, which he would have done in any protracted visit, he would not have set down such an absurdity. It is more probable that he may have touched there on some official voyage, that he saw the radiant plumage of the dead birds there, or elsewhere, and that he repeated the traveler's tale about them.

What follows is mainly silence for some years, unless a fine sonnet can be connected with the famous Grotto. Juromenha, whose guesses Prestage regards more highly than recent scholars are in the habit of doing, and who was certainly not always uninspired, did not hesitate to make the connection. But at the very best we cannot be sure. At the end of his service in Macão, if it was Macão, Camões found himself at odds with a superior, who ordered him back to Goa to be tried, apparently for malversation, in the city where that art was most efficiently practised. Sometime in 1559 his ship was wrecked near the mouth of the Mekong, the river of Cambodia, and one of the seven or eight greatest rivers of the world. He gives us an odd piece of philological information in this connection, for he translates the native name of the stream as "Captain of the Waters," in which he is followed by the Dutch explorer Linschoten, who came out in the Portuguese Service in 1583, perhaps with the 1572 Lusiads in his dunnage. Camões got safe to shore with the manuscript of the Lusiads, and was apparently kindly treated by the natives. But nothing could better illustrate the difficulties of Sixteenth Century navigation than the fact that it took him many months to reach Goa after the wreck, in which, incidentally, he lost every material part of his fortune and some believe a Chinese concubine. The attractive legend that he wrote the noblest of his lyrical poems, unsurpassed by any poet, while a castaway on the banks of the Mekong, must, it seems, be given up. The mere physical difficulties which would necessarily prevail in a native village in a tropical forest would seem to be a compelling argument. At Goa, the Mandavi, with its superfluous crocodiles, would do just as well for a river of Babylon as the Mekong, which, in the Lusiads, he describes as kind and compassionate. These adjectives could hardly apply to anything in or near Goa. On the other hand, as previously mentioned, he alludes elsewhere to Goa as the modern Babylon. On his arrival there he was cast into prison, and he could have heard from Lisbon that Caterina de Ataide was dead. If she was his Beatrice, the combination of prison and personal loss would have been hard. But in this region of gossip and tradition, we are hardly certain that he was in prison. And, indeed, we do not know what the charges against him were. Apparently, they were permanently quashed, though his complaints in the Lusiads make it clear that he considered himself the victim of abominable injustice. One may hazard a guess that he was not well qualified for administrative employment. It seems at once the most reasonable and the gentlest judgment.

Almost instantly, he was in prison again, this time for debt. A humorous versified appeal to high authority practically clinches it. But he was presently extricated, and for a time seems to have led a not unpleasant life in the big unprofitable town. A group of agreeable friends appear to have gathered, an Ataide, an Almeida, a Lopes Leitão, and Heitor de Silveira, evidently a close relative of the hero mentioned in the Lusiads. There were literary amusements, of which the record remains for what it is worth, and, we may add, dalliance, platonic or otherwise, with the colonial ladies, for whom he had expressed such contempt when he first arrived in India, not to mention native possibilities. One of the prettiest of Camões' lyrics is addressed to a barbarian slave-girl, whose sweetness and gentleness evidently deserved the anonymous immortality which his poem conferred. Chateaubriand, as the critics inform us, admired this poem and translated it. It is curious that one must agree with Chateaubriand. A rather hideous foot-note to the affair must be mentioned. A horrible set of verses on the amours of Luiz de Camões with a black slave was discovered and printed by Juromenha.

Even if one knew more about Goa, it would be hard to say more than this, that intrigue and self-interest were the leitmotiv of such existence as was existed there. Fortune hunters suffer from an occupational disease, namely, myopia. And the Portuguese settlers paid very little attention to their neighbors, except as they were uncomfortable enemies or useful allies. It is an odd fact that, although Camões speaks of many petty kings, he only mentions the Great Mogul once (by name), though the fascinating and exciting Akbar the Great was on the throne of Delhi for a great part of the Poet's residence in the East. The squabbles for preferment and promotion perhaps absorbed Camões as they absorbed his inferiors. And, accordingly, it is pleasant to find his hand evident in a less ignoble connection. An old gentleman, who may have been his teacher in Portugal, brought out a scientific work on Oriental drugs and medicinal plants at Goa in 1563. For this book Camões provided an introductory ode on the new Chiron, which is addressed to the Viceroy. This, as the scholars have noticed, is the first work of his hand to get into print. And after this debut we are in the dark about him again for four stricken years.

In 1567, in spite of the reversion of the collectorship of Chaúl, which was granted him and would yield a princely salary when it fell in, for reasons which we can only guess, he determined to return to Portugal. A certain Pedro de Barreto, who had been commissioned Captain of Mozambique, offered him passage so far, and lent him some money. The subsequent quarrel was evidently about the money. At any rate Camões found himself penniless in Mozambique for two years, in as bad a case as he had been in Cambodia. The epigram was duly made that, for two hundred cruzados, Camões lost his liberty and Pedro de Barreto any right to be honorably remembered. Fortunately the martyrdom ended when the "Santa Clara," with Heitor de Silveira and the historian Diogo de Couto aboard, reached Mozambique. These gentlemen, and several others, pooled their resources and bought the poet out of the clutches of Barreto. He and the Lusiads sailed for Portugal with his deliverers. Juromenha's Hugoesque rhetoric is for once more than pardonable. He observes that when on April 7, 1570, the "Santa Clara" entered the mouth of the Tagus she carried the richest cargo that had ever reached Lisbon from the Gorgeous East. It may be added that Silveira died as they crossed the bar and that the pest was on the city.

It could have been no particularly cheerful homecoming. Camões had not returned a nabob. And seventeen years make havoc of one's acquaintance. His mother was still alive, and we may properly infer that he had some powerful friends still. However, the times were as threatening as our own. Calvin and Luther were dead, but Europe had now definitely split into two savagely opposed camps. And the Turk loomed terribly in the East. Portuguese power in North Africa was a shadow. And thoughtful men must have viewed with horror the fact that Philip II was a fearfully powerful neighbor and second in succession to a throne occupied by a boy whose religious scruples, psychological difficulties, and physical deficiencies combined to make him a celibate. Great wars threatened, nor were they long in coming. The year after Camões' return brought the tremendous triumph of Lepanto when Spain and Venice wiped out Turkish sea power and carried Philip to yet more dangerous heights. And 1572, in which the Lusiads saw the light, is also the year of St. Bartholomew. About all we know of Camões in this two-year interval is that he was granted a ten-year copyright for his book in September 1571 and that on July 28, 1572, the King awarded him a pension of 15000 reis, which while not magnificent, was not, according to competent students of the period, the pittance which sentimental tradition requires.

Something was stirring in the Latin soul at the time. For two other famous epic poems were published within five years—Erçilla's Araucana, three years before (in part), and Tasso's Jerusalem Delivered, two years later. Nothing like them in stature has been printed since in Portugal, in Italy, or in Spain. Epic poetry was, so to say, in the air. We have alluded casually to the Lusiads several times in this essay, and it is now time to say something that will bring things together. On the face of the returns, a theory acceptable to many seems substantially correct. The idea of a national epic apparently swam into Camões' ken before he was twenty-four, though, contrary to equally respectable opinion, the notion of stringing his episodes on the thread of Gama's marvelous voyage may not have been part of his original plan. Where, or when, he wrote the greater part of it, is sheer conjecture, though many cantos must have been complete when he swam ashore through the Cambodian breakers. Couto's evidence has been adduced to show that he was polishing the poem during his Mozambique captivity. But "Couto's evidence" is under suspicion like everyone else's, for it may be a 17th Century forgery. Images and allusions found in the Lusiads are scattered about his lyrical works, and two actual lines of the epic, both in Book I, are to be found, one in Eclogue VII and one in Canzone X. But they don't help us greatly with respect to the time of composition. It has been reasonably inferred that the invocation and the valediction, both naturally addressed to the young King, were written after Camões returned to Portugal.

But after all, such investigations don't matter much. What counts is the poem itself.

It is a strange one. As has been pointed out a hundred times, the hero is not a man but a nation. Vasco da Gama is a great captain, and his voyage is the most magnificent of exploits. But he is not Aeneas who made Rome. The idea is quite different. Portugal made Gama—Portugal that with so little did so much. Gama and his voyage are no more than rather special aspects of the glory of Portugal. No aspect of that glory is ignored, to such an extent that Camões has no hesitation in repeating himself. He doesn't quite fight all his battles o'er again, though foreign critics have not been wanting, who found that the iteration in Book VIII of much that has been said in Books III and IV is only saved from being damnable by sheer genius of the poet, if it is saved. But it is fair to say that few can escape the infection of that intense patriotism. Ironic fate willed that the poem should appear only six years before the ghastly catastrophe of Alcazar-Kebir, one of the most spectacular reversals of a situation in history. But no creature with a shadow of human sympathy, native or foreign, can fail to respond to the noble expression of what can be one of the most splendid emotions, even if in our time it has been degraded to the vilest purposes.

The poem may be said to be modeled as far as construction goes on the Aeneid. It begins with "an announcement of the subject" and an invocation to Dom Sebastião, and then turns to the fleet of Gama, which, having rounded the Cape, is sailing up the east coast of Africa, bound for India. The Gods of the Olympian Pantheon hold a conclave concerning the Expedition, a circumstance which offended the faithful in Camões' own time and the faithless two centuries later. Jupiter declares the decree of Fate, Venus and Mars favor the Argonauts, and Bacchus, envious for his Indian laurels, opposes them. The voyagers reach Mozambique where Bacchus stirs up the natives against them, and the Portuguese defeat these evil-minded with great slaughter. Thence the fleet proceeds to Mombassa, where further mischief is plotted by Bacchus. Warned by Mercury in a dream, Gama sails to Melinde farther north, whose king proves friendly. In the vein of Aeneas or Odysseus, Gama, by request, gives the monarch a description of Europe, relates heroic or tragic events in the history of Portugal, and concludes with an account of his own voyage. This narrative requires three full books and is adorned with tremendous episodes, such as the tragedy of Ignes de Castro, the prophecy of the Old Man of Belem, and the magnificent legend of "the great vision of the guarded mount," Adamastor, the Spirit of the Cape, something which only the greatest of poets could have dreamed. Speeded on his way by the kindly king, Gama heads across the ocean for India, and is already in the antechambers of the East when Bacchus stirs up the sea-gods against the fleet. Neptune orders Eolus to loose the winds, which burst forth as a sailor is telling the famous story of the Twelve of England to keep the midwatch awake. And we have the first description of a typhoon by a man who had been in one, however much it may owe to Ovid. Venus and the Nereids persuade the winds to give over their fury by familiar methods. The Western Ghats above Calicut appear at last, and Gama goes ashore to visit the Zamorin, the local overlord. An interpreter, a Moor of Barbary, fortunately turns up, as Marina did in Mexico, through whom Paul da Gama, Vasco's brother, explains to one of the native governors the significance of episodes which are painted on the banners of the fleet, many of which had previously been related at Melinde. Bacchus intrigues with the Mahometans, who in turn stir up the Hindu chiefs against the Portuguese. And Vasco da Gama is held captive by one of the governors. By playing on the covetous nature of his captor, he makes good his escape, rescues two of his men by holding a number of eminent citizens as hostages, and sails for home. Venus, much troubled by the sufferings of her favorite Portuguese, commands Tethys and the Nereids to entertain the wanderers on an island, a regular Venusberg, which she magically causes to block their way in the sea. But she has first seen to it that Cupid has shot every one of the ladies with the golden-headed arrows. This episode is at once quaint, sensuous, delightful, and intensely diverting. At the end of the marriage feast, whose pagan aspects Camões (perhaps by order of the censor) excuses as a mere allegory of Fame, a nymph sings the future glories of Portugal till 1548, and Tethys takes

Gama and his men up a mysterious mountain where a miraculous model of the Universe on Ptolemaic principles is suspended. She leads them from sphere to sphere inward and then shows them all the kingdoms of Asia, with a side glance at the voyage of Magellan. The poem ends with the wanderers return and an exhortation to Dom Sebastião, which is as splendid advice as was ever ignored by a king.

To the writer, quite apart from magnificent imagery and verse which is at once melodious and luminous, one of the great and attractive qualities of the poem is a sort of pervading sense of newness, which Camões feels himself and induces in others. Dante knew about the Ganges and Chaucer about Cathay. But the Ganges was only a larger Adige and Cathay was no more than a remoter France. Their imaginations, and don't think for a second that I am running them down, worked differently. But Camões, as has been often said before, was the first highly imaginative European to visit the Tropics and the Orient. Everything was astonishing and incomparably strange. And he had the intelligence to perceive that nothing imagined could compete for an instant in interest with what his own singular single eye had beheld. Hence veracity reigns in every syllable, even if he did believe one or two travelers' tales. And even that dependence on the ancient Classics, which was one of the thought-forms of the Renaissance, cannot and does not overcome the factual and the actual. The sense of newness is triumphant, though some may feel that he should have described his great storm in his own way, as he could have done, instead of paraphrasing Ovid. Be that as it may, when that storm is done, the Melindian pilot's words have the simplicity of power, without which dramatic ingenuity descends into the pit of bathos:

Terra é de Calecú, se não me engano.
(That land is Calicut, or I mistake).

The longer one dwells with Camões the more one learns to admire his realistic veracity, the brilliant birds levying tribute on the green nutmeg, the threads of the trimurti on the Brahmin's bosom, the Zamorin chewing his betel, the Borneo trees dripping camphor, the violent flames, presumably of the Mountain of Ternate, and the slim smokes above the volcanoes of Sumatra (it has been acutely inferred from the contrast that he must have seen both), the blue breech-clouts of the African shore, the polyandrous marriages of Malabar, the crease of the Malay, and the assegai of the Moor. The world has grown exciting for its own sake in a way hitherto unknown. And the most passionate of patriots had discovered the pleasure of the exotic. There may be some point in the fact that Ben Jonson appears, according to the Oxford Dictionary, to have been the first to use that term in English, some nineteen years after Camões' death. It was the kind of word which was needed when "deserts vast and antres idle" began to capture the fancy. As Camões saw, it seems to me, he helped to make Europe see.

At any rate, such a poet as Tasso was instantly impressed, as is proved by a stately sonnet. And Latin Europe seems to have agreed with the Italian almost at once, though that may not have helped Camões much, prematurely old, as I believe may be properly inferred, and with a pension which appears to have been irregularly paid. Whatever the difficulty, the stipend was renewed again on June 2, 1578. And there is a legend that Camões sang for his supper and had already completed three books of an epic on the forthcoming Conquest of Africa, when the news of Alcazar-Kebir reached Lisbon.

Everything which the man who wrote the Lusiads believed in went down with the headstrong, handsome, subnormal young King. For Philip II of Spain could and did support his claim to the throne against two helpless native competitors when the old Cardinal Henry, Dom Sebastião's successor, died early in 1580. The fragment of a letter, which expresses absolute desolation of spirit, appears to be the latest surviving relic from the pen of Camões. It has been quoted many times and has to be. But no amount of repetition can destroy the quintessence of agony: "I loved my country so much that I shall die with her." The Poet did not delay long. A few months later, as Philip's armies advanced to take away Portuguese liberty for sixty years, Camões died, poverty-struck, according to every testimony, and certainly heartbroken, on June 10, 1580.

In this meager and derivative sketch, I have tried to stick

to such fact as I could find in a wilderness of frequently brilliant guess-work. The literature is enormous and is not at my fingers' ends. What a tyro owes to casual pickings from great scholars like Professor Prestage and Professor Aubrey Bell, not to mention the wonderful Senhora de Vasconcelos and others big and little, will be at once apparent to anyone who has the faintest familiarity with the subject. Nevertheless, as my betters have done, I may attempt to sum Camões up once more. Obviously, he was high-minded, brave, tender, humorous, passionate, and "capable of magnificent indignation." Warmth of feeling, rather than depth of thought, is the striking quality of his poetry, but the warmth is more than enough. He had his gay and even frivolous side, which, as has been noticed, is borne out by little poems, which suggest that he was humanly interested in cakes and ale and even fine raiment. But at all times he appears to have had "a knack for misadventure," whether in love or any other aspect of existence. That Camões was a highly cultivated man, familiar with a great deal of Portuguese, Spanish, Italian, and Latin Literature, goes without saying. That he was "an abyss of learning," I do not believe. Rather, he was a soldier and a poet, who read when he could to excellent purpose. In any case, he saw hard service in both capacities. And when he speaks of himself as one whose arm was made to manage weapons and whose mind was given over to the Muses, the antithesis tells a great deal of his story, if not all. "No one can explain him completely, and it is just as well." What matters is that there is a halo for ever about some girl or other, whoever she was, that the masculine and splendid lines which celebrate a young soldier who was fed to the sharks in the rough sea of Abyssinia still can wake a drowsy modern, that Adamastor towers over Gama's fleet, that we feel the agony by the rivers of Babylon. No wonder it is easy to love him.

II.

WARNING WITH RESPECT TO THE NOTES

ANY READER who consults the notes in this volume should be fairly warned. These comments and illustrations are in no sense the work of a profound scholar, though they would not exist at all if there had not been many profound scholars before this compiler. Many of them are gleanings, often at third, fourth, or fifth hand, from the harvests of persons who have dealt with the life and times of Camões and who have occasionally endeavored to indicate the dimensions of his mind and the direction of his thought. In particular the editor has leaned heavily on Juromenha, Burton, Senhora de Vasconcelos, Lencastre, and our own distinguished Camonian, Professor J. D. M. Ford, all of whom have been forced to pay Danegeld. Their riches have been carried off bodily, and their suggestions have been followed sometimes slavishly, sometimes capriciously. When he has seen what he supposed to be light, the compiler has occasionally gone farther than they cared to go, or has come to different and not necessarily better conclusions. And he has drawn on every field of knowledge with which his friends or he had any familiarity. He has himself explored a considerable part of the Golden and Silver Ages of Latin Literature and to some extent investigated such works of other times as Camões might be guessed to have laid under contribution. But he admits at once that he does not pretend to have covered the field. Nor does he see how his betters could. Researches of this order resemble the archeological excavation at some imperial site, and deductions from the artifacts which are from time to time dug up may easily be faulty. Nevertheless, if a shadowy notion of Camões' myriad mind (oddly limited as it may in some respects appear) and omnivorous interests is suggested to the reader, these scribblings will have served their purpose.

Inaccuracies which are bad and failures to understand which are worse may doubtless be found in these observations. "Who can contend against an infinity of motes?" However, it is hoped that some little light may come through chinks in the iron curtain which hangs between the 16th Century and the 20th, even though Camões himself made in another connection a remark to this effect: "Nothing is sure of things so long gone by."

For the convenience of the Reader the notes to each book are printed at the end of the division in question, as in the Dent Dante. No asterisks or ghastly little numbers appear in the text of the translation. But if the Reader is puzzled or curious at any point, he will often find that the solution of some minor mystery has been attempted, if he will turn to the remarks on the stanza and line which give him pause.

I refer constantly to two editions of the Lusiads and hope I have made my obligations clear. They are:

Os Lusiadas, edited by F. de S. Lencastre, Lisbon, 1927.

Os Lusiadas, edited by J. D. M. Ford, Harvard University Press, 1946

References to the two great Portuguese historians João de Barros and Damião de Goes are to the most modern editions, as follows:

Barros, "Da Asia, Decadas I-IV" (Camões could only have used I-III), edited by Hernani Cidade and Manuel Murias, Lisbon, 1945 (by Decade, Book, and Chapter).

Goes, "Cronica do Felicissimo Rei Dom Emanuel," edited by Texeira de Carvalho e Lopes, Coimbra, 1926 (by Part and Page).

Nearly all places mentioned in the Lusiads have been located and are to be found on one, or occasionally on several, of the three accompanying maps, which have been prepared by Mr. John T. Westlake. Mr. Westlake's capacity in such matters was fully tested while he was engaged in the more exacting occupation of making satisfactory representations of regions where Americans, only a few years ago, found themselves involved in the uncongenial intricacies of battle.

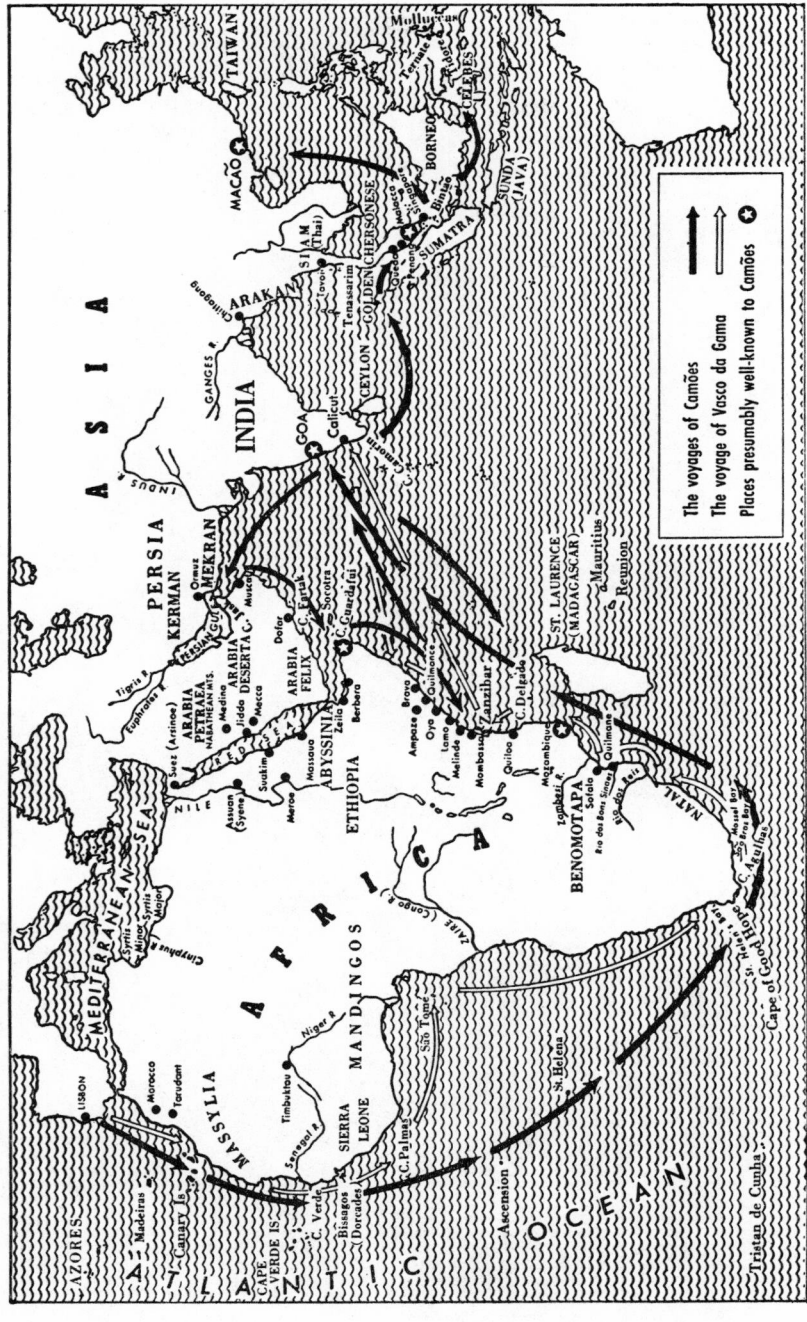

THE LUSIADS
OF
LUIZ DE CAMÕES

BOOK I

ARGUMENT

The Portuguese navigate the Eastern Seas. The gods hold council. Bacchus opposes the voyage. Mars and Venus favor the travelers. These last arrive at Mozambique, whose governor intends to destroy them. Encounter and our first battle with the heathen. They weigh anchor and, passing by Quiloa, moor at Mombassa.

THE LUSIADS

THE FIRST BOOK

ARMS, and those matchless chiefs who from
Of Western Lusitania began   [the shore
To track the oceans none had sailed before,
Yet past Taprobané's far limit ran,
And daring every danger, every war,
With courage that excelled the powers of Man,
Amid remotest nations caused to rise
Young empire which they carried to the skies;

2

So, too, good memory of those kings who went
Afar, religion and our rule to spread;
And who, through either hateful continent,
Afric or Asia, like destruction sped;
And theirs, whose valiant acts magnificent
Saved them from the dominion of the dead,
My song shall sow through the world's every part,
So help me this my genius and my art.

3

Of the wise Greek, no more the tale unfold,
Or the Trojan, and great voyages they made.
Of Philip's son and Trajan, leave untold
Triumphant fame in wars which they essayed.
I sing the Lusian spirit bright and bold,
That Mars and Neptune equally obeyed.
Forget all the Muse sang in ancient days,
For valor nobler yet is now to praise.

3

I And you, my nymphs of Tagus, who created
Within me such a genius new and glowing,
If ever yet your stream was consecrated
In humble verses which were my bestowing,
Grant me a music great and elevated,
Give me the style magnificent and flowing,
For thus your springs, so Phoebus doth ordain,
Shall never envy Hippocrene again.

5

Give me sonorous fury vast and strong,
No country reed or any pan-pipe base,
But the loud trump, whose notes to war belong,
Which burn the breast and lighten in the face;
And equal to their actions make my song,
Who gave such aid to Mars, your glorious race,
That it may be sown and sung throughout the earth,
If but my verse possess such precious worth.

6

And thou, the nobly born high guarantor
Of our old Lusitanian free estate,
And, no less certainly, fair omen for
This little Christendom that shall be great,
New terror for the lances of the Moor,
Our Century's miracle decreed by Fate,
Vouchsafed the world by God, Who all commands,
To give its better portion in God's hands;

7

O youthful branch, tender and flourishing,
Branch of a tree Christ loveth best of all,
Whatever in these western regions spring,
That men "Most Christian" or "Imperial" call,
Behold thy scutcheon doth declare the thing,
Pattern of victory that could once befall,
For as armorials Christ left to thee
The wounds that once He suffered on the Tree.

Strong King, whose haughty realm, in his career,   I
The new-born sun has first of all in sight,
Sees from the center of the hemisphere,
And leaves the latest when he takes his flight,
Who art, we trust, to yoke and strike with fear
The sullen horsemen of the Ishmaelite,
The Orient Turk and all the heathen train,
The water of the sacred stream who drain;

9

Descend a little from thy majesty
That I thy kindly countenance may know,
Appearing as through life thou art to be,
Till to the eternal temple thou shalt go.
And cast thine eyes kindly and royally
Upon the ground. Thou shalt discover so
Fresh proof of love of patriot acts divine,
Now sung abroad in the sweet-cadenced line.

10

Love of country, thou shalt see, not dominated
By vile reward but a deathless thing and high.
My prize must not be basely estimated,
Who still my native land would magnify.
Hark and behold their glory celebrated,
Whose lord thou art at height of sovranty,
And thou shalt judge which is the better case,
To rule the earth or govern such a race.

11

Hark! Thou shalt never see, for empty deed
Fantastical and feigned and full of lies,
Thy people praised, as with the foreign breed
Of muses that still vaunt them to the skies.
So great and true those acts that they exceed
Utterly all such fabulous fantasies,
And Rodomont and the vain Roger too,
And Roland's tale, even if that were true.

5

I   Instead I give you Nuno grim and dire,
Whose prowess well for King and Realm was shown,
With Egas and with Fuas. Homer's lyre
I covet, for the like of them alone.
For the Twelve Peers, Magriço I desire
Among the Twelve of England shall be known,
And offer likewise Gama's noble name,
Who for himself snatched all Aeneas' fame.

13

For if, in lieu of Charles the King of France
Or Caesar, equal glory you would see,
Mark well the first Afonso then, whose lance
Tarnished whatever foreign fame might be,
Or him who left his land the inheritance
Of freedom with his splendid victory,
Or the second John unconquered, or, in a word,
The fourth and fifth Afonsos, or the third.

14

Nor shall my verses let their memory wane,
Who once beyond the realms of morning went,
And by their good swords could such height attain
They kept your banner still armipotent:
Pacheco strong, the dread Almeidas twain,
For whom yet Tagus grieves with sad lament,
And Albuquerque stern and Castro brave,
And all who scaped dominion of the grave.

15

While them I chant, who cannot celebrate
Your worth, great King, for I am not so bold,
Take in your hand the bridle of the state,
Making matter for an epic yet untold.
They feel already the tremendous weight
(The fear whereof makes the whole world grow cold)
Of hosts and deeds as splendid as may be,
On Afric's coasts or on the Orient sea.

16

The Moor looks ever on thee, chill with fear,

In whom he can foretell his deadly check.

The Hindu rude, but seeing thee appear,

Beneath the yoke already bends the neck.

Tethys, the whole domain of azure clear,

As for a dowry, has begun to deck.

So moved by beauty and by youth is she

That for her son-in-law she welcomes thee.

17

On their likeness from the Olympic dwellings gaze

Two grandsires, souls with world-wide glory fraught,

One golden from angelic peace's rays,

One from the bloody battles that he fought.

In thee they trust to see renewed their praise,

The memory of heroic works they wrought,

And keep a place for thee till time's extreme

In the temple of eternity supreme.

18

But for such little space as time may halt

Ere thou rule folk that would thy subjects be,

In kindness this new enterprise exalt

So that my verses may belong to thee.

Thine Argonauts, shearing the silver salt,

Thou shalt behold, and they shall also see

Thou hast beheld them whom wild oceans hem.

So grow inured to be invoked by them.

19

Already through the open sea they sailed,

Thrusting unquiet waves to either side.

And 'twas a gentle breath the winds exhaled,

That made the vessels' hollow sails spread wide.

White wakes all over the great seas they trailed,

Where through the deep the sharp cutwaters plied,

Cleaving the sacred wave where to and fro

The rushing cattle herds of Proteus go;

I   When the gods, upon Olympus full of light,
The very seat of human government.
Gathered together in their Council bright
To read the future of the Orient.
Ascending gorgeous Heaven's crystal height.
Together up the Milky Way they went,
Summoned by the Thunderer, whose will was told
To them by the grandson fair of Atlas old.

21

Of all the seven orbs they left the reign,
Granted to them by Higher Sovranty,
Vast Power, Which by thought only can maintain
The rule of Heaven and Earth and wrathful Sea.
There in a moment were they met again,
All those whose seats 'neath cold Arcturus be,
Lords of the South and of those regions wide
Where dawn is born, or the clear sun may hide.

22

The great and sacred Sire was seated there,
Who shook the bolts of Vulcan, crepitating.
His crystal throne with shining stars was fair.
His look was high and stern and dominating.
And from his face there breathed divinest air,
Our poor clay into deity translating.
And all his crown and gleaming sceptre shone
With strangest gems clearer than diamond stone.

23

On glittering thrones inlaid with pearl and gold
Of other gods are seated the whole train.
But lower than Jove's place their station hold,
As reason and good order may ordain.
In first rank sit the honorable and old,
Below them deities of lowlier strain,
To whom thus Jove his purposes made known
And there was weight and danger in his tone:

"Eternal natives of the gleaming, bright,   I
Starbearing Pole and the clear firmament,
If you have not forgotten yet the might
Of Lusitania's race bellipotent,
Then this word should be wisdom in your sight,
For to it the Fates visibly consent.
Because of them, men shall forget for aye
Assyrian, Persian, Greek, or Roman sway.

25

"To them was granted, as yourselves could see,
To take, so few but guiltless of deceit,
From the strong Moor in warrior panoply
All the lands watered by the Tagus sweet.
And against dread Castile continually
Kind Heaven showed them favor so complete
That they were always able in the end
Trophies of splendid triumph to suspend.

26

"O Gods, I speak not of their fame of yore,
That with the race of Romulus they held,
When with Viriathus in the Roman War
So high the praises of their actions swelled.
Also the mighty memory I pass o'er,
Which unto honor bound them and compelled,
When they chose that stranger chief, who feigned to
Divinity's true spirit in a hind.   [find

27

"Now mark! Delivered to sea-change unclear,
To tracks unknown in cockboats they resort,
And Notus' force, or Afric's, never fear,
But still attempt what higher may import.
For, having seen such regions, thence they steer,
Where day now lengthens out and now grows short,
And so incline their purpose and are drawn
To look upon the cradle of the Dawn.

9

I "This they were promised by Eternal Fate,
And nothing can gainsay that judgment dread,
That for long ages they should dominate
Waters that gaze on the sun rising red.
At sea they suffered winter obdurate.
And the crews are overwearied and half dead.
It is no more than justice might require
That they be shown this new world they desire.

29

"And since, as you have seen with your own eyes,
On their voyage fearful peril they outwore,
And tested out what climes under what skies,
And the fury of the winds such hate that bore,
Let them on Afric's coast, as I devise,
Like friends, find hospitality therefor.
And, the weary fleet new-fitted as is due,
They shall go forth on their long road anew."

30

Such were the very words that great Jove spake.
And in his turn each of the gods replied.
Differing as to the courses they might take,
Rendering or harking reason on each side.
But our sire Bacchus no accord would make
With Jove's desire. Too clearly he descried
Men would forget his every Orient deed,
Once men came there of Lusitania's breed.

31

There would come, for he had heard the voice of Fate,
From Spain a people, terrible in war,
O'er the high seas, and they would subjugate
As much as Doris bathes of India's shore,
And with new victories they would make less great
Old fame of his or other conqueror.
Sorely it irked him thus to lose the fame
For which yet Nysa venerates his name.

For lo, o'er Indus he had once prevailed   **I**
And still, by fortune and occasion good,
As conqueror of India had been hailed
By whosoever drink Parnassus' flood.
Now at the thought of some dark urn he quailed,
Where, buried deep, his name for hardihood
In waters of oblivion should be drowned
Once Portugal's strong sailors reached that ground.

33

Against him Venus bright the cause sustained
Of Lusitania's race, whom she held dear
For virtues which she saw in them ingrained,
Like her loved Romans of a bygone year,
The noble star, the courage never stained,
That was well proved in the country of Tangier,
And the language, which, if one lets fancy range,
One takes for Latin with but little change.

34

These things moved Cytherea. And beside
She could see clearly the decree of Fate,
That her glory would be sounded far and wide
Wherever the war-loving race grew great.
Thus one for fear of infamy denied,
And the other for the honors of her state
Affirmed, disputing. High doth the quarrel reach,
Since there are many friends to favor each.

35

As the fierce North or South in the profound
Depth of the wood, where thick the trees engage,
The dark grove's boughs hurls crashing to the ground,
With headlong force and with unmeasured rage,
And the whole mountain roars with echoing sound,
The high range thrills, while rends the foliage,
So raged the tumult that was agitated
By gods upon Olympus consecrated.

I But it was Mars who on the goddess' part
   Her suit most sternly 'mid them all would press,
   Whether his former love so urged his heart,
   Or that a gallant race deserved no less.
   Up on his feet among them did he start,
   And all his look declared his bitterness.
   The strong shield at his neck he cast aside,
   All full of menace and of angry pride.

37

The visor of the diamond helm he wore
He raised somewhat, the better to speak clear
His purpose, and he stood Jove's seat before,
Armed at all points, portentous, and severe.
A sharp stroke he delivered, furthermore,
With his staff against the sacred throne. For fear,
While the sky shook, Apollo lost his light
For a brief space, like one turned white for fright.

38

And thus Mars spake: "Father, whose empire here
All things obey, for them thou didst create,
If these who seek a second hemisphere,
Once dear to thee for gallant acts and great,
Thou wouldst not see the butt of gibe and sneer,
Since long ere this thou didst decree their fate,
Then hark no more, being a judge so just,
His reasons, who, it seems, we cannot trust.

39

"For now, were it not visible and plain
That reason by huge fears is set aside,
It would be well for Bacchus to sustain
The sons of Lusus he once magnified.
And may this wicked plot of his prove vain,
Which only springs from his accursèd pride;
For alien envy has no power to seize
What men have merited and Heaven decrees.

"And thou, our Sire, in overwhelming might,　　**I**
From what thou hast determined to see done,
Never turn back. 'Twere weakness in our sight
To shrink from the adventure thus begun.
Let Mercury, who swifter in his flight
Than the swift wind or well-smoothed shaft can run,
Show them the land where there are tidings true
Of India and their forces can renew."

41

The mighty Sire, when brave Mars said his say,
Consented wholly and inclined his head,
Content with all that in his meaning lay,
And nectar over all the gods he shed.
Whereon down the resplendent Milky Way
Presently every god departing sped,
Having taken leave with high imperial grace.
And each one went his way to his own place.

42

While these events were making high above
In the skied Olympian realm omnipotent,
Our valiant men their way through Ocean clove,
Past boundaries of the South and Orient.
'Twixt Ethiopia and the famed isle they drove,
Named for Saint Laurence. The sun flaming bent
Over those gods whom, by his aspect stern,
Typhéus could for dread to fishes turn.

43

And them the winds so gently onward bear,
As they were men whom Heaven holdeth dear.
Cloudless the weather and serene the air,
Nor was there danger anywhere to fear.
Already beyond Prasso's cape they fare,
Where ancient Ethiopia's coasts appear.
When the sea discovered to them his new-found
Islands, the which he laved and girded round.

I Vasco da Gama, the captain strong and tried,
Who still took up such valorous enterprise,
With a heart all audacity and pride,
And whom his fortune watched with kindly eyes,
Could see no reason there to turn aside.
Lands uninhabited he might surmise,
And so determined further on to press,
But things befell far other than his guess.

45

To them appeared then in close company
Some little shallops bearing thence away
From the isle that next the mainland seemed to be.
With big sails set o'er the broad sea came they.
Our folk were gladdened, and with mirth and glee
Could but mark well what made their spirits gay. [ing,
"What men might these be?" they thought wonder-
"What customs? What their laws? And who their

46   [king?"

Their ships are builded in the manner due,
Narrow and long, and for that reason fleet.
The sails wherewith across the sea they flew
Were palm-leaf mats, which skillfully they pleat.
The people had the veritable hue,
Phaëthon gave the world in lands of heat,
In rashness and audacity who dealt,
As the Po knew and Lampetusa felt.

47

In clothing of a cotton weave they fare,
Of many various colors, striped and white.
A sort of sash knotted behind they wear,
And on the shoulders airy drapery light.
From the waist up their bodies are all bare.
Buckler and blade they carry for the fight.
Their heads are turbaned. As o'er sea they go,
Sonorously their Moorish horns they blow.

With their garments and their arms the sign they gave   I
For the Lusitanians to shorten sail.
Already the swift prows lean o'er the wave
Till, near the isles, their canvas they can brail.
Soldier and sailor at the hard task slave,
As here were ended all their labor's tale.
They take in sail along the yard and furl,
And, anchor-smitten, high the waters hurl.

49

Scarce were they anchored when that stranger race
Swarmed up the bulwarks, clinging by the cord.
Gay were their faces, and with kindly grace
Our Chief great-minded welcomed them aboard.
At once he had the tables set in place,
And liquor of Lyaeus' vine they poured
In crystal cups, a vintage which the sect
Whom Phaëthon scorched in no way would reject.

50

In Arabic they asked us, while they dined
So gaily, where our voyage had begun,
Who we were, and whence, and what we sought to
And what the seas that we had overrun.   [find,
Lusus' brave children, with discreetest mind,
In such sort answered as might best be done:
"We are Portuguese who from the Sunset hail,
And to find out the Sunrise lands we sail.

51

"We have navigated the whole ocean o'er,
Belonging to the Antarctic and the Bear.
And we have circled all of Afric's shore
And seen strange skies and countries everywhere.
All powerful the King whom we adore,
So well beloved by all that we would dare
Not only the wide ocean for his sake
But cheerly sail the Acherontic Lake.

15

I   And hence we go to seek at his behest
Those Orient lands where Indus' waters flow.
And through the utmost oceans we have pressed
Where only ugly-favored seals may go.
But now, unless your people think it best
Not to speak truth, 'tis right that we should know
Who you may be and in what land you dwell,
And if of India you have aught to tell."

53

"We are," one of the islanders replied,
"To land and law and nation strangers here.
The natives are a race unsanctified
By law or sense, whom Nature thus did rear.
By that most certain faith we all abide,
Which Abraham's shining progeny made clear,
Who is the lord of all this world's empire,
Son of a Jewess and a heathen sire.

54

"The isle in which we dwell, though it be small,
Is a safe anchorage for the region round.
Quilóa and Mombassa here must call,
Sofála too, when o'er these waters bound.
And since 'tis necessary to them all,
We seized the isle for our own stamping-ground,
And to answer everything of which you speak,
The name by which it goes is Mozambique.

55

"And since from so far off your ships have plied,
Seeking Hydaspian Indus' fiery strand,
Here you may have a pilot, who, to guide
Your fleet o'er sea, wisely will understand.
But it were good a little here to bide
And take the sweet refreshment of the land.
What's needful, he who over us holds sway,
And who himself will greet you, will purvey."

When he had said these things the Moor withdrew I
Unto his ships with all his company.
He parted from the Captain and the crew,
Showing his high respect as needs must be.
While this was doing, Phoebus bolted to
Bright day and crystal chariot under sea,
Leaving his charge by his sister to be kept,
Who lit the wide world while her brother slept.

57

In the weary ships the long night they outwore.
There was wild pleasure hardly to be thought
In finding tidings of that far-off shore
For so long time so passionately sought.
And every man in his mind pondered o'er
That folk, and customs with such strangeness fraught,
Wondering how votaries of a lying creed
Thus through the whole wide world could sow their
58   [seed.

The brilliant radiance of the moon on high
Over the silver waves of Neptune shone.
And all the stars marched onward with the sky,
That seemed a field with the white daisies sown.
And quiet all the winds infuriate lie,
Hidden in caverns sombre and unknown.
Yet in the fleet good watch kept every crew
As this long while had been their wont to do.

59

But when the Dawn, coming in dappled state,
All down her shoulders shook her lovely hair,
In the clear skies opening the rosy gate,
So to awaken bright Hyperion's heir,
The whole fleet they began to decorate
With flags and dressed the ships with awnings fair,
With gaiety and festival to greet
The Island Lord who came to view the fleet.

I From the shore he headed, full of mirth and gay,
   To see the Lusitanian galleons light.
   He brought refreshment, deeming our array
   Came of that nation full of all despite,
   Whose dwelling in the Caspian region lay,
   And who rose up the Asian Lands to smite,
   Till they at length, for so did Fate ordain,
   From Constantine had wrenched away the reign.

61

   The Captain, with a courtesy benign,
   Greeted the Moor and all his company,
   And gave a present of gold pieces fine,
   Which he had brought for such necessity,
   As likewise candied sweets and burning wine,
   Unknown to them before, which makes for glee.
   The gifts the Moor accepted with good will,
   And further ate and drank with better still.

62

   Lusus' seafaring sons, where they abode
   Manning the shrouds, all in great wonder gazed,
   Noting how strange the manner and the mode,
   The speech involved and barbarously phrased.
   But the cunning Moor himself confusion showed,
   By color, dress, and the strong fleet, amazed.
   He asked the Captain of each circumstance
   And if from Turkey we were come perchance.

63

   He said yet more, for he desired to see
   Books which our law, precept and faith express,
   To know if with his own they might agree.
   That we were Christian he might lightly guess.
   Viewing and noting all things curiously,
   He begged the Captain with much eagerness
   Of those portentous arms to make a show,
   Which would be used in fight against the foe.

64

Our valiant Captain answered him apace   I
Through one who that dark speech could understand:
"Great Sir, you are to hear all of our case:
My own, our faith, the weapons of our hand.
I am not of the region or the race
Of the gross peoples of the Turkish land,
But come from Europe practised in great wars,
And now I head for famous India's shores.

65

"His faith I follow, to Whose mandate clear
Visible and Invisible submit,
His, Who created either hemisphere
And all that hath, or hath not, sense and wit.
Insult and all dishonor He knew here.
Insufferable foul death, He suffered it,
From Heaven to Earth descending to the end
That mortals might from Earth to Heaven ascend.

66

"Of this God-Man, the Infinite and High,
I bear no books that you would have me show.
I stand excused for written words, for why
Should I bring on paper what the soul should know?
But if you would behold our armory,
It shall be granted, since you wish it so.
And as a friend our weapons you shall see,
But, I trust, never as an enemy."

67

He spoke and bade the soldiers diligent
Display their arsenal in the Moor's view.
Harness was brought, breastplates magnificent,
The fine-linked mail, the strong plate-armor too,
And painted shields with various ornament,
Bullets, and iron muskets tempered true.
Bows and the quivers full of bolts appear,
And the sharp partizan and sturdy spear.

I Fireballs they bring, and every sulphurous pot
That can do mischief horrible and dire.
But unto Vulcan's sons he granted not
Their terrible artillery to fire.
To fright poor timorous folk would be a blot,
Nor what a noble nature would require
To show his power. Reason is still to keep.
'Tis weak to play the lion 'mid the sheep.

69

Because of what he noted there displayed,
And the Moor watched everything with eye intent,
Sincerest hatred in his spirit stayed,
And will toward us wholly on evil bent,
Which neither bearing nor his face betrayed.
Rather, with laughter and feigned merriment,
He had in mind gently to cheat us, till
He might at length unveil what he might will.

70

Pilots our Chief requested of the Moor,
The Indian voyage to direct and guide.
To them a mighty profit would inure
For whatsoever travail might betide.
These the Moor promised, with the intention sure
In his soul, poisonous and unsanctified,
If possible to kill him that same day,
Rather than give him pilots for his way.

71

So furious was the hatred and despite
That suddenly against the strangers wrought.
Too well he knew they followed the true light
That unto us the Son of David taught.
Oh Secrets of Eternity, to whose height
Reaches in vain the power of human thought!
For there must still be some perfidious foe
To plague them who Thy perfect friendship know.

Thereupon, from the ships, with all his train   I
The Moor departed, treacherous and fell,
With greatest courtesy but false and vain,
For all was feigned, however affable.
The straight way home his longboats took again
Through Neptune's waves. There he was greeted well
By a great gathering with obsequious grace,
For here the Moor was come to his own place.

73
The mighty Theban from his ethereal seat,
He who was born out of his father's thigh,
Beheld the advent of the Lusian fleet
And likewise how the Moors were plagued thereby.
In thought he conjured up a treacherous cheat
By which he trusted that they all might die.
And the thing mulling in his soul the while,
Unto himself he spake after this style:

74
"Is it by Fate already foreordained
That many a great and famous victory
Shall by these men of Portugal be gained
Against what warrior tribes in India be?
Has this for my great father's son remained,
Possessed of every generous quality?
To see Fate favor them must I endure,
Whose deeds will wholly my great name obscure?

75
"For once already have the gods decreed
To Philip's son throughout that realm such might
That captive the whole region he could lead
Under the yoke of Mars the fierce in fight.
Must more be borne? And must Fate grant indeed
Such strength and skill to an armament so slight?
And shall, like Rome and Macedon, my fame
Give ground before the Lusitanian name?

I   "It shall not be. Ere to his goal he get
So dread an ambuscade, adroit and sly,
Shall for this Captain presently be set
That on no Orient Coast shall he lay eye.
Forthwith to Earth I shall go down to whet
In Moorish breasts their indignation high,
For ever by the shortest way he goes,
Who the advantage of the just hour knows."

77

So saying, in great wrath and halfway mad,
Down he descended to the Afric shore.
A god, in human form and feature clad,
He went by Prasso, known to him of yore.
The better to weave tricks astute and bad,
All of the natural lineaments he wore
Of a Moor known to fame in Mozambique,
Old, wise, and in great favor with the Sheikh.

78

Entering in time and hour that suited well
With the appearance by his fraud contrived,
To the Sheikh his story he began to tell,
Of pirates lately on his shores arrived.
For so the rumor runs, that they who dwell
Along the coasts are of their all deprived
By these who pass, whose custom is, where'er
They anchor, first to proffer friendship there.

79

"Further know this, for I have heard," said he,
"These Christians are most bloodily inclined,
And have wrought ruin over the whole sea,
And rob and burn after their savage kind.
A long time they have planned this treachery
Against us. The whole purpose of their mind
Is but upon our coast to rob and slay
And captive lead woman and child away.

"To land for water here, as well I know,   I
In a little while their Captain's will is bent,
And with him many of his men alsó,
For fear is ever born of base intent.
Armed, with thy men, to face him thou shouldst go.
In hidden ambush hold thine armament,
And as they come ashore without a care,
They shall be taken in the ambush there.

81

"And if so hap they are not by this feat
Given utterly to death and to damnation,
Yet have I fashioned forth in my conceit
A fair ruse pleasant in thy contemplation.
Send them a pilot who is skilled to cheat,
Wise, and adept in treacherous conjuration,
One who shall lead them to some coast, where they
Shall be defeated, slain, or cast away."

82

When Bacchus in such words had put the case,
The wise Moor, who in treason had grown grey,
Clasped him about the neck in close embrace
And would advice with noblest thanks repay.
And he accordingly prepared apace
His warlike armament for that affray.
As for the Portuguese, it was his thought
To turn to blood the water which they sought.

83

Yet further devilment he did devise.
A Moorish pilot for the ships he found,
Wise, keen, and skilled in wicked enterprise,
Who for such act was of a trust most sound.
He with the Lusitanian, comradewise,
Should lead him through such seas to such a ground
That, should he 'scape thence, on some farther shore
He must go down and never rise up more.

84

I   The Nabatéan heights already flared
Before Apollo with his radiant brand,
When Gama to his men his purpose bared,
To go in arms for water to the land.
And in the boats the crews were well prepared,
As if they knew the treachery in hand,
For the deceit was easy to surmise,
And the prophetic spirit never lies.

85

Gama beside had tidings from the shore,
Borne by the pilot whom he sent ahead,
And who was answered with the sounds of war,
A thing which all he had in mind gainsaid.
For this, and since 'tis foolish, furthermore,
To trust a foe in treacherous practice bred,
Gama went armed with preparation strong
And three boats only took with him along.

86

But the Moors, along the beaches standing by,
That we from springs we sought might be withstayed,
Lay close with buckler and the assegai,
Or with curved bow and poisoned shaft arrayed,
And waited till our soldiers should draw nigh,
With men well hidden in the ambuscade.
And, to make labor easier, they deploy
Some few ahead to act as a decoy.

87

Along the sandy foreshore gleaming white,
The warlike Moors in high defiance strode,
With shields and lances perilous in fight,
The better the brave Portuguese to goad.
Nor suffered long those generous men of might
The dogs to run about, their teeth that showed.
They leaped so swiftly to the beach before
That none could say who was the first ashore.

As in the bloody cirque, some lover, proud   I
Because he sees his charming sweetheart there,
Seeks out the bull, faces him, shouts aloud,
Runs, gambols, whistles, and defies him fair; [bowed,
But the fierce beast, in the nick, his horned front
Right at him with a bellow and a blare,   [bound,
Eyes closed, storms forward, bound on desperate
Tosses, gores, kills, and hurls him to the ground;

89

So on the boats flamed out the fire of war
From the implacable and furious guns.
The lead ball slays. Rises the savage roar.
The whistling echo shocks the air and stuns.
And now is broke the courage of the Moor,
For cold his blood in the vast panic runs.
And those who lay in hiding fled dismayed
And died in that uncovered ambuscade.

90

Yet were the Portuguese but ill content.
Following up victory, they wrecked and slew.
The people without walls or armament,
They smote with shot and flame and overthrew.
On the Moor's heart weighed heavy the event,
Who had hoped to buy more cheap what now fell due.
Weak age, the mother with the nursing child,
Now curse that battle with blaspheming wild.

91

The Moors shot many an arrow in their flight,
But forceless in their hurry and their fear.
With stick and stone and shard, they strove to fight.
Such arms were lent by desperation drear.
The greater part, abandoning in fright
Their isle, made for the terra firma near.
The narrow ocean arm, they clove it fast,
That girds the isle, and quickly overpassed.

I In overladen dugouts many fled,
And others, swiftly swimming, sought to flee.
Under the curving wave sinks many a head,
And many drink and vomit forth the sea.
Heavily fall the crushing salvoes dread
On keen prows of that brutish enemy.
Thus Portugal took vengeance in good time
On the foes' malice and perfidious crime.

93

Now they return victorious to the fleet
With a rich prize and all the spoils of war,
At pleasure seek a place for watering meet,
Nor find resistance or defenses more.
Among the Moors, so broken in defeat,
Their ancient hate burns higher than before,
And, seeing wholly unavenged their woe,
They trust their second snare will trap the foe.

94

For now the ruler of that wicked land
Sought to make peace, as one repenting quite,
Nor did the Lusitanians understand
That under forms of peace he meant to fight.
For the false pilot, promised to their hand,
Who kept in mind that counsel of despite,
To guide them to their deaths, as sign he sent
Of peace and honorable arbitrament.

95

Our Chief, who thought it fitting to prepare
For his departure on the accustomed road—
For the weather favored and the wind stood fair
To seek out Indus' much-desired abode—
Welcomed the pilot who came to him there,
And every kindness to the fellow showed.
Gama, who heeded well the envoy's tale,
While the wind blew, gave orders to make sail.

And so away the gallant fleet has gone.　　　　　I
The waves of Amphitrite they divide.
The band of Nereus' daughters hastens on,
Delightful, sweet, and faithful, at their side.
The Captain not as yet had pitched upon
The knot of falsehood that the Moor had tied.
But the man with many questions did he ply
On India and the coasts that he passed by.

97

But the Moor in every treachery expert,
Taught him by Bacchus of the evil mind,
Death and captivity and new-found hurt,
Ere he reached India, for him designed.
A tale of Indian ports did he concert,
And all things that the Captain sought to find.
And since whate'er he said was truth, they thought,
The stalwart crews on their part feared for naught.

98

And furthermore, with the same false intent
As Sinon, whose deceit the Phrygians quelled,
He said an isle lay near, or settlement,
Where an old Christian people long had dwelled.
To this the Chief an ear most eager lent.
Such pleasure at this news within him welled
That the Moor with splendid gifts he did entreat,
Thither where that people lived, to steer the fleet.

99

And that same thing the false Moor meant to do,
For which the trusting Christian begged and pled;
For that island is the home of a vile crew
Who in the path of base Mahomet tread.
He would forge death for them by trick untrue,
For in this isle more power and men are bred
Than are in Mozambique. It has to name
Quilóa, largely trumpeted by fame.

27

I Thither away merrily sailed the fleet.
But the goddess whom in Cythera they adore,
Seeing them from the certain road retreat
To rush on death none ever dreamed before,
Considered that in no way was it meet
The men she loved should die on some far shore,
And with head winds she turned them quite aside
From the course plotted by the rascal guide.

The wicked Moor, seeing that he could not
Longer that well planned villainy maintain,
Other iniquity began to plot,
And constant in his purpose did remain.
He said that the thwart currents from the spot
They sought did all too forcefully restrain,
But another isle was near, and in that place
Were Moors and Christians both of the same race.

Nevertheless he lied on every head,
Cleaving utterly to his Sheikh's order clear.
For never in that land were Christians bred,
But only those Mahomet who revere.
The Captain trusted all the Moor had said,
And tacking round bade toward the isle to steer.
But the guardian goddess for her part denied
His entry to the port. He moored outside.

The isle lies no great distance from the land.
A narrow channel separates the twain.
And on the island doth a city stand,
Easily seen because it fronts the main,
Full of fine buildings from the mason's hand.
And far away a man may see it plain.
And there an ancient king rules over all,
Whose isle and city men Mombassa call.

104

The Captain, having made his landfall there,   I
Was strangely happy, for his hope was high.
To see baptizèd men was all his care,
According to the traitor pilot's lie.
And from the King, by this time well aware
What men we were, boats with his message ply.
Bacchus thereof long since had made him sure,
Coming in guise of yet another Moor.

105

The message seemed the greeting of a friend,
But underneath the venom was complete,
For the thought was all that enemies intend,
Though in the sequel was unveiled the cheat.
Oh, great and heavy perils without end!
Oh, road of life where nothing sure we meet!
For where we think our hope is most secure,
Life holds but little that can long endure.

106

At sea by such rough storms and griefs forespent!
So many a moment when Death stands alert!
Ashore such strife and treacherous intent,
Where horrible necessity can hurt!
How can weak man escape the harsh event,
And how misfortune from brief life avert,
Where calm Skies rage not nor take arms alway
Against so mean a creature of the clay?

NOTES

BOOK I

1.   1. The imitation of the first line of the Aeneid (a stock 16th Century opening) is obvious, but not uninteresting, for Virgil may be said to have been as important to Camões as he was to Dante. The Roman was at all times present in the mind of the Portuguese, who quotes or imitates his great predecessor in at least eighty places in the Lusiads. Horace, Ovid, and Lucan were also much admired by the Poet. The editor has indicated Camões' indebtedness, in all cases giving credit to previous investigators.

    4. Tapróbané was the Greek name of Ceylon. It is derived from the Sanskrit word Tamraparni (Cambridge History of India, I, 424). Burton notes and rejects Milton's pronunciation of the word in Paradise Regained, IV, 75,

> And utmost Indian isle, Tapróbané.

With respect to Sir Richard Burton an odd point must be raised. He adored Camões and for nineteen years was sporadically engaged in translating him and making notes. But he was almost perfectly shameless in his commentary, as Mr. Edward Glaser has abundantly proved. Burton appropriated for himself, without giving any but the faintest credit to his predecessors, the results of their labors. Faria y Sousa and, I have no doubt, Correia are transferred bodily into his notes almost always without mention. Perhaps he regarded them as public property. I have endeavored not to follow his example.

For Pomponius Mela Tapróbané was the beginning of a new world (Geography, III, 7). Apparently Camões knew the work of this writer. He speaks of him in V, 50.

2.   To the literal-minded this stanza might seem hyperbolical. The only Portuguese ruler who ever was in Asia was Henry of Bourgogne, "Count" of Portugal, who appears to have visited the Holy Land. Many of the Kings from John I on fought in North Africa. But none of them seems to have visited the Asiatic conquests. Camões unquestionably views such conquests as due to the Kings even if they were not present.

3.   3. Philip's son, Alexander the Great.

    Trajan, the last expander of the Roman Empire (98–117 A.D.).

4.   1. The nymphs of Tagus appear to be Camões' own invention (Lencastre).

8. Hippocrene, the "horse-spring," sacred to Pegasus on Mt. Parnassus.

5.   2. Tityrus' "country reed" (Virgil, Eclogue 1, 2) is in Camões' mind, as is the "pan-pipe base" (Ibid., 10). So also Eclogue VI, 8.

5. Camões might remember Sallust's remark (Conspiracy of Catiline, Cap. III) that it is difficult to write history because deeds must be adequately expressed by words.

6. ff.   1. The person addressed is King Sebastian (1554–1578), the obstinate and nearly idiotic fanatic who was responsible for the ruin of Portugal at Alcasar-Kebir in Morocco in 1578. More information about him will be found in the notes to X, 156, and in Camões and the History of Portugal, at the end of this volume. Camões, it may be noted, was a liberal. This stanza finds its parallel in the Octaves to King Sebastian (Juromenha, II, 310).

7.   4. The Holy Roman Empire and the French Kingdom.

5. The Arms of Portugal are blazoned with several heraldic allusions to the Crucifixion, the Cross itself, the five shields which symbolize at once the Five Wounds of Christ and the five Moorish Kings defeated by Afonso I at Ourique in 1139, and the Thirty Pieces of Silver. See III, 54.

8.   6. Sullen horsemen of the Ishmaelite. This stock phrase for a Moslem (torpe Ismaelita) occurs in Elegy XI, Juromenha, III, 210.

7–8. The contrast appears to be between Mohammedans and the heathen idolaters, i.e., Hindus, who are purified in the waters of the Ganges, the sacred stream. Camões refers to their faith in the Ganges in X, 121. Perhaps "the Orient Turk" is an allusion to the Grand Mogul.

10.   7–8. Burton notes that this couplet was carried on the colors of a Portuguese infantry corps after the Battle of Vittoria in 1813.

11.   5. This gibe at Boiardo and Ariosto and the Romantic Epic in general has its diverting aspect if one considers Book IX of the Lusiads. There Camões proves himself the equal of the Italian poets at their own game. All three of the heroes mentioned appear in Ariosto, and Rodomont the boaster and Roland in Boiardo. There are many points where Ariosto (1474–1533) has something in common with Camões. In spite of his professed dislike for the Italians, Camões evidently admired and imitated them. Some of these convergences are duly indicated in the notes.

12.   1. Nuno Alvares Pereira, "Portugal's Scipio" and the victor of Aljubarotta under John I in 1385. He appears in IV, 23–33 and in VIII, 28–32. See Camões and the History of Portugal.

31

2. Egas Moniz, the heroic friend of Afonso I, whose self-sacrifice is twice described once in III, 35 and again in VIII, 17.

Fuas Roupinho, an Admiral under Afonso I. See VIII, 16–17.

5. The Twelve Peers of the Charlemagne Legend.

6. The story of Magriço and the Twelve of England is related in VI, 43 ff.

7. Vasco da Gama (c. 1460–1524), the discoverer of the sea-route to India, and the principal figure in the Lusiads, the real hero of which is, of course, the Portuguese nation. He was fierce, brutal, and incredibly successful. Camões has softened the harsh aspects of a character, whose savage cruelty in India in 1502 was rough even for the 16th Century. He was subsequently viceroy and died at his post.

13. 1. Charlemagne. The Charlemagne of legend rather than of history (as Burton rightly says).

2. Afonso I, an almost legendary hero who became "Count" of Portugal in 1128, was proclaimed King in 1140, and occupied the throne till 1185. His victories, among them the Battle of Ourique, greatly expanded the country, and his capture of Lisbon in 1147 was an important step in the expansion. See III, 28–84, and Camões and the History of Portugal.

5–6. John I, the victor of Aljubarrota, 1385, perhaps the most spectacular of Portuguese kings. He fought off the Spanish threat and in a reign of nearly fifty years restored the country he had saved. See Camões and the History of Portugal. See also IV, 2–50.

7. John II (reigned 1481–1495), a very great king, who carried on the ideas of Henry the Navigator.

8. Afonso IV (reigned 1325–1356) one of the victors of the battle of the Salado in 1340, and the persecutor of Ignes de Castro. See III, 118–135. Afonso V (reigned 1438–1481), who campaigned with some success in North Africa, whence his soubriquet "the African." Afonso III (reigned 1248–1279), the usurper who gave continental Portugal its present frontiers.

14. 5. Duarte Pacheco Pereira conquered the Malabar Coast for King Manuel (reigned 1495–1524). See X, 12–25 and notes.

6. Francisco de Almeida, first Viceroy of India (1505). His son Lourenço was his second in command. See X, 26–38.

7. Afonso de Albuquerque (1453–1515), Captor of Goa and Malacca, and the ablest, justest, most intelligent, and most enterprising of the Portuguese governors. He had the abilities of Cortez, but was an honest man. See X, 40–47.

8. João de Castro (1500–1548), governor in 1545. See X, 67–72.

15. 4. Arrian (Anabasis of Alexander, I, 11) speaks of Alexander as producing much labor for epic and lyric poets.

16.   8. This line is an adaptation of Virgil (Georgics, I, 31), teque sibi generum Tethys emat omnibus undis.

17.   2. Burton points out that the two grandfathers of the wretched Sebastian were John III (1503–1557) of Portugal, called the Peaceable, and the Emperor Charles V (reigned 1519–1556).

18.   8. This line is an adaptation of Virgil (Georgics, I, 42), votis iam nunc adsuesci vocari.

19.   8. The cattle herds of Proteus are fish. Proteus was a sea-god, the son of Oceanus and Tethys, or of Neptune and Phoenice. He was the Shepherd of the Ocean, "the Carpathian wizard." The phrase "gado de Proteo," cattle-herds of Proteus, occurs in Canzone XIV (Juromenha, II, 225). A full account of Proteus may be found in the Odyssey, IV, 383–424, imitated by Virgil in the Georgics. And in Horace (Odes, I, 11, 7–8) Proteus drives his flock to visit towering peaks (in the great flood).

20.   8. The grandson of Atlas is Mercury. See Ovid (Met., I, 682, Heroides, XVI, 62), also Horace (Odes, I, x, 1), where we read, "Mercuri, facunde nepos Atlantis."

The whole passage is mainly Ovidian (Met., I, 168–185). Professor Ford, who cites this passage, points out that the Aeneid (Book X) is in the picture. And Virgil was imitating the Iliad, Book IV.

21.   1. The spheres of the Ptolemaic system were (at length) eleven in number. This is in allusion to the seven spheres of the Seven Planets described by Ptolemy. See note to X, 77.

23.   The arrangements for seating the gods remind one of Claudian's account of a similar council in De Raptu Proserpinae, III, 8 ff.

26.   3. Viriathus, murdered in 139 B.C. by order of a Roman general after ten years of successful revolt. See VIII, 6, 36.

4. Sertorius, an adherent of Marius in the war with Sulla, was a skillful soldier and good administrator, who held Lusitania for his party and was assassinated in 72 B.C. See III, 63, IV, 33, VIII, 8 Plutarch who wrote his life describes the milk-white hind and other artful devices of Sertorius.

27.   Camões is paraphrasing Horace (Odes, I, iii): ——————— nec timuit precepetem Africum decertantem Aquilonibus.

28-29. Jupiter's speech may have something of Valerius Flaccus' Argonauticon, I, 528–535.

30.   5. Bacchus is rather inconsistently cast as the divine enemy of the Portuguese, for the legend is that they are his descendants or at least descendants of his henchman Lusus. But see III, 21, note. The mythical conquest of India by Bacchus is frequently alluded to in the Poem. It is perhaps connected with obscure traditions of the descent of the Aryans into India. It may be noted that in the Odyssey (XIII,

33

128–130) Poseidon is particularly severe upon the Phaeacians who are his descendants.

31. 4. Doris, the daughter of Oceanus and Tethys, and mother, by her brother Nereus, of the fifty Nereids.

8. Nysa. There are at least ten towns of this name in the old authors, most of them sacred to one Bacchus or another. Nysa according to Pliny (V, 15) was Bacchus' nurse. He named a town in Syria for her. But Pliny writes elsewhere (VI, 23): "Most people also assign to India the city of Nysa and Mount Merus (thigh in Greek) which is sacred to Bacchus (this being the place from which originated the myth of the birth of Bacchus from the thigh of Jove)." Alexander's army came to a town called Nysa on the Indian frontier, whose people had legends that could easily be equated with Greek mythology (Cambridge History of India, Vol. I, 354 and Arrian, Anabasis of Alexander, V, 1 and Indica, 5). It may be observed here that Bacchus plays the role played by Hera in the Odyssey and Juno in the Aeneid. The whole passage (Stanzas 30–32) closely parallels Virgil's description of Juno's fears in Aeneid, I, 12–33.

32. Oddly enough, almost the last Greek Classic poet, Nonnus (Fifth Century A. D.), wrote an epic on Bacchus in India, which was first printed in 1569, probably too late for Camões to have availed himself of it.

35. The simile of the Winds in Iliad, XVI, 765–771, is the ultimate fons et origo of this passage.

37. 7. The touch about the pallor of Apollo is Ovidian (Met., X, 185). The god turns white when the quoit strikes Hyacinthus.

42. 6. Saint Laurence, now called Madagascar. Professor Ford, who quotes Ovid, Met., V, 321 ff., points out that Camões has scrambled several inconsistent myths. Venus and Cupid took the form of fishes when they fled from Typheus in the War between the Gods and the Giants. The zodiacal sign, the Fishes, is a memorial of this episode. And the sun is entering that sign (late February, 1498), when the voyagers arrive on the shores of Melinde, as the commentators note.

43. 5. Prasso, the Green Cape, the Promunturium Prasum of Ptolemy (IV, 9, 2), was farthest south for the Greeks. It was their Cape Verde in the Second Century, A.D. It is 15° south for Ptolemy, which is the latitude of Mozambique. Ford equates it with Cabo das Correntes on the Mozambique coast. But there seems to be some doubt as to the situation of Ptolemy's promontory. All that need be said here is that Camões borrowed the name for some headland not too far south of Mozambique.

6. Æthiopia—the Æthiopia above Egypt of Ptolemy.

46. 6. Phaëthon, the son of Apollo and Clymene, lost control of his father's sun-chariot, whence he was hurled down by one of Jove's thunderbolts. He fell into the river Po. But before his death he had scorched Africa black. His sister Lampetia was so troubled that the gods went to the unusual length of changing her into a poplar tree. Camões has combined the lady's name with that of one of her sisters, Phaëthusa. The form Lampetusa is unknown to Ovid but appears to occur elsewhere. See Ovid, Met., II, 156–400. Claudian might support Ovid here as in many places (De Tertio Consulatu Honorii, 122–125). Burton cites Aeneid, X, 185 ff., as well. The sisters Lampetia and Phaëthusa are keepers of the Cattle of the Sun (Odyssey, XII, 132).

47.   Burton, who knew the East Coast of Africa well, has explained the costume and weapons of the natives perfectly. I have followed the suggestions of his note to the best of my abilities. He further states that the stanza is absolutely true to life as he had himself seen it. This is the sort of thing that makes one love Burton and would have made Camões love him.

49.   6. Lyaeus, an epithet applied to Bacchus. It appears to mean "the unlooser of anxieties."

51.   8. Acherontic. "Sad Acheron of sorrow black and deep" is one of the rivers of Hades in Greek mythology.

52.   4. The seal or sea-calf is practically a synonym for ugliness with classic writers (Virgil, Georgics, IV, 395; Ovid, Met., I, 300). It is perhaps worth noticing that Camões mentions no sea-beasts unknown to the classic poets, and that in general his reaction to wild nature was not like that of our time. He must have seen monkeys, crocodiles, boas, cobras, tigers, and whatever India, Burma, South China produce. A man who had been shipwrecked at the mouth of the Mekong in the middle of the 16th Century would only view great beasts like the rhinoceros or the huge wild bull as hideous inconveniences, not as exciting features of outdoor experience. We should go a thousand miles to see such a creature. He would unquestionably have gone a hundred to avoid the spectacle.

53.   5. Burton notices that this account of Mohammedanism and Mohammed does not correspond with such facts as yet remain.

54.   4. Quilóa, Mombassa, Sofala, Mozambique. All four of these East African towns appear in Paradise Lost, two of them in the same line, which, with other evidence, seems to show that Milton was familiar with the Lusiads. Milton apparently accented the second syllable of Quilóa like Fanshawe before him, as Burton observes. Which of the two immediately adjoining Kilwas Camões means, I do not know. It may be pointed out that East and West really met when Gama touched at Mozambique.

55.   2. Hydaspes, an affluent of the Indus, now called the Jhelum.

The name is ultimately derived from the Sanskrit Vitasta and reached the Greeks through Persia. It has several forms in Greek. Thus Ptolemy called it the Bidaspes. Horace brings it into his most famous ode (Odes, I, xxii) as a symbol for what is immoderately far away.

59.   4. Hyperion's heir is, of course, the Sun Helios in a myth older than Apollo. Camões might have found the term thus translated, in the Greek, but it is in Valerius Flaccus (Argonauticon, II, 34–37).

63.   1–4. Damião de Goes (I, 75) might be Camões' historic source for the Moor's curiosity about religious works.

68.   6–8. Damião de Goes (I, 75) says that, contrary to Camões' statement, Gama fired a few shots.

69.   Barros (I, iv, 3) explains the immediate reaction in Mozambique. The Portuguese were at once recognized as Christians by the man who saw them first, a Moor from Fez.

73.   The mighty Theban is Bacchus. His mother Semele, when pregnant, desired to look on Zeus, her child's father. She was burned to a cinder by the spectacle. But Jupiter kept the unborn child alive in a cleft in his thigh, until he was sufficiently developed to be born. Hence the epithet, "the child of two mothers." This was a good joke among the Greeks and Romans. Pliny writes of a painting by a pupil of Apelles, who represented Jupiter in labor with Bacchus (XXXV, 40). Claudian (De Laudibus Stilichonis, III, 227–229) has some singular remarks about the occasion when Jupiter lay in and Bacchus was born. And Martial, whose works Camões apparently knew well, alludes to these singular obstetrical difficulties (De Spectaculis, XIII and Epigrams, V, lxxii).

This tirade is modeled on Juno's speech in Aeneid, I, 37–49. There may be also a tang of Statius (Thebais, IV, 670–676) if Statius may be said to have a tang.

75.   7. Rome. The allusion is to Trajan's eastern conquests (Burton). He reached the Persian Gulf.

77.   1–2. A close imitation of Virgil, Aeneid, I, 50–52.

5. The classic epics are full of disguised gods. It is useless to specify.

78.   5. Burton notes that the Argonauts had touched at four places on the African Coast, Saint Helen's Bay, São Bras (Mossel Bay), Rio dos Reis (perhaps the Limpopo), and Rio dos Bons Sinaes. This last might be a mouth of the Zambezi. But see note to V, 77, 4.

79.   Burton notes that these words have the very turn and twist of Africa, just as the remarks of the Catual (VIII, 85, and VIII, 92) have the aphoristic ring of Oriental talk.

84.   1. The Nabatéan heights are the mountains of Northern Arabia, and mean the East. The verse is a reminiscence of Ovid, Met., I, 61.

Burton found the phrase in Ariosto (Orlando Furioso, XV, 12) and thinks Nabatéan equals Oriental generally.

86.　3. In Carta Escripta d'Africa (Juromenha, IV, 155) the writer describes himself as equipped with a shield and assegai, when he wandered outside the walls of the city. The word assegai, now commonly associated with South Africa, according to Webster, is of Berber origin.

87.　Barros on the storm of Dabul (II, iii, 4) might be the model for Camões' account of the landing at Mozambique.

88.　7. Mr. Barnaby Conrad, a painter, a novelist, and an experienced bull-fighter, informs me that Camões has fallen into error here. The superstition that the bull closes his eyes when he charges he thinks is unfounded, although it has been believed for centuries. But if the creature's surprising rapidity in following his enemy did not prove the contrary, the camera does.

91.　4. A variation on Aeneid, VII, 508, where wrath lends arms, Also Aeneid, I, 150, where fury performs for wrath (Ford).

94.　4. Burton noted the paraphrase of Cicero, "sub nomine pacis bellum latet." And Claudian (De Sexto Consulatu Honorii, 307) has "Mars gravior sub pace latet."

96.　2. Amphitrite, daughter of Oceanus and Tethys, and one of Neptune's two wives. She is the mother of Triton and is sometimes called Salatia.

　　3. Nereus, brother and husband of Doris. The fifty Nereids are their daughters.

98.　2. Sinon, the lying Greek (Aeneid, II, 57–144) who persuaded the Trojans to drag the Horse within the walls. The Troad is part of Phrygia. Hence Trojans are often called Phrygians.

　　4–5. Gama's expectation of finding Christians on the East Coast of Africa is evidently due to the legends of Prester John. But Covilham almost certainly got some account of Abyssinia back to Portugal before Gama sailed.

99.　5. Quilóa. See note to Stanza 54.

106.　8. Canzone X (Juromenha, II, 208) has the same line. (Ford.)

BOOK II

ARGUMENT

Inspired by the Demon, the King of Mombassa deter-
mines to destroy the voyagers. He hatches his treasons
under the appearance of friendship. Venus appears before
Jupiter and intercedes for the Portuguese. He promises
to grant them his favor and prophetically reveals to her
certain of their exploits in the Orient. Mercury appears
to Gama in a dream and warns him to flee from peril
in Mombassa. Gama weighs anchor and arrives at
Melinde where the king welcomes him and shows him
kindly hospitality.

THE LUSIADS

THE SECOND BOOK

NOW for the brilliant star the time came round,
He who distinguishes the hours of day,
When he had reached his far desirèd bound,
Veiling from men his clear celestial ray.
In his secret oceanic house profound,
The god of night opened his gates straightway,
And the heathen people hastened from the town
To the ships, that scarce had got their anchors down.

2

Among them one who harbored in his breast
That mortal treachery thus to speak was fain:
"O Captain valorous, you who have pressed
Over the salty road and Neptune's reign,
The King who rules the isle doth joy protest
And in your coming has such pleasure ta'en
That for him cannot be greater desire
Than to greet you, see you, grant what you require.

3

"And since he holds it in especial dear,
And a thing of fair report, yourself to meet,
He prays that you, setting aside all fear,
Will enter in the harbor with the fleet.
And since from your laborious journey here
Your men must suffer weariness complete,
He says you should restore their strength on land,
For this man's very nature must demand.

II   "And if to seek out the rich merchandise
The Golden East brings forth be your design,
Cinnamon, cloves, or other burning spice,
Or drugs that are both sovran and benign,
Or if you look for shining gems of price,
Whether hard diamond or ruby fine,
Here you will find such treasures so abound
That here the end of your desires is found."

5

Our Chief to the ambassador replied,
Grateful for what the King vouchsafed to say,
That, since the sun now under sea would hide,
He might not enter yet and thus obey.
But when tomorrow's sunrise came to guide
And without risk should show the fleet the way,
He would, unfearing, his desire accord,
As fitted, dealing with so great a lord.

6

He asked if Christians in that land there were,
As heretofore to him the pilot told.
The skilled ambassador, who did not err,
Said that the better part Christ's faith did hold.
For thus from the Chief's breast the flatterer
Hoped to root out all thought of caution cold,
So that the Captain might put all his trust
In a people unbelieving and unjust.

7

Gama from among his knaves (he had a few),
Men guilty proved for deeds of vile disgrace,
For the very reason that they well might do
Unchancy work in such a dubious case,
Chose a sharp-witted pair, and bade the two
Forthwith spy out the Moorish traitors' place,
Their city and their power, and haply find,
Christians, whom but to see so gripped the mind.

Through these his presents to the King he sent   **II**
So that he still might cleave to honesty
Continual, pure, sincere, and excellent,
Though much unlike what it appeared to be.
Now from the ships the legion of them went,
The base and wicked, and cut through the sea.
With many a well-feigned smile they came to greet
Ashore the two who landed from the fleet.

9

After they had delivered to the King
The presents and the messages alsó,
They went all through the town, discovering
A great deal less than they desired to know.
For the Moors, suspicious above everything,
What they would gladly see forebore to show.
Where malice rules, there lightly fear will start,
Which fancies falsehood in another's heart.

10

But he whose countenance is wont to wear
Perpetual youth, born of the mothers two,
He who that web of falsehood did prepare
Which should the wanderers utterly undo,
Was in a dwelling in the city there.
False human guise and gear he wore anew.
Seeming most like a Christian, he had made
A splendid altar before the which he prayed.

11

There the high Holy Spirit painted fine,
As it were a portrait, had the artist placed,
With a white dove worked into the design
Above that phoenix sole, the Virgin chaste.
The twelve Apostles' company divine,
Their faces all sore troubled, had been traced
As when from Heaven tongues all fiery broke,
And various languages forthwith they spoke.

II   And thither were the two companions led
Where Bacchus waited for them with his cheat.
And on their knees their prayers to God they said,
Who in the universe hath power complete.
Perfumes in odorous Panchaia bred
Bacchus was burning, excellently sweet.
Thus at long last the false god came to do
His homage and must venerate the True.

The Christians twain were welcomed for the night
And with an honest favor entertained,
Seeing not at all the trickery and sleight
Put on them by false sanctity and feigned.
But when the sun sowed wide his rays of light
O'er the world, and on the horizon scarlet-stained
A man could see all in a moment brighten
The rosy forehead of the child of Titan,

Then from the shore with the King's message went
The Moors to bid them come. With them attend
Those two whom on his errand the Chief sent,
To whom the King had seemed so sure a friend.
And since the Portuguese was now content
There was no peril he need apprehend,
And Christian people had their dwelling there,
Up the salt channel he desired to bear.

His envoys told him they beheld ashore
High altars and a priestly anchorite,
And there had slept, nobly provided for,
While day was hidden in the cowl of night.
In King and people they saw, furthermore,
Only such true contentment and delight
That nobody could nurse suspicion here,
After good faith so perfect and sincere.

At this the noble Gama with good will   **II**
Showed to the Moors who came aboard fair cheer,
For a man's spirit must be trustful still
When all seems certain as this might appear.
The faithless people the whole flagship fill,
Leaving the boats they sailed beneath the sheer.
Happy were they, who clearly could surmise
That they were sure of their desirèd prize.

17

On land with all precaution they procured
Weapons and shot so that, when in the bay
They presently should see the shipping moored,
In fury they might fall on them straightway.
And by this treachery they were well assured
The Portuguese to the last man to slay,
And thus upon those heedless vengeance wreak
For evil they had done in Mozambique.

18

They weighed the anchors that so firmly grip
With the wonted sailors' ho and yo-heave-ho,
But only foresails to the winds let slip
When steering past the well-staked shoal they go.
But Venus sweet, o'er that brave fellowship
Who kept watch always to avert all woe,
Seeing the ambush huge concealed from view,
From sky to sea down like an arrow flew.

19

Nereus' white nymphs she bade come instantly,
Likewise the whole troop of the blue array,
For, since herself was born of the salt sea,
The powers of every ocean must obey.
And she made clear to all their company,
Why she was come and with them sped away
To halt the fleet, ere it should reach the shore
And thereby be undone for evermore.

II   Across the waters with all speed they pressed.
Their silver flukes aloft the white foam threw.
There Doto clove the combers with her breast
In greater rage than she is wont to do.
Nisa skimmed lightly. And from crest to crest
Of the curling seas, headlong, Nerina flew.
And the waves, curving over in dismay,
Before the hasting Nereids, made way.

21

On a Triton's shoulder (her look was wrath complete),
Raging, did lovely Cytherea fare.
But her ferryman scarce felt the burden sweet,
So proud he was such charming freight to bear.
Already they drew near the warrior fleet,
Whose canvas stiffly swelled with stirring air.
At once they parted and a circle wove
About the swift ships where ahead they drove.

22

The goddess halted with her regiment
Right at the flagship's prow. She and her brood
Of nymphs, the barrier's passage to prevent,
Strong winds that vainly filled the sails withstood.
Back on its course the sturdy vessel went,
As her soft bosom pressed the rugged wood.
The other nymphs around her stop and stay,
And from the foe's shoal push the ship away.

23

As by their hill the ants, who all foresee,
Bearing their burdens disproportionate,
Work in a spirit of fierce enmity
Against the freezing winter, which they hate,
And there they toil in dreadful drudgery,
Displaying vigor wholly desperate,
Even so the squadrons of the nymphs contend
To save the Portuguese from that bad end.

Back on her track perforce the tall ship drew,   **II**
Despite her company, who with a shout
Tried a new tack. Enraged were all the crew.
Starboard and port they shifted helm about.
The master on the quarter-deck, who knew
His mystery so well, in vain cried out,
Seeing a threatening reef that lay ahead,
The which of shipwreck put him sore in dread.

25

Rose terribly the yelling yo-heave-ho
From the rough sailor while he hauled and heaved.
And the roar among the Moors spread fear and woe,
As if some monstrous battle they perceived.
The reason of that wrath they did not know,
Nor of that haste what was to be believed,
But fancied their design was all seen clear,
And they would get their quittance now and here.

26

And lo! A many darted in a flash
To the swift prows, moored to the ships that lay.
And others dive and high the waters splash
Where, plunging in the sea, they swim away.
Starboard and port over the side they dash,
For what they see compells them in dismay.
To chance the sea more with their purpose stands
Than to be captives in their foemen's hands.

27

As where in some wild place a fen is found,
And frogs (the Lycian tribe in times gone by),
Careless, on the water's edge squat all around,
But, if they think they see a man draw nigh,
Here and there leap, while the pool thrills with sound,
And from the peril they discern they fly
To shelter in the harbor that they know,
And but their heads above the surface show;

II   So fled the Moors—and the pilot, whose intent
Was into danger vast the ships to steer,
Fled too. O'erside into the brine he went.
That his false arts were known was all his fear.
Lest on that stubborn shoal they should be shent,
Where they could lose sweet life that is so dear,
The flagship forthwith anchored in the place,
And the ships near her struck their sails apace.

Gama, who watched with an attentive eye
The Moors' unlooked-for actions, noticed too
In the very nick the pilot swiftly fly,
And guessed what that vile people thought to do.
The wind was neither contrary nor high,
Against the fleet no countercurrent drew,
And yet the ship could make no way ahead.
It seemed a miracle, and this he said:

"Oh! mighty chance, strange, and incredible!
Oh! miracle too clear and evident!
Oh! new-found unsuspected treason fell!
Oh! hypocritic foe malevolent!
What man so wise in a trap set so well
Could hope to 'scape the perilous event,
If the Sovran Watcher, yonder from the Height,
Came not to help our feeble human might?

"For Providence Divine has shown us here
Scant safety in these ports we may attain.
We have beheld too well how things appear,
And confidence has been deceived again.
Since prudent human wisdom sees not clear
The way through falsehood that so well can feign,
O Sacred Guardian, men must think of Thee,
Without Whom they have no security.

"If to this wandering people in their woe
Thy Spirit doth in charity incline,
Which saved us whole and did Thy Mercy show
Amid a folk perfidious and malign,
Then to safe harbor where the truth they know
Conduct us, as Thy Wisdom may design.
Or lands we seek, discover to our sight.
For we sail but to do Thee service right."

33

Fair Venus heard how sadly he complained
In piteous words, and was much moved thereby.
The troop of nymphs she left, who there remained,
Grieved that their patroness so soon must fly.
The shining circle of the stars she gained,
Passing onward to the third sphere of the sky.
And thence to the Sixth Heaven she took the road,
Until she came unto her sire's abode.

34

As, flushed with effort, she climbed upward there,
So beautiful her look and features were
That the stars and Heaven and all the neighboring air
And whoso saw her fell in love with her.
In eyes where cradled rests her infant fair
Living inspiring spirit was a-stir,
Whereby the icy poles she wholly burned,
And into flame the frozen sphere was turned.

35

And to enamor her great sire the more,
Who ever loved her well and held her dear,
As for the Trojan, the same guise she wore
When she in Ida's forest would appear.
Had the hunter seen who lost man's shape of yore,
Beholding Dian in the water clear,
Never had the famished hounds their master slain.
He would have died before of amorous pain.

49

II   Curled threads of gold were radiantly besprent
    All down her neck which darkened whitest snow.
    Her milky bosom quivered as she went,
    With which love plays, though none can see him so.
    From her white flanks the flames shot imminent,
    Wherewith her boy sets every soul aglow.
    And all desires around her limbs were twined,
    As these were pillars which the ivies bind.

                37
    With delicate lawn those parts were covered o'er,
    Whose natural defence is bashful fear.
    If the veil hid, yet it revealed the more,
    No miser of red lilies, too austere.
    But that desire might twofold burn, she wore
    Adornment of transparency so clear.
    And they understood throughout all Heaven above
    Vulcan his jealousy and Mars his love.

                38
    Indeed she seemed by her angelic face,
    In which some sadness mingled with the smile,
    Like a lady whom a lover without grace
    In loving play entreats in evil style,
    Who weeps and the same moment laughs apace,
    'Twixt pain and pleasure balancing the while.
    But less in sadness than in tender jest
    The goddess without peer her sire addressed:

                39
    "O powerful, my sire, I thought alway
    In aught wherefore with loving heart I prayed
    To find thee gentle, amorous, and gay,
    Although some reason thwart against it weighed.
    But since I now behold thy anger play
    Against me, guiltless, who no error made,
    Do now what unto Bacchus seemeth just,
    And I shall know how luckless was my trust.

"This people, which is mine, for whom I cry **II**
With tears, which, as I see, fall all in vain,
Though I love them I but do them injury,
Since you hate all whereof I am most fain.
For them I pray you, and I sob and sigh
And against my happiness the fight sustain:
Because I love them, they must suffer still.
If you protect them, I will wish them ill.

41

"Aye, let them die at the hands of that vile race,
For since I was—" At that the soft look fled
And burning teardrops watered all her face,
As on the opening rose the dew is shed.
Her teeth clenched. She was silent for a space
And could not speak sad words she would have said,
Yet yearned to speak. But the great Thunderer,
Leaning forward in his power, prevented her.

42

Such tenderness was hers. Much moved thereby,
For a tiger's heart must have been touched for sure,
With joyful look, as when the lofty sky
He calms once more and clears the air obscure,
With passion, while he sought her tears to dry,
He kissed her sweet face, clasping the white neck pure
So warmly that, if none were by but he,
A second Cupid might have come to be.

43

To his own he pressed that well-belovèd face,
Made lovelier by her tears and by her sighs,
As a young child, with his nursemaid, in disgrace,
For her caresses but the loudlier cries.
To calm her angry spirit, all the case
He showed her of the future enterprise.
What fortunes in the womb of fate there were,
After this manner, he revealed to her:

51

II "For thy Lusitanians, my daughter fair,
Of any peril stand thou not in fear,
For naught with me a greater weight can bear
Than that those sovran eyes should shed a tear.
Thou shalt see, child, I promise and declare,
The Greek and Roman glory wiped out clear
By the surpassing acts which these men's hands
Are to perform throughout the Orient lands.

45

"For, if Ulysses, by fair words' resource,
'Scaped in Ogygia endless servitude,
If Antenor the Illyric gulfs could force
To find the wellhead of Timavus' flood,
And if devout Aeneas laid his course
Through Scylla and Charybdis' channel rude,
Thy people greater toils shall undergo
And unto all the world new worlds shall show.

46

"Fortresses, cities, bulwarks huge of height,
Built by their hands, my child, thou shalt behold,
And the tough Turk, so terrible in fight,
By them still backward in disorder rolled.
India's free kings secure, by this King's might,
Thou shalt see wholly conquered and controlled.
And they, when all as masters they command,
Shall give a law far nobler to the land.

47

"Thou shalt behold him, who so swift his way
Toward Indus, by great perils girt, doth take,
Scare Neptune till he tremble in dismay,
When without wind the curling waters break,
Miracle never seen until that day,
For in dead calm the sea shall heave and quake.
O noble race, whose thoughts are high indeed,
If the very elements must fear their breed!

"Behold! the land that water once denied II
Becomes a harbor for them of the best,
Where, after their far voyage, resting ride
The galleons that come sailing from the West.
And all this coast, where that damned homicide
Was plotted once, shall be at their behest
And pay them tribute, for they know aright
That against fearful Lusus none can fight.

49

"Thou shalt behold the nobly-known Red Sea
When he turns yellow pale for terror pure,
And Ormuz' realm, for all its majesty,
Defeat and subjugation twice endure,
And pierced with shafts of his own archery,
There shalt thou look upon the savage Moor.
For he who goes against thy chosen's might,
When he resists, against himself shall fight.

50

"Thou shalt see in Diu the impregnable
Thy favored folk two sieges undergo.
Their worth and fortune they will show right well,
Doing great feats of arms against the foe.
And thou shalt see huge Mars for envy swell
Of Lusitania fierce that works such woe.
They shall behold the Moor, whose dying scream
Shall for Mahound against the Skies blaspheme.

51

"Thou shalt see Goa from the Moslem ta'en,
Which shall throughout the Orient far and nigh
Henceforward as the sovran mistress reign,
By the victor people's triumph set on high.
There, in her pomp and power, she shall constrain
With the harsh bit all those who magnify
Their heathen idols, and so in every land
That would in war thy chosen folk withstand.

II "Thou shalt see them at the fort of Cananor,
With a handful and scant strength, keep up the fight.
Calicut, likewise, they shall topple o'er,
That was so populous and had such might.
In Cochim shall his reputation soar,
Whose pride and insolent mind attain such height
That never lyre for victory could raise
The chant that should express his name and praise.

53

"Ne'er with such fierce pitched war Leucadia flamed,
What time Augustus of the spirit true,
In internecine strife for Actium named,
The faithless Roman captain overthrew,
Who from Dawn's races, from the Nile far-famed,
And from the mighty Scythic Bactria drew
The wage of triumph and enormous spoils,
Taken in the fair Egyptian's wanton toils,

54

"As thou shalt see when Ocean flames indeed
With fires thy folk have lit where they make war.
Captive idolater and Moor they lead,
With various nations whom they overbore,
Till the rich Golden Chersonese concede
Defeat, and they sail past far China's shore.
And the Earth's remotest islands one and all,
With the whole sea, are at their beck and call.

55

"Thus, child, they'll show their manner and their state,
For more than man's their fortitude will be.
And never shall be seen courage so great
From the Gangetic to the Cadiz Sea,
Nor from the Boreal Ocean to the Strait
Which the wronged Portuguese found latterly,
Though all who ever knew peril and pain
Of old throughout the world should rise again."

56

So saying, he bade Maia's sacred son
Descend to earth, with the commandment clear
To find safe harbor and a pleasant one,
In which the fleet might enter without fear.
Lest in Mombassa some fresh risk be run
By the brave Captain if he lingered near,
He bade the god in dream to him disclose
The land where he might quietly repose.

57

Already the Cyllenian down the air
Was hurling. On wing'd feet to Earth he flies
And in his hand the fateful rod doth bear,
Wherewith he lulls to sleep outwearied eyes,
Or from Hell summons spirits that despair,
And the winds obey it. In his wonted guise
Mercury upon his head his helmet wore,
And thus descended on Melindè's shore.

58

And Rumor he took with him to proclaim
How worthy was the Portuguese and rare.
For favor hung on his illustrious name,
That made him loved and courted everywhere.
And thus was spread the legend of his fame
Among the friendly people here and there.
Already in Melindè will grows warm
To know us and our pressure and our form.

59

Then straightway to Mombassa did he go,
Where all the fearful ships at anchor lay,
And bade them from the harbor of the foe
And lands suspect at once to take their way;
For skill and valor make but a poor show
Against their hellish urge, who would betray.
Naught avail courage, subtlety, and sense,
Not guided by celestial Providence.

II Half way along her road had gone the night,
While with strange fire the stars in Heaven keep
This world in its immensity alight,
And the one pleasure of mankind was sleep.
The famous Captain, overwearied quite
From night watch in anxiety so deep,
To give his eyes some little rest is fain,
While others at their posts their guard maintain.

In dream to him did Mercury appear,
Uttering these words: "Fly, Lusitanian, fly
From treachery the false King is weaving here
To work destruction and your death thereby.
Calm are the waters and the weather clear.
Fly now, for the wind favors and the Sky.
And elsewhere is a king of friendlier mind,
With whom in safety shelter you shall find.

"Here you are nothing but the feast arrayed
For his stallions by Diomedes the fell,
Who trained his beasts so that their meal they made
On flesh of folk he entertained so well.
The altars where sad captives with the blade
Were slaughtered by Busiris horrible,
You will attain, if you delay too long.
Fly from these brutes and their perfidious wrong!

"Forthwith the length of all the coastline run
Till on a greener country you shall light,
Hard by the region where the flaming sun
Has equal made the length of day and night.
The King there, with kind acts in friendship done,
Will cheerly give the fleet a welcome right.
Safe shelter he will grant you, and beside,
To India, a wise and trusty guide."

64

This Mercury said, from slumber rousing swift   **II**
The Admiral, who started up awake
And saw in cloudy darkness, through a rift,
A sudden ray of sacred sunshine break.
He thought how in that land of evil shift
Clearly it skilled not more delay to make,
And bade the master, with a courage new,
Shake out the canvas to the gale that blew.

65

"Make sail," he said, "for the wind blowing wide,
Since the Skies favor and 'tis God's intent.
The Bright Throne's messenger I have descried,
Who here, to speed us on, his course has bent."
The mariners' hurly rose. To either side,
Shouting their chanteys, cheerily they went.
And high apeak the anchors up they hove
With all the lusty vigor that they love.

66

At the moment when the anchors home they brought,
Under cover of gross dark, the hidden Moor
Then privily to cut the hawsers sought,
That the ships might run aground to ruin sure.
But the Portuguese, alert, not to be caught,
With the eyes of lynxes kept a watch secure.
And the Moors, when they perceived their trick we
Fled fast. They did not row. Rather they flew. [knew,

67

But swiftly now the sharp cutwaters go,
Through the wet silver roads cleaving the way.
And fairly for them doth the Southwest blow
With motion smooth and easy as he may.
Of peril past the talk goes to and fro,
For great affairs but slow from memory stray,
When out of the fell clutch of circumstance
Life has been saved by some brave stroke of chance.

II   Already once had shone the burning sun.
Another day was toward. Far off in view
Two ships appeared to them, that made their run
Before the wind so pleasantly that blew.
That they were Moors was plain to everyone.
They hauled the wind to overtake the two.
And one for terror of the ill he feared,
To save his crew, right for the beaches steered.

69

The other who remained had not like skill
And fell into the Lusitanian's clutch.
But he from cruel Mars sustained no ill
Nor did he suffer furious Vulcan's touch.
Since his weak human spirit, conscious still
Of his scant crew, cowered and feared so much,
He showed no fight at all, which, had he done,
Yet greater risk thereby he would have run.

70

In Gama the desire had risen high
For a pilot to the India he sought.
He hoped for one in the Moors' company,
But things befell far other than he thought.
For, as to the right region of the Sky
Where India lay, no man could teach him aught.
But they all told how near Melindè stood,
Where surely he might get a pilot good.

71

And the Moors praised the king as being kind,
Of free conditions and a heart sincere,
And greatness and humanity of mind,
With qualities men mightily revere.
To think it true the Chief was well inclined,
For the Cyllenian had showed it clear
In the vision of the night. And on they speed,
As the Moor declared and as the dream decreed.

'Twas the delicious time when Phoebus' light   **II**
His sign seeks, who away Europa bore,
And both the Bull's horns with his heat doth smite,
And, from Amalthéa's, Flora all her store
Pours forth. The swift sun, circling in the height,
Revives the memory of the day once more
When He, the Master of us all and one,
Set first His seal on the works that He had done.

73

Then it was the squadron to the shore drew nigh,
(Melindè's kingdom standing full in view),
With awnings decked, that served to signify
How well to keep the Holy Day they knew.
Fair did the pennons whip, the standard fly.
A man far off might see that purple hue.
And all the drums and timbrels raised the blare
As the happy warriors made their entrance there.

74

At once was thronged the whole Melindian shore
With folk who came at the glad fleet to gaze,
A kinder folk, more truthful, furthermore,
Than in those lands, whence late they came their ways.
The Lusitanian ships moored right before.
Firm in that ground the heavy anchor stays.
They sent ashore one captured Moor alone,
Unto the King their coming to make known.

75

The King, who that nobility could guess,
That Portugal up to such greatness led,
The freedom of his port conceived no less
Than what a gallant nation merited,
And, with sincerity and gentleness
That honor every spirit nobly bred,
Entreated them to hasten to the land
Where all his realm should be at their command.

II   This offer wholly as good faith appears.
The words are trusty with no double sense,
Which the king sent the gallant cavaliers
Who had passed such tracts of earth and sea immense.
With meat of fleecy lambs their board he cheers,
And fatted barnyard fowl likewise presents,
With every sort of fruit the region breeds.
Yet the good will the goodly gift exceeds.

77

The Admiral received in high content
That pleasant envoy and the word he bore,
And forthwith in his turn his present sent,
Destined for such a purpose long before—
Fine branching coral, scarlet and purple blent,
Colored like flame, whereby men set such store.
It grows 'neath water, and is soft while there,
But, taken thence, it hardens in the air.

78

He sent a man (a speaker skilled was he),
With that good King to make a compact true.
If from the ships he came not instantly,
Delay as guilt he should not misconstrue.
The envoy left, who knew his mystery.
When near the presence of the King he drew,
In such a style as Pallas' self can teach,
And in such words as these, he made his speech:

79

"Great King, to whom Justice Supreme could grant
From bright Olympus the right to govern here
A people who are brave and arrogant
And love thee not the less because they fear;
As a strong port and refuge in our want,
Known throughout all the Orient far and near,
We look to find thee. So we may have indeed
A certain remedy in our sore need.

"We are not buccaneers, who, as they stray   **II**
Among defenceless cities unaware,
With fire and steel the wretched people slay,
Coveted wealth out of their hands to tear.
But from proud Europe we have made our way,
And to the uttermost of lands we fare,
Huge wealthy India. This we undertake,
So ordered, for our splendid sovereign's sake.

81

"What barbarous custom and device they used!
Stiff-neck'd the generation of that land,
That not alone their ports to us refused
But the mere refuge of their wastes of sand!
Why of such wicked will were we accused?
Why of so few in such great terror stand
That they, with armed plot and snare well-feigned,
The sight of our own death for us ordained?

82

"Gentlest of kings, we look to find in thee
A firmer faith, and comfortable aid
We likewise hope for from thy charity,
Alcinoüs to the Ithacan dismayed.
Safely unto thy port we crossed the sea,
By the divine interpreter conveyed,
For, since he sent us, it is now seen clear,
Thine is a rare heart, human and sincere.

83

"And, King, I beg, do not at all suspect,
Because our Captain of exalted mind
Comes not to see or serve thee. Indirect
Dealing he has not seen, nor has divined.
For thou must know this is but the effect
Of the order of his King, which, well inclined,
He keeps, who bade him never leave his post
With the fleet in any port on any coast.

II   "For this should always be good vassal's part,
As with the limbs o'er which the head holds sway.
Ask not (for on a royal throne thou art)
That any man his king should disobey.
But, finding grace and kindness in thy heart,
He promises his gratitude alway,
Whatever shall by him and his be done,
So long as rivers to the ocean run."

85

He ended. And together all men nigh
Thereupon fell a-talking at their ease,
And gave our courage commendation high,
Who, 'neath such skies, had crossed so many seas.
The noble King beheld in his mind's eye
The obedient spirit of the Portuguese
And our King's worth could loftily assay,
Who was obeyed so well so far away.

86

He, with a smiling face and aspect kind,
Said to the envoy, whom he now held dear:
"Pluck out all base suspicion from your mind,
And let your people feel no chilly fear.
Your worth, your acts, in such wise are combined
As to the whole world nobly shall appear.
And whosoever does you harm in aught
Is one incapable of noble thought.

87

"That some of you ashore no foot will set,
According to accustomed precedent,
Though it weighs strangely on my mind as yet,
With such obedience I am well content.
But since 'tis the condition to be met,
Then I am one who never will consent
That such true loyal hearts should do such ill
To their own souls, merely to serve my will.

"However, when the sunrise comes anew II
Tomorrow, pinnaces I shall array,
And come your formidable fleet to view,
Which I have much desired this many a day.
And if the ships have suffered hurt undue,
Because of seas, strong gales, and the long way,
Here you may have, without least cause for fear,
A pilot, stores, and various naval gear."

89

Thus spake the King. Therewith Latona's son
In the sea hid him. And the envoy went
With the tale of things so happily begun
In his light shallop to the armament.
There joy now filled the heart of everyone,
Thus to have won true solace and content,
Reaching the land they sought for far away.
That night they feasted and all hearts were gay.

90

No lack of fires of artifice they knew,
That emulate a comet's tremulous light.
And well the bombardiers their work could do,
Who earth and sea and sky with thunder smite.
The bombs that from the blaze all flaming flew
Displayed the Cyclops' labor to the sight.
Others in song, wherewith the Heavens they rent,
Touched many a nobly sounding instrument.

91

And from the shore they instantly replied
With fiery serpents and tremendous sound.
Blazing wheels high aloft in circles ride.
Explodes the hidden sulphur finely ground.
With a loud voice to Heaven the people cried.
The sea with fires was burning all around,
The land no less. Such was the gay ado,
As if a contest were between the two.

II But the skies wheel with motion never failing
And wake mankind unto their toil to wend.
Already Memnon's mother comes, light trailing,
And to the longest slumber puts an end.
Now the dark shadows haste away, exhaling
The frozen dews that on the flowers descend.
Melindè's King betook him to his barge,
To view the fleet, seaward that rode at large.

93

Behind him you could see along the shore
Folk, who came but for sport, light-hearted, stream.
Bright the fine purple of the smocks they wore,
And fair their garments all silk-woven gleam.
And palm-tree branches in their hands they bore,
Instead of warlike darts or bows that seem
Mimics of Luna's horns, boughs fit to be
The veritable crown of victory.

94

A gleaming galley, hung with awnings fair,
Silken and dyed with many a various stain,
Melindè's royal Majesty did bear,
With his realm's chiefs and nobles in his train.
Well-adorned costly robes the King doth wear,
As art permits and custom may ordain,
On his head a cotton turban, fold on fold,
Splendid with broidery of silk and gold.

95

His robe, rich damask, for a king to don,
And Tyrian-colored, which they rate so high;
Fine gold, his collar, but, in comparison,
The workmanship the metal could outvie;
And at his belt, brilliant as diamond, shone
A noble dagger fashioned cunningly.
Seed pearls and gold, the history to complete,
Covered the velvet sandals on his feet.

A servant bears a silken target round,   II

Nailed on the point of a tall gilded spear,

To ward the sun's heat off lest it confound

Proud royalty or peradventure sear.

At the prow strange noise that had a merry sound,

But harsh of note and horrible to hear,

Issued from the curved trumpets, music sore,

Which, inharmonious, made a hellish roar.

97

The Lusitanian's splendor was no less,

As with his boats, departing from the fleet,

Followed by a glittering and noble press,

He went Melindè's Majesty to greet.

Fashioned in the mode of Spain was Gama's dress,

Albeit of French tailoring complete.

Of Adrian Venice satin, his attire

Was wrought, and crimson, which all men admire.

98

And studs of gold to bind his sleeves has he,

Whence the sun flashes, dazzling to the eyes.

On his soldier trunk-hose is embroidery

Stitched with the ore fortune to most denies.

With points of the same, designed most artfully,

His doublet slashes he adjusts and ties.

His golden sword the Italian taste recalls.

And to one side, slanting, his cap-plume falls.

99

Those of his following, shimmering with the dye

Which from the matchless murex men prepare,

Display the changing hue that charms the eye

And differing sort of fine apparel wear.

Such bright enamels might a man descry,

Who looked on all the brilliant vesture there,

As the fair nymph, Thaumas' girl, is wont to show

In the splendor of her many-colored bow.

II And straightway the sonorous trumpets' sound
Makes every spirit glad, rebellowing loud.
And the Moors' boats choke all the waters round
As, trailing pennons, through the sea they crowd.
The cannon echoes horribly rebound,
And puffs of smoke the sun's face overcloud.
The guns go off again, again, once more,
And the Moors clap hand to ear against the roar.

Already in the Captain's shallop stands
The King, who in his arms our Chief doth take
And with the courtesy good sense demands,
As from a king, right fairly him bespake.
Pleasure mixed with astonishment expands
In the Moor's face, seeing our mode and make,
As a man thrilling with esteem profound
For them who came so far, for India bound.

Then he made offer, in great words and high,
Of his whole realm, whatever might pertain,
And if our Chief lacked victual and supply,
Let him ask as one who asks his own again.
Further, he said he knew from Rumor's cry
Portugal's name ere he perceived them plain.
And he had heard how on another shore
With men of his confession they made war.

He said all Africa rang with the sound
Of mighty actions that their hands had done,
What time the diadem of all that ground
Where once dwelt the Hesperides they won.
In words of compliment he did abound,
But Portugal's merits less descanted on
And more on that which he by rumor knew.
In this sort Gama answered thereunto:

"Thou, only thou, unto the Portuguese
Hast pity shown, O King of noble mind!
We know all sorrows and adversities
And put to test the ocean's fury blind.
Eternity the Holy, may it please,
Who rules the wheeling Heavens and Mankind,
For the good deeds done unto us by thee,
Better to pay than in our power may be.

II

105

"Thou only, of all those whom Phoebus brands,
To men from the great Deep hast ministered.
From wild Eolian tempests, at thy hands
We find release, kindness, and faithful word.
Long as the sun gives light to all the lands,
Or the great Pole pastures his starry herd,
Where'er I list to dwell, in pride and fame,
Memory shall keep the praises of thy name."

106

He spoke. And forthwith to the oars they bent,
Heading for the fleet the Moor desired to see.
And in a circle round each ship they went,
That all he might observe sufficiently.
To the sky thundered Vulcan's armament,
As the fleet saluted with artillery,
Loud blared the trumpets sounding sweet and high,
To which the Moorish slughorns made reply.

107

But after he had had all this in view,
The generous Moor, who shook and was afraid,
Hearing the guns that erst he never knew,
Which such terrific power to him displayed,
Issued forthwith the order to heave to
And anchor the light bark which them conveyed,
Wishing with Gama to have further word
Concerning all the matters he had heard.

II Since various talk the Moor pleased passing well,
He prayed that he might be enlightened more
About the famous battles that befell
Against the folk Mahomet that adore.
He also wished to know what peoples dwell
Far on the ultimate Hesperian shore,
And who their neighbors in that place might be,
And the tale of all the wet roads of the sea.

"But, first," he said, "courageous Chief, make plain
To us distinctly and in order due
The climate of your land, the region main
As of this world that it pertains untó,
There where you dwell. Tell what your ancient strain,
Whence its beginnings your strong kingdom drew.
And from the first your deeds of war relate,
Which, knowing not, I yet must know are great.

"And let your world-wide wandering be told,
Into the toils of savage seas betrayed,
And what strange barbarous rule you might behold,
Rough Africa unto herself has made.
Tell, for the horses with the bits of gold,
That draw the young sun's chariot rich inlaid,
Come from the regions of the dawning chill,
And the winds sleep and the sea-waves are still.

"And as the time seems ripe, why even so
Is my desire to hear what you relate,
For who is he, by fame, who doth not know
That actions of the Portuguese are great?
Nor so far distant from us flames the glow
Of the clear sun that you should justly rate
Our rough Melindian hearts as apt to treat
Below its worth so marvelous a feat.

"Proud giants did their powers to war commit   **II**
In vain against Olympus bright and pure.
Piríthoüs and Theseus, lacking wit,
Stormed Pluto's realm, the dreadful and obscure.
Great deeds on earth, of these the compeers fit,
Have been, superb and fearful to endure.
If they dared Hell or Heaven to engage,
These others bore the brunt of Nereus' rage.

113

"Herostratus burned down the sacred fane
Of Dian, built by the wise Ctesiphon,
Supposing thus a wide repute to gain
'Mid men for what the world would comment on;
For to such acts deceitfully constrain
Hopes of a name that flouts comparison.
But this is truth. Who glory would ensue
Deeds that deserve long memory must do."

NOTES

BOOK II

1.   Perhaps this stanza owes something to Petrarch's Sonnet IX:

> Quando 'l pianeta chi distingue l 'ore . . .

6.   1. Lencastre notes that at the time there were almost certainly many persons in Mombassa, whom the Moors could easily take for Christians, and who in fact might be so, namely Abyssinians and the so-called Christians of St. Thomas from India. But Burton's commentary is full of his amused astonishment at the fact that the Portuguese at first thought that Hindus (of whom there must have been many in Mozambique) were Christians, because they were not Mohammedans.

7.   With respect to this curious practice of carrying criminals along for dangerous or discreditable jobs, Damião de Goes (I, 97) has some remarks. Gama dropped a number of them at various points at which he touched on the way out, but did not pick them up on his return. A more ghastly fate than theirs cannot be imagined. Gama sent several such unfortunates on dangerous missions at the Rio dos Reis (de Goes, I, 72).

10.   1. Bacchus.

        3. Why he was called the son of two mothers has been explained in I, 73, note.

11.   4. The same phrase and order in the description of the Virgin occurs in the second line of the 197th sonnet. The expression, though common form, evidently pleased Camões.

        5. The Day of Pentecost and the tongues of fire, Acts, II.

12.   5. Panchaia an Island off Arabia Felix, (Ovid Met., X, 307–310): Let the land of Panchaia be rich in balsam, let it bear its cinnamon, its costum, its frankincense sweated from the tree, its various flowers, so long as it bears the myrrh tree.

        Professor Ford quotes Virgil (Georgics, II, 139): Panchaia rich in frankincense-bearing sands.

        Tibullus (III, 2, 23) also talks about "Panchaia merces."

        Burton says Panchaia is Dofar, in Southeast Arabia. It was an

El Dorado for Greek and Roman. Gold-smelting was believed to have been invented there (Pliny, VII, 56).

7-8. The conceit in this couplet has been cavilled at. But god may pray to god in Homer, e. g. Odyssey, III, 51-61, when Athena prays to Poseidon.

13.   8. Aurora, the goddess of dawn and daughter of the Titan Hyperion, loved Tithonus, the son of Laomedon founder of Troy. By her he had Memnon, one of the heroes of the Iliad. Tithonus was granted immortality but he unfortunately neglected to ask for eternal youth. He prayed for death, but Aurora instead changed him into the Cicada, an insect, which, for the Provencal poets of the 19th Century, became the symbol of their renaissance.

19.   3-4. Dame Venus, Love's Lady,
            Was born of the Sea.

20.   3. Camões' Nereids, Burton succeeds in linking up with the Iliad and Aeneid, but Nerina seems to be the Portuguese's own invention.

21.   Triton carries Venus on his shoulders in Claudian (De Nuptiis Honorii, 128-130).

22.   Athena and Hera in Valerius Flaccus (Argonauticon, IV, 682-683) force back the Cyanean Rocks from the ship Argo in much the same manner.

23.   Burton says that this simile is a classic commonplace ultimately derived from Homer. I appear to have missed it in Homer, but Virgil is certainly in the picture (Aeneid, IV, 401-407). And Horace has his version of the simile of the ants (Satires, I, 1, 32-35).

24.   This stanza could be a reminiscence of the difficulties of Argo off Lemnos in Statius (Thebais, V, 412-415) and in Valerius Flaccus (Argonauticon).

        5. According to Damião de Goes (I, 67) the master was a certain Pero de Alemquer.

27.   The Lycian peasants were discourteous to Latona, mother of Apollo and Diana. She changed them into frogs (Ovid, Met., VI, 339-381).

33.   6. Camões is punctilious about his astronomy. Venus goes onward to her own sphere, the third, and thence to her father's, the sixth (Lencastre).

34-56.   An elaborate imitation of Aeneid, I, 223-304, where the interview of Venus with Jupiter is described. Parts of this passage are actual translation. But Camões goes beyond the Virgilian simplicity. Jupiter's prophecy of the greatness of Portugal parallels the prophecy of the greatness of Rome, and at the end Mercury is dispatched on an errand similar to that on which he goes in the Aeneid.

35. 3. The Trojan is Paris, to whom Venus, Juno and Minerva appeared naked in the woods of Ida.

5. The hunter is Actaeon, who enraged Diana when he inadvertently discovered her bathing. She changed him into a stag. And his own dogs devoured him.

36. 7–8. This conceit is a dreadful, but the translation is reasonably close. 20th Century poetry may have to be forgiven a good deal some day.

37. Statius may be in Camões mind: "The wicked power that commends the girdle" (Thebais, II, 283–284). Alcina when she seduces Ruggiero in Orlando Furioso (VII, 28) wears a similar costume. And the whole passage descriptive of Alcina may be compared with Camões' account of Venus. Claudian knows all about the girdle of Venus (De Nuptiis Honorii, 122–127).

40. This seems to be a variation on a speech of Juno's in Ovid, Met., II, 518–520.

41. 7–8. The speech of Africa in Claudian's De Bello Gildonico follows the same rhetorical pattern.

42. 1–4. cf. Aeneid, I, 254–256.

3–4. One of the most beautiful similes in Homer (Iliad, XVI, 297–302) may be the origin of this sadly diminished cliché.

5–8. The embrace in the Lusiads is much warmer than in Virgil.

45. 1. Ulysses, otherwise Odysseus, Homer tells us, was for eight years a captive of the nymph Calypso in her island of Ogygia. He was finally released owing to the good offices of Pallas Athene.

3. Antenor, one of the sons of Priam, according to Virgil, escaped after the sack of Troy, explored Dalmatia (Illyria), and founded Padua. The Timavus is apparently a river on the Venetian-Istrian border (Aeneid, I, 242–243).

6. Scylla and Charybdis. Scylla is a rock and Charybdis a whirlpool in the Straits of Catania. Scylla had been a beautiful nymph who scorned the attentions of Glaucus. He asked Circe to aid him in his love-making, but she fell in love with him herself and changed Scylla into a hideous monster. Charybdis is said to have stolen the oxen of Hercules and to have been changed into a whirlpool for her pains. For Scylla, see VI, 24, note.

47. On a later voyage (1524, year of Camões' birth, when Gama went out to be Viceroy), Vasco da Gama exhibited extreme presence of mind, when an earthquake convulsed the sea during a dead calm. His reported words may be translated: "How delightful! The very sea is afraid of us" (Ford). This is surely what may be called the Caesar or Cortez touch. Men, who in terrifying moments have such odd flashes, have also, right or wrong, a knack for empire building. Camões, who seems to know Pliny pretty well, has overlooked Pliny's notion that earthquakes and inundations may be connected (II, 83).

49.   Ormuz, in the Persian Gulf. The story of the arrows that boomeranged is to be found in the historical work of João de Barros. Albuquerque finally took Ormuz in 1514.

50.   1. Diu, still a Portuguese colony, besieged by the natives in 1538, and again in 1546–47.

51.   Goa, still a Portuguese colony, seized by Albuquerque in 1510 and capital of the Indian colonies ever since. Here stood the statue of Vasco da Gama, which a century after the discovery was torn down in riots against the discoverer's descendant, the Viceroy Francis da Gama. It is supposed to have had at its height as many as 100,000 inhabitants. The whole east coast of Africa, both coasts of India, Malaya, Indonesia, and Macão were governed from Goa.

In his biographic sketch of Robert Byron, Christopher Sykes (Four Studies in Loyalty) quotes a remarkable passage from his friend's "Essay on India":

"From an eminence above the Delhi plain rises a line of sunlit domes and towers, pink and cream against the azure sky—the new capitol of India. Few capitols can surpass the magnificence of this architectural monument to the English dominion. Yet on the west coast of India, surrounded by palm trees and lagoons, lingers a ghostly parody of this magnificence, the epitaph of another and earlier European dominion. There athwart a road leading from a broken wharf that was once a street, stands another arch, planned for the reception of other Viceroys and upholding, in a creepered niche, the effigy of Vasco da Gama. In the Council House at Panjim may be seen the cracked portraits of these other Viceroys, imperious in ruff, corselet, and peruke of the 16th, 17th, and 18th Centuries. Up at old Goa, the secular buildings have sunk to mounds beneath the palm trees. But in the series of gigantic churches that still stand; in the twisted Manoeline of St. Francis; in Bom Jesus, where the body of St. Francis Xavier lies embalmed in a tomb supplied by the Grand Duke of Tuscany; in the crypt of St. Monica's, floored with Persian tiles of the 17th Century that moulder untended and moss-grown in the damp; in the vast aisles of the cathedral, where a few brown-skinned canons in purple and lace still perform their rites to the accompaniment of a mechanical organ; in the bat-stunk dome of St. Cajetan's, a church modelled on St. Peter's—may be read the tale of the Portuguese Empire in India, sprung up by decree of Albuquerque and, after a century of wealth and might, doomed to fall into perpetual decline.— Misfortune comes to the complacent, brought not by some moral law, but because complacence is the parent of incompetence. The last half of the 19th Century saw this disease fasten on Englishmen like cholera." This passage is quoted by the kind permission of Mr. Sykes and his English and American publishers, Collins, Publishers, London and William Sloan Associates, New York.

52. 1. Cananor, the scene of lots of fighting during the conquest of the West Coast of India. There was a great sea fight there in 1504.

3. Calicut, the first Indian city seen by the discoverers. See VI, 92 and note.

4. Cochin and Cananor were more friendly to the Portuguese than Calicut. And Cochin was an especially loyal tributary. Cabral established a factory there in 1500. The unnamed hero, Lencastre and Ford agree, is Pacheco. See I, 14 and X, 12-25 (notes).

53. 1. Leucadia, an island near Actium, where Augustus defeated Antony and Cleopatra in 31 B. C. Camões says nothing to show he knew about Sappho's suicide there (Strabo, X, ii, 9).

2. Bactra, now Balkh in Northern Afghanistan.

The imagery in this stanza derives from the Aeneid, VIII, 675-688.

54. 5. The Golden Chersonese is the Malay Peninsula. Albuquerque conquered its capital Malacca in 1511.

55. 6. The wronged Portuguese is Magellan. Burton, quoted by Ford, noted the anachronism of referring to Magellan in the past in 1498, but defended it. Homer must be permitted to nod occasionally.

56. 1. Maia's sacred son is Mercury, who from his birth on Mount Cyllene in Arcadia is often called the Cyllenian as in Stanza 57. Horace calls him "almae filius Maiae" (Odes, I, ii, 42-43).

57. The description of Mercury in this stanza might be drawn from Iliad, XXIV, 339-348, from Odyssey, V, 42-49, from Odyssey, XXIV, 1-10, from Aeneid, IV, 238-246, from Statius' Thebais, I, 302-308.

8. Melinde, now Malind. One of the many towns whose names Milton may have borrowed from Camões.

Rabelais, as Professor Francis M. Rogers has pointed out to the compiler, has several remarks on the Portuguese discoverers. Thus in Gargantua and Pantagruel, I, 5 (Modern Library Edition, magnificently translated by Jacques Le Clercq), this doggerel occurs:

> Drinking made our magnates wealthy.
> Drinking makes our bodies healthy.
> Thus Bacchus won the giant realm of Ind!
> Thus Vasco found that mine of gold Melinde.

In Book IV, 1, Rabelais describes Pantagruel's voyage to India via the Northwest Passage, which is much more convenient than "the usual Portuguese course." Another point where the orbits of Camões and Rabelais touch will be noticed at the proper place, V,

39, note. By a curious coincidence the great Frenchman died at the moment when the great Portuguese sailed for the Orient.

60.   Lucretius, Catullus, and Claudian all light the moon with alien or illicit fire. Catullus (Ode to Diana, XXXIV) looks like the source. Perfectly lovely too!

61.   2. Burton notices the Virgilian imitation (Aeneid, III, 44 and 639).

62.   2. One of the labors of Hercules was to feed Diomedes, a king of Thrace, to his own carnivorous horses. Pomponius Mela in his account of Thrace (II, 2) explicitly describes Diomedes.

3. Busiris, King of Egypt, sacrificed all foreigners. Hercules sacrificed Busiris, his son, and the attendant priests on Busiris' own altar. Strabo quotes Eratosthenes to the effect that Busiris is merely a reflection of Egyptian chauvinism (XVII, 1, 19). Both these amiable kings appear in Ovid, Heroides, IX, 67–70. Faria y Sousa (Mr. Glaser informs me) quotes Georgics, III, 5, for Busiris. But almost any classic poet would do as well.

65.   1–4. This passage is an abridgment of Aeneas' address to his men as they leave Carthage (Aeneid, III, 573–576).

67.   3. Burton says this wind is the N. E. Monsoon Trade, but the word "galerno" may mean merely favorable. Hence Professor Ford suggests southwest.

72.   2. His sign is that of Taurus the Bull. Jupiter in the form of a bull kidnapped Europa, the daughter of Agenor, King of Phoenicia. In Crete he reassumed the god, and the princess bore him Sarpedon, Minos, and Rhadamanthus. Professor Ford points out that the sun entered the Sign of the Bull on April 5, 1498, and that Gama sighted Melinde on Easter Sunday, April 15, 1498. Almost the same words as those describing the sun entering Taurus are used by Camões in Canzone VII. If the Portuguese version of Petrarch's Trionfi, attributed to Camões by some, is really by him, which I do not believe, then we have another parallel.

4. Amalthea, the nymph, fed the infant Jupiter with goat's milk. "Hence, some authors have called her a goat," one of whose horns became the symbolic horn of plenty. The horn of Achelous is a connected myth. His also became a horn of plenty. Flora (Greek, Chloris), the Goddess of Flowers, married to Zephyr the West Wind, who with his sweet breath brings the flowers and fruits.

5–8. Easter Day, according to Professor Ford.

76.   4–8. These verses are a sort of realistic travesty on the gift of Dido to the fleet of Aeneas, Aeneid, I, 633–636.

77.   5–6. Ovid has this description of coral twice, in Met., IX, 750–753, and XV, 416–417, quoted by Ford. Pliny (XXXII, 11) says

that in India coral is as much prized as pearls in Europe. He adds the detail about its hardening in the air. In the letter, alleged to be from the King of Calicut to King Manuel, coral is one of the items specified as desired by the Hindu Prince.

78.   Lencastre states that the ambassador was Fernão Martins, who is elsewhere represented as being familiar with Arabic (V, 77).

80–81. The first four verses of each of these stanzas are strongly reminiscent of the speech of Ilioneus to Dido, Aeneid, I, 527–529, which in turn is reminiscent of Polyphemus' question to Odysseus in Odyssey, IX, 252–255.

82.   4. Alcinoüs, the King of the Phaeacians, who entertained Ulysses and sent him home to Ithaca. There is a certain propriety in the comparison, for Gama is about to relate his adventures to the King of Melinde, just as Ulysses related his to Alcinoüs.

84.   1–4. The simile is of course drawn from the parable of Menenius Agrippa in Livy, II, 32.

8. So long as rivers, etc. In the dubious Eclogue XII, a similar expression may be found (Juromenha, III, 132). But such a classic commonplace is probably no argument. The original is in Aeneas' speech to Dido, Aeneid, I, 607.

89.   1. Latona's son is Apollo.

90.   6. The tribes of the Cyclopes were the smiths and armorers who forged Jupiter's thunderbolts. This stanza and the next must be one of the earliest accounts of fireworks. But Claudian (Mallii Theodori, Panegyris, 327 ff) talks of something that could have been pyrotechnics.

91.   4. If proof were needed that Camões was familiar with Lucan's De Bello Civili, the somewhat enigmatic phrase which I have translated "hidden sulphur" would supply it (III, 682). Lucan wrote "tecto sulpure." Mr. Duff remarks that the epithet has never been explained. But Camões seems to have lugged it over literally into Portuguese.

92.   1. Dawn calling men to their labors suggests Aeneid, XI, 182–183.

3. Memnon's mother, Aurora, the dawn. See note, II, 13, 8.

93 ff. This passage has a sort of parallel in Carta Escripta d'Africa (Juromenha, IV, 157) in which the arrival of a Moorish army is vividly described.

4. See Ovid, Met., II, 5: materiam superabat opus (Ford). A classic commonplace (Plutarch, Pericles, Pliny, XXXIV, 18).

Camões in his Eclogue I has a slight variation on a much too threadbare theme (Juromenha, III, 6).

This passage may well have been in Milton's mind when he wrote the great lines:

> Or where the gorgeous East with richest hand
> Showers on her kings barbaric pearl and gold.

96.   Such an oriental device as the parasol seems to have astonished Camões. Yet classic writers with whom he appears familiar mention it repeatedly. Strabo while noticing the splendor of Indian dress embroidered with gems and gold speaks of umbrellas (XV, i, 54). Pliny alludes to palm-leaf sunshades (XIII, 7). Arrian (Indica, 16) knows about parasols. So does Plutarch (Themistocles). And Claudian (De Quarto Consulatu Honorii, 341) makes Theodosius adjure his son Honorius not to employ one. The Crusaders must have seen them, and Professor R. T. Hill refers me to Le Pelerinage de Charlemagne in which a parasol is employed by the Emperor of the East. Damião de Goes (I, 75) perhaps was in Camões' mind when he expressed his views on Oriental music.

99.   7. Thaumas' daughter was Iris, the goddess of the rainbow and messenger of the gods.

100.   1–4. Mr. H. M. Landon, one of the most enthusiastic of Camonians, has pointed out traces of the language of Catullus in this stanza (Catullus, LXIV, 262–264). The most resounding of these lines is parodied by Persius (I, 99). Camões probably knew both.

103.   4. The region alluded to is Northwest Africa, where the daughters of Hesperus kept watch over the golden apples.

104–105.   These stanzas are a paraphrase of part of Aeneas' address to Dido, Aeneid, I, 597–600 and 605–610.

108.   8. Wet roads is a direct translation of "humidos caminhos" which in turn is a direct translation ὑγρὰ κέλευθα (Odyssey, III, 71).

109.   Invitations to begin a tale are pretty well standardized in the classic epics. Very likely Camões remembered Alcinoüs and Odysseus, Dido and Aeneas, and Lucan's Caesar and Acoreus. But we may be pretty sure that Dido and Aeneas were foremost in his mind (Aeneid, I, 753–756).

111.   This stanza is modeled on Dido's reply to Ilioneus, Aeneid, I, 565–568.

112.   1. The Giants, a race related to, but later than, the Titans, made war on Jupiter. They were defeated and many of them were imprisoned under volcanoes.

3. Pirithoüs, the King of the Lapithae, was the sworn friend of Theseus. There is an enormous growth of myths about the two, but the allusion here is to their descent into Hell to carry off Proserpina, the Queen of Pluto. The god captured them, and they were only released by the efforts of Hercules.

113.   1. Herostratus, Erostratus, or Eratostratus, is said to have burned down the temple of Diana at Ephesus, which was one of the seven

wonders of the world. The first recorded pyromaniac, he performed this exploit that his name might be remembered. Diana was unable to avert the disaster because she happened to be away that night, presiding over the accouchement of the mother of Alexander the Great (Plutarch, Alexander).

2. The only thing known about the architect of the temple is his name, Ctesiphon, which, according to Strabo (XIV, i, 22), should be Chersiphron. Pliny is of the same opinion twice (VII, 38, XXXVI, 21). Architect and pyromaniac have suffered the same fate. No one knows the right name of either.

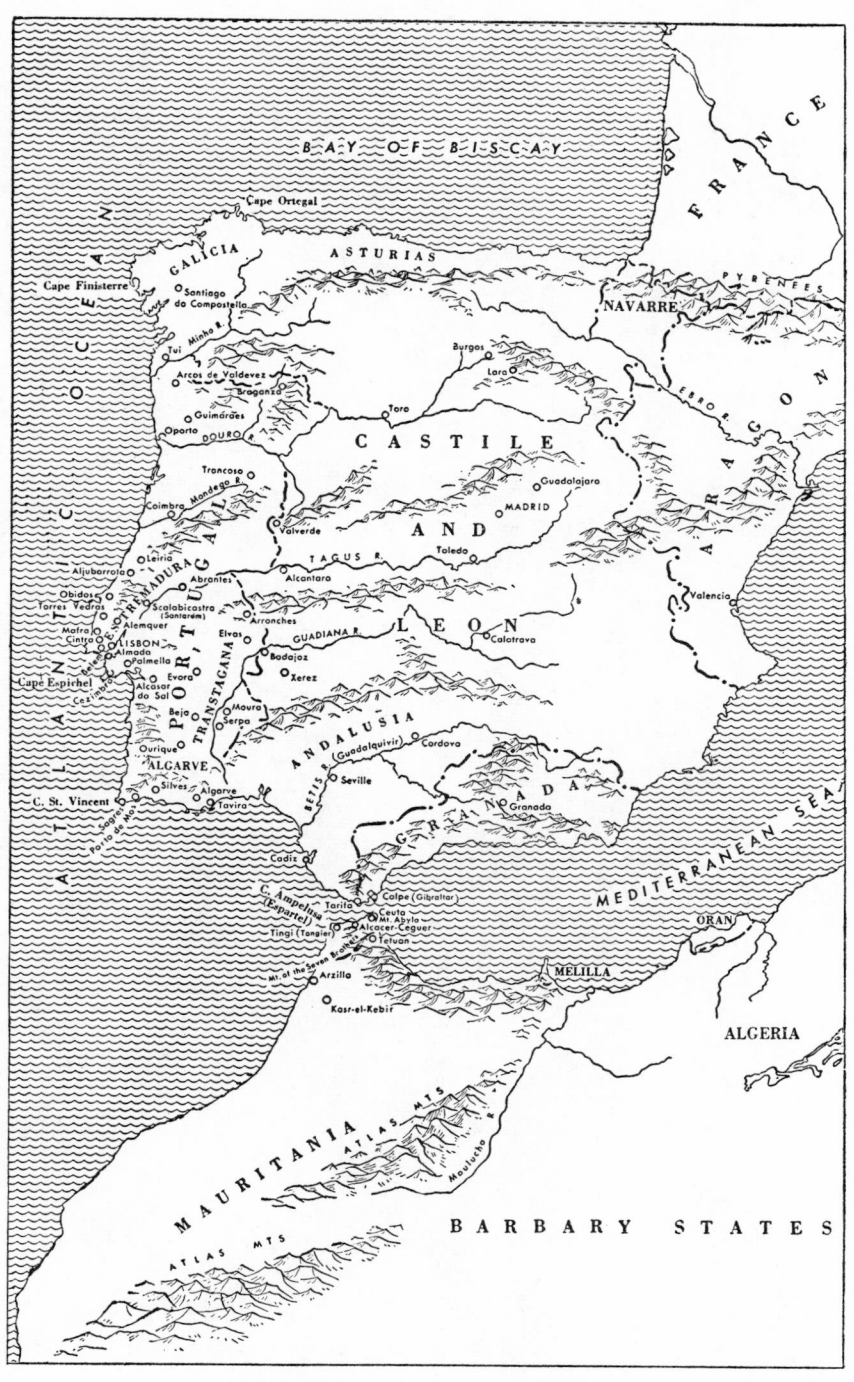

BOOK III

ARGUMENT

Vasco da Gama's conversation with the king of Melinde, in which he gives him a description of Europe and an account of the origins of the kingdom of Portugal, of her kings (till the time of Dom Fernando), and their principal actions; the notable deed of Egas Moniz; how Dona Maria the queen of Castile came to Portugal to get help before the battle of the Salado; and the love and disastrous fate of Dona Ignez de Castro, together with certain events under Dom Fernando.

THE LUSIADS

THE THIRD BOOK

D O THOU instruct me now, Calliope,
  What to the king great Gama might declare.
Immortal song and voice arouse in me,
Whose human heart toward thee such love doth bear.
So may healing's great inventor ne'er to thee,
Who barest Orpheus to him, O most fair,
Deny due love, though apt his faith to break
For Daphne's, Clytië's, or Leucothoë's sake.

2

O Nymph, give my desires effectual force,
As well with Portugal's desert may keep.
Let the world know, where Tagus runs his course,
Waters of Aganippe spirt and leap.
Leave Pindus' flowers—already in his source
Of sovran lymph I feel Apollo steep
My soul—if thou wilt not, I shall proclaim
Thy fears for thy loved Orpheus' darkened fame.

3

Now eagerly all men stood listening by
To hear what noble Gama might relate,
Who, after giving thought to his reply,
Looked up again and made his answer straight:
"Thou hast commanded, O great King, that I
My nation's splendid lineage should narrate.
Thou dost not ask me for some foreign story,
But plainly bidst me speak my people's glory.

III   "To praise another's acts may well assort
With all that is to taste and custom dear.
I dread my people's honors to report,
Lest praise suspect but ill in me appear.
However long the time, 'twill prove too short,
If all is to be told, I think and fear.
What thou hast asked I hold my duty chief,
And will do that I ought not and be brief.

5

"Further I speak as one compelled thereto,
Nor can speak false in what I am to say,
But the more these high deeds I reveal to you
The more upon the tale I must delay.
However, even as you bid me do,
What you desire to know I will display,
And first our giant continent explore,
And after tell the tale of bloody war."

*   *   *   *   *   *

6

Between that zone where Cancer sway doth hold,
The shining sun's northerly bound and mete,
And that which is as greatly feared for cold
As the equatorial country is for heat,
There lies our Europe, arrogantly bold,
And to the north and toward the sun's retreat
Salt waves of ocean circle constantly,
While to the southward lies the Inland Sea.

7

And toward the region of the birth of light,
It borders Asia, but the stream that glides,
Curving and cold, from the Riphéan height
To Lake Maeotis, all the tract divides,
As does that sea of terror and despite
That knew the fierce Greeks, where no trace abides
Of Trojan triumph now, and sailors see
Only the vestige of a memory.

In the part that toward the Pole Star nearest goes,   **III**
The mountains, Hyperborean called, are found,
And the hills where Eolus for ever blows,
Which, from the winds' name, have become renowned.
Apollo's light, on earth that flames and glows,
So little strength has got in all that ground
That snow perpetual on the mountains clings,
And the sea is frozen always, and all springs.

And here there dwell of Scythians great store,
Who, as to Man's antiquity, of old,
Their part in bickering contention bore
With who the Land of Egypt then did hold.
But they too well could real truth ignore.
Errors of human thought are manifold,
And who right knowledge on the point would glean
Must seek it in the province Damascene.

They call the countries of those regions wide
Chill Lapland and the unplowed Norroway,
And Scandinavia's island, whose chief pride
Is triumph Italy cannot gainsay.
And so long as the bitter wintertide
Freezes not the sea, men navigate that bay,
Which is an arm of the Sarmatic Main,
Between the Swede, the Prussian, and cold Dane.

Strange folk dwell 'twixt the Tanaïs and that sea,
Muscovites and Ruthenians and Livonians,
Sarmatians erst. On heights Hercynian be
Those Marcomans who now are styled Polonians,
And subject to imperial Germany
Are Saxons and Bohemians and Pannonians,
And other races, whom the Rhine's cold wave
And the Danube and the Ems and Elbe lave.

III   Between far Danube and the shining strait
Where Helle left her name and life, there dwell
The men of Thrace, whose courage is so great,
In the country that ferocious Mars loves well.
Hemus and Rhodope are subjugate
Unto the Ottoman, whose powers compel
Byzantium at his most unworthy will,
Unto great Constantine foul injury still.

Hard by them live the Macedonian race,
Whose lands are washed by Vardar's freezing flood,
You also, splendid lands, the native place
Of noble customs, genius, fortitude,
Who nurtured souls in eloquence and grace,
And thoughts of fancy in her noblest mood,
By which great Greece, you are to Heaven preferred,
No less by arms than by the written word.

Dalmatians dwell hard by. That gulf beside,
Where in old time Antenor built his wall,
Amid the waters, in her pomp and pride,
Stands Venice, whose beginnings were so small.
An arm of land, through the sea reaches wide,
Valiant the various nations to enthrall,
Strong arm of men whose lofty thoughts accord
No less with noble arts than with the sword.

The realms of Neptune all that land confine,
Save only where great Nature's bulwarks stand.
And 'tis divided by the Apennine
Where their Sire Mars gave glory to the land.
But since no more the Gatekeeper Divine
Old power and skill in battle can command,
The land is poor, for all its former might.
So in humility doth God delight!

Beyond that land lies France, whose legend blown   **III**
With Caesar's triumphs through the world did sweep,
Well watered by the Seine and by the Rhone,
And cold Garonne and the Rhine river deep.
And near by rise the mountains that are known
By the nymph Pyrenè's name, who there doth sleep,
Ensepulchred. They burned, men say, of old,
And the rivers ran with silver and with gold.

17

And here may be discovered stately Spain,
As it were the head of Europe's commonweal,
Whose fame magnificent and noble reign
Have known strange turnings of the fatal wheel.
Yet restless Fate her honor could not stain,
Howe'er she might in force or treason deal,
Nor filch audacity and fortitude
From the brave spirits she is wont to brood.

18

Spain fronts Tangier and such a port doth bear
As who to block the Inland Sea is fain,
By the famed strait that got a name so fair
From the strong Theban's utmost toil and pain;
Grown great from divers nations dwelling there,
Whom the wide waters of the sea contain,
And all so brave and noble, for the rest,
That every country thinks itself the best.

19

There is the Aragonese, whose fame grew bright
When the restless Neapolitans he quelled;
Navarre and the Asturias, who in fight
Against Mahomet's breed the bastion held;
There the Galician shrewd, and, great in might,
The high Castilian, whom his star impelled
Spain to restore and rule the commonweal,
Betis, León, Granada, with Castile.

85

III   And there, as crown of Europe it might be,
You may behold the Lusitanian reign,
Where the land ends and where begins the sea,
And in the Ocean Phoebus rests again.
And they have flourished, by just Heaven's decree,
In arms against the brutal Moorish strain.
They hurled him forth, and they permit him not
To live in peace where Africa burns hot.

21

This is my well-loved country of content,
To which if Heaven grant me safe return,
And of my venture the accomplishment,
Why then for me may this light cease to burn.
And Lusitania traces her descent
From Lusus or from Lysa, who, we learn,
Were ancient Bacchus' sons or comrades dear
And were the first men to inhabit here.

22

And here was born that shepherd, whose sole name
Showed he could play the man with actions fair,
Whose fame is tarnished by no other fame,
That being more than Rome herself could dare.
And duly the light-footed Ancient came,
Who makes his own dear children's flesh his fare,
To raise us high, for such was Heaven's decree,
And breed a great realm. Thus it was to be.

23

There was a King in Spain, whom men did call
Afonso, with the Moors that fought the fight
And took from many life and land withal,
With blood-stained weapons, and by force and sleight.
Wild rumor from Herculean Calpe's wall
Flew with his name unto the Caspian height,
And many keen a warrior name to win,
To pawn their lives with him, came marching in.

And with one inward passion did they flame,   **III**
In Faith, which, matched with Glory, still does more.
And many were the countries whence they came,
Leaving their homes and well-loved native shore.
After great acts that won them proud acclaim
Had proved that they were mighty men of war,
The great Afonso wished such deeds should bear
Fair prize and good reward in equal share.

25

Of these, one Henry, thought the second son
Of a certain King of Hungary most wise,
Won Portugal by lot, although not one
Illustrious, or dear in the world's eyes;
And further great Castile would have it done,
For sign of his deep love, that marriage ties
Should bind his child Teresa to the Count,
Who with her held the land as paramount.

26

He, after warring with the progeny
Of the slave Hagar, whom he overthrew,
Won in the neighboring lands the mastery,
Doing what his great spirit urged him to,
And, for his deeds of brave audacity,
Shortly a son God granted as his due,
Who the proud name would furbish yet more bright
Of Lusitania's kingdom strong in fight.

27

When Jerusalem the Holy, conquest's hand
Had taken, Henry home was fain to fare.
He had beheld the Jordan's bed of sand,
That saw God's flesh washed in his waters there.
For Godfrey their desires would not withstand,
After Judea's fall, who would repair,
Homeward to their own seignories once more,
Having so aided him in that great war.

III   When to his ending and his limit late
Had come the great Hungarian full of fame,
Compelled by strong necessity and fate,
He gave his soul to God from Whom it came.
His son remained in childhood's tender state,
His father's copy, for he seemed the same,
Matchable with the best of earth entire.
Men hoped for such a son from such a sire.

29

The old tale goes, if false I cannot say
(Nothing is sure of things so long gone by),
That his mother on the realm her hands did lay,
Nor, scornful, second wedlock would deny.
She disinherited and sent away
The orphan, and did clearly signify
That the whole kingdom and its glory were
Her own, the dowry her sire gave with her.

30

But Prince Afonso (for they named him so
After his grandsire) now beheld his land,
In which he had no share, to ruin go
Under his mother's and her lord's command.
He felt fierce battle in his bosom glow,
Considering how to get his realm in hand.
And when the causes to his mind he brought,
Then the effect followed resolvèd thought.

31

At Guimarães they painted all the plain,
For civil war made flow their own best blood,
Where a mother, but a mother all in vain,
Her own son's right to love and land withstood,
And fight in field against him would deraign.
But against God and loving motherhood
How much she erred, that proud dame could not see,
So strong in her was sensuality.

O cruel Procne! Witch Medea fell!   **III**
Who on your sons, for what their sires did ill
And others' guilt, avenged yourselves so well,
See how Teresa was more wicked still.
Vile lust and her ambition horrible
Were chief beginnings of her evil will.
Scylla for lust had her old sire undone.
Teresa, moved by both, would slay her son.

33

But the illustrious Prince in battle beat
His stepsire and his mother inhumane,
And in a trice the land was at his feet,
That first against him would the fight maintain.
Howe'er, his mind subdued by anger's heat,
He had his mother bound with the harsh chain.
In brief space God took vengeance for her woes.
All reverence man unto his parents owes!

34

For now the proud Castilian came apace,
Revenge for wronged Teresa to ensue.
Few were his Portuguese that foe to face,
But he was one no labor could subdue.
His human courage in that desperate case,
And aid of angels added thereunto,
Not only gave him strength such wrath to fight
But hurled the savage foeman into flight.

35

But the bold Prince in Guimarães ere long
His enemies encircled with their ring
In infinite numbers. For they made them strong
After this fashion, who yet felt the sting.
Egas the faithful tutor from such wrong,
At peril of his own life saved his King,
Uncaptured. Or else evil had he fared,
Being for battle wholly unprepared.

89

III This overwell the loyal vassal knew,
Who saw his lord could not keep up the fight.
He gave to the Castilian promise true
His Prince would come and do him homage right.
And from the dreadful siege the foe withdrew,
Since Egas' word of honor in his sight
Sufficed. That great youth's heart could ill allow
Necessity to other will to bow.

37

Now came the time appointed to fulfill
All the Castilian monarch's expectation,
When the Prince must submit to the King's will,
And, as he hoped, accept his obligation.
When Egas saw his pledge unhonored still,
A thing beyond Castile's imagination,
He judged that restitution must be made
And dear life answer for his word betrayed.

38

With wife and children then he took his way,
For thus to pay his forfeit he designed,
And all unshod and wretched of array,
Moving less to vengeance than to pity kind.
"If you would vengeance take," so did he say,
"Great King, on my rash confidence of mind,
Here to you now I make my offering plain
And with my life my promise will maintain.

39

"You see how here these sinless lives I lead,
My children, like their mother, innocent,
If great and generous spirits can indeed
From slaughter of the weak derive content.
Here are my hands and tongue that guilty plead.
On them alone try the experiment,
Exploiting death and torture to the full,
In the mode of Sinis or Perillus' bull."

As the condemned, with the headsman face to face,   **III**
Who yet alive the cup of death hath drained,
Lays neck on block, out of all hope of grace,
And there awaits the dreadful stroke ordained;
Before the angry monarch, in like case,
Egas awaited what must be sustained.
But the king, seeing honor of such rarity,
The less was moved to wrath and more to charity.

41

O brave fidelity of Portugal!
O vassal who to all things could submit!
Was the Persian's action more heroical,
Who slashed his features and his nostrils slit?
A deed the great Darius above all
Admired, who said a thousand times of it
That Zópyrus unharmed to him meant more
Than to have taken Babylons by the score.

42

Now Prince Afonso marshalled in array
His Lusian host, with noble fortune bright,
Against the Moors, who harbored in that day
Beyond clear Tagus, river of delight.
Already in Ourique's meadows lay
The army, full of arrogance and fight,
Before their enemy the Saracen,
Although they had but scanty store of men,

43

Resolved that nothing was to trust unto
Save highest God, their Heavenly Governor.
Of christened folk the number was so few
That for each man of them were Moors five score.
And it might seem, after reflection due,
Rather rashness than true bravery in war,
A contest of such sort to have begun
That made the odds a hundred men to one.

III   Five Moorish kings are there to back the foe,
Of whom the foremost Ismar has to name.
All five of them the toils of battle know,
Whence they have won their portion of good fame.
And in their train their warrior ladies go,
Whose model is that bright heroic dame
From whom the Trojans had such help in war,
With all her maids who loved Thermodon's shore.

45

Serene and chilly light of morningtide
Had chased the stars already from the Pole,
When Mary's Son appeared, Christ crucified,
Unto Afonso and inspired his soul.
The Prince, adoring, to the Vision cried,
Inflamed by holy faith entire and whole:
"Unto the faithless! Unto the faithless, show
"Thyself, Lord, not to me, Thy power who know!"

46

The soul of every Portuguese thereby
Was set on fire, so great the miracle.
And as their rightful King they raised on high
The good Prince whom they all loved passing well.
Shouting aloud, they smote the very sky
Before the strong host of the infidel,
"Royal! Right royal!" yelling one and all,
"For Afonso, the high King of Portugal!"

47

As in the hills, when cry and shout excite,
The mastiff, in his rage, against the bull,
Makes the attack, where the creature on the might
Of his tremendous horn now counts in full;
Yelping, less stalwart, yet of foot so light,
The dog at flank or ear doth rend and pull
Till, tearing at the throat, he grips him fast,
And the brave beast's brute strength goes slack at last;

So in the new-made King did courage flare,   **III**
For God and for the people fired alike.
And right at the barbarian aware,
With the army all in fury, did he strike.
At that among those dogs arose the blare
And howl. They beat to arms, and bow and pike
Snatch up. The heathen rage. The bugles call,
And clang of weapons thunders over all.

49

And just as when a flame, where fields are dry,
Is lighted, and the whistling north wind blows,
And, by the fury of the gale whipped high,
Racing, the fire through dusty thickets goes;
And some company of shepherds, who hard by
Are sleeping soft, awake from their repose,
When they hear the crackle of the kindling blast,
Gather their flock, and to the town flee fast;

50

Even so the astonished Moors in disarray
Took arms haphazard, in wild scurry pressed.
They fled not. Sure of victory were they,
And their war-jennets in the ranks they dressed.
The Portuguese smote furious in the fray
And with the lances pierced the foeman's breast.
Some fell half-dead, and some their outcry made,
Calling upon the Koran to give aid.

51

There terrible encounters might you see,
To get possession of a towering height,
And the great beasts galloping fierily,
Neptune revealed, who once the ground did smite,
And dreadful blows of force exchanging free.
And in all quarters flame the fires of fight,
But the Portuguese, mail, plate, and corselet hew,
Shatter to bits, break, split, destroy, cleave through.

III   On the field heads are rolling everywhere,
Legs, arms, that neither sense nor master know.
Of others, pulsing entrails are laid bare,
All pale their hue and with death's look of woe.
The accursèd host was beaten then and there.
Rivers of blood spilled in the battle flow.
Changes the color of the field of fight,
Grown crimson and no longer green and white.

The Portuguese stayed master of the field
To take their trophies, and good prize they gained,
While the Spanish Moors in flight, defeated, reeled.
There, for three days, the noble King remained.
'Twas then they painted on the proud white shield
What still our claim to victory has sustained,
The azure targes five, emblazoned fair,
In token of the five kings conquered there.

On those five shields the thirty pence he drew,
For which aforetime our dear Lord was sold,
Blazoning memorial, in various hue,
Of Him Whose favor could so well uphold.
Five he limned on all five. And that the due
Number of pence may properly be told,
Of five blue shields, the midmost men count twice,
With the pence drawn cruciform in the device.

The noble King, when some brief time had run
After that giant and triumphant fight,
Went to storm Leiria, which had been won
Some short while since by those he put to flight.
Arronches strong he likewise pounced upon.
Scalabicastro, still with glory bright,
Fell to him also, whose sweet fields well-seen,
Thou, shining Tagus, waterest, serene.

Having subdued these cities in their pride,   **III**
He added Mafra quickly to his share.
In the Mountains of the Moon, known far and wide,
Strong arms quelled Cintra of the icy air;
Cintra, where in the fountains naiads hide,
For ever fleeing from the gentle snare,
Whom Love entraps there with some soft deceit,
In the waters kindling still his burning heat.

57

And thou, proud Lisbon, who, the whole world
Art easily the queen of cities all,   [through,
First builded by the eloquent chief who knew
The craft whereby the flame on Troy must fall,
Thou, to whom vasty seas their homage do,
Didst homage to the power of Portugal,
Helped though we were by that strong armament,
Which from the quarters of the north was sent.

58

They march from German Elbe and the Rhine,
Though some from frozen Britain take their way.
Destruction for the Moslem they design.
Such holy will the greater part display.
Entering the mouth of Tagus the benign,
They join with great Afonso's their array,
Whose fame had risen to the Empyréan.
So were besieged the ramparts Odysséan.

59

And five times over the moon hid her face,
And as many did the same at full present,
Before at length was yielded up the place
To the rough leaguer that the town had pent.
Desperate and bloody was that battle's case,
So hard each party clove to their intent,
The savage conquerors that would greatly dare,
And the vanquished full as firm in their despair.

III And thus at length to yield them they consent
In the town which never in the days of old,
However great his force, the neck had bent
Before the courage of the Scythian cold,
Whose power so wide among the nations went
(Ebro in fear, like Tagus, might behold),
He who at last all Betis took in hand
And gave the name Vandalia to the land.

61

Was there perchance some town so full of fight
It dared resist, when Lisbon overthrown
Could not withstand the overwhelming might
Of men whose wingèd fame so far had flown?
Estremadura offers homage right.
Obidos, Alemquer, where murmurous moan
Sounds among boulders, which the waters chill
Wash round, and Torres Vedras do our will.

62

You lands that lie on Tagus' further shore,
Famed for the gifts of Ceres tawny-tressed,
Submit that superhuman strength before,
Of all your forts and ramparts dispossessed;
Laborious Moor, thyself thou cheatest sore,
If hope to hold good land is in thy breast;
For Elvas, Moura, Serpa, nobly known,
With Alcacer do Sal their master own.

63

Look on the noble city. Long ago
Rebel Sertorius surely harbored there,
Where now the silver-shining waters flow.
Afar relief to fields and men they bear
On arches fine, that make a royal show
And tower by the hundred high in air.
Yet the town fell to guile and courage high
Of Gerald whom no fear could terrify.

64

And now Afonso unto Beja went,
Trancoso's ruin greatly to repay,
In quiet ill-disposed to rest content
And so in fame to lengthen his brief day.
The city could not long that fate prevent,
But when it was surrendered, then straightway
Our people, by their furious anger moved,
On all things living the hard sword-edge proved.

65

Along with these Palmella to him fell,
With Cezimbra rich in fish, and in that hour,
Because his lucky star still served him well,
He got the best of overwhelming power.
This the town knew, whose lord by sight could tell,
He, bringing succor, thought in haste to scour
Along the foot-hills, nor foresaw at all
What desperate sort of battle would befall.

66

Badajoz' Moorish King came on in pride,
With his four thousand horsemen full of fire
And countless foot, with golden arms supplied,
All warriors in glorious attire.
But as in May a proud bull, in full tide
Of passion for his cow and mad desire,
Blinded with brutal lust, if man he scent,
Charges the passerby improvident;

67

Afonso suddenly himself did show,
And hurled against them marching heedless there,
Smote, slew, and wrought a fearful overthrow.
Then fled the Moor, whose life was all his care.
His army on his heels was fain to go,
O'erwhelmed in the black panic of despair.
And those who launched disaster on its course
Were but a solitary sixty horse.

III He followed up that victory without stay,
For the great and indefatigable King
Gathered throughout his kingdom an array
Whose custom was still to be conquering.
Siege unto Badajoz he went to lay
And had his heart's desire in everything,
Who fought with such brave strength, skill, martial
That the town joined its fellows in defeat.   [heat,

But Great God, Who a long while may refrain
From punishing a man who merits it,
Tarrying in case he may from sin abstain,
Or for hid cause unknown to human wit,
If till then He did constantly sustain
The King, who never shrank from risk a whit,
No longer would the accomplishment defer
Of his mother's curse, whom he held prisoner,

For in the town he once beleaguered round
He was beleaguered by the Leonese,
For he had made his conquest on the ground
Which they possessed and not the Portuguese.
Costly his pertinacity he found,
As many a time and oft in life one sees,
Breaking his leg on a gate-iron, as he flew
To fight, where he was beat and taken too.

O famous Pompey, never be cast down
Before the ruin of thy acts divine,
Seeing thy sire-in-law seize thy renown
And triumph by just Nemesis' design.
Though the cold Phasis, though Syene's town,
Where shadows neither north nor south incline,
Though Boötes locked in ice, though Line a-flame,
One and all, still must tremble at thy name;

72

Though rich Arabia, and the savage seed
Of Heniochia and famed Colchian shores
Of the Golden Fleece, though Cappadocia's breed,
Judea that one God loves and adores,
And soft Sophenians, though those dread indeed,
The Cilicians, and Armenia that pours
The waters of two rivers forth, whose fount
Springs otherwhere from a huge holy mount;

73

And though, yet further, from the Atlantic Sea
To Scythic Taurus, that uptowering height,
Men saw thee conquer; let it not trouble thee
If Emathia's field beheld thee lose one fight.
Afonso thou wilt look on, valiantly
Worsting them all, then himself worsted quite.
Thy stepsire won, for Heaven willed it so,
As his son-in-law wrought the King's overthrow.

74

To his own at last the Great King came once more,
Of Heavenly Judgment having felt the pain,
After proud Saracens beset him sore
In Santarem,' although their siege was vain.
And when at length St. Vincent's corpse they bore,
The holy reverend Martyr, home again
Translated to the Odysséan town
From the promontory sacred in renown,

75

The tired old man, that hope might be made good,
Gave his commandment to his stalwart son,
Those lands that lie beyond the Tagus flood,
With his host and train of war to overrun.
Sancho, all full of fire and hardihood,
Went forth and straightway stained vermilion
The stream that through Seville still rolls its flood
With the Moor's shameless and barbaric blood.

III   And with this victory grown covetous,
The youth would never rest until he made
Like ruin for the Moor, as perilous,
Who around Beja had his leaguer laid.
Nor tarried long a Prince so prosperous
Ere he achieved the end for which he prayed,
And the Moor, stricken by a stroke so stern,
Could only for some future vengeance yearn.

77

Now from his mount they swarm, who altered shape
Before Medusa and upholds the sky;
From Ampelusa and from Tingi's cape,
Once country of Antaeus, they draw nigh.
Ábyla's dweller has no mind to 'scape,
For, to the Mauretanian horn's shrill cry,
All of that kingdom hasten sword in hand,
From what was once the noble Juba's land.

78

And, at the head of all that company,
Came the Miramoline to Portugal.
Thirteen stout Moorish kings with him had he,
Of those ruled by his rod imperial.
And doing as much evil as might be,
He did his worst where worst it might befall,
And in Santarem to leaguer Sancho went,
Though not too fortunate in the event.

79

And there the fights were sharp, with many a ruse
Of battle tried by the fierce Moor malign,
But his grim engines were of little use,
Or driving battering ram, or hidden mine;
For not one whit Afonso's son did lose
Of courage or of generous design,
Foreseeing all with judgment and with heart
And showing fight in every threatened part.

But the old man, whom hard years burdened so   **III**
That he at length with quietness must dwell,
Was in the town where green those meadows grow,
Which the Mondego river waters well,
And came the case of Santarem to know,
And his son besieged by the blind infidel.
Out of the town he sped without delay.
Age could not snatch that lightning speed away.

81

He, with a splendid force to battle bred,
Rushed to his son's aid. When were joined the two,
The Portuguese, with wonted fury dread,
Speedily routed all that Moorish crew.
The field, which thick in every part lay spread
With mantles and with caps of various hue,
Horses and trappings, battle's rich rewards,
Was paved with the dead bodies of their lords.

82

The remnant of their army hastily
In panic flight from Lusitania sped.
But the Miramoline fled not. Not he!
For, e'er he thought to flee, his life had fled.
To Him Who granted them the victory
Prayers of unmeasured gratitude they said,
For in strange fortunes, it is seen aright,
God's favor better than mankind can fight.

83

Afonso old, a great prince without fail,
Triumphed in victories magnificent,
Till he who could against all men prevail
Down to defeat in his time's fulness went.
Presently the cold hand of sickness pale
Touched the poor body, sickly now and spent,
And his long years, in the accustomed way,
To Libitina sad their debt must pay.

III　And the tall promontories made their moan,
　　And forlorn river waters, flooding wide,
　　Rise up to overwhelm the plowlands sown,
　　And shed their tears in pity where they glide.
　　But over all the earth so great had grown
　　The legend of his acts of martial pride
　　That in his land echoes will still complain,
　　Calling, "Afonso! Afonso!" but in vain.

85

Sancho the stalwart stripling, who remained
To imitate his father in his might,
While yet that father lived, repute attained
When Betis all with blood was painted bright.
And victory o'er the barbarous host he gained
Of Andalusia's sovereign Ishmaelite.
And at Beja's bootless siege the heathen folk
Had clearly known how heavy was his stroke.

86

But later on, when he our King was made,
His reign not lengthened yet to many a year,
Then unto Silves city siege he laid,
Whose fields the Saracen was wont to ear.
And men of valor came to bear him aid,
From an army of the Germans passing near,
Who men-at-arms and weapons did not lack,
And meant to win new-lost Judea back.

87

Now on that sacred venture they were bent
To succor Frederic Red-beard in his war,
When with huge force to save the town he went,
Where long ago Our Lord his torment bore,
What time Guy's host, by burning drought forespent,
Unto great Saladin, the place gave o'er.
There for the Moors abundant springs outburst,
For lack of which Guy's soldiers knew such thirst.

But the fair fleet that came arrayed so well,
And winds opposing to our harbors blew,
Would back the King in battle terrible,
Though bound in Holy Wars their deed to do.
And much as with his father it befell,
When Lisbon in like case he overthrew.
With German help, he conquered Silves town
And the bold burghers slaughtered and put down.

89

If trophies of Mahomet he alway
Raised up, he brooked not the strong Leonese
In quiet in his countryside should stay,
So well inured to war's severities,
Till he the yoke upon the neck did lay
Of Tui the superb, who also sees
Whelmed by like fortune many cities round,
By thine arms, Sancho, humbled to the ground.

90

But he 'mid victor palms a victim fell
To dreadful death. And true heir they proclaim
One of his sons, who with all men stood well,
Third King, Afonso, second of the name.
From Alcacer do Sal his men expel
The Moors. This time they wholly overcame.
Aforetime to the Moors the place was lost,
Which act they purchased at a fearful cost.

91

Afonso dead, there followed next in line
Sancho the Second, mild and negligent,
So given o'er to carelessness supine,
He bent to those whose will he should have bent.
And so to favorites did he incline
That he quite lost the kingdom's government,
Another sought. For he was ruled so ill
He yielded all to wicked favorites still.

III   Sancho was not so deep in infamy
As Nero, who once took to wife a lad,
And later, foully and incestuously,
With his mother Agrippina commerce had.
He burned not his own town. Such cruelty
He practised not on men, or usage bad.
He was no Heliogabalus depraved,
Or Sardanapalus by soft vice enslaved.

Nor did his people ever agonize,
Like the Sicilians 'neath their tyrant's reign.
Nor did the King like Phalaris devise
Every variety of ghastly pain.
But the proud realm, used to another guise
Of kings who could true sovranty maintain,
No longer her obedience would accord
To one no better than some other lord.

And hence it was, Boulogne's Count a brief while
Governed the realm, who to the kingship rose,
When his brother Sancho, to his leisure vile
Delivered, came at length to lifetime's close.
And him the 'brave Afonso' did they style,
For, when he had the kingdom at dispose,
He thought to widen it. His pride disdained
To be within such trivial bounds contained.

From the Algarve marches, which in dower
To him had come, the Moor forthwith he threw,
Recovering greater part, by his arm's power,
From them who Mars' good favor never knew.
Lusitania, free and sovran, in that hour,
With strength and warlike art he 'stablished true,
And their strong nation could at last compel,
Whose country now to Lusus' children fell.

After came Denis, who might well appear   **III**
A worthy heir of brave Afonso's name.
For in his time eclipse obscured the clear
Alexandrine liberality and fame.
He made the whole realm prosper in good cheer
(A golden age of peace celestial came),
When constitution, custom, law and right,
In a quiet world, gave forth a brilliant light.

Minerva's noble offices to do,
In Coimbra first the hearts of men he led,
And every muse from Helicon he drew,
The herbage of Mondego's meads to tread.
All things desirable that Athens knew
Superb Apollo gathers here instead,
And here his tresses, wreathed with gold, are seen,
With spikenard, and with laurel evergreen.

And noble cities he built up again
And fortresses and keeps of strong estate,
And as it were wholly restored the reign,
Erecting lofty walls and houses great.
But when harsh Atropos had cut in twain
His thread of days, already waxing late,
He left a son who ill his sire could heed,
Afonso Fourth, yet strong and good at need.

Ever he studied the Castilians proud,
With a misprizing heart, serene and strong.
For Lusitanian spirits are not cowed,
Though small their powers, by odds however long.
But when the Mauretanians in a crowd
To the conquest of Hesperia would throng,
There the Castilian marches to invade,
'Twas proud Afonso's part to bear them aid.

III   Ne'er with Semiramis like human tide
Choked the Hydaspes regions with their surge.
Nor Attila that all Italy terrified,
He who proclaimed himself God's awful scourge,
Such an array of Gothic force did guide
As the fearful and barbaric Moor could urge,
Whose powers in the Tartessian fields unite
With all Granada's overwhelming might.

Castile's high King, when he had seen it plain,
That host resistless and armipotent,
Feared more the last fate of the men of Spain,
Lost once ere this, than his death imminent.
The succor of the Portuguese to gain,
The belovèd lady of his heart he sent,
His wife, who was the dear child, furthermore,
Of him to whom she came ambassador.

The beautiful Maria entered there
Her father's halls magnificent and high,
With little mirth, however she were fair,
The tears for ever welling in her eye.
She had let fall all her angelic hair
About her shoulders white as ivory,
And to her sire, who welcomed her, content,
These words she spake, making a great lament:

"As many peoples as were ever bred
Africa over, men of savage strain,
Hither Morocco's mighty Lord has led,
Intent to seize the noble land of Spain.
None ever saw power swell to such a head
Since first dry land was washed by the salt main.
So high their fury and their rage appear
They fright the living and strike the dead with fear.

"And he whom for my lord thou gavest me,   **III**
The frightened land against such ill to ward,
With his small powers, the sacrifice must be
Under the hard stroke of the Moorish sword.
Robbed of her King and Kingdom, thou shalt see
Thy daughter, if no succor thou accord,
A widow grieved, doomed to a life obscure,
Lordless, dethroned, and with no fortune sure.

105

"Therefore, O King, at whose name, in pure fear,
Mulucha's waters as they run congeal,
Quickly bear aid, without more tarrying here,
To the unhappy people of Castile.
If now your countenance look kind and clear
And of right father love be sign and seal,
Father, help swift, for if no haste is made
You may not find the man you think to aid."

106

Not otherwise timid Maria spake
Than Venus, in her spirit grieved, when she
Pleaded with Jupiter for her son's sake,
Aeneas, where he ploughed across the sea;
Which so much pity in his heart could wake,
That, laying by his dread artillery,
The Father in his kindness granted all
Which she had asked, as though the gift were small.

107

But now armed squadrons of the men of might
Evora's fields have thickly overrun.
From lance, sword, armor, the sun flashes bright.
Neighs every steed with rich caparison.
And flagged sonorous clarions excite
Hearts, that to peacetime usage have been won,
To take up shining weapons. The sound fills,
Rebellowing, the hollows of the hills.

III In the army's center and in noble state,
Where, royal, the armorial banners fly,
Above them all, magnanimous and great,
Afonso towered, with his head held high.
His look alone could fire and animate
Whatever heart peril might terrify.
With his fair daughter, the land's royal dame,
Thus to the kingdom of Castile he came.

109

In the fields about Tarifa at the last
Their force together joined the Afonsos twain,
Facing a heathen multitude so vast
There was no room for them on hill or plain.
No heart so high and strong but was downcast
By the presentiment that all was vain,
Unless the man had clearly seen and known,
Christ battles with the strong arms of His own.

110

But Hagar's grandsons as it were deride
The army of the Christians, weak and small.
The land, as their own portion, they divide
Among their host, ere to their hand it fall.
For, as they held by title falsified
The famous name of Saracen withal,
By such false reckoning they asserted then
Claim to fair heritage of other men.

111

As the barbarous and most huge-limbed of giants,
Who (there was cause) Saul's spirit overbore,
When the unarmored shepherd, whose reliance
Was courage and his slingstone, stood before,
With haughty words of arrogant defiance,
The ill-clad fragile youth insulted sore,
And, when the sling was whirled, was undeceived
By who in faith, more than man's strength, believed;

So the perfidious Moor mocked and spake ill   **III**
Of the Christian army. Nor could he foretell
That Loftiest Fortitude would help them still,
Unto Whose powers yielded terrific Hell.
With God to aid and with his soldier skill,
Castile advanced and on Morocco fell.
The Portuguese thought scorn of all the game,
Who made Granada's kingdom fear his name.

113

The lances and the swords clang loud and high
On armor. 'Tis brave slaughter that they make.
According to their faith, the battle cry,
Or for Mahomet or Saint James, they wake.
The screeches of the wounded wound the sky.
Their blood flows down into a ghastly lake,
Where other men, half-dead, are drowning laid,
Though with their lives they had escaped the blade.

114

Portugal 'gainst Granada smote and slew,
Assailing with a courage so immense
That quickly the foe's power he overthrew,
For naught avails steel breastplate or defence.
Such triumph purchased at price less than due
Little enough the strong of arm contents.
He went to succor the Castilian good,
Where still against the Moor in fight he stood.

115

The burning sun already took his way
To Thetis' house, and to the west inclined.
That glorious and memorable day,
Departing, left the Vesper star behind,
When the hateful Moorish powers, in disarray,
Broke before monarchs of such stalwart kind,
With loss so vast that memory ne'er before
Saw in this world such triumph in a war.

III For the great Marius not the fourth part slew
Of them who in that victory were slain,
When waters, which had taken on the hue
Of foes' blood, thirsty troops he forced to drain;
Nor the Punic chief who from his birth-hour knew
How to be Roman power's most savage bane,
When on great Rome he wrought such slaughter dread
And filled three corbs with seal-rings of the dead.

If you alone compelled such throngs to go
To the kingdom of Cocytus void of light,
When you had laid the Holy City low
And a people stubborn in their ancient rite,
Vengeance was yours, for Heaven wished it so.
'Twas not, great Titus, your arm's proper might.
But thus the prophets once had prophesied,
To which truth Jesus later testified.

When with a triumph so magnificent
Afonso home to Lusitania sped,
His soul in peace with glory to content,
Which he knew how to win in warfare dread,
That grievous unforgettable event,
Which from their sepulchres might wake the dead,
Befell and sank in misery and shame
A girl who after death a queen became.

Thou alone, purest Love, whose cruel might
The hearts of men constrains and troubles so,
Wast cause whereby she perished in despite,
As if she were a traitor and thy foe.
They say thy thirst is never quenched aright,
Terrible Love, by tears and human woe.
Therefore, harsh tyrant, is thy heart inclined
To wet thine altars with life-blood of mankind.

Sweet Ignes, thou wast only gathering there   **III**
The lovely fruits of youth, in peace secure
And the spirit's error blind, without a care,
Which Fortune suffers not long to endure.
In dreamlike meadows of Mondego, ne'er
Unwatered by thine eyes of beauty pure,
The hills, the very grass-blades, didst thou tell
What name within thine heart was written so well.

121

Ever to thee thy Prince's thoughts replied,
Those thoughts that harboring in his soul he knew.
Ever before his eyes they made thee glide,
When from thine own most lovely he withdrew,
By night, in deep delicious dreams that lied,
By day, in fantasies away that flew.
And what he dreamed or what was clear to sight
Fashioned the memory of dear delight.

122

Bride-bed of princess or of lady rare
Was what he had rejected utterly.
True Love, thou hatest all things else whate'er,
Once a fair countenance has conquered thee.
When the old sire considered with due care
Love that was of so strange a quality,
He thought of grumbling crowds and fancy bred
In his son's mind, who had no mind to wed,

123

And to slay Ignes formed his firm intent,
Thus from her toils his son to liberate.
Foul death, he thought, and bloody punishment
Alone strong love, hot-flaming, could abate.
But what delirious madness could consent
That the good sword-blade, fit to bear the weight
Of Moorish rage, should be raised up to wreak
Its wrath against a girl so sweet and weak?

III   The headsmen dread dragged her the king before,
Already unto mercy turned thereby,
But the crowd's fierce unreason overbore,
Persuading that a grim death she must die.
She with a piteous voice lamented sore
The suffering and the yearning agony
Of her Prince and of her children left behind,
Which more than her own death could bruise her mind.

Lifting her eyes to heaven, crystal-clear,
All full of tears that might to pity move—
Her eyes! As for her hands, one of those drear
And murdering ministers, the cords he rove—
Looking thereafter on his children dear,
Whom she had cherished with such tender love,
Whose orphaned state a mother needs must dread,
Unto their grandsire hard these words she said:

"If all the brutish animals, whose mind
Nature from birth has formed to cruelty,
As also all the fowls of wildest kind,
Though in airy rapine all their practice be,
With little children, as we often find,
Give evidence of tenderest sympathy,
For so to Ninus' mother they appeared,
And likewise to the brothers, Rome that reared,

"Do thou, who hast a human breast and brow
(If it be human that a girl be slain,
Forceless and frail, except as she knew how
To keep his love, who well her own could gain),
Take pity on these little creatures now,
Who wilt not pity her dark mortal pain.
May mercy move thee, as for them and me,
Since innocence so little weighs with thee.

"If that to deal out death with fire and steel   **III**
Is thine, the Moorish strength who broke and bent,
It should be thine in clemency to deal
And grant her life, who will die innocent.
But if such innocence the pang must feel,
Doom me to sad perpetual banishment
In Scythia cold or burning Libya, where
I shall in tears eternally despair.

"Set me where there is every use unkind,
'Mid lions and 'mid tigers. I shall see
If among them that mercy I may find,
I might not find in all humanity.
There, with firm love and with sweet will of mind
Toward him, for whom this death hangs over me,
I'll rear his relics, standing in thy sight,
To be their wretched mother's sole delight."

The King would pardon her, compassionate,
Because her every word had pierced him through.
But the stubborn-hearted people and her fate
(For so Fate willed it) would no mercy do.
Those who approved that deed infuriate,
At once the swords of the fine steel they drew.
You make brave show, you hearts of butcher kites,
Against a lady, and have proved you knights.

Even so against Polyxena, fair maid,
Of her mother old, last consolation glad,
Condemned to die by great Achilles' shade,
With the drawn sword, came Pyrrhus fierce and bad;
But she, whose eyes a tempest might have laid
(Like a soft patient lamb's the look she had),
Watched her grieved mother, who must shriek and rave,
And to hard sacrifice herself she gave;

III   So against Ignes came that murderous crew.
In the alabaster bosom that sustained
Such beauty Love with love his spirit slew,
Who after death queen's state for her ordained,
The brutes their swords in her white breasts imbrue,
Whereon the tears of the sad girl had rained,
And in mad wrath themselves incarnadine,
Nor any vengeance yet to come divine.

133
That day, O Sun, all thy irradiance clear
From such as they well might'st thou turn aside,
As from Thyestes' board of dreadful cheer,
Who ate his babes, as Atreus' hand might guide.
And you, you hollow valleys, who could hear
The last word that her cold lips feebly cried—
Aye! All too well you heard—abroad proclaim,
Re-echoing long while, her Pedro's name.

134
Like the blanched daisy, which ere season due
Is plucked, although so beautiful and bright,
By some small damsel's wanton fingers, who
In her hair wreathes it and maltreats it quite;
And its scent fails, while withers all its hue;
So lay in death the lady ghastly white,
Her living snow and rose and color clear
Withered and gone with life that is so dear.

135
Mondego's maids her tragedy obscure,
Lamenting long, in memory kept alway
And tears they shed became a fountain pure,
Which shall for ever as memorial stay.
"The Loves of Ignes," name that doth yet endure,
They called the place where Love had once his day.
How fresh the spring watering the flowers appears,
Whose name is Love, whose waters are their tears.

Nor was it long ere, for that mortal pain,
Pedro the plans for his revenge could lay.
Once in the Kingdom he began to reign,
His hand could reach those murderers runaway.
From Pedro curst he got them back again.
Those Pedros, who were foes to human clay,
Alliance made, harsh and injurious,
Like Augustus, Antony, and Lepidus.

137

Pedro was enemy inveterate
Of murder and adultery and stealing.
To torture wickedness in wrath and hate
Was to his spirit very balm and healing.
Just, hard, he kept the cities of the state
Safe from all arrogance and evil dealing,
And, thieves chastising, more to death did do
Than gipsy Hercules or Theseus slew.

138

To Pedro, stern and just, Fernando slack
Was born (Oh! what a breach in nature here!),
An idle creature, who all thought did lack
And brought the Kingdom close to ruin sheer.
For when Castile his devastating track
Took through the land unguarded, very near
Portugal came to wholly perishing.
Strong men are weakened by a weakling king.

139

Either it was sin's wages clear as day,
For from her husband Leonor he stole
And wedded her himself, carried away
By the false beauty that deceived his soul;
Or else his heart delivered to the sway
Of the vile vice, to which he gave him whole,
Grew frail and soft; for 'tis a commonplace:
Strong men grow feeble if their loves are base.

III   Many for that sin have suffered pain and blame,
According to God's will and judgment due.
They knew it who to rape fair Helen came,
As likewise Appius and Tarquinius knew.
For what to sacred David proved his shame?
What Benjamin's great people overthrew?
Hard schooling in like case they undertake,
Pharaoh for Sarah, Shechem for Dinah's sake.

And that strong souls are weakened and undone
By lawless love in its insanity,
This well appears in great Alcmena's son,
Wearing the soft disguise of Omphalé.
Mark Antony's dimming fame is blown upon,
So deep in Cleopatra's love was he.
And, Punic victor, you too were compelled,
Who the Apulian peasant-girl beheld.

But who in snares love softly sets can know
The art which happily may break the hold,
When caught by roses and pure human snow,
By the clear alabaster and the gold?
Or 'scape from the strange woman's beauty so,
Face of Medusa, if the truth be told,
Ever the warm heart of her captive turning
Not into stone but into passion burning?

Who has seen gentle eyes and countenance kind,
Sweet excellence, angelically bright,
Which of itself ever transforms the mind,
Can he be hardy to resist such might?
Guiltless Fernando they will surely find,
Who all the tests of love have tried aright.
But the fancy free that felt no pang before
Will only blame his wickedness the more.

NOTES

1.   1. Calliope, the epic muse, invoked for a similar purpose, Aeneid, IX, 525.

5. Apollo is the god of medicine as well as of the sun (Ovid, Met., I, 521). The god is made to say: Inventum medicina meum est.

6. Virgil, Eclogue, IV, 56, is perhaps Camões' authority for making Calliope the mother of Orpheus.

8. These three ladies were at one time or another beloved by Apollo. Daphne escaped him by changing into a bay tree. He abandoned Clytië, a sea nymph, for Leucothoë. Clytië betrayed this third affair to Leucothoë's father, who buried his daughter alive. Clytië is changed into the sunflower, and Leucothoë became the plant which produces frankincense. This is all Ovidian.

2.   2. Aganippe, a fountain at the base of Helicon.

5. Pindus, a mountain. Both Aganippe and Pindus are sacred to, and symbols of, the Nine Muses.

7–8. This couplet, though common form, may perhaps owe something to Statius' lament for Lucan, Silvae, II, vii, 39–41.

4.   8. Professor Ford makes this appropriate remark: "Vasco da Gama is certainly not brief in his account of Portuguese history; it occupies the rest of this canto and all of Cantos IV and V." But Homer, as Professor Ford earlier notices, lets Ulysses spend four books of the Odyssey on his adventures. For a brief summary of the facts, see Camões and the History of Portugal at the end of this volume.

Burton finds his usual satisfaction in making fun of Macedo on the subject of Vasco's "brevity." Macedo—to judge from Burton's quotations—must be one of the most absurd of commentators, in spite of tremendous competition.

7.   2. The river in question is the Tanaïs, now called the Don.

> Lo! where Maeotis sleeps, and hardly flows
> The freezing Tanaïs through a waste of snows,
> Dunciad, III, 87–88.

Ammianus Marcellinus has a similar account of the Don rising in strange mountains and winding its way to Azov (XXII, 8, 27).

Lucan (De Bello Civili, III, 272–276) calls the Tanaïs the border between Europe and Asia. See also Arrian, Anabasis of Alexander, III, 30; Pliny, IV, 24; Pomponius Mela, I, 1; and Strabo, VII, iv, 5.

3. The Riphéan heights could be the Urals or the Caucasus or any other unknown ranges, but it has been observed that the Don does not rise in mountainous country.

4. Lake Maeotis is the sea of Azov.

5. The sea in question could be the Black Sea or the Aegean or both. The line may be a reminiscence from Petrarch, Trionfo d'Amore, Capitolo IV, which is curiously mistranslated in the Triumpho do Amor (Juromenha, V, 25). In any case Camões seems to be following Strabo who strangely enough includes part of the Black Sea in the Aegean. Strabo, II, v, 24.

8. This line appears to be Ovidian (Met., XV, 422 ff.).

8.   2. Hyperborean, an adjective applicable to those who live "back of the North Wind."

3. Eolus, the god of the winds and the inventor of sailing.

4. Professor Ford says that the hills named for the winds are the Riphéan Mountains. This name in Greek signifies, among other things, gust or blast.

9.   Burton, whose learned note at this point saved his successor from a transcendent howler, explains the contest between the Scythians and Egyptians for the honors of superior antiquity. Burton says the story comes from Ammianus Marcellinus, XXII, 15. Scythian is a vague term for northern Barbarian, applied indiscriminately to Slavs and Tartars.

8. This commonplace about human fallibility is perhaps in echo of Aristo, (O. F., I, 7, 2): Ecco, il giudicio uman come spesso erra.

10.   3. Scandinavia is an island for Pliny, IV, 13.

4. An allusion to the Gothic successes against the late Roman Empire. Like the story about the Scythians in 9, this too might come from Ammianus Marcellinus, whose history ends with the Gothic victory of Adrianople, 378 A. D.

11.   3. Sarmatians, another vague term, like Scythian, for northern barbarians, though actually now made tolerably explicit.

Hercynian, the general region of the Black Forest, plus the whole European Urwald right into the heart of Russia.

4. The Marcomans (Marchmen or Frontiersmen) were dwellers on the northern banks of the headwaters of the Rhine and the Danube.

6. Pannonian, Hungarian. Most of the information in this stanza seems to come from Strabo, VII, i, 3.

12.   2. Helle in the myth fell from the golden ram into the Hellespont.

3. Thrace is the home of Mars for most classical poets.

5. Hemus and Rhodope are ranges in what we now call the Balkans. Hemus is the Great Balkan, Rhodope Despoto Dagh (Ford).

14.   2. Antenor is the Trojan refugee who built Padua. Camões might remember Claudian (De Tertio Consulatu Honorii, 119–125) in this account of the Adriatic shore, as also Pomponius Mela, II, 4.

15.   Burton says the first lines are from Petrarch, Il bel Paese. Ariosto's hand is visible here also, he believes (O. F., XXXIII, 9, 35).

5. The Gatekeeper is of course the Pope.

Strabo (VI, iv, 1) is almost certainly supplying details.

16.   6. Pyrene, a nymph beloved by Hercules, gave her name to the Pyrenees. Ford cites the Punica of Silius Italicus, III, 420, ff. There is no reason why Camões might not have read this work. But I do not think he did, for he ignores dozens of details which would have fitted nicely into the Lusiads. The Punica would have enabled Camões to make Viriathus a general under Hannibal. Pliny rejects Pyrene as completely fabulous (III, 1).

7–8. Rivers flow with gold in Lucretius, V, 911. But Strabo is skeptical about forest fires that bring precious metals to the surface (III, ii, 9).

17.   4. The fatal wheel of fortune. Herodotus (I, 207) is perhaps ultimately responsible.

18.   4. The Theban is Hercules who wrenched the mountains apart to make the Strait of Gibraltar.

19.   8. Betis, the Guadalquivir, Andalusia.

Leon and Castile (with Aragon) belonged to Ferdinand and Isabella in Gama's time. They conquered Granada in 1492.

20.   6. It may be pointed out here as well as anywhere else that Gama at no point considers the possible prejudices of his listener, the King of Melinde, who as a Moor himself could hardly have enjoyed much uncompromising condemnation of his creed and his people. Such considerations did not enter the European system of thought at the time, if they ever have. Burton thinks the King is not a Moor but an Arab and would therefore be delighted by strictures against Moghrabis. Gama's tactlessness has troubled Portuguese commentators, as I find at third hand.

21.   1–4. There may be a recollection of the Odyssey (VII, 224–226) here. Odysseus says, "May life leave me when I see my dwelling."

6. The origin of the eponymous hero Lusus appears to be due to a mistranslation of a passage in Pliny (III, 3), who says that the name Lusitania is derived "from the Lusus or Lyssa of Father Liber (Bacchus)." These two common nouns were mistaken for the names of persons, who were accordingly invented to fill the bill. The two words (of which the second is Greek) mean respectively sportiveness

and drunken excitement. Pliny's etymology is, of course, absurd, but to him Lusitania meant the land of drunken gaiety, not the land of Lusus. To this day the French say "jolly as a Portuguese." The expression would seem to have a history.

22.   1. That Shepherd is Viriathus, the first Lusitanian rebel against Rome. In the Portuguese there is a mild play on words. Viriathus is assimilated to Latin *vir*, a man.

        5. The Ancient is Saturn who devoured the gods, his children. Saturn's name in Greek is Chronos, son of Coelus or Uranus, and the God of Time who devours his children,

        Daughters of Time the enigmatic days.

23.   2. Alfonso, Alfonso VI of Castile and Leon (reigned 1065–1109), who was the much put-upon liege lord of the Cid Campeador, Roy Diaz of Bivar. His western offensive seems to have been better organized than his campaigns against Valencia.

        5. Calpe, Gibraltar.

        Camões at this point does not mention the real liberator, Ferdinand the Great of Castile and Leon, whose capture of Coimbra in 1064 went a long way to create free Portugal. Alfonso VI was his successor.

25.   1. Henry of Burgundy (ruled 1095–1112), Count of Portugal, and husband of Teresa, natural daughter of Alfonso VI of Leon and Castile. His Hungarian origin is completely mythical, though some Hungarian lady may have married into what was actually a very noble French family. The story might be due to some scribe's mistake. It would be easy to write Hungaria for Burgundia.

26.   2. The progeny of the slave Hagar refers, of course, to the followers of Mahomet, who as an Arab was believed to be descended from Ismael the son of Hagar the concubine of Abraham. Of him it is written: "He will be a wild man; his hand will be against every man, and every man's hand against him." Things seem to have worked out that way.

        Camões, as noticed by Burton, draws a distinction between Hagarenes, the descendants of Hagar, and Saracens the descendants of Sarah. The etymology is fanciful, but there seems to have been a real distinction once. Saracen was first applied to Arab nomads, who have always felt themselves superior to their sessile brethren.

27.   5. Godfrey of Bouillon, successful leader of the First Crusade (1096–1099). Professor Ford gives 1103 as the date of Henry's arrival at Jerusalem. But Dr. Livermore (History p. 50) says he never went there.

29.   3. Teresa apparently did seize the power but was expelled after a reign of sixteen years.

31.   1. Guimarães, not far from Oporto. The battle was fought at nearby São Mamede in 1128.

32.   1. This alludes to one of the less pleasing Greek legends. King Tereus of Thrace married Procne, daughter of King Pandion of Athens. Later he fell in love with her sister Philomela, violated her, and cut out her tongue to prevent discovery. However, he was detected, and Procne in revenge served him Itylus, her child and his, as a special delicacy at dinner. Philomela became the nightingale, Procne the swallow, and Tereus the hoopoe, a bird of beautiful appearance and "filthy habits." The penalty seems insufficient (Ovid, Met., VI, 425–674). Pliny (X, 34) reports that in his time swallows never visited Bizyes in Thrace because of the crime of Tereus. Camões apparently has no recollection of the more ancient myth of Philomela and Zethus (Odyssey, XIX, 518).

Medea was a Colchian sorceress whose history is at least as unpleasant as Procne's. She had helped Jason to win the Golden Fleece, but, embittered by his unfaithfulness, murdered two of their children (Ovid, Met., VII, 1–424, not to mention Euripides, Seneca, and Valerius Flaccus).

7. Scylla, not the same as the beloved of Glaucus, loved Minos, who besieged her father Nisus, King of Megara. The fate of the city hung on a purple lock in Nisus' hair. Scylla removed it and the city fell. But Minos repudiated the lady and the gods changed her into a lark. Her father became a hawk and pursues her on every opportunity (Ovid, Met., VIII, 1–151). A minor poem of Virgil's, Ciris, is devoted to the history of Scylla. And in the Georgics (I, 404–409) the punishment of Scylla is described.

34.   4–8. The chronology of this period offers a wonderful opportunity for scholars who like controversy. See Lencastre. It is hard to decide whether these lines refer to the battle of Valdevez in 1128 or to the tournament of Arcos de Valdevez in 1140. The tournament took place instead of a battle which was due between Afonso I and Alfonso VII of Castile. The Portuguese chroniclers say their knights swept the decks.

35.   The chronology remains confusing. It must have been early in Afonso I's career that this episode took place.

6. About all that is known of Egas Moniz is to be found in the text. Burton says somewhere that he wrote poetry.

39.   8. Sinis, one of the robbers slain by Theseus. He bent branches to the ground, tied his victims to them, released the boughs, and thus tore the unfortunates to pieces (Ovid, Met., VII, 440–2).

Perillus, who made the brazen bull in which Phalaris of Agrigentum (6th Century B. C.) roasted his enemies. Pliny (XXXIV, 19) reproaches Perillus because he degraded sculpture to the purposes of torture. Perillus was the first victim of the device he designed. Phalaris was the last. Burton cites Claudian. (In Rufinum, I, 253) for Perillus. But the same writer (De Bello Gildonico, 186–189) is more to the point, and Ovid (Tristia, III, xi, 39 ff.) better still.

41.   7. Zopyrus' adventures are related in Herodotus (History, III, 153–160). The remark of Darius is exactly translated (History, III, 160). It may be noted in passing that, although Camões would seem to have read Herodotus, his knowledge of history has strange gaps in it. I don't think that a personality or an episode of the Peloponnesian War is mentioned in the Lusiads. But Camões knows the story of Alexander and Roman history reasonably well.

Burton says that Zopyrus is a corruption of Dadukya, Datis, and that his name appears on the Behistun Inscription. In the English translation of the inscription such a name does appear, but it seems a long way from home.

42.   5. Ourique (1139) was a resounding victory, but according to Ford and others by no means decisive. Almost certainly it was not fought at the town of Ourique in the Algarve. Livermore suggests Chão de Ourique not far from Santarem, of which Ismar, one of the Moorish "kings," was governor.

43.   5–8. Plutarch (Life of Alexander) criticizes Alexander at the Granicus in much the same terms.

44.   1. The five Moorish kings appear to have been invented by the chroniclers (Ford).

2. Ismar was only Governor of Santarem (Ford).

6. The great and worthy dame is Penthesilea, slain, according to tradition later than Homer, by Achilles.

8. The Amazons of antiquity lived along the Thermodon River in Asia Minor. Professor Ford thinks there is some reason to believe that female soldiers actually fought at Ourique. Virgil in describing Camilla has something to say of Penthesilea and the Thermodon (Aeneid, XI, 659–663). Pomponius Mela (I, 19), Plutarch (Life of Theseus), and Valerius Flaccus (Argonauticon, IV, 601–602) repeat the same clichés.

45.   Lucifer chases the stars from the Pole in Statius, Thebais, V, 290–291.

47.   One may fancy a connection between Virgil's simile of the Umbrian hound and the stag and this passage. But the mastiff, Spanish type, was the original bulldog. See Aeneid, XII, 749–755. Virgil himself no doubt had the hound in Iliad, VIII, 338–342, in mind.

48.   5. Burton notices the Moslem shout of battle. So did Lord Byron in another connection:

Hark! through
All sounds it pierceth—"Allah! Allah Hu!"
Don Juan, VIII, 8, 7–8.

49.   Perhaps this stanza has some affinity with Virgil's picture in Georgics, II, 298–311, as also Aeneid, X, 405–411. Virgil, no doubt, had in mind some passage in Homer, such as Iliad, XI, 155–162.

51.   3. Neptune's creation of the horse is a myth which pleased Camões in especial. The sea-god smote the earth with his sceptre, and the creature sprang full-formed from the cleft. Ovid, without mentioning the horse, alludes to this episode (Met., VI, 75).

53.   5. The shields of the five imaginary kings take the place of the cross azure that once stood on the arms of Portugal, with the five pence crosswise on each shield. The method of making up the necessary thirty pence seems inconvenient.

55.   3. Leiria, scene of the first important Cortes and site of Dinis the Ploughhand's forest.

6. Scalabicastro, a pedantic variation on the Roman name for the town now called Santarem. Scalabiscus Colonia was known to Ptolemy (II, 5). Afonso I retook it from the Moors in 1147.

56.   3. The Mountains of the Moon, so-called as early as Ptolemy (II, 5), on whose northern slope lies

4. Cintra, a mountain town, not far from Lisbon and famous for its beauty.

5. Naiads are the nymphs of rivers and springs. They have nothing to do with salt water.

57.   3. The eloquent chief is Ulysses, legendary founder of Lisbon. The curious reader, if there be one, is referred to the notes on VIII, 4.

5–8. These allies were a large detachment of the Second Crusade. They were of great assistance in the siege of Lisbon, which fell in 1147. The advance to the Tagus was on in earnest now.

59.   1–2. This is an imitation of Ovid (Met., VII, 530–532):
Dumque quater iunctis explevit cornibus orbem
Luna, quater plenum tenuata retexuit orbem.

60.   4. Scythians, northern barbarians in general at the time of the collapse of the Roman Empire.

7. Betis, as explained above, Andalusia (Vandalia).

61.   5. Obidos, a few miles north of Lisbon. Estremadura is the name of the Portuguese province of which Lisbon is the capital. It is not to be confused with the Spanish province which has the same name.

6. Alemquer appears to be one of Camões' favorite places like Coimbra and Cintra. Sonnet C (Juromenha, II, 51) alludes touchingly to Alemquer. Juromenha is sure the place had some special meaning

for him, though the belief that Camões was born there gets no support from the poem.

      8. Torres Vedras, famous in Napoleon's Peninsular War.

62.   2. Ceres, the great corn-goddess.

      7. Elvas, Moura, Serpa, and

      8. Alcacer do Sal are all in the land south of the Tagus.

63.   1. The noble town, Sertorius' stronghold, was Evora.

      3. Professor Ford points out that the aqueduct was built in Camões own time by John III. This enterprise in the 16th Century had all the grandeur of something like T. V. A. in the 20th.

      8. Geraldo sem Pavor took Evora in 1166.

64.   In passing it may be observed that a pattern of circumstance develops before the eyes of any reader of the Lusiads who will from time to time consider the map. The great offensive against the Moors, beginning as early as the 10th Century, gradually worked down the Tagus and northward and southward, till in due course, after several centuries of fighting, continental Portugal attained her present boundaries. Though he is guilty of some exaggerations and inaccuracies, Camões seldom departs from the main stream of fact.

65.   1. Palmella and

      2. Cezimbra, both on the coast. The epithet "rich in fish" is an exact translation of an Homeric epithet.

66.   1. Badajoz, a Spanish frontier town, famous in the Peninsular War.

      5–8. The simile appears to be modeled on Ovid, Met., XIII, 870 ff.

69.   8. Teresa was banished. It does not appear that Afonso imprisoned her. Burton states that the moral remarks in this stanza are perhaps derived from St. Augustine, whom he quotes. But I am not convinced, nor, I think, was Burton.

70.   1. Afonso's misadventure at Badajoz took place in 1169.

71.   Burton points out that much of stanzas 71, 72, and 73 has been derived from Lucan's De Bello Civili, II, 585–595.

      4. Thy sire-in-law, Julius Caesar.

      5. Phasis, a river in Colchis whence Jason stole the Golden Fleece (roughly, Georgia). In a crude form of goldwashing a fleece was used. The grains of gold adhered to the fleece (Strabo, XI ii, 19).

      Syene, Assuan in upper Egypt. As it is almost directly on the Tropic, the sun in season is vertically overhead at noon and no shadow is cast. Strabo, Pliny, and Ammianus Marcellinus could have supplied this grace note.

      7. Boötes, the northern constellation, whose brightest star is Arcturus.

72.   2. Heniochia, part of Georgia. Colchian shores, Georgia, home of the Golden Fleece.

3. Cappadocia, in central Eastern Asia Minor.

5. Sophenians, inhabitants of Greater Armenia.

6. Cilicians. Cilicia is the extreme southeast coast of Asia Minor and was once celebrated for bad Greek and worse pirates.

8. Two rivers, the Tigris and Euphrates, which rise in Armenia, in the legend, on Mt. Ararat. Compare Dante, Purgatorio, XXXIII, 111–113, which is supposed to derive from Boethius, V, Metre 1. I owe this reference to Mr. H. M. Landon. A line almost exactly like 8 may be found in Elegy XXIX, Juromenha, III, 255.

73.   2. Taurus, a classic name for a range in Eastern Asia Minor, but sometimes loosely applied to all the mountains from Syria to, and including, the Himalayas.

4. Emathia, a stock poetic name for Thessaly and adjoining Macedonia, in Roman poets, e. g., Lucan, De Bello Civili, I, 1. Milton calls Alexander "the great Emathian conqueror." Emathia's field is Pharsalia where Caesar defeated Pompey.

8. The King's son-in-law, Fernando II of Leon, defeated Afonso at Badajoz in 1169. The contrast between Caesar and Pompey as father-in-law and son-in-law goes back to Catullus (XXIX, 24): "Gener socerque perdidistis omnia." Ovid plays on it, and so does Virgil, if Catalepton VI be his.

74.   3. Santarem, a stronghold on the Tagus frontier, endured innumerable attacks.

5. Martyr Vincent, a more than usually well-documented saint, for, as the handbooks state, St. Augustine bears witness for him, and Prudentius wrote a hymn in his honor. He is said to have perished in the persecution of Diocletian in 304 A. D. Relics of St. Vincent were kept for centuries apparently on the Cape which bears his name, and under Afonso I were translated to Lisbon. Cape St. Vincent is the Sacred Promontory of Strabo and Ptolemy, the World's western limit. There is a certain point in the fact that Sagres near Cape St. Vincent, which Burton says gets its name from "Sacrum Promontorium," became the headquarters of Henry the Navigator, who is here recommended to the Papal Curia as a suitable candidate for canonization.

75.   5. Sancho I campaigned as far as Seville, up the valley of the Guadalquivir, as early as 1176, and again in 1178.

77.   1. Atlas is the Titan who carries the sky on his shoulders, and was turned to stone by Perseus, who showed him the head of Medusa.

Quantus erat mons factus Atlas . . .

. . . . et omne

cum tot sideribus Caelum requievit in illo.

(Ovid, Met., IV, 656 ff.).

125

3. Ampelusa (the Cape of Grapes), a cape on the African coast opposite Gibraltar, now Espartel. Both Pomponius Mela and Strabo begin their account of Geography in the West, Strabo at Cape St. Vincent and Pomponius at Ampelusa. Tingi, Tangier.

4. Antaeus, the giant who doubled his strength whenever he touched his mother Earth. Hercules outwrestled him by holding him aloft in the air till his strength departed.

5. Abyla, now Ceuta opposite Gibraltar.

8. Juba, an African king who allied himself with the Senate against Julius Caesar. He and Cato of Utica are alleged to have fallen on their swords together, when their cause was lost in 46 B. C. Some of the details in this stanza seem to come from Pomponius Mela, I, 5 and 6.

78.　　2. Miramoline, commander of the faithful and Emperor of Morocco. He invaded the Tagus region at least three times after Afonso's misfortune at Badajoz. It appears that the Miramoline died during the third campaign on June 24, 1184 (Livermore, Page 89).

80.　　3. The town is Coimbra, the site of the famous university. It is watered by the Mondego.

4. The banks of the Mondego were the scene of the love affair between Ignes de Castro and Pedro the Doer of Justice (III, 118 ff.).

83.　　8. Libitina, Venus in her paradoxical aspect as goddess of death. Plutarch (Life of Numa Pompilius) is in doubt whether Libitina is Proserpina or Venus, but favors Venus. Libitina came to mean the litter on which dead or wounded gladiators were removed from the arena.

Afonso I, the Great, died in 1185. He was evidently as great a man as Camões makes him out to be. See Camões and the History of Portugal.

84.　　This noble stanza is signal proof of the impossibility of trans- lating great poetry. Burton compares it to Georgics, IV, 460–63. The translator believes that Ovid (Met., XI, 44–49) was also in some sort a model. Both passages are concerned with the death of Orpheus. Burton further says that there was a great flood in December, 1185, at the time of Afonso's death.

85.　　1. Sancho I (1185–1211) was by no means so successful in war as represented by the poet. His true glory is the last ten years of his reign, when he earned the soubriquet "o Povoador," the town-maker.

86.　　3. Silves, in the extreme south.

4. The Third Crusade (1189–1193) proved exceptionally con- venient for Sancho I. The leaders were Frederick Barbarossa, Richard Coeur de Lion, and Philip Augustus of France. The final conquest of Algarve the southernmost Portuguese Province did not come till the reign of Afonso III (1248–1279).

87. 2. Frederick Barbarossa (1152–1190). Camões, like Barbarossa, is believed to have had a red beard.

5. Guy of Lusignan, forced to surrender by (6) Saladin in 1187, at the Battle of Tiberias.

90. 4. Afonso II (1211–1223), the Fat, was apparently a very able king indeed. See Camões and the History of Portugal.

91. 2. Sancho II (1223–1248), called Capelo, the Cowl. He was deposed by his brother Afonso III in 1245. According to modern opinion, the real issue was a quarrel about religious matters. Hence the bad press that has been the fate of an anticlerical king, incidentally a mighty warrior, who before his misfortune had nearly completed the conquest of the Algarve. See Camões and the History of Portugal.

92. 2. Nero has also had a bad press. Apart from his private irregularities, it is alleged that he was responsible for the great fire of Rome in 64 A. D.

7. Heliogabalus (reigned 218–222), the most singular and least interesting of Roman Emperors.

8. Sardanapalus, the last Assyrian King of Nineveh and, rightly or wrongly, a byword for effeminacy. Strabo reports him as saying that it was best to eat, drink and be merry, for nothing else was worth the snap of a finger (XIV, v, 9).

3. Phalaris, the 6th Century B. C. tyrant of Agrigentum. See note to III, 39, 8. Pliny (VII, 57) calls Phalaris the first Greek tyrant.

94. 1. Boulogne's Count, the usurper Afonso III. Professor Ford points out a curious error of Camões. Afonso III, notwithstanding his military record, was never called "the brave," which was the soubriquet of Afonso IV. See Camões and the History of Portugal.

95. 1. The Algarve marches are in the extreme south. And the seven castles on the arms of Portugal signify the strongholds of the Algarve. As stated in the text, Afonso III gave Portugal her present frontiers. The statement that he acquired by marriage some rights to Algarve, whose conquest Sancho I had begun, seems to be legendary. He no doubt completed the task, but he should not have full marks for work most of which had been performed by his brother and his victim.

96. 1. Dinis (1279–1325) might have been dwelt on more by Camões. A fine poet, a good soldier, a first-rate administrator, he founded the University of Coimbra. The epithet, "o Lavrador," the Ploughhand, was honestly earned. See Camões and the History of Portugal.

97. 8. Spikenard. Ficalho says that this plant is Gnaphalium sanguineum (Lencastre), but "baccaro," the word here translated "spikenard," has several meanings.

98.　5. Atropos, "the blind fury with the abhorred shears."

　　　8. Afonso IV, the Brave, apparently as unpleasant and brutal as his father was brilliant and humane.

99.　5. Mauretanians, Moors of Morocco.

100.　Semiramis, an historical princess of Assyria (c. 800 B. C.). The myths about her are nearly all discreditable to her character. Among other things, she is supposed to have invaded India. See VII, 53.

　　　2. Hydaspes, the Jhelum, an affluent of the Indus. Ptolemy calls it the Bidaspes (VII, 1, 26).

　　　3. Attila, "the Scourge of God," was defeated by the allied Romans and Visigoths at Chalons in 451 A. D. Camões makes an odd slip here. Attila was King of the Huns, and his armies were not Gothic, though some Goths fought for him.

　　　There could hardly have been enough ships in the Mediterranean to transport the army which the Emperor of Morocco led into Spain, 60,000 horse, 400,000 foot. The Chronicles always exaggerate. 20,000 in all would be ample.

　　　8. Tartessian fields, Tartessus, the region at the mouth of the Guadalquivir near Cadiz. It is perhaps the Biblical Tarshish whence Solomon obtained much wealth. The paradox may be noticed, that part of Spain was once a Mexico. The name is in Pomponius Mela, Strabo, and Pliny. Ptolemy ignores it.

101.　1. Castile's high king, Alfonso XI of Castile (1312–1350).

　　　4. As Burton notices, the Castilian feared the fate of Roderick.

　　　5. Dona Maria was badly treated by her husband (Livermore, A History of Portugal, 159).

103.　Perhaps Claudian's rhetoric (In Rufinum, II, 144–151) colors Maria's speech.

105.　2. Mulucha, a stream in Morocco, the modern Muluya, which in Roman times was the border between the two Mauretanias. Pomponius Mela, Strabo, Pliny, and Ptolemy know it.

106.　Ovid has a passage (Met., XIV, 585 ff.) with which this stanza is affiliated.

109.　1. Tarifa, near Gibraltar.
　　　Battle of the Salado, 1340.

115.　2. Tethys' house, the Ocean.

116.　1. Marius (155–86 B. C.) won the battle of Vercelli in 101 B. C. against the Cimbrians. Plutarch (Life of Marius) has the anecdote of the drinking water purchased with blood.

　　　5. Hannibal (247–183 B. C.) won the battle of Cannae in 216 B. C. The story is that he sent three pecks of the golden rings worn by Roman knights to the Senate of Carthage (Livy, XXIII, 12, 1). Silius Italicus speaks of this (Punica, VIII, 675–676). And Juvenal points

the inevitable antithesis between the ring filled with poison which killed Hannibal at Brusa and the rings of the dead knights at Cannae (Satire X, 162–166). Why drag in Pliny, XXXIII, 6?

117. 2. "Cocytus named of lamentation loud," one of the rivers of Hell.

6. Titus, the son of Vespasian, who took Jerusalem in 70 A. D. and was later Emperor himself (79–81 A. D.). Josephus (The Wars of the Jews) is perhaps Camões' source.

The slaughter at the Salado has unquestionably been exaggerated.

118. 5. The tragic episode of Ignes de Castro is much admired by the Portuguese. The whole business is a chemical mixture of fact and fable extremely hard to separate. The episode of the crowning of the corpse of Ignes is narrated by the chroniclers with great detail, but has the earmarks of the legendary. See Camões and the History of Portugal.

Burton notes that his pet aversion, Macedo, considers the episode "the most disjointed and incoherent passage in the Lusiads."

119. 1. Again Camões leans on Virgil (Eclogue VIII, 45).

5. He likewise remembers Eclogue X, 28–29.

120. 2. A parallel to this line in the dubious translation of Petrarch's Trionfi may be found in Juromenha, V, 41.

122. 8. This may be a gentle hint to King Sebastian, whose celibate views early caused much alarm and finally resulted in national disaster.

125. 1–2. Professor Ford indicated the resemblance of these lines to Virgil, Aeneid, II, 405–6:

Ad caelum tendens ardentia lumina frustra,

Lumina, nam teneras arcebant vincula palmas.

And the same idea in almost identical words may be found in Ciris (402–403), a poem believed to be by Virgil.

126. 4. Statius' account of the birds of prey as seen by Amphiaraus and Melampus (Thebais, III, 508–509) could have been swimming in Camões' ken.

7. Semiramis is intended, who, having been exposed at birth, was fed by doves. But, as the ubiquitous and omniscient Professor Ford has noted, Ninus was the name of Semiramis' husband. Her son was Ninyas.

8. Burton characteristically refers to Colonel Sleeman's "account of wolf-reared boys (never girls) in India" in support of the legend of Romulus and Remus.

128. 5–7. Camões had not forgot Horace, Odes, III, xi, 47–48.

129. 1–4. These lines are strongly reminiscent of Ovid, Heroides, X, 1–2, in which Ariadne rails against the cruelty of Theseus.

131. 1. Polyxena, daughter of Priam and Hecuba, sacrificed according to one of the legends to placate Achilles' spirit. See Ovid (Met., XIII, 446 ff., quoted by Ford) and Virgil (Aeneid, III, 321, ff.).

7. Camões might have had in mind Juvenal's hateful words:

. . . . sed torva canino
Latravit rictu.

Satire X, 271-272

133. 3. Thyestes, who had injured his brother Atreus, was tricked into eating the flesh of his own children by Atreus. Camões could have derived the legend of Thyestes' feast from a dozen places, Ovid, Heroides, XVI, 208-209 for one. Seneca's drama is a possibility too.

7. Pedro (reigned 1357-1367) called the Doer of Justice. See Camões and the History of Portugal for a brief notice of a very curious man, also Stanza 137 of this book.

134. The simile of the daisy seems to be a variation on the same theme in Virgil's account of the death of Pallas (Aeneid, IX, 433-437).

135. Burton describes with gusto the garden of the palace at Coimbra where the famous fountain flows. He was pleased too by a secular cedar on which he saw inscribed words to this effect:

I shaded beautiful Ignes.

136. 5. Pedro curst, Pedro the Cruel (reigned 1350-1369), King of Castile. He was the son of "the beautiful Maria" by Alfonso XI, the hero of the Salado. His daughter Constance was the second wife of John of Gaunt. There has been an attempt to whitewash him, but it is still satisfactory to know that his brother stabbed him to death.

6. The two Pedros had the same soubriquet, "Doer of Justice."

7-8. Camões is quoting Plutarch's opinion (Life of Antony) of the Second Triumvirate.

137. 8. Hercules and Theseus were both slayers of outlaws.

138. 1. Fernando "the Fair" (reigned 1367-1383), who has been well described in three words: "ambitious, unscrupulous, and incapable."

The King of Castile besieged Lisbon in 1373 (Livermore, History, 169).

139. 2. Leonor Teles, mistress and queen of Fernando, who for her sake refused to marry the Castilian Princess Leonor. This had much to do with the troubles which were not finally settled till Aljubarrotta, 1385.

140. 3. Paris and his Trojans.

4. Appius Claudius kidnapped Virginia, whose father stabbed her to save her from the tyrant, Sextus Tarquinius, the violator of Lucrece.

5. David and Bathsheba.

130

6. The repulsive action of the men of Gibeah,
                    when the hospitable door
        Exposed a matron to avoid worse rape.

8. Pharaoh, supposing Sarah to be Abraham's sister, got into serious difficulties.

Shechem, who behaved very well in his affair with Dinah, was murdered by her brothers, who used more than usually unpleasant Oriental methods.

141. 2. Alcmena's son, Hercules, whom Omphale compelled to wear her garments while she put on his lion skin and carried his club. In Ovid's Heroides IX, 65 ff., Deianira expresses herself freely on Hercules' infatuation with Omphale. And in the Fasti (II, 303 ff.) the story is told at length. Other sources are of course possible. But Ovid appears so often as the obvious one that one is gradually persuaded.

7. Hannibal. According to Burton the legend of the Apulian maid is derived through Petrarch from Plutarch (Trionfo d'Amore). The Portuguese translation of the Trionfi (by some thought to be by Camões) duly deals with this (Juromenha, V, 17). But Pliny (III, xi, 103) speaks of the Apulian town Salapia (now Salpi) famous for Hannibal's affair with a courtezan.

142–143. These stanzas have some special interest as expressing with less power, but with no less explicitness, the same regret of which we become aware in the greatest of Camões' lyrical poems, "By the Rivers of Babylon." The poet, faithful in thought to what, in spite of his imperfect sympathy with Platonism, he would have called the "Idea" of his unknown Beatrice, had, without much doubt, turned aside into the house of the strange woman, the "barbara escrava," and perhaps Dianeme, who, some suppose, may have been a Chinese girl. Evidently Camões had moments of bitter self-reproach, with respect to these episodes. The two stanzas at least suggest such a moment, as the tremendous redondilhas do in an overwhelming way.

BOOK IV

ARGUMENT

Gama continues his account to the King of Melinde and relates the history of Portugal's wars with Castile about the succession to the throne after the death of King Fernando. The military exploits of Nuno Álvares Pereira. The victory of Aljubarrota. The efforts made in the time of King John II to discover India by sea. How King Manuel pursued this end and decided on Gama's voyage. Preparations, embarkation, and departure from Belem.

THE LUSIADS

THE FOURTH BOOK

AFTER the storm, tempestuous and drear,
And shadow of night and shrieking winds that
Comes on the morning hour, serene and clear, [blow,
With hope of harboring safely from the woe.
Quelling gross darkness, doth the sun appear,
That stills all dread conjecture. Even so
In the great Kingdom did such change betide
After the hour when King Fernando died.

2

For, if our folk were mightily inclined
Toward some one who should make his vengeance
On those who wrongfully their pockets lined   [good
Because of the last King's ineptitude,
In little space the very man they find
In John, though but a bastard of the blood,
For ever glorious, whom they King declare,
And Pedro's only veritable heir.

3

That this was true, the mandate of the Sky
Divinely did by clearest tokens show
In Évora, when a girl baby's cry
Named him aloud ere speech the child could know.
Rising in the cradle, her voice lifting high
(Clear proof it was that Heaven willed it so),
"Portugal!" she called aloud, and thereupon
Her hand raised, "Portugal! for the new King, John!"

IV But now throughout the Kingdom's whole extent
Men's hearts were altered by their hatred keen,
And cruelties, absolute and evident,
Wrought by the people's wrath on all sides seen.
To massacre the kin and friends they went,
The minions of the adulterous Count and Queen,
Now that the dame's incontinent turpitude
Was clearlier seen in state of widowhood.

5

But he, his cause dishonored at long last,
In the woman's presence by cold iron died,
And with him many to destruction passed,
For the mounting flame burned all as it ran wide.
One, like Astyanax from the high tower cast,
Found naught availed his order sanctified,
One not her order, altar, honor meet,
And one lay naked, piecemeal in the street.

6

In long forgetfulness now let them rest,
Mortal barbarities that Rome once knew,
Fierce Marius' cruelty, and savage zest
Of Sulla when his enemy withdrew.
But for this reason Leonor confessed
Her lust for the dead Count, for all to view,
And against Portugal let loose Castile,
Calling her daughter heiress of our weal.

7

Beatrice was that daughter, who had wed
Castile, that now to seize the Kingdom came,
The daughter of Fernando as was said,
If it be conceded to uncertain fame.
Castile was well persuaded on that head,
Saying the girl her father's rights might claim,
And gathered a great host of war in hand
From various provinces and many a land.

They come from all that country called of yore   **IV**
By Brigo's name (if true) and still so known,
From lands Fernando and the Campeador
Took from the Moorish tyrants for their own.
They did not value well the risks of war,
Whose rough plows till the meadows of León,
Because they are a people who for sure
Were excellent in battle with the Moor.

9

The Vandals, ever mindful of their dread
Renown of old, likewise alliance gave,
Of Andalusia the front and head,
Which Guadalquivir washes with his wave.
And where the Tyrians once inhabited,
They armed for fight, those island-dwellers brave,
Who, for their veritable sign of war,
Hercules' columns on their banners bore.

10

And thither from Toledo's realm repair
The levies of that old and noble town,
Girded around by Tagus calm and fair,
Out of the Conca mountains pouring down.
Nor did your fear prevent your hastening there,
You rough Galicians of unclean renown,
Taking up arms to fight against a foe
Whose hard strokes you had tested long ago.

11

And war's black furies stirred up all the race
Of Biscay, who lack wit to understand
Learning polite, and who in any case
Endure but ill wrongs at a stranger's hand.
Guipuscoa and Asturias apace,
From mines of iron which enrich their land,
Armed with their own steel haughty native hordes,
In order in the fight to help their lords.

IV John, from whose breast the strength of spirit grew
As once strength grew from Hebrew Samson's hair,
Although his powers to him seemed all too few,
Began the land's slight forces to prepare;
And, not that lack of policy he knew,
With his chief nobles would his counsel share,
But to discover what their thoughts might be,
For many minds breed much diversity.

13

They lacked not reasons, such as would oppose
Common opinion, to self-will inclined,
In whom, all changed, the ancient courage shows
As unfamiliar treason of ill kind.
For the inert cold terror overcrows
Right natural fidelity of mind.
King, country, they deny, and will deny,
If it suit, like Peter, Very God on high.

14

But such erroneous thought could never dwell
In the stout Nuno Álvares, who still,
Though in his brothers he saw treason well,
Sternly rebuked every inconstant will.
In words more forceful than delectable,
He spake to all men whom such doubts might fill,
Hand on sword, wrathful, with no grace of style,
But the whole world threatening, land and sea, the
15   [while:
"What? Has the glorious race of Portugal
Bred men who will not like good patriots fight?
What? In this province, princess of them all
In world-wide war, is there one man in sight,
Who to defend her disobeys the call,
Refusing faith, love, soldier skill, and might
Proper to Portugal, for no reason known?
Does he hope to see his country overthrown?

138

"What? Have you ceased to be their right descent, **IV**
Who, with the great Afonso's flag before,
Proved themselves fiery and armipotent
And this same martial nation overbore,
When they beat back so vast an armament,
Whose soldiers with their banners fled the war,
And seven counts illustrious were ta'en,
Beside what other booty they might gain?

17

"And how, then, were they constantly restrained,
These, with whom now again you have to do,
By Denis and his son, those chiefs unstained,
Except by your brave sires and grandsires too?
If Fernando's sin and folly has attained
Such height as makes his weakness govern you,
Your ancient force, this new reign home will bring,
If it be true men alter with their King.

18

"You have such a King that, if your valor show
Equal to his you now have raised on high,
All whom you will you well may overthrow
And beat them worse than in the times gone by.
But if my words cannot persuade you so,
Because your fears possess and terrify,
Then let this panic dread tie every hand,
For alone against the foreign yoke I'll stand.

19

"I only, with my men and this beside"
(Which saying, forth he drew the sword half way),
"Will against hateful foes defence provide
For the country none has conquered to this day.
With the King, and with the Kingdom sadly tried,
And the mere loyalty which you gainsay,
I'll beat not only these our present foes
But whosoever shall my King oppose."

IV As in Canusium youths who yet remained,
Cannae's sole relics, come together there,
Scarce from surrendering themselves refrained
To the might of Afric and her fortune fair,
But young Cornelius presently constrained,
Sword in hand, all that company to swear
Never the arms of Rome to cast aside
While yet they lived or till in arms they died;

21

So Nuno stirred their spirits and compelled.
When they heard him his last argument impart,
Gone was the fear importunate that held
Frozen within the courage of the heart.
On the beasts of Neptune, galloping, they yelled,
Shaking and brandishing aloft the dart.
And all around the shouts full-throated ring:
"He'll set us free. God save the glorious King!"

22

Many of the people give their suffrage to
A war which will the fatherland maintain.
Many their weapons furbish or renew,
Wasted with rust of a pacific reign.
They quilt the helms, try plates if they be true,
And each man as it likes him arms again.
Others get thousand-colored tabards wove
With verses and the emblems of their love.

23

From cool Abrantès, out marched John the bold,
Together with his troops that flash and gleam,
Abrantès that from Tagus' fountain cold
Enjoys the flooding and abundant stream.
The headship of the vanguard one did hold,
Who fit to rule the greatest hosts would seem,
Even such countless Orient armies vast
As once o'er Hellespont with Xerxes passed.

Nun' Álvares the very scourge I call
Of arrogant Castile. So men acclaimed
Long since the fierce Hun chieftain first of all,
So by the French and the Italians named.
Command of the right wing of Portugal
Was given to another knight far-famed,
Skilled to command and well to rule the fight,
A Vasconcellos, Mem Rodrigues hight.

IV

25

On the other flank, matchable in degree,
Anton Vasques of Almada had command.
Later the great Count of Avranches was he.
He led the troops that marched on the left hand.
And in the rearguard there were plain to see
The shields and towers that in our banner stand,
Where, by his steady courage, John the King
Made Mars his glory seem a trivial thing.

26

Along the walls, in timorous dismay
And almost frozen in their loving fear,
Wait mothers, sisters, sweethearts, wives, who pray
And promise pilgrimage and meagre cheer.
And now already the battailous array
Unto the host of enemies draws near,
Who make them welcome with a mortal shout,
And all at once are troubled by great doubt.

27

Harbinger trumpets with their blasts reply,
And the whistle of the fife and tambour's sound.
The standard-bearers shake their flags on high,
Whereon is every various color found.
Ceres, her fruits, for now the year grows dry,
Grants to the farmers on the threshing ground,
Since in Astraea stands the August sun,
While Bacchus from the grape makes sweet must run.

IV A signal the Castilian trumpet blew,
Horribly thundering, wild, and full of dread.
Ortegal heard. Guadiana's waves withdrew,
For very fear, back toward their fountainhead.
Douro and Transtagana the sound knew.
And to the sea bewildered Tagus fled.
And mothers, who the ghastly sound might hear,
Clutched to their bosoms little children dear.

29

And many a blanched face, whence kind blood had
The heart to succor, there a man might see!   [flown
For fear when faced with perils overgrown
Is greater oft than peril e'er can be.
And if not, so it seems. For rage alone
To smite and beat some stubborn enemy
Prevents our feeling loss, howe'er severe,
Of bodily limbs or life that is so dear.

30

Now, closing fast, doth doubtful war commence.
On either side the vanguard moves to fight,
These for their country risen in defence,
And these in hopes to capture it outright.
There great Pereira, all brave confidence
Locked in his breast, first makes his fame shine bright,
And shocks and slays till all the field lies sown
With those who would make others' land their own.

31

Through the thick air, all various shot, bolts, darts,
Are hurling with a strident hissing sound.
'Neath hard hoofs of great steeds with burning hearts
The earth shakes. Clamors from the vales rebound.
The lances smash. Tremendous thunder starts,
As armèd men go crashing to the ground.
The foes upon fierce Nuno's handful fall
In swarming squadrons, which he made look small.

His brothers came against him on that day   **IV**
(Bad case and cruel), but he felt no dread.
Little he errs who would a brother slay,
That against King and Country would make head.
And of those traitors, in the first array,
Were very many who the battle led
Against their sires and brethren (hateful thought),
As in the wars Caesar and Pompey fought.

33
Sertorius, Coriolanus without stain,
Catiline, whoever in antiquity,
Against your own dear country, with profane
Courage, once chose to play the enemy,
If in the darkness of King Pluto's reign
Subject to heaviest punishments you be,
Say to the King that there have been withal
Traitors from time to time in Portugal.

34
Our vanward men are there hurled back in flight,
So thick upon them do the foemen throng.
But there stands Nuno, as on Ceuta's height
There stands a lion terrible and strong,
Watching the horsemen gird him left and right,
Who toward the Tetuan country ride along,
And they make shift to plague him with the spear;
He rages, troubled somewhat, not in fear;

35
Heavily he eyes them, but wild instinct keen
And anger suffer not the beast to fly,
Who hurls where thickest set the spears are seen,
And all around him lances multiply;
So stands that champion, staining all the green
With strangers' blood. Some of his men must die,
For spirits with all gallantry endued
Lose their force, fighting such a multitude.

IV When John beheld that the attack was grave
Where Nuno fought, like a captain wise and ware,
Thither he raced, saw all, and fresh heart gave
By his presence and his voice to all men there.
As a lioness that has whelped, savage and brave,
Who knows her cubs, left lonely in the lair,
While she went forth their provender to find,
Are stolen by Massylia's shepherd hind,

37

And mad she runs, roaring, and every roar
With thunder shakes the Seven Brothers height;
So John with many a chosen warrior
Rushed to bear up the forefront of the fight:
"O brave companions, O brave men of war,
Whom none can ever equal in my sight,
Strike for your land, for all the hope and chance
Of liberty depend upon the lance!

38

"Here you may see your king and your compeer
Who in the van made haste to stand with you,
Despite the foe in arms and bolt and spear.
Portuguese, strike! Strike in, as ye are true!"
So saying, the heroic cavalier
Four times his great lance brandished, and then threw
The weapon strongly, and, at that single cast,
There were very many men who breathed their last.

39

For lo, his men, burning with noble shame
And honorable fire, hotly contest
Which one of them shall win the martial game
And with brave spirit face the peril best.
The iron is reddened in the bloody flame.
They hack the cuirass through to pierce the breast,
And at one moment buffets get or give,
Like men who care not if no more they live.

144

40

Many they sent the Lake of Styx to view,
In whose bodies death and steel found entry wide.
There Santiago's master quittance knew,
Who had maintained the fight with gallant pride.
And that other, having wrought his wild battue,
Calatrava's cruel master, likewise died.
And there Pereira's brothers runagate
Fell also, cursing Heaven and cursing fate.

41

Hordes of the low and nameless crowd descend,
With many a noble, to the Deep profound,
Where, for their souls, who from this world must
Hungers perpetual the three-mouthed hound. [wend,
And better, hostile pride to break and bend,
The banner, for nobility renowned,
Of the infuriate Castilian foe
Under the feet of Portugal sank low.

42

One fester has that savage battle grown,
Sword-cuts, blood, death, and shouting far and wide.
All flowers take on a color not their own,
Because of the vast multitude that died.
Men flee. Men fall. And all their wrath is flown.
It is lost labor with the lance to ride.
And the Castilian for a beaten man
Now knew himself, baffled in all his plan.

43

Unto the conqueror he left that plain,
That he left not his life there, well content,
Followed by such as of his host remain.
Fear, wings, not feet, unto the flying lent.
In their profoundest hearts they nursed the pain
Of death and of an enterprise misspent,
Bruises, dishonor, and a sorrow sore
That others triumphed with their spoils of war.

IV Some in their flight with blasphemy abuse
Whoever first on earth to battling fell.
And others still the cruel thirst accuse
Of a spirit envious and insatiable.
He who to rob another's goods doth use
Plunges unhappy men in pains of Hell,
Thus many a wife and many a mother leaving
Without her lord or son, for ever grieving.

45

The victor John the customary days
In triumph on the field of fight remained,
And then with gifts and pilgrimages pays
His dues to Him Who victory ordained.
But Nuno, who desired no other praise
Than that his fame henceforth should be maintained
In the folk's memory for victorious war,
Went to the lands on Tagus' further shore.

46

His destiny into his hand played still.
The effect was like what the mind might devise,
For the marches of the Vandals to his will
Yielded a victory and a noble prize.
And now the Betic banner of Seville,
With various chiefs, all in a moment lies
Under his feet with no defense at all,
O'erwhelmed by the main strength of Portugal.

47

Long time Castile in sad subjection went
Because of this and other victories,
Till at last peace, on which all men were bent,
The victor to the vanquished foe decrees.
And afterward our Sire Omnipotent
Desired that the two royal enemies
In marriage should two English ladies lead,
Sweet, fair, and famous princesses indeed.

The strong heart used to battle ill can bear   IV
The lack of enemies to work them woe.
On land was none to conquer anywhere,
And Ocean's wave he went to overthrow.
He was the first of all our Kings to fare
Forth from our land, that Africa might know,
By force of arms, how much our Christian creed
The law of false Mahomet doth exceed.

49

A thousand swimming birds her silver sail,
Where Thetis rages, never at her ease,
Spreading afar their wide wings to the gale,
Near the last limit set by Hercules.
Against Mount Ábyla he would prevail
And the great citadel of Ceuta seize,
Hurling forth Mahomet vile and saving Spain
From risk of Julian's base device again.

50

But Death consented not that Portugal
Should long have Fortune's hero at command,
Rather, in the choirs of Heaven imperial,
Desiring he should come to take his stand.
God took him, but, to be our rock and wall,
Granted him children who could rule the land
And make it larger than in time gone by,
A noble progeny of princes high.

51

King Edward's fortune hardly was so great
During the years he held the lofty reign,
For the unkindly time would alternate
In good and evil and delight and pain.
Who ever saw a wholly happy state,
Or Fortune firmness constantly maintain?
And did not this same law of Destiny
Press hard on monarch and on monarchy?

IV He saw his saintly brother captive led,
That Ferdinand who sought adventure brave.
To save his wretched men from leaguer dread,
Himself a hostage to the Moor he gave.
And for mere love of country his life sped,
Though princely born, as might become a slave,
Who for his life strong Ceuta gave not o'er.
Though life be dear, he loved his country more.

53

Codrus, the foeman's triumph to forestall,
Consented rather that himself should die;
Regulus, that his nation might not fall,
Preferred the loss of his own liberty.
But he, to end Spain's terror once for all,
In prison perpetual resolved to lie.
Codrus and Curtius, whose deeds with terror strike,
And the true Decians never did the like.

54

Afonso held the realm's sole title clear,
In our Hesperia a fair martial name,
For pride of the barbarian frontier
He changed to base and miserable shame.
Invincible had been that cavalier,
But once to view Iberia he came.
And Africa will say it could not be
That any beat a king as dread as he.

55

For he could pluck the golden apples where
The Tirynthian alone had plucked before,
The yoke that he compelled his neck to bear
Has not been shaken yet by the brave Moor.
The palm and the green laurel did he wear,
Of victories in the barbaric war,
When the foe came strong Alcacer to hold,
Tangier thick-peopled, and Arzilla bold.

By force and arms he storms them nonetheless,   **IV**
Adamantine ramparts razing to the ground,
For the Portuguese with wonted fury press
To wreck whatever in their way is found.
And miracles of highest knightliness,
In noble histories fit to be renowned,
In that emprize wrought many a cavalier,
That made the fame of Portugal shine clear.

57

But later on, touched by ambition's hand
And pride of rule, the bitter and the bright,
Against the Arragonese King Ferdinand
For the strong realm of Castile he went to fight.
A multitude of foes throughout the land
From Cadiz to the Pyrenéan height,
Most proud and various nations, thither drew,
Who to King Ferdinand their homage do.

58

But quiet in a peaceful land to wait
Pleased not his young son John, who thought to aid
His sire, whose spirit was inordinate,
Nor was the effort small that he essayed.
And at long last, out of his perilous strait,
With cloudless brow, serenely undismayed,
The father 'scaped, sore pressed and red with blood,
Though even now doubtful the victory stood.

59

For the bold lad, full of ambition high,
A strong and gentle knight, brave to the core,
Did fearful hurt upon the enemy
And all that day stayed on the field of war.
So Octavian was beat, while Antony,
His comrade good, away the victory bore,
When on the men, great Caesar's blood who spilled,
At Philippi their vengeance they fulfilled.

IV Later when darkness and eternal night
To the calm Heavens would Afonso bear,
The Prince, who long held the realm's oversight,
As second John and thirteenth king, fell heir.
And he, to keep perpetual honor bright,
Dared to attempt more than a man can dare,
And this it was he dared, to find the way
To the red Dawn's limits, which I seek today.

61

And forthwith his ambassadors he sent
Through Spain, through France, through famous Italy.
In the noble harbor aboard ship they went,
Where sepulchred lies dead Parthenopé.
In Naples is Fate's power made evident,
That gave her o'er to various mastery,
Yet in time's fulness made her great again
Under the rule of mighty men of Spain.

62

Through Sicily's high seas the ships they guide
To sandy beaches of the Rhodian isle
And the steep foreshores where great Pompey died,
Which therefore have been famous this long while.
Memphis they reach, and countries watered wide
By swelling inundations of the Nile,
And from Egypt Ethiopian heights ascend,
Where yet Christ's sacred ritual men defend.

63

And they went over waters Erythréan
Through the which, shipless, Israel's children came.
Behind them lay the mountains Nabatéan,
Which Ishmael's son made noble with his name.
And they sailed round those odorous coasts Sabéan,
Whereof Adonis' mother spread the fame.
And Arabia the Blest to them was known,
Who left the Arabias of the Waste and Stone.

To Persia's gulf they came, where yet mankind   **IV**
Babel's confusion keep in memory,
And Tigris and Euphrates flow combined,
Proud of the springs of their nativity.
Next they go forth those purest floods to find,
That themes for mighty histories yet shall be,
The streams of Indus, o'er that Ocean's wave
Whose passage Trajan ventured not to brave.

65

Kerman, Mekran, and India, they saw,
And stranger peoples utterly unknown,
With differing habits and a various law.
Each region breeds and cherishes its own.
Nor is it easy homeward to withdraw
On those long roads with difficulty sown,
There, dying, in the country they remain,
Nor see their dear-loved fatherland again.

66

And surely it would seem that Heaven bright
Reserved a venture with such peril fraught
For Manuel's merits, for unto the height
Of great endeavor on his soul it wrought;
Since Manuel succeeded John by right,
Both in his realm and loftiness of thought,
And, when the Kingdom's charge fell to his hand,
Desired yet more vast Ocean to command.

67

Now Manuel, from the noble sentiment
Of that to which he was in duty bound,
Derived from his forerunners (whose intent
Was to make greater Portugal's dear ground),
Not for a single moment would be bent,
For as the hour when the light dies came round
And all the stars aloft arose to shine,
Yet would invite to sleep at their decline,

IV He laid him down upon his golden bed,
That place of the most sure imagination,
And turned for ever over in his head
His blood and office's great obligation.
Sleep o'er his eyes accustomed influence shed,
Yet did not check his spirit's operation,
For as, outwearied, gently she came o'er him,
Morpheus in various forms appeared before him.

69

It seemed to him that he had climbed so high
He must have touched on the first sphere at last,
Whence many various worlds he could descry
And, of strange folk and savage, nations vast,
And near the place of Dawn's nativity,
As far away as farthest sight could cast,
'Mid the long range of huge and ancient mountains,
He saw spring forth two clear and noble fountains.

70

Wild fowl and savage beasts and monstrous kine
Live on those mountains where the forests grow.
Thousands of trees with various shrubs combine
To block all passage where no man can go.
Those desperate heights, as enemies malign
Of any traffic, all too clearly show,
For not since Adam sinned until our day
Has human foot across them broke the way.

71

From the waters issued (or so fancy told)
Two beings, who, far-striding, near him drew.
Each of the pair appeared exceeding old,
Rustic, perhaps, yet honor was their due.
Down from their locks the drops of water rolled,
Which wetted all the bodies of the two.
Their skin was of a brown and blackened cast,
And their thick beards were all unshorn and vast.

Each of the twain upon his brow did wear   **IV**
A wreath of herbs and sprays we do not know.
And one of them approached with weary air,
As who had had the longer way to go.
Likewise the water seemed from otherwhere
To have come hither with an altered flow,
As Arcadian Alphéus in Syracuse
Seeks the embraces of his Arethuse.

73
He, as the person of chief dignity,
Thus to the King from far his thought made plain:
"Know a great cantle of this world shall be
Awarded to your crown and to your reign.
And we, whose fame so far abroad doth flee,
Whose necks to bow none ever could constrain,
Warn you 'tis time for you to make demand
For the great tribute given by our hand.

74
"I am illustrious Ganges. In the earth
Of Paradise I have my cradle true.
And this, O King, is Indus, he whose birth
Befell among the heights you have in view.
Fierce warfare is the price that we are worth.
But if your ends you constantly pursue,
Unfearing, after victories untold,
You'll bridle all the nations you behold."

75
No more the famed and sacred river said,
But in a moment disappeared the two.
Manuel awoke with a sudden shock of dread
And perturbation in his spirit grew.
Phoebus meanwhile his shining mantle spread
O'er the dark sleep-bound hemisphere anew.
And Dawn breaks, painting Heaven as she goes
With hues of scarlet flowers or modest rose.

IV The King his lords to council summoned there
And of the figures in the vision told.
The holy ancient's words did he declare,
Which all must needs for a great wonder hold.
Measure they took the navy to prepare,
Whereby, with noble courage high and bold,
His messengers, plowing the oceans through,
Might visit stranger airs and climates new.

77

Though I the issue could but ill detect,
That what my heart desired was soon to be,
For part in great affairs of like effect
My soul prophetic long had promised me,
I knew not for what reason, or respect,
Or for what virtue in me some might see,
Into my hands, a king so wise and great
Should give the key of projects of such weight.

78

But with sweet word and, as it were, with prayer,
Which doth in kings more than command constrain,
He said: "Things glorious and hard to bear
Only with labor and travail men attain.
But life brings fame and reputation fair
To who can lose it bravely and is slain,
Who never to weak fear is given o'er,
And, though his course is brief, endures the more.

79

"I have chosen thee from the whole retinue
For an adventure worthy thy degree.
Hard, splendid labor glory's beams strike through,
I know thou wilt think light as done for me."
I could no more: "Little it were to do
To go against steel, fire, and snow for thee,
For more it grieves me, O most noble King,
That this poor life should be so small a thing.

"Bring such titanic ventures to the mind   IV
As for Hercules Eurystheus found of yore,
Nemea's lion, the vile Harpy kind,
The hydra fierce, the Erymanthian boar,
At length descent through shadows void and blind
Where the Styx river waters Hades' shore,
For what vast peril, savage test, may be,
Body and soul, O King, are ripe for thee."

Forthwith he thanked me in the noblest strain.
High compliment to my good will he paid.
For virtue praised springs up and lives again,
And praise to noble action can persuade.
And therewithal would follow in my train
One who his friendship and his love obeyed,
Yet no less apt for name and fame to pine,
Paulo da Gama, this brother dear of mine.

So too would Nicholas Coelho go,
Who had endured through many travails sore.
Both of them valor and good counsel know,
Well tried in arms and hardy men of war.
Of youths in whom visions of valor grow,
It was my fortune to enlist a corps,
All of high courage. He must be strong of heart,
Who in like enterprise would play his part.

And Manuel did well such worth requite,
That with more loving zeal they might prepare,
Their souls with brave words seeking to excite
Against what future dangers were to dare.
So once they brought the Minyae to unite,
Who in their bark prophetical would fare
For the Golden Fleece to battle, first to brave
On their adventure high the Euxine wave.

IV   In the fair port of Odysseus' city stand,
Eager and straining, the ready ships complete,
Where, with salt Neptune, tumbling the white sand
And mingling waters, rolls the Tagus sweet.
Nor is there any fear in all the band,
That checks their young vivacity and heat.
Every soldier, every sailorboy, is bound
To follow after me the world around.

85

And all along the beach the soldiers press,
In various manner clad and various hue.
Nor is the splendor of their courage less,
That shall discover all earth's regions new.
On the strong ships winds stilled to gentleness
Move, wavelike, the aerial standards through.
They promise, when they reach great seas afar,
To be like Argo, each a heavenly star.

86

And after everything was set in train
To furnish what such enterprise demands,
To furnish forth our spirits we were fain,
For Death, who still in sight of sailors stands.
And from the loftiest Power, Who can sustain
By His transcendent look the angelic bands,
Favor we begged to guide us and to aid
By inspiration these beginnings made.

87

From the sacred temple, seated by the sea
Upon the beach itself, we came once more,
Named for the place where for humanity
The Godhead was made human flesh of yore.
I tell thee, King, when it comes over me
What distance I have wandered from that shore,
Then is my bosom choked with doubts and fears,
And scarcely may my eyes keep back their tears.

88

The people of the city on that day

To see their kin and friends from all sides pressed,

Though some came but to witness the display,

But every face seemed saddened and distressed,

As we, with a most virtuous array,

A thousand strong, true men of God professed,

In slow procession, His Name upon our lips,

In solemn prayer, went marching to the ships.

89

So long a voyage and the doubt so high,

The people all for dead men gave us o'er.

Women lamented with a piteous cry,

And not a man but he was groaning sore.

Mothers, sisters, wives, whom their loves terrify

Too easily, only increased the store

Of desperation and of chilly fear

That we would not return for many a year.

90

A mother spoke: "Son, who I thought would be

My dear defender and my one delight

When weak age should have overtaken me,

Now I must die in pain and in despite.

Why do you leave me in my misery?

Wherefore should you abandon me outright,

But to prepare your burial grim and dark,

And to become a meal to feed the shark?"

91

Or one with hair all torn: "Sweet husband mine,

Without whom Love will have my life, no less,

Why risk that life which is my life, not thine,

On oceans raging in their storm and stress?

Why for a journey full of doubt resign

Our sweet affection to forgetfulness?

Is it thy hope the wind that lifts the sail

Should bear away love and contentment frail?"

IV So spake they. And yet other matters spake,
Out of their love and piteous charity,
Old men and children that followed in our wake,
To whom age grants but scanty bravery.
The nearby mountains, echoing, answer make,
As they were moved by noble sympathy.
And tears, that all the milk-white sands bedewed,
Were equal to the grains in multitude.

93

But never once would we lift up our eyes
To wife or mother, knowing it for true,
We must not grieve, nor in the enterprise,
Thus well launched, cease our purpose to ensue.
I had decided to embark, likewise,
Without leave taken as men wont to do,
Which though it be love's usage of good will,
To who departs or stays makes sharp the ill.

94

But an old man of venerable air,
Who on the seafront stood among the crowd,
Turned his eyes toward us with a steady stare
And thrice his head as one in grief he bowed.
We on the water heard him clearly there,
For the voice charged with grief was somewhat loud.
With wisdom only to experience due,
Out of his much-tried breast these words he drew:

95

"Glory of empire! Most unfruitful lust
After the vanity that men call fame!
It kindles still, the hypocritic gust,
By rumor, which as honor men acclaim.
What thy vast vengeance and thy sentence just
On the vain heart that greatly loves thy name!
What death, what peril, tempest, cruel woe,
Dost thou decree that he must undergo!

96

"Dreadful disquiet of his life and soul!   IV
Spring of adultery and abandonment,
Empires and realms and wealth consuming whole,
And, as we know, only too provident!
Thy powers for high and noble men extol,
More worthy of their curse malevolent,
And call thee fame and glory's plenitude,
Names whereby witless men their souls delude.

97

"What new disasters dost thou now prepare
Against these kingdoms and against their seed?
What peril and what death for them to bear,
Under some mighty name, hast thou decreed?
What mines of gold now dost thou promise fair?
What kingdoms?—promise lightly made indeed!
What fame dost thou propose? What legend glorious?
What palm? What triumph? And what war victo-

98   [rious?

"Thou art indeed the Madman's right descent,
Whose wickedness and itch to disobey,
Not only from the realm pre-eminent,
Drove thee forth in sad banishment to stay,
But all thy state of innocent content,
Simple, still, more than human, stole away—
Thy Golden Age—and gave thee wholly o'er
Unto the Age of Iron and of War.

99

"Thou who now into pleasant vanity
Art swept away by fantasy so light,
Thou who to cruelty and savagery
Now giv'st the names of courage and of might,
Thou who dost value in such high degree
Contempt of life, which should in all men's sight
Still be esteemed, for One in time gone by,
Who gave us life, was yet afraid to die;

IV   "Hast thou not ever near thee Ishmael's breed,
     With whom to carry on perpetual war?
     Does he not cleave to the false Arab creed,
     If it be but Christ's faith thou fightest for?
     If further lands and treasures be thy need,
     Of towns and fields, has he not thousands more?
     And is he not in arms courageous still,
     If praise for triumph earned be all thy will?

"Wilt thou raise up the foeman in the gate,
While seeking out another worlds away,
Whereby unpeopled is the ancient state,
Weakened afar, and falling to decay?
Wilt thou rush on unknown ill and dubious fate,
That Fame may flatter thee and great things say,
Calling thee Lord, with plenteous plaudits dinned,
Of Araby, Ethiopia, Persia, Ind?

"My curse on him who first on the dry tree,
In the waters of this world, set up the sail!
Worthy of the Deep's eternal pain was he,
If the just creed I trust in does not fail!
May no high judgment's wise authority,
Nor singing lyre, nor genius bright, prevail
To grant thee either memory or fame,
But with thee die the glory and the name!

"Iapetus' child the fire from Heaven bore,
The fire that entered every human breast,
The fire that kindled all the world to war,
To death, to shame. What a huge cheat confessed!
Prometheus, to our vantage it were more,
And the world by trouble were not so oppressed,
Had thy great image never known the fire
That still has moved him, thrilled by vast desire!

"The poor youth had not guided otherwise IV
His sire's high car, nor would the stripling flee
With the great Architect through empty skies,
Who famous made a stream and named a sea.
There is no high and hateful enterprise,
By fire, steel, flood, heat, cold, though it may be,
The sons of men have ever left untried.
Desperate condition! Fate unsanctified!"

NOTES

2.   6. John I (1357–1433), certainly a remarkable figure. He was the illegitimate son of Pedro the Doer of Justice, by Teresa Lourenço, with whom Pedro had an affair, apparently shortly after the death of Ignes de Castro.

3.   7–8. Burton says that "the loyal and loquacious child" was the eight-months-old daughter of Estevão Anis of Evora. He also speaks of "her Delphian adroitness," for the principal contenders for the crown were both named John, John of Avis and John de Castro, and so for that matter was the Spanish claimant, John of Castile. He also notes the three rejected stanzas in praise of bastards.

4.   1. The Count of Ourem, whom John stabbed to death, not in the presence of the Queen regent but in a nearby room. Portuguese etiquette, as in the case of Ignes de Castro, forbids assassination in the presence of royalty, though John of Avis, like his great-grandson John II, never hesitated to do his own dirty work.

5.   5. Dom Martin, Bishop of Lisbon, who took the wrong side, suffered like Astyanax, the son of Hector, who was hurled by the Greeks from a tower in Troy. Virgil and Ovid tell the story. So does Seneca.

        7. According to Lencastre, this victim was the abbess of a nunnery who was murdered while clutching the altar.

        8. Some person unknown, but one of many torn piecemeal by John's mob.

6.   3. Marius, the leader of the liberal party against Sulla who led the aristocrats, in a series of conflicts from 100 to 86 B. C. Camões perhaps remembers Lucan's gory intermezzo on the struggle between Sulla and Marius (De Bello Civili, II, 63–233). Nor is it impossible that he had Ariosto (O. F., III, 33) in mind.

7.   1. Beatrice was officially Fernando's daughter, and perhaps actually, but her mother's unfaithfulness was notorious.

8.   2. Brigus, an eponymous and undoubtedly fictitious hero, from whose name the fanciful derived the name of Burgos (Ford).

        3. Fernando, Ferdinand the Great of Castile (died 1065), who

has some claims to be considered the beginner of the expulsion of the Moors from Portugal (Ford).

Campeador, the Cid, Roy Diaz of Bivar (died 1099), the captor of Valencia and hero of the famous epic.

6. The classical periphrasis could have a dozen models, but Statius (Thebais, IV, 116–117) will do as well as any.

9.   5. The Island of Leão, i.e., Cadiz, supposed with probability to have been colonized by Phoenicians, as Pomponius Mela (II, 6) attests. Pliny (IV, 22) could give Camões the same information.

10.   6. The Galicians are for some reason a subject of ridicule in Spain and Portugal. This Camões remembers. He ignores the circumstance of his own descent from a noble Galician family, exiled in 1369, as the commentators point out.

12.   5–8. A shadowy resemblance to Nestor's advice to Agamemnon might be detected here (Iliad, II, 364–368).

14.   2. Nuno Álvares Pereira, often called, perhaps because of his habit of praying at inconvenient moments, "the Holy Constable."

In the Octaves to Dom Constantino de Braganza (Juromenha, II, 305) the expression "scourge of the arrogant Castilian" also occurs. See Camões and the History of Portugal for Pereira.

17.   8. Camões seems to be quoting Claudian here (De Quarto Consulatu Honorii, 302):

Mobile mutatur semper cum principi vulgus.

20.   5. Scipio Africanus rallied what remained after Cannae in 216 B. C., and, as Burton notices, Scipio was only twenty-four at the time, as was Nuno Pereira in his great hour. Livy describes the scene at Canusium (XXII, 53).

22.   Either Virgil or Lucan could provide Camões with a model description of a nation springing to arms after a long period of peace (Aeneid, VII, 623–640, De Bello Civili, I, 239–243). So could Statius (Thebais, III, 580–589).

4. To apply the adjective pacific to the troubled reign of Fernando has its oddity.

23.   5. Nuno Álvares Pereira.

24.   8. Mem Rodrigues de Vasconcellos, of whom not much is known except that he fought valiantly at Aljubarrota, even after being wounded. (Lencastre).

Burton properly points out an intranslatable pun in this stanza between Hunno, a Hun, and Nuno, the Constable.

25.   3. Avranches in Normandy (Ford). According to Professor Ford, Antão Vasquez de Almada was never Count of Avranches. Camões confuses him with his nephew Alvaro Vaz de Almada, who

is reputed to have been one of Twelve of England as was Antão. See VI, 42 ff.

6. By this time the Seven Castles of the Algarve had been added to the five shields and the thirty pence. The flag of the Portuguese Republic still preserves the heraldic record of the Reconquest.

27.   7. The Battle of Aljubarrota was fought on August 14, 1385, as Ford points out, about a week before the Sun entered the sign of Virgo (Astraea).

28.   3. Ortegal, a cape in northern Galicia. But it could be Finisterre, also in Galicia (Ford).

The image of a stream turning back for psychological reasons is a favorite with Camões. Thus, in the great "Redondilhas" on the Rivers of Babylon, the river retreated when it heard the music of the flute. It is of course an imitation of some classic account of Orpheus' powers. But Pliny (II, 106) alleges that rivers flowed backwards at Nero's death in his own time.

Transtagana, a region in Portugal south of the Tagus. The word is a Latinization of Alemtejo, the common name.

8. The babe is clutched to the bosom even more rhetorically in Valerius Flaccus (Argonauticon, II, 199–203).

The stanza as a whole harks back to Aeneid, VIII, 511–518, but its first line makes one think of Aeneid, XI, 474–475—bello dat signa rauca cruentum bucina. And Burton sees Lucan's hand (De Bello Civili, VII, 460–505).

29.   3–4. This seems to be Ovidian (Heroides, XVI, 351–352):

> Terror in his ipso maior solet esse periclo,
> quaque temere libet, pertimuisse pudet.

But Plutarch speaks of the suppression of pain by anger (Life of Coriolanus), and Camões, who had lost an eye in battle, knew what he was talking about.

30.   The Battle of Aljubarrota decided the question, whether or no Portugal should be annexed to Castile, in the negative for two centuries. Camões does not mention the circumstance that the founder of his house in Portugal fought for Castile in this battle.

31.   Aljubarrota seems to have been decided by new weapons. Some eight hundred English archers and (presumably) Genoese crossbowmen more than made up for the long odds (nearly four to one) against the Portuguese. This stanza may have some shadowy connection with Statius' account of the darts in Thebais, VIII, 412–420.

32.   1. If all his thirty-one brothers came against Nuno Pereira, he deserves more credit for firmness than most heroes.

The stanza as a whole is clearly an echo of Lucan, De Bello Civili, VII, 550–554.

33.   1. Sertorius, see I, 26 and VIII, 8. Coriolanus, the hero of Shakespeare's tragedy.

2. Catiline, Cicero's adversary, killed at Pistoria in 62 B. C.

It is noticeable that Camões ignores Greek traitors such as Alcibiades and Themistocles in this connection.

34.   3. Ceuta, opposite Gibraltar. The legendary treason of Julian is connected with the place. If it was once fatal to Gothic Spain, it was to be equally fatal to the Portuguese Empire.

6. Tetuan, not far from Ceuta.

The great simile of the lion has every appearance of being based on personal experience, but the form if not the substance is Virgilian (Aeneid, IX, 545–555 and again, IX, 791–796). Valerius Flaccus (Argonauticon, I, 757 ff.) might play his part too.

35.   The brooding anger of the lion could have a connection with Odyssey, IV, 791–793.

36.   5–6. Ovid (Met., XIII, 546–548), Statius (Thebais, IV, 315–316), Valerius Flaccus (Argonauticon, I, 489–493 and III, 737–739), and Claudian (In Rufinum, I, 227) all have lionesses or tigresses in pursuit of hunters who have stolen their whelps. Carrying off cubs seems to have been a favorite amusement. American forest rangers appear to enjoy it today. Camões might have modeled this passage on any or all of the poets listed above.

8. Massylia, roughly the Atlas region.

37.   2. The Seven Brothers are known by corresponding names to all four of the classic geographers whom Camões follows, and would seem to be the Jebel Mousa near Ceuta. Burton thinks they are in the Dahra region east of Oran.

40.   3. The Grand Master of the Military Order of Santiago, Don Pedro Moniz (Burton). Lencastre says he was Mem Rodrigues de Vasconcellos, that he survived the battle, and that he fell at Valverde.

5. Calatrava's "cruel" master, so-called I know not why. Lencastre says he was a brother of the hero Nuno. It should be remarked that the military orders (soldier monks in theory) played a tremendous role historically in Spain and Portugal.

41.   The three-mouthed hound is, of course, Cerberus.

7–8. Burton quotes a picturesque account of Antão Vasques de Almada, who came dancing up to John on the field, with the banner of Castile round his waist like a sash.

44.   2. Tibullus (I, x, 1) wishes to know who was the first inventor of ghastly swords.

45.   5–8. These lines and the following stanza allude to the Battle of Valverde, a little later than Aljubarrota but in the same year.

46.   3. Again a reference to the Battle of Valverde (Lencastre).

47.   7. The bonds between Portugal and England had always been close since Dinis the Ploughhand.

It is amusing to learn that these princesses were daughters of John of Gaunt, "time-honored Lancaster." John I married Philippa, the Duke's daughter by Blanche, who was Chaucer's patroness. Henry of Castile, later Henry III, married Catherine, the Duke's daughter by his second wife, Constance of Castile (Lencastre). The Duke laid claim to the throne of Castile himself.

49.   5. Ábyla, Ceuta. The nearby height is the African Pillar of Hercules.

8. Count Julian is alleged to have betrayed Ceuta to the Moors to punish King Roderick for seducing his daughter.

50.   Professor Ford points out that Camões has a gift for understatement. John I, the Great, had been on the throne for forty-eight years when he died. What the length of a normal reign ought to be must be left to the imagination. It may be noted that many of the kings of Portugal seemed to have a knack for longevity.

51.   1. The statement in the foregoing note does not apply to King Edward (Duarte), named after his great grandfather, Edward III of England. He reigned only five years (1433–1438).

Perhaps the moral of the stanza derives from something in Ovid. But Herodotus, who appears to have been the Father of Clichés, as he certainly was not the Father of Lies, seems to be the first on record to deliver himself of these particular commonplaces. Plutarch rolls them over his tongue (Aemilius Paulus). Claudian repeats them all (In Probini et Olybrii Fratrum Consulatum, Panegyris, 11 ff.). The remarks about unstable happiness may be found elsewhere in Camões, e.g. Eclogue VII, Juromenha, III, 95, and again in Lusiads, V, 80.

52.   1. Ferdinand the Constant was captured by the Moors in 1436 and died in captivity. As Burton observes, he had no choice in the matter, because Duarte refused to ransom him.

53.   1. Codrus, the last king of Athens, arranged to have himself slain in the besiegers' lines because an oracle had foretold that only by the king's death could the city be saved. Horace hits him off in a splendid phrase, "pro patria non timidus mori" (Odes, III, xix, 2).

3. Regulus, captured by the Carthaginians in 255 B. C., and the hero of Horace's great ode. Sent by the Carthaginians to persuade the Romans to make peace, he successfully argued against such a step and returned to Carthage where he was tortured to death. Cicero

dwells on him lovingly (De Finibus, II, xx, 65 and De Officiis, III, xxvi, 99).

5. Curtius, who leaped into the chasm in the Forum, which could only be closed if Rome's greatest treasure were cast into it.

6. A dynasty of Roman heroes. The first Decius died in battle against the Latin League, his son against the Gauls, and his grandson against Pyrrhus (Cicero De Finibus, II, xix, 61).

54. 1. Afonso V (1438–1481), called "the African," because of his campaigns in Morocco, which were successful in appearance only.

55. 2. The Tirynthian is Hercules. Canzone XIII has the same images.

3–4. This is another of Camões' unhappy passages. Six years after the publication of the Lusiads, the Portuguese were practically expelled from North Africa.

7. Alcacer in Morocco, captured by Afonso V in 1458 (Ford).

8. Arzilla, captured 1471, as was Tangier (Ford).

57. 3. Ferdinand the Catholic, Columbus' patron.

58. 2. His young son, later John II. Ford points out that the Battle of Toro in 1476 was a serious set-back for Portugal. Burton (always full of matter) quotes Queen Isabella as saying: "But for the cockerel the cock was lost." When John died nineteen years later, the Queen is said to have remarked, "The *Man* is gone."

59. 5–8. Suetonius describes Augustus' defeat at Philippi (Twelve Caesars, Caesar Augustus, Cap. XIII). So does Plutarch (Life of Antony). And Pliny (VII, 45) might have something to do with it.

60. 4. John II, as already observed in these notes, pushed the projects of Henry the Navigator to their logical conclusion, for which the wholly inferior Manuel (Professor Livermore remarks that it is no wonder he is called "the Fortunate") got credit which he was not entitled to.

61. 1. Among the emissaries whom John II sent out were Pedro de Covilham and Afonso de Paiva. As may be imagined, their experiences were harsh. Covilham actually reached Calicut by land eleven years before Gama got there by sea. Paiva died on his way to Ethiopia, but Covilham finally met the Negus, and Abyssinia re-entered history. But Covilham never got home. According to Barros (I, iii, 5), Covilham and Paiva started from Santarem, May 7, 1487. And Beazely (Encyclopedia Brit., s. v. Dias) says that Covilham's letters describing his visit to the Malabar Coast and to the East Coast of Africa as far south as Sofala reached John II at the same time that Dias announced the discovery of the Cape.

4. Parthenope, one of the Sirens, and a name for Naples. Strabo (I, ii, 13) speaks of her tomb. Pliny (III, 5) knows about it. Silius Italicus (XII, 33) is quoted by Strabo's editors (Bohn Edition). Ariosto (O. F., XXXIII, 56) brings his tribute to the Siren. And even English readers remember "Dead Parthenope's dear tomb."

5. Naples became the possession of Ferdinand of Aragon.

62.   3. Pompey was slain in Egypt.

7. Abyssinia.

63.   1. Erythréan (Greek for red), the Red Sea.

3. Nabatéan mountains, in Northern Arabia, and symbolic of the Orient.

4. Sabéan coasts, the biblical Sheba, now Yemen or south-western Arabia. Herodotus (History III, 113) has this to say of the region: "The whole country is scented with them (spices) and exhales an odor marvelously sweet." Camões must have seen the coast. Milton's lovely phrases may be cited:

> Sabéan odors from the spicy shore
> Of Araby the Blest.

6. Adonis' mother was Myrrha. Her father was Cinyras, as he was also the father of Adonis. Myrrha was transformed into the shrub whence myrrh is obtained (Ovid, Met., X, 312 ff.).

64.   8. Trajan got as far as the Persian Gulf, but doubtless never intended to reach India. There is no record of his ever shrinking from anything, though Dio Cassius (LXVIII, 28 and 29), quoted by Cary and Warmington (The Ancient Explorers), has preserved a remark of Trajan's to the effect that he would have conquered India, if he had been a young man.

65.   1. Kerman, a province in southern Persia. Mekran lies just east of Kerman and is separated by the ramparts of the Indus Valley from India proper.

7–8. As mentioned above, neither Paiva or Covilham ever returned.

66.   3. Manuel (reigned 1495–1521), called the Fortunate. Vasco da Gama's voyage laid the foundation of his Eastern Empire. Cabral discovered Brazil. In general Manuel was not grateful to the great men like Pacheco and Albuquerque.

69.   2. The first sphere, the first of the eleven concentric spheres of the Ptolemaic system. This is the sphere of the Moon.

71.   Perhaps Manuel's vision of the two great Indian rivers owes something to Aeneas' vision of the Tiber (Aeneid, VIII, 26–35).

72.   3–4. Pliny (V, 10) makes an odd remark about the Nile, to the effect that it is somewhat fatigued by the distance it has raced.

7. The river-god Alpheus pursued Arethusa under the sea to

Syracuse. In Eclogue VII, which is a sort of abridgment of the Metamorphoses of Ovid, Camões devotes half an octave to this episode. There are dozens of allusions to the Alpheus-Arethusa affair in Latin poetry, but Virgil (Aeneid, III, 694-696) will serve.

74.   1. As Professor Ford points out, Camões' notions as to the sources of the Ganges and the Indus are not to be taken too seriously.

       4. The advice given by the Ganges to Manuel resembles that given by the Tiber to Aeneas (Aeneid, VIII, 36 ff.).

75.   3. There is impeccable historical evidence for Manuel's praiseworthy habit of rising early. Damião de Goes (IV, 202) speaks of it as one of the King's characteristics.

78.   2. Burton quotes the Latin aphorism: Preces regum leges sunt. He says that Gama carried letters from Manuel to Prester John and the King of Calicut. Oddly enough, at the same time Columbus was given a letter to Vasco da Gama, to be delivered if the navigators met on the coasts of Asia.

       It may be noted that Damião de Goes (I, 44-45) represents Manuel as making many complimentary remarks to Gama.

79.   5. Barros (I, iv, 1) says that Vasco da Gama promised the King to go through fire and steel and water for him.

80.   2. Eurystheus, the tyrannical king who imposed the twelve labors on Hercules. Of these the four mentioned in 3. and 4. are child's play, but the descent into Hell, which was undertaken to capture Cerberus, the three-headed watch-dog, might prove more of a tax upon heroic powers.

81.   4-8. Burton speaks of the strange contest between the brothers Gama. Paul insisted that Vasco, his junior, should have the command. He carried his point. Paul da Gama died at Terceira in the Azores on the return trip in 1499 (Livermore, History, 230).

       The fleet consisted of four vessels, three "ships" and a supply-boat. The three "ships" were the "São Gabriel" (flagship), commanded by Vasco da Gama, the "São Raphael," commanded by Paul da Gama, and the "Berrio," a caravel commanded by Nicholas Coelho. The supply-boat (commanded by Gonçalo Nunes, de Goes, I, 67) according to the "Roteiro," or log, of the great voyage, was deliberately broken up at the Cape so that only three ships reached India. There were approximately 160 men (de Goes says 148, of whom only 55 came home) on the expedition, of whom half are said to have died of scurvy (see V, 81) on the East Coast of Africa. De Goes probably got his figure of 148 men from the Roteiro (Ravenstein, The First Voyage of Vasco da Gama, p. 123). Thus the navigation of the unknown Indian Ocean was brought off by three ships worked by less than thirty men apiece. "The São Raphael" was abandoned on the return trip.

What is the difference between a "ship" and a caravel? A caravel, lateen rigged, would sail closer to the wind. Ship evidently means the ancestral form of the full-rigged ship.

82.   1. Nicholas Coelho, of whom little is known. But he got home with the news first. And Manuel is said to have been the first to spy the returning ship.

83.   5. The Minyae, Thessalians, the Argonauts, who went with Jason on the quest of the Golden Fleece in the Argo. A timber from the oracular oak of Dodona was built into the bow of the ship and gave advice on many occasions when it was much needed. Valerius Flaccus (Argonauticon I, 2) calls Argo "fatidicam ratem" which in Portuguese becomes "fatidica nao." It would seem that Camões had read at least part of a stilted but spirited epic.

84.   1–2. It may be mentioned at this point that the ships of Vasco da Gama's fleet were specially designed and built for his expedition. There was nothing slipshod about Portuguese methods in the Age of Discovery.

5. Tagus sweet. Sweet is in contrast to salt Neptune, i. e., fresh.

85.   8. In Valerius Flaccus (Argonauticon, I, 4) Argo becomes a constellation. His early 19th Century editor and translator, Dureau de la Malle, points out that this constellation is visible as far north as Cadiz. He cites Manilius in three places (Astronomicon, I, 412 and 415, V, 13, V, 40–45) for Argo's translation to the skies.

87.   The church at Belem (Bethlehem) near Lisbon.

90.   8. The image goes back to the Odyssey (XV, 480, XXIV, 290–291). The stanza as a whole seems to be based on the complaint of the mother of Euryalus (Aeneid, IX, 481 ff.).

91.   It is perhaps not fanciful to see in this stanza some reminiscence of Camões with respect to March 23rd, 1553, when the "São Bento" sailed for the Orient and he was certainly thinking of the lady who had got him into trouble, whether or not Fate permitted him to see her.

93.   Euryalus, in Aeneid, IX, 284–292, could not bear his mother's tears and left without taking leave.

94.   Here begins the famous passage of the Old Man of Belem. Burton compares it with a long tirade in Lucan (De Bello Civili, II, 68–233) and with Horace and "impias rates." He further cites the Portuguese Cicero, Osorio, but I don't think to much purpose. But, as the most recent editors of Barros (Lisbon, 1945) state, there was a good deal of conservative opposition to the overseas policy of the King. Damião de Goes (I, 44–45) describes the objections of these isolationists.

98.   1. Madman, Adam. Ovid described the Iron Age in Met., I, 125–135.

101.   1–4. Traces of Plutarch (Life of Fabius) perhaps appear here. The passage reminds one of Fabius' tirade against Scipio, whom he reproached for stripping Italy of men in the Hannibalic War.

   8. This is very near to laesa majestas. When Cabral established himself at Cochin, a year or so after Gama's voyage, King Manuel adopted the title, "Lord of the Navigation, Conquest, and Trade of Ethiopia, Arabia, Persia, and India" (The Cambridge Short History of India, p. 486). No irony could be more severe.

102.   Mr. Edward Glaser, who has made an elaborate study of Faria y Sousa, an early commentator on the Lusiads, has pointed out in a memorandum to the translator that the curse on the inventor of ships is a commonplace in 16th Century Hispanic literature, as indicated by an article by Mr. B. B. Ashcom (Hispanic Review, XI, 1943, pp. 328–333). Mr. Ashcom believes that the origin is Medea's curse in Euripides' tragedy. But Faria y Sousa noted the same idea in Propertius (I, xvii, 13–14) and Seneca, from one or both of whom Camões probably derived it. Ovid has the image of the dry tree (Met., I, 95).

103.   1. Iapetus, the son of Coelus, a Titan who begat Prometheus and Epimetheus. Prometheus stole the fire and was chained by Jupiter on the summit of the Caucasus where the vulture perpetually devoured his liver, which was perpetually restored.

104.   1. The poor youth is Phaëthon who fell from the chariot into the Po.

   2. The Architect is Daedalus who invented wings to escape from Crete with his son Icarus.

   4. The Po is famous because of Phatëhon's disaster. The Icarian Sea is named for Icarus. The line is apparently a translation from Ovid (Tristia I, 1, 90) though the whole story is told in Met., VIII, 195 ff. Horace, too, might play his part (Odes, I, iii, 34–35):

> Expertus vacuum Daedalus aëra
> Pinnis non homini datis.

BOOK V

ARGUMENT

Vasco da Gama continues the history of his voyage and describes to the King of Melinde the departure from Lisbon, the various coasts they touched, and the people they saw as far as the Cape of Good Hope; the affair of Fernando Velloso; the fable of the Giant Adamastor; the continuation of the voyage to Melinde. This brings the account to an end. Peace is established, and a genuine friendship has arisen between Gama and the King.

THE LUSIADS

THE FIFTH BOOK

SUCH words the noble ancient standing there
Cried out aloud, what time our wings we spread
To the serene and favorable air.
So from the harbor well-beloved we sped
And, as at sea it is the custom fair
When making sail, the welkin overhead
We rent with our "Fair Voyage." And the blast
Pushed, as his wont is, hard on every mast.

2

'Twas the season when the Eternal Light of Day
Through fierce Nemea's beast his course would run,
And this world, which with time consumes away,
Sickly and slow, through its sixth age went on,
Having counted, as the custom is to say,
Some fourteen hundred circles of the sun,
And ninety-seven, in which last, incomplete,
The sun wheeled, when to sea put forth the fleet.

3

Little by little was exiled our sight
From hills of our own land that lay behind.
There was dear Tagus, there cool Cintra's height,
Toward which our eyes for a long while inclined.
But the spirit in the land of our delight
Stayed yet, for there abode what hurt the mind,
Until at length all vanished utterly,
And we saw nothing but the sky and sea.

V   Thus we went forth to break those oceans through,
Where none before had ever forced the way.
We saw the new isles and the climates new
Henry the Great discovered in his day.
Mauretania's heights and cities full in view,
Lands over which Antaeus once held sway,
We had upon our left. On the right hand,
Although not certain, we might guess at land.

5

And we sailed by Madeira's island vast,
That from the giant forest takes its name,
The first of all we peopled in the past,
Known for the name rather than any fame.
But though it be of all this world the last,
Those Venus loves advance no nobler claim.
Were it hers, she would forget in little while
Cythera, Cnidus, Cyprus, Paphos' isle.

6

Now past Massylia's desert coast we go,
Where Azenegs put cattle out to hay.
Fresh water's taste that folk can never know,
Nor yet sufficiency of grass have they.
This is a land in which no fruit can grow,
Where iron in birds' gizzards wastes away.
The region knows extremest poverty,
Which Ethiopia parts from Barbary.

7

Our course beyond that limit did we hold,
The sun attains, who north his car would guide.
There also dwells that race, to whom of old
Clymene's son the hue of day denied.
There the black Senegal with current cold
That region of strange nations waters wide.
Cape Arsinarius' name no more is heard,
Which in our tongue today is called Cape Verde.

Past the Canary Islands on we bore,   **V**
The Fortunate Isles (for once so named were these),
And sailed amid the maids of Hesperus hoar,
Who hence were known as the Hesperides,
Regions to which our navies long before
Had come and looked on novel prodigies.
We made a port hard by, the wind being fair,
And went ashore to get provision there.

9

The isle we harbored in its name doth take
From that Saint James who was a soldier too.
And he it was who for the Spaniards' sake
Helped them brave slaughter on the Moor to do.
Thence, to sail over that enormous lake
Of the salt ocean, while the north wind blew,
We set our course, and left behind the ground
Where such a sweet refreshment we had found.

10

We circled Afric where it stretches wide
And, for us, ever to the east doth bear—
Jalofo's province, which the blacks divide
Among the various nations dwelling there,
Mandinga's greatest, whence we are supplied
So well with the rich metal shining fair.   [weaves,
There men drink Gambia's stream that winds and
And which the Atlantic huge at length receives.

11

Next past the Dorcades our course inclined,
The dwelling of those sisters anciently,
Who, though the three of them were wholly blind,
Yet used a single eye among the three.
Thou, and no other, whose locks crisply twined
Set fire to Neptune yonder in the sea,
Into the foulest of all things must turn,
And fill with vipers all the sands that burn.

177

V With the sharp prow still southward headed right,
Into the greatest of all gulfs we drave,
Leaving behind Leone's saw-toothed height
And the Cape of Palms, for such the name we gave.
The giant stream is here, where still must smite,
On shores we know and hold, the roaring wave,
Likewise that island, whose name sanctified
Derives from him who touched his Savior's side.

13

Congo's vast kingdom is established there
(Erewhile by us brought to Christ's faith), where-
Runs the long current of the crystal Zair, [through
A river which no ancient ever knew.
And from the Pole familiar of the Bear
At length in those vast oceans I withdrew,
For I had overpassed the burning bound,
Where the limit which divides the world is found.

14

We had discovered earlier in our way
A new star set in the new hemisphere,
Unknown to others, for, all ignorant, they
Of earlier times thereof heard nothing clear.
We saw those regions of less splendid ray,
Which, starless, not so beautiful appear,
Near the fixed Pole, where none yet comprehends
If other land begins or the sea ends.

15

Our course across those regions we had ta'en,
Through the which, passing twice, Apollo makes
A pair of winters and likewise summers twain,
What time from Pole to Pole his way he takes.
Through calamity and calm and hurricane,
Mad Eolus still over Ocean wakes,
We saw the Bears that Juno's wrath defied
Bathing themselves in Neptune's waters wide.

16

At length to tell the perils of the sea,
Things inconceivable to human wit,
The sudden bolt that crashes fearfully,
Lightnings whereby the flaming airs are lit,
Black squalls, and the night's dark intensity,
Bellow of thunders that creation split,
Were not less labor than erroneous choice,
Supposing that I had an iron voice.

17

But I beheld those things, which sailors rude,
Who long experience for their mistress own,
Count ever truth and perfect certitude,
Judging things by appearances alone.
But they with more intelligence endued,
Who see world mysteries, only to be known
By science or pure genius, reason still
Such things are false or else conceived of ill.

18

And I have clearly seen that living light,
A holy thing, as mariners consent,
In time of storm with wicked winds at height
And dark tornado making sad lament.
Nor was it less miraculous in our sight,
And surely 'tis a terrible event,
As in a pipe, the sea-mists to descry
Drawing up to Heaven Ocean's waters high.

19

I do not think that my sight cheated me,
For certainly I saw rise up in air
A smoke of fine and vaporous subtilty,
That whirled perpetual, as the wind might bear.
To the high pole rose the spout, as one might see,
And yet it was so tenuous and rare,
Discovery by the eye was scarce allowed.
It seemed the very substance of a cloud.

V   Little by little waxing, the thing grew
Till it was thicker than the mightiest mast.
Here it might thin or thicken out anew,
As it sucked up the sea with gulpings vast.
With the rolling wave it undulated too.
On its head a dense cloud darkened, overcast,
That swelled apace and still more ponderous showed,
For water it took up, a monstrous load.

21

As the red leech on the bullock's lip his fill
Sucks of strange blood, his hot thirst to abate
(For the ox, unthinking, at the fountain chill
Drank in the creature), and insatiate
The leech keeps at it and enlarges still,
Gorging itself, swelling, and growing great;
So the huge column, drawing up water, swelled,
Together with the black cloud it upheld.

22

But, after, having drunken its whole due,
It lifts the foot on the sea surface set,
And, raining out of Heaven, fades from view,
Making the ocean waters yet more wet,
To the waves the waves returning, that it drew,
Though it has robbed them of their salty whet.
Now let the men well skilled in letters see
How mighty nature's mysteries may be.

23

If old philosophers, who went to find
The secrets of so many lands afar,
Had witnessed, spreading sail to every wind,
As I have seen, the miracles that are,
What noble works they would have left behind!
What influences sweet of sign and star!
What qualities and what strange things uncouth!
All in good faith and everything pure truth!

24

But now the planet that hath post of right   V
In the First Sphere, moving with hasty tread,
Five times full-faced, or half, had been in sight,
While the armada over Ocean sped,
When a seaman, from the foretop's towering height,
Whose eye was keen, cried out: "Land! Land ahead!"
The crew in rapture to the bulwarks ran,
The easterly horizon line to scan.

25

In manner of a cloud began to show
That range of mountains which we saw before.
The heavy anchors were ready to let go,
And sail was struck as closer in we bore.
And that we might with greater sureness know
Where now we were, on what remotest shore,
By the astrolabe, that novel instrument,
Which skill and wisdom jointly could invent,

26

Our landing near a spacious plain we made.
Then wild to seek strange matters out the crew
Immediately all through the region strayed,
That a strange people's footsteps never knew.
But with the pilots on the beach I stayed
To find what country we had journeyed to,
Determining by the sun's height the part,
Thus to complete my universal chart.

27

We ascertained that we had passed entire
Through the fish Capricorn's gigantic bound,
Standing 'twixt him and the cold Antarctic gyre,
Which of this world is the most secret ground.
And lo, a black-skinned man of aspect dire,
I saw, by my companions hemmed around,
Whom, without more ado, by force they caught,
While on the hill sweet honeycomb he sought.

V   The man's whole countenance was full of woe,
As one who ne'er was in such dread extreme.
His speech we knew not, ours he could not know,
A savage worse than brutish Polypheme.
To him rich fleece of Colchis did I show,
The gentle metal, above all ores supreme,
And silver fine and the hot burning spice,
But all to move the brute could not suffice.

Things of less worth I bade them let him see,
As beads of crystal that one looks quite through,
Certain small bells that jingled merrily,
A cap vermilion of a pleasant hue.
That this last pleased him in a high degree,
From his nods and from his becks, was clear to view.
I bade them loose him, and with all that gear
He went to his own people, who dwelt near.

But all his fellows came on the next day,
Mother-naked all, and of the deepest black.
Down the steep mountain spurs they took their way,
Seeking such baubles as their friend brought back.
Of such kind fellowship they made display,
Fernão Velloso ventured up the track,
So to explore the customs of the land,
And went into the jungle with that band.

Velloso in his strength was confident,
And certain of his safety in his pride.
But after a great length of time was spent,
In which I sought to know what might betide,
As I looked up, with all my thought intent
On the adventurer, down the rough hillside
He hove in sight and hurried toward the shore
A great deal faster than he went before.

Thither Coelho's boat made haste to steer   V
And take him off, but ere it reached the land
An Ethiopian who knew not fear
Grappled him, lest he 'scape out of their hand.
Others thrust in. We saw Velloso clear,
Surrounded, and not one by him to stand.
I sprang to help. As to the oar I bent,
There stood revealed a whole black regiment.

33
From their thick cloud, the arrow and the stone
Upon the rest of us, unmeasured, rain
And not in vain nor to the wind are thrown.
Scars of the wound this leg got yet remain.
But we, like men who injury have known,
So strict an answer gave them back again
That in more places than their caps they wear
Vermilion color earned in that affair.

34
And now, Velloso being safe and whole,
Back to the fleet we presently returned,
Having bad faith and wickedness of soul
In that vile, ugly, bestial folk discerned,
From whom, concerning India our goal,
We knew that there was nothing to be learned,
Save that we were a long way from it yet.
Hence I commanded that the sails be set.

35
To Velloso said a comrade (all men were
Smiling somewhat upon him with good cheer),
"Hola, old friend, after you climbed that spur,
Did you find coming down was less severe?"
"It was," replied the brave adventurer,
"But I saw so many of the dogs were here
That for the nonce some little haste I made,
Knowing your plight without my hand to aid."

183

V When they had passed the mount those wretches black
Of whom I speak, for so did he declare,
Would let him go no further on their track,
Swearing, if he turned not home, to slay him there.
And against us coming up to fetch him back,
As he returned, their ambush they prepare,
In hope to send us all to darkest Hell
And thus to spoil us easily and well.

37

But now five suns had gone upon their way
Since we had parted thence, those seas to plow,
None save our brethren sailed before our day.
And the winds for us blew prosperously now,
Until one night as at our ease we lay,
Keeping our watch above the cutting prow,
A cloud that darkened all the atmosphere
Above our heads did suddenly appear,

38

So terrible and with such darkness stored
That in our hearts woke terror overgrown.
And bellowing afar the black sea roared,
As if it broke in vain on reefs of stone.
"O Power," I cried, "exalted and adored,
What divine menace, mystery unknown,
Will the new sea and region now make plain,
For it looms larger than the hurricane?"

39

I had not finished when a form appeared,
High in the air, filled with prevailing might.
The face was heavy, with a squalid beard.
Misshaped he was but of enormous height.
Hollow the eyes, and bad and to be feared
The gesture, and the color earthen-white,
And, thick with clay, the lank hair twisted hangs.
And the mouth was black and full of yellow fangs.

So huge of limb he was, I swear to thee,   V
That the thing's equal only could be found
In the Rhodian's colossal prodigy,
One of the Seven Wonders world-renowned.
And the voice seemed to thunder from the sea,
As he spoke thickly with a ghastly sound.
Our hair stood up on end, our flesh went cold,
Only to hear the monster, and behold.

41

"O braver race than all who undertake
Throughout the world whatever great affair,"
He cried, "Who from those cruel wars you make
Rest never, nor from travail, nor from care;
Since now through my forbidden bounds you break
And to sail through my vasty oceans dare,
Which long while I have guarded nor allowed
By strange or native shipping to be plowed;

42

"Since you would pierce mystery inviolate
Of Mother Nature and the Ocean Sea,
Permitted unto none, however great,
Worthy of ageless fame though he may be,
The penalty of your inordinate
And arrogant insolence, now learn from me:
Everywhere, every sea and every shore,
You are to subjugate in desperate war.

43

"Know that henceforth whatever ships shall track
With reckless courage on the course you sail
Will deem this region the demoniac
Home of the tempest and unmeasured gale.
And for the first fleet standing on this tack,
That seeks o'er seas forbidden to prevail,
I'll impose penalty foreseen by none,
Till grief looms greater than the risks they run.

185

V "Here I shall take, if hope prove not a cheat,
From him who found me fearful recompense.
Nor even so will vengeance be complete,
That punishes your stubborn insolence.
If what I think be true, each year your fleet
Shall look on many a shipwreck, and immense
Variety of ruin shall befall,
Till death itself shall be least ill of all.

45

"As for that foremost great adventurer,
Whose fame and luck shall lift him to the sky,
In this my strange, eternal sepulchre
God's viewless purposes will have him lie.
His Turkish naval spoils, proud though they were,
And prosperous, the conqueror shall lay by.
Nor I, for wrong done, threaten him, alone,
But Mombassa and Quilóa overthrown.

46

"Here will another come, of fairest fame,
A knight, a lover, and of liberal mind,
Bringing with him that most delicious dame,
Love, of his mercy, for his love designed,
Whom their sad fortune and dark fate shall claim
Here in my country, angry and unkind,
Which, though it let them through rough shipwreck
'Tis but the sight of greater ills to give.   [live,

47

"Starving to death, they shall see children dear,
Begot and born in love beyond compare,
And the fierce Caffirs, envious of her gear,
From the sweet lady all her vesture tear,
And limbs, so beautiful and crystal clear,
Naked in the sun and frost and windy air,
After the long march when her delicate feet
Have suffered the beach sands' ferocious heat.

"Their eyes shall see, such as escape again   V
From so much misadventure and distress,
The lovers in their misery remain
Deep in the hot implacable wilderness.
There, when for bitter tears of grief and pain
The very stones seem not so merciless,
Those two, in close embrace, their souls shall free
From the fair prison of their agony."

49

Yet more the ghastly monster would have said,
Touching our fate. But I rose up before
And asked him: "Who art thou, whose shape of dread
Has filled me with astonishment so sore?"
Twisting his mouth and the black eyes in his head,
With a bellow and a horrifying roar,
Heavily, harshly his reply he made,
As one on whom the answer gravely weighed:

50

"I am that vast cape locked in secrecy,
That Cape of Hurricanes your people call,
Of whom Pomponius, Strabo, Ptolemy,
Pliny, the whole Past, lacked memorial.
I round out Africa's extremity
In my hid headland, where the shore lines fall
Away, toward the Antarctic Pole prolonged,
Which your audacity has deeply wronged.

51

"I was Earth's child, like those of ruthless might,
Egeus, Enceladus, and Hundred Hands.
I am Adamastor, and I fought the fight
With him who rattles Vulcan's thunder brands.
I piled not mountain height on mountain height,
But, to make Ocean bow to my commands,
Captain by sea was I, and thither went
To come to grips with Neptune's armament.

V   "The love it was of Peleus' consort high
That made me such a venture undertake,
Misprizing every goddess of the Sky
Only for the Lady of the Waves' sweet sake.
Her, 'mid her Nereids, once I happed to spy
Coming naked up the beach, and felt awake
Desire within with such prevailing power
I know no greater yearning to this hour.

"And since there was no way to have her charms,
With my huge ugliness and look unmeet,
I thought to take her by main force of arms
And before Doris laid my case complete.
Doris spoke for me, troubled by alarms,
But my love answered with chaste laughter sweet:
'How shall sufficient her affection prove,
A nymph who must sustain a giant's love?

"'But that we may deliver all the sea
From such a war, devices I shall find,
Mine honor saved, to 'scape the penalty.'
My go-between brought answer in this kind.
I, who could never fall by treachery,
For lovers are magnificently blind,
Now found my inmost heart filled up and thronging
With the abundance of my hope and longing.

"Like a poor fool the battle I gave o'er.
And lo! as Doris promised, on a night
Appeared to me a long, long way before,
Naked, alone, sweet grace of Thetis white.
From afar I ran, like one in madness sore,
With arms outstretched to clasp the life's delight
Of this my body, and those eyes so fair
I fell a-kissing, and her cheek and hair.

56

"What grief do I not know, who this recount!　　V
I deemed my love was in my arms, no less,
But found I had embraced a rugged mount,
Full of rough woods and thickset wilderness?
And with the high crag standing front to front,
When I thought that face angelical to press,
I was unmanned and, dumb, still as a stock,
Became a rock joined to another rock.

57

"O nymph, the loveliest in all the sea,
Although my presence ne'er thy pleasure wrought,
Why labor in that gin to capture me,
Whether it were mount or cloud or dream or naught?
Thence half-way mad in fury did I flee,
Because of hurt and shame upon me brought,
To seek another world she could not know,
Who made such mockery of my grief and woe.

58

"And in that hour, all of my brethren's band
Sank beaten in the extremity of ill,
And the false gods, in safer state to stand,
Buried them, each under some mighty hill.
Against high Heaven can avail no hand.
And I, for my own sorrows weeping still,
Began to feel at last what punishments
The hateful Fates kept for my insolence.

59

"This flesh of mine was changed into hard clay.
My bones, of crags and rocks, took on the cast.
These limbs you see, this form and body, lay
Stretched out in the great waters. And at last
Into this promontory faraway
The gods transmuted all my stature vast.
And, that I might endure redoubled ill,
The seas of Thetis circle round me still."

V   He told his tale, and, weeping wild, before us
In a twinkling he had vanished from our view.
The black cloud broke, and, moaning and sonorous,
Far-ranging sound over the ocean flew.
Raising my hands to the angelic chorus,
Who this long while had given guidance true,
I prayed God in his mercy to withhold
Those evils Adamastor had foretold.

61

Phlegon and Pyroïs the bright car once more
Drew onward, yoked with their companion pair,
When all the towering land arose before,
To which the giant huge was changed whilere.
And as we coasted on along that shore,
We plowed the waters of the Orient there.
Beyond a little northward did we stand,
Till for the second time we sought the land.

62

The people dwelling in that wilderness,
Though they of course were Ethiopians still,
Seemed better human feeling to profess
Than those who erst had treated us so ill.
And to us down the sandy beach they press,
Dancing in festal manner of good will,
Their women with them, and the gentle kine
They pasture there, fat and exceeding fine.

63

As for those sunburnt women, they bestride
The backs of steers that slowly lurch along,
The beasts in which they take especial pride,
Beyond all other cattle in the throng.
And pastoral hymns, in prose or versified,
They raise in their own speech, concerted song,
With such sweet sound as rustic pipes may use,
After the mode of Tityrus his muse.

64

These people all much gaiety displayed,   V
As in their dealings wholly kind were they.
Their sheep and fowl they brought along to trade
Against our trinkets which they took away.
But my men found that nothing could be made
From any word whatever they might say,
That gave us the least light on what we sought.
So we made sail and home the anchors brought.

65

Now in a mighty arc had we swept by
Afric's dark coast-line, and the prow inclined
To seek the burning center of the sky,
And the Antarctic Pole lay far behind.
Also we left that isle where formerly
The fleet had come, which was the first to find
The Cape of Tempests and, that being found,
Established in the isle their certain bound.

66

And thence we plowed along for many a day
Between the calms and grievous hurricane,
On the high sea still breaking the new way,
Led on by hope that yet was full of pain.
With the sea a while we held contentious fray,
For, since the sea must change and change again,
We found a current of a strength so dread
The ships were powerless to forge ahead.

67

The force was of unmatchable degree,
And back upon our track the fleet it threw,
For there against us galloped the whole sea,
Though favorably the wind behind us blew.
The South, much wronged (for so he seemed to be)
That with the waves such battle was to do,
As though in anger, then increased his blast,
Whereby we overcame that current vast.

V   And now the sun the great day brought anew
When the three Kings of Orient were fain
That new-born King to seek for and ensue,
Who in Himself doth other Three contain.
That day a harbor of that self-same crew
I lately spoke of, we made shift to gain,
Near a great stream, and named it, furthermore,
After the day when there we came to shore.

69

Victual we had from the people of the place,
And from the stream fresh water, but, in sum,
Of India we could never find a trace
In the speech of those, like ourselves almost dumb.
What lands we passed! O King, view well our case!
Forth from those rude folk we might never come,
Or ever find good news, or any least
Sign of the longed-for Chambers of the East.

70

Consider well that, girt with grief and pain,
It was our lot continual to go,
Fainting for hunger, broke by the hurricane,
Through seas and regions that we did not know!
So sick of hope deferred that must constrain
The spirit to the extremity of woe,
And always under the unnatural sky,
Whose nature is to hate humanity.

71

Our rotting provender to ruin went,
Bad for weak men, prolific of disease,
And beyond that, nothing that brought content;
For any hope was but a cheat and tease.
Would you believe it, if our armament
Of soldiers had not been right Portuguese,
That they would prove them loyal utterly
Unto their King and their King's deputy?

72

Would you believe they would no violence do   V
Against their Captain, if he said them nay,
And turned not pirates, as compelled thereto
By hunger, wrath, and desperate dismay?
Most certainly these things have been proved true.
There was no travail that could make them stray
From what is Portugal's most noble part,
Perfected discipline and loyal heart.

73

We left that port and the fresh stream. Once more,
Our course to plow salt water, did we lay,
And toward the great main ocean, from that shore,
We headed the whole fleet some little way,
So that the soft but chilly winds that bore
From southward might not trap us in that bay,
Where the curved coastlines deeply inward fold,
And whence Sofála sends her wealth of gold.

74

When this was passed, then the light steering-gear,
Committed to St. Nicholas to ward,
Compelled the prow of every ship to veer
Coastward, where thundering Ocean bayed and roared.
And the heart, balancing twixt hope and fear,
Which must depend upon a fragile board,
And whose supreme desire is always thwarted,
By something strange was suddenly transported.

75

This it was. As we stood in handily
To shore, where beach and valley were in view,
In a stream running to the open sea,
Were sailing boats that entered or withdrew.
And certainly in ecstasy were we
To have found men that navigation knew,
For among them we thought that we might well
Get some new tidings, as indeed befell.

V Ethiops they are, but, as it might appear,
   With a superior race some commerce share.
   A little Arabic a man may hear,
   Mingled with the gibberish they gabble there.
   And delicate tissue that is woven sheer
   From cotton thread, wound on their heads, they wear.
   And with a loin cloth, always azure-dyed,
   Their custom is their privy parts to hide.

77

In the Arabian tongue, which ill they spake,
Whereof Fernão Martins knows well the sense,
They said that ships, as great as ours in make,
Plowed their seas, coming from the regions whence
The sun arises. And their course they take
South where the land curves, swelling and immense,
Then sunward from the south, where a land lay,
With folk like ours, the color of the day.

78

And there we felt the spirit of good cheer
With the people, but with good news even more.
The stream where we found evidence so clear
The name of the Good Signs thereafter bore.
And a pillar on the beach we let uprear,
For some I brought to mark out such a shore.
'Tis named after the angel full of grace,
Who once led Tobit to Gabellus' place.

79

And here from weeds and barnacles and scale,
The pestilent creation of the sea,
We cleansed the hulls, which, from the ocean trail,
Had all of them grown foul as foul could be.
And from our neighboring hosts, who did not fail
In shows of pleasure and of gaiety,
Ever we had the accustomed provender,
And clear of any treacherous thought they were.

But the happiness of such a hope immense

As then we had could not stay pure and clear,
For Nemesis now, as a recompense,
Loosed on us dreadful misadventure here.
Thus Heaven serene disposes of events.
Men are born under heavy and severe
Conditions. Sorrow has a lengthy range.
But it is natural that good should change.

81

For by a cruel and disgusting pest
(I ne'er saw fouler) many came to die,
And in a far and alien land at rest
Their bones ensepulchred for ever lie.
Who could believe, if sight did not attest?
The gums within the mouth swelled horribly,
And all the flesh about them tumid grew,
And as it swelled apace, it rotted too.

82

And with a loathesome odor did it rot,
The stench infecting all the air around.
Physicians well-instructed we had not,
Nor among us was a skillful surgeon found.
Some who in this but little art had got
Would cut away the flesh that proved unsound,
As it were dead. And it was right to do,
For he would die, in whom that proudflesh grew.

83

So in that thickset wilderness obscure
We left for ever friends who perished there,
Who, 'mid such risks and fortunes insecure,
With us in every venture did their share.
How easy for a corpse is sepulture!
Whatso'er wave, strange mountain whatso'er,
Receive, as they received our comrades then,
At length the bones of all illustrious men.

195

V   Thence away from that harborage we bore,
    Higher in hope, deeper in discontent,
    And, seeking clues that could be trusted more,
    Along the coast, cleaving the sea, we went.
    We moored off Mozambique's ungenerous shore,
    Of whose bad faith and wicked devilment
    You will hear tales, and of base plots and plans
    Used by Mombassa's scarcely human clans.

At length to your safe harbor we were sped,
Where kindness and your courtesy benign
Can heal the quick and bring to life the dead,
By the high mercy of the Throne Divine.
Here you have rested us and comforted,
Quieting thought with a new anodyne.
You may behold, if you have harkened well,
That I have told you all you bade me tell.

Dost thou think, Sire, this world has e'er possessed
A race that ran a course of such a reach?
Or that so far Aeneas ever pressed,
Or wise Ulysses of the skillful speech?
Did either dare deep Ocean thus to test,
For all the verses men have written of each,
Or seek out by his virtue and his art,
Of what I saw—and shall see—the eighth part?

He who drank deep of the fountain of Aonia,
About whom rose strange contrarieties,
As between Smyrna, Rhodes, and Colophonia,
Athens and Chios, Argos and Salamis;
And that other, once the glory of Ausonia,
With voice divine sounding great harmonies,
Hearing which, his Mincius was slumber-bound,
But Tiber started proudly at the sound;

Let them sing, flatter, scribble, and inflate   V
Their demigods, always in terms too high,
Forged Cyclops, Circes, Seers, elaborate,
Sirens who make men sleep with melody;
With sail and oar, let them still navigate
Among Ciconians, and where memory
Of friends no more the lotus-eaters keep,
So likewise lose their pilot in the deep;

89

Of winds released from wineskins, let them feign,
And of their amorous Calypsos tell,
Of Harpies who the banquet foul and stain;
Let them descend 'mid naked shades in Hell.
Though greatly they refine their fables vain,
And though theirs be imagined ne'er so well,
Mere truth I speak in naked purity
Triumphs over all high-flying poetry.

*   *   *   *   *

90

On the words of the wise captain eloquent
All of them hung, as they were drinking there,
When the long tale of many a great event
He ended, full of actions high and fair.
And the King praised courage pre-eminent
Of kings whose fame in war went everywhere,
Likewise our people's ancient fortitude
And loyalty of heart and noble mood.

91

And the crowd, wondering, told the tale again,
Noting each circumstance that edified,
Nor from staring at our people could refrain,
Who on such voyages had wandered wide.
But now the Delian stripling turned the rein,
The which Lampetia's brother ill could guide,
In Thetis' arms to find his sweet content,
And the King o'er sea to his great palace went.

197

V How sweet is honor and the splendid name
   Won by our actions when afar they sound!
   The brave who toil for memory's acclaim
   Would match or beat the chiefs of old renowned.
   On envy of some other's storied fame,
   Men oft and oft their great achievements found.
   And others' good approval thrills and warms
   His spirit, who courageous acts performs.

93

'Twas not Achilles' famous victories
That Alexander in his heart admired.
Rather the poet's numerous verse could please,
And that he praised, and only that desired.
The famous trophies of Miltiades
Sleeplessness in Themistocles inspired,
Who yet declared naught gave him such delight
As the voice fit his actions to recite.

94

Gama had sought to make it well appear
That both those voyages men magnify
To such acclaim possessed no title clear
As his, that startled both the Earth and Sky.
Yes, but the chief who cherished and held dear
The Mantuan Lyre, in grace and favor high,
With gifts and honors, spread Aeneas' name,
And so gave wings unto the Roman fame.

95

Portugal has brought forth her Scipios,
Caesars, Augusti, Alexanders too,
But ne'er on them the gifts of grace bestows,
Whose lack keeps them but harsh and tough of thew.
Octavius was accustomed to compose
Sweet artful verse, when griefs around him grew.
Nor would Fulvia have said this was a lie,
When left for Glaphyra by Antony.

Caesar in triumph subjugated France,
But Arms in him the Arts did not repress.
One hand, the pen, the other held the lance,
Cicero yet matching in persuasiveness.
For Scipio, 'tis a known circumstance
That in playwriting he had great address.
Alexander with such zeal his Homer read,
He kept him on the pillow of his bed.

V

97

In short there was no captain of great name
Who was not skilled and learnèd, though from Greece
Or Latium or a barbarous land he came,
Unless it were perchance some Portuguese.
And this I cannot mention without shame,
For few there are whom the sweet verses please
In a land where prose and rhyme are held so low.
No man can praise an art he does not know.

98

Therefore, and not from natural defect,
Here can no Homer and no Virgil be,
Nor, if the case stands so, need one expect
Achilles fierce, Aeneas good, to see.
But the worst of all is that this chance neglect
Has made us men of such austerity,
So harsh, so rude, in genius so remiss,
That little or naught our people care for this.

99

Let Gama thank the Muses, whom the flame
Of patriotic passion thus could move,
Harping, to hail his race's name and fame
And all his warfare and the toil thereof.
For he, and such as with him kinship claim,
Would never take Calliope for love,
Or Tagus nymphs, who might have turned aside
From weaving gold to spread his glory wide.

V   For love fraternal and the will sincere
That Lusian acts their due of praise should win
Conceived the nymphs of Tagus, sweet and dear,
And is their only cause and origin.
However, let none fail to persevere,
Who nurses dreams of noble works within,
Lest, if some byway here or there he choose,
He should thereby virtue and honor lose.

NOTES

BOOK V

2.   This stanza dates the voyage. It is the sixth age of the world, and the 1497th year of that age, meaning the Christian era. The sun is in the Lion (Nemea's beast, slain by Hercules), that is to say July. Gama actually set sail on the 8th (Livermore, History, 229). The notion that the universe is running down is as old as literature and as new as the Second Law of Thermodynamics. Lucretius (II, ad finem), "watching nature go astern," was perhaps the first Roman to give currency to the idea. Pliny (II, 46) exclaims: "But now men's customs are waxed old and decay." Elsewhere (VII, 16) he expresses this pessimistic view and refers the reader to Homer's opinions.

3.   Valerius Flaccus' account of the sailing of Argo (Argonauticon, I, 494–497) might play a role in this stanza.

4.   4. Henry the Navigator, "never so-called till the 19th Century." Some curious remarks might be made with respect to nicknames conferred after death.

6. Antaeus, Hercules' victim.

8. John II had certainly guessed at the existence of Brazil some years before the expedition of Gama. And it has been supposed by some that it was better than a guess. It is not impossible that a stray Portuguese navigator had seen the Americas before Columbus.

5.   2. Madeira means "wood" in Portuguese. It was one of the earliest Portuguese colonies.

8. These Greek islands were all sacred to Venus. She boasts of several of them in Aeneid, X, 51–52.

6.   1. Massylia, the Atlas region.

2. Azenegs. The word is applied to the Berbers in Portuguese.

6. "The ostrich's digestive powers are exaggerated."

8. Barbary, the land of the Berbers, separated from Abyssinia by thousands of miles of the Sahara.

7.   1. Those limits, the Tropic of Cancer.

4. Clymene's son was Phaëthon, whose unhappy conduct of his father's car blackened the face of Africa. See I, 46, IV, 104, notes.

5. Senegal, a famous African river which Henry's men had reached before the middle of the 15th Century.

8. The Greek geographers, Ptolemy for instance, knew about Cape Verde, presumably from Phoenician navigators.

8.   4. Hesperides, perhaps the Cape Verde Islands.

9.   2. Professor Ford points out the not undiverting fact that Camões has confused his apostles. The island was named for Saint James the Less, not the Patron Saint of Spain. It is one of the Cape Verde group. To this day it is the boast of citizens of Santiago that Vasco da Gama made their island a port of call.

   5. It is not uninteresting that at this point the voyagers sailed right across the Gulf of Guinea instead of timidly hugging the shore.

10.   3. Jalofo's province. One guess is as good as another, but the Mandingos had become the greatest power in the Central Niger region as early as 1240.

11.   1. The Dorcades are supposed to be the Bissagos off the Guinea Coast (Ford).

   2. The sisters are the Graiae, sisters of the Gorgons. Perseus stole their single eye in order to force them to direct him to the Gorgons' lair. In Ovid, Met., IV, 775, only two sisters are mentioned.

   4. Medusa, who enraged Athena by meeting her lover Neptune in the temple of the virgin goddess. It was for this reason that the snaky hair and other attractions were added unto her. The drops of blood that dripped from her severed head, as Perseus flew with it back to Greece, became the serpents of the desert.

   . . . . . not so thick swarmed once the soil
   Bedropt with blood of Gorgon . . .
                              Paradise Lost, X, 526–527

The source is probably Ovid (Met., IV, 614–620). But Lucan has a vivid version of the fate of Medusa, ending up with a catalogue of the serpents of Africa, which, depending on the special weakness of the reader, may produce either delirium tremens or mal-de-mer (De Bello Civili, IX, 696–937).

12.   3. Sierra Leone, probably so-called from some fancied resemblance of the mountain to a lion or lions. There are no lions there, according to Burton, who makes the point.

   5. The giant river is the Niger.

   7. St. Thomas, a Portuguese possession in the Gulf of Guinea, which John II populated with the children of unhappy Jews expelled from Spain in 1492.

13.   3. The Zaire is the Congo.

   4. The burning bound is, naturally, the Equator.

Valerius Flaccus, in spite of his artificiality, seems to have felt what his Argonauts might be expected to feel:

> Quod primum ingentibus ausis
> Optavistis, ait, veterumque quod horruit aetas
> Adsumus en, tantumque fretis enavimus orbem.

Argonauticon, V, 314–316.

14.   2. The new star is believed to be the Southern Cross. Camões also speaks of it in the great Elegy III.

15.   1–4. The voyagers have passed through the two Tropics.

5. Eolus, god of the winds and inventor of the sail.

7. The Bears, Callisto, one of Jupiter's innumerable loves, and her son, Arcas, changed into the Constellations by Jupiter. Juno prayed the sea-gods that the Bears might never bathe in the ocean. Seeing the Bears set must have been an eerie experience for the 15th Century navigator. Ovid is always talking about the Bears who are forbidden to enter Ocean (Met., II, 171, Met., XIII, 293 and 726). The same image may be found in Virgil (Georgics, I, 244–246). The first mention of this oddity in the behavior of the Bears is in Odyssey, V, 275.

16.   8. The iron voice is a Virgilian borrowing (Georgics, II, 44, and also Aeneid, VI, 625–627). But the original seems to be Iliad, II, 490, where Homer speaks of "the voice unwearied and heart of bronze."

17.   This may be a variation on Ariosto (O. F. VII, 1), who says that the vulgar do not believe strange things. With Camões it is the instructed who are sceptical.

18.   1. St. Elmo's Fire. Linschoten (quoted by John Masefield, Captain Dampier's Voyages, I, 410, Note 3) saw "a certain sign the Portuguese call corpo santo, or the holy body of Brother Peter Gonsalves, but the Spaniards call it St. Elmo." Camões, in his first letter written in India, alludes in a curious way to the Portuguese patron of the flame. "News about Ladies," he says, "is as necessary in a letter as sailors at the Feast of Holy Brother Peter Gonsalves." Ariosto (O. F., XIX, 50 ff.) has an elaborate description of St. Elmo's fire. St. Elmo was a Sicilian saint.

5. This must be the first realistic account of a waterspout, but Burton refers to Lucan's casual phrase about whirlwinds that suck up water in De Bello Civili, VII, 156, also to Lucretius, De Natura Rerum, VI, 424 ff. There is no evidence that Camões knew this last passage, which is quite unlike his. Pliny (II, 50) has an account of the whirlwind and waterspout.

22.   6. This observation, whether Camões' own or another's, is interesting. His statement that "the water content of the spout is fresh" is, of course, correct, and must be a very early record of the phenomenon.

24.   2. On Ptolemaic principles the First Heaven belonged to the Moon.

25.   7. The improved Mariner's Astrolabe had only been in use for about twenty years (Ford). One gathers that the region where they landed was St. Helena's Bay, about ninety miles north of the Cape. The superiority of Portuguese navigation has been noticed by Professor Morison. Vasco da Gama went ashore so as to get a really accurate observation. He was incapable of the astounding blunders of Columbus.

30.   7. Professor Ford notes that Velloso is a real person. Both Barros and de Goes mention him, and de Goes (I, 69) speaks of him as a boaster. Later in the Lusiads he tells the Tale of the Twelve of England (VI, 41–69) and he is the discoverer of the nymphs in IX, 69.

31.   8. De Goes (I, 70) has a very similar expression to describe the men fleeing to their boats.

37.   Gama was held up by strong winds for four days after sighting the Cape. But Camões apparently was in a hurricane there, of which he has made the discoverer a present.

39.   1. The invention of Adamastor would be enough by itself to put Camões among the world poets. The making of a myth is beyond the powers of all but the greatest. The very name Adamastor is unknown in classic literature. But see note to V, 51. Herman Melville, one of Camões' greatest admirers, makes a strange comparison in his famous story, Billy Budd. He equates the terrifying figure of Adamastor with the overwhelming ideas which frightened Europe in 1789. The genius of the French Revolution was "an eclipsing menace, mysterious and prodigious," like the shape that towered above the fleet of Gama. The analogy is still good for those of us who look uneasily at "mighty workings" in Europe and Asia. Miss Constance Biddle kindly drew my attention to this passage.

"This Cape is a most stately thing, and the fairest Cape we saw in the whole circumference of the earth, and we passed by it the 18 of June." Narrative of Sir F. Drake's Voyage, Hakluyt, Everyman Edition, I, 74.

41.   The speech of Adamastor may owe some features of its design to that of the prophetess in Aeneid, VI, 83 ff. In a note to the translator, Mr. J. R. Fonseca has pointed out a curious parallel. There is certainly a family resemblance between the apparition of Adamastor to Gama and that of the Afrit to the Fisherman in the Arabian Nights. There is at least a possibility that Camões might have heard the story during his years of military service in Morocco. If Burton noticed the resemblance, I missed it in his commentary.

43.   5. The allusion is to Cabral's expedition of 1500, when, after

the discovery of Brazil, a number of the ships bound for India were lost in a hurricane off the Cape (Lencastre and Ford).

44.   2. Bartolomew Dias rounded the Cape in 1488. He was lost at sea in 1500 on Cabral's voyage to India, and off the Cape.

45.   1. Francisco de Almeida (1450–1510), who with his son Laurence did heroic service for Portugal, while the father was viceroy. Their careers are elaborated upon in X, 26–38.

46.   Manuel de Sousa de Sepulveda and his wife Leonor de Sa, daughter of the Governor, wrecked in Natal, near Inhambane, the year before Camões went to the Indies. The affair evidently and naturally made a deep impression in Portugal. Camões' mother was one of the innumerable de Sas. Could there have been some connection? Various commentators give details.

48.   5. A classic cliché of this nature must of course turn up somewhere else in Camões. In Eclogue IV, it may be found (Juromenha, III, 51). The actual circumstances of the episode are so horrible that one is almost grateful to Camões for softening them. Dona Leonor died almost immediately after the outrage. Her husband went mad and disappeared in the bush (Lencastre). The ghastly affair became in due course the subject of Jeronimo de Corte Rial's epic, Naufragio de Sepulveda in 17 books, which this translator will not read.

49.   5–8. These lines appear to be modeled on those which describe Proteus when he replied to Aristeas in the Georgics (IV, 450–453).

50.   2. Cape of Hurricanes was the name Dias gave. John II, who had not been there, renamed it Good Hope. According to Barros (I, iv, 3) Gama got around it with little trouble.

The four geographers, Pomponius Mela (floruit, 45 A. D.), Pliny (23–79 A. D.), Strabo (floruit 10 A. D.), Ptolemy (Second Century), were apparently studied by Camões. Or if he did not study them himself he had pumped the brains of men who had. Dozens of details in the Lusiads are directly or indirectly derived from them.

51.   Egeus, properly Aegeon, ("hundred-fold Aegeon" in Statius, Thebais, IV, 535) is all over the war of the Gods and Giants. Hundred Hands, I take to be Briareus.

2. Enceladus, the strongest of the giants, is confined in the crater of Aetna (Aeneid, III, 578 ff.).

4. Jupiter, who hurls the thunderbolts forged for him by Vulcan the blacksmith of the gods.

After a vain search for the name Adamastor in Classical literature, it occurred to the translator that the word must be an invention and was perhaps bad Greek. But that did not help. Nor was the mystery cleared up at first sight by the fact that the name occurs in the genealogy of Gargantua (Rabelais, Gargantua and Pantagruel, II, 1, Modern Library Edition, page 168), as "the son of Porphyrio and father of Antaeus." This clue I owe to Professor Francis M. Rogers of Harvard. And a clue it proved to be. Professor Ivan Linforth of the University of California, to whom I took my troubles, pursued the quarry and discovered that Rabelais had written or printed Adamastor in error for Damastor, who is one of the Giants in Claudian's Gigantomachia (100 ff.) and, like Camões' monster, a brother of Aegeon and Briareus. How did the Frenchmen and the Portuguese come to make the same blunder? It is tempting to believe that Camões knew his Rabelais, which the French say all virtuous young men should. But it seems too good to be true. In any case, whether Camões borrowed the name from Rabelais or invented it himself, the fact that he ignored the anomalous character of the word is one more of the numberless straws which show that his Greek was sketchy.

52.   1. Peleus' consort high is Thetis, the mother of Achilles.

6. Perhaps in this line Camões had in mind Ovid's account of how Peleus seized Thetis naked in her cave (Met., XI, 229 ff.).

53.   3. Doris, the mother of the Nereids.

55.   Burton quotes with the queer satisfaction of the anthropologist from the scholiast: "To kiss the eyes is a recognized poetical practice, but to kiss the hair is an act so brutal that it denotes the Savage."

56.   7–8. Camões plays with this image in Canzone VII (Juromenha, II, 199). Burton, with his usual ingenuity, remembers Ovid (Heroides, X, 44–50). The Latin lines are almost certainly the fountain and origin of the Portuguese paraphrase.

58.   Horace's account of the defeat of the giants (Odes, III, iv) might be in Camões' mind.

59.   Perhaps the image of Adamastor sprawled out in defeat on the great waters goes back to Tityos (Odyssey, XI, 576–581), as the comparable image of Satan overthrown in Paradise Lost (I, 194–199) almost certainly does:

>. . . . . his other parts besides
> Prone on the flood, extended long and large,
> Lay floating many a rood, in bulk as huge
> As whom the fables name of monstrous size,
> Titanian or Earth-born, that warred on Jove,
> Briareos or Typhon . . .

In Claudian's Gigantomachia (91 ff.) Pallas the brother of Damastor is changed slowly into stone by the Gorgon's head on Athena's aegis.

61.   1. Phlegon (the Burning One) and Pyroïs (the Fiery) are two

of the four horses that draw the chariot of the Sun. (Ovid, Met., II, 153–154). The other two are Eoüs (Eastern) and Aethon (the Blazing).

The region is thought to be São Bras about "halfway between Capetown and Port Elizabeth" in the general vicinity of Mossel Bay.

63.   8. Tityrus, the shepherd who appears in the first line of the first Eclogue of Virgil, and also in the last line of the last Georgic, "which is glory enough for any shepherd." Barros tells of these native dances (I, iv, 3). So does Damião de Goes.

65.   6. Dias, first to round the Cape (1488), unless we count the Phoenician expedition sent out by Pharaoh Necho nearly two thousand years before, was blown far to the east and correctly inferred that he had got around the southernmost point of Africa.

66.   The allusion is perhaps to Cape das Correntas, named for its tremendous currents (Lencastre). But the stanza is not too explicit.

68.   1. On the Feast of the Epiphany (Ford), January 6, 1498, Gama reached the Rio dos Reis, according to Lencastre, the Save between Lourenço Marques and Inhambane. It could be the Crocodile River (the Limpopo) or several other streams. This is north of Natal. But the people seem to have been the same and well-disposed. Nearly two centuries later Sir William Dampier in his report on Natal dwells on the friendliness of the natives (Voyages of Captain Dampier, ed. John Masefield, Vol. II, 321).

72.   This stanza perhaps refers to a mutiny in the fleet, which appears to have broken out while they were sailing up the East Coast.

73.   8. Sofala, near Beira, south of Mozambique. It is one of the places Milton mentions in Paradise Lost, and he adds that it is by some "thought Ophir." Beazely states (Encyclopedia Britannica, s. v. Dias, Bartholomew) that Covilham had reached Sofala some ten years before. Thus Vasco da Gama had really got to known country at this point, and East and West had met.

74.   2. Saint Nicholas, in addition to his other duties, is the patron saint of sailors. A celebrated Serbian ballad narrates how he laid a storm when he heard the prayers of three hundred pilgrims on their way to Mount Athos.

6. Perhaps Camões remembers Juvenal's objections to trusting to a hewn plank (XII, 57–58 and again, XIV, 289).

76.   4. The gibberish (linguagem—dialect), according to Lencastre, was Swahili, a sort of Bantu lingua franca spoken from Suez south to Quilimane, and also in the Congo basin. Camões' remarks are borne out by modern handbooks. Thus the Encyclopedia Britannica speaks of the tongue as "much mixed with Arabic." The race who speak it,

if they can be called a race, are a negro stock with a strong infusion of Semitic blood. And to this day the language is useful in a great part of the continent.

77. 2. Fernão Martins is historic, according to Lencastre, who, however, says that Damião de Goes gives him another name, Martins Afonso. Damião (I, 71) says this man knew many tongues.

8. These white men are almost certainly Arab traders from the Red Sea (Lencastre).

78. 4. The River of the Good Signs, possibly the Zambesi. I deduce this from Livermore (History, 229). But Professor R. T. Hill agrees with another school who believe that it is near Quilimane about a hundred miles northeast of the mouth of the Zambesi. And Ravenstein, in The First Voyage of Vasco da Gama (a translation of the so-called Roteiro) held the same opinion fifty years ago.

80. 8. This commonplace about Fortune's mutability is all over classic literature. Lucan may be in the picture—mutantur prospera vita (De Bello Civili, VIII, 631). So may Herodotus (History, I, 5), who was talented in the manufacture of such aphorisms.

81. 1. The pest was scurvy. It may be added that, however repulsive, this passage supplies so accurate a clinical account as to interest several leading physicians whom I have consulted in the connection. It must be one of the earliest accounts of a disease, which was something of a novelty. Lord Stanley in The Three Voyages of Vasco da Gama (page 70) notes that Gaspar Correa's account of scurvy, which could have been on Camões' desk, is perhaps the first mention of the disease at sea. Scurvy was a penalty of long voyages. And the Portuguese invented that form of activity. In Hakluyt, Everyman Edition, Vol. IV, 238 (Voyage of Thomas Stevens, 1579), the account of scurvy is practically identical.

5. This is typical Ovidian rhetoric. See Met., I, 400.

According to Castanheda, 100 of Gama's 160 men died of the disease (Karl Vogel, Scurvy, Bulletin of the New York Academy of Medicine, August, 1933, Second series, Vol. IX, No. 8, p. 460). Damião de Goes, who gives another figure, says nearly half died at this time (I, 76). On the way home, the Argonauts suffered from the malady again, and no more than seven or eight men were available to work the ships. Anson's account of his difficulties off the west coast of South America in the 18th Century vividly suggests what scurvy meant to an active commander.

83. 5. Camões in this line appears to have modified Virgil, who says that the loss of burial is easy for a corpse (Aeneid, II, 646). The line may be compared with one in Elegy X (Juromenha, III, 203).

Burton as usual sees many analogies, Odyssey, IX, 62, Horace, Odes, I, xxviii, and Aeneid, V, 871.

86. Barros (I, iv, 11) makes much the same boast for Gama.

87. 1. Homer.

2–3. The seven cities of Greece, each of which claimed the honor of being Homer's birthplace. Camões elsewhere plumps for Smyrna.

5. Virgil. Ausonia, a name for Italy.

7. Mincius, a stream which flows into the Po near Mantua, celebrated in the Eclogues.

8. The contrast with the Tiber is perhaps too rhetorical.

88–89. The attack on Homer and Virgil reminds one of the attack on Boiardo and Ariosto in I, 11. In each case Camões is severe on the fabulous aspect of the poetry under fire.

It may be noticed that Camões gives what is almost an abstract of the Odyssey here, comparable to the Odyssey's abstract of itself in XXIII, 310–343. He leaves out the Lestrygonians and Phaeacia, not to mention the slaying of the Suitors. Virgil for once plays second fiddle, the death of Palinurus and the episode of the Harpies being the only specifically Virgilian touches in the passage.

Perhaps there is some special interest in the stanzas if, as I rather think he did, Camões believed that Dichtung was Wahrheit. The notion that poets always exaggerate Camões could have found in Claudian: si qua fides augentibus omnia musis (De Sexto Consulatu Honorii, 475).

88. 3. Cyclops, Polyphemus. Circe, the enchantress of the Odyssey who changed the crew of Odysseus into swine, "a task of no particular difficulty."

4. The Sirens sang their intended victims to sleep.

6. The Ciconians destroyed part of the fleet of Odysseus.

7. The land where the lotus narcotized the nostalgic.

8. Palinurus was lost overside in the Aeneid. Vasco da Gama seems to imply that the discipline of Aeneas' navy was not up to current Portuguese practice.

89. 1. The crew of Odysseus opened the wineskins in which Eolus had shut up the contrary winds.

2. Calypso, the island-goddess who kept Odysseus prisoner for eight years.

3. The table manners of the Harpies left much to be desired.

4. Both Odysseus and Aeneas descended into Hell to consult about their voyages.

91. 5. The Delian stripling is Apollo, who was born in Delos and had a temple there.

6. Lampetia, the sister of Phaëthon, changed into a poplar tree after her brother's death. This is the correct form of the name. Elsewhere Camões calls her Lampetusa, perhaps a syncretism between her name and that of her sister Phaëthusa who suffered the same arboreal transformation.

92. The praise of praise in this stanza finds a parallel in Plutarch (Life of Coriolanus).

93. 2. Alexander envied Achilles not his battles but his poet (Arrian, Anabasis of Alexander, I, 12.).

5. Miltiades, the victor of Marathon (490 B. C.).

6. Themistocles, the victor of Salamis (480 B. C.), who fortified the three harbors of Athens. Plutarch (Life of Themistocles) quotes his remark that the trophies of Miltiades would not let him sleep. His statement as to his preference for the voice that most eloquently praised his achievements is in Cicero (Pro Archia Poeta, IX, 20), where Camões probably found it. In the beginning of Elegy III Camões quotes another Ciceronian anecdote (De Finibus, II, xxxii, 104) about the Athenian: "Themistocles—when Simonides or someone offered to teach him the art of memory, replied that he would prefer the art of forgetting."

94. 6. Augustus was the patron of Virgil, the poet of Mantua.

95. 7. Martial (XI, 20), at his scabrous best, describes the verses Augustus wrote on Antony's affair with Glaphyra and Fulvia's exorbitant reaction. Nothing could be funnier or more unprintable. Antony made Glaphyra's son King of Cappadocia. Professor C. W. Mendell called my attention to the source from which Camões drew. Montaigne, Camões' contemporary, employed the epigram for a different purpose.

96. 3. This is a favorite figure with Camões. See VII, 79, 1–8. And in Elegy IV (Juromenha, III, 178) it occurs once more. Mr. Harold Landon has drawn my attention to Sonnet CXCII, in which we have it again:

Agora toma a espada, agora a penna.

In a remarkably thorough paper, Mr. Edward Glaser has traced the figure all over Renaissance literature, Sa de Miranda, Ercilla, Bernardo Tasso, Juan de Valdez, et al. The repetition of a commonplace has little charm for us. We prefer what we call originality.

5. Scipio Aemilianus, adopted son of the son of the conqueror of Hannibal, the younger Africanus. He destroyed Carthage, but it would be difficult to prove that he ever wrote a play. The invariably helpful Professor C. W. Mendell has admirably dissected Scipio's reputation as a playwright in a letter to the writer of this note. The style of Terence's comedies is so excellent that his patrons Laelius and Scipio

were supposed to have written them for him. Needless to say, the Scipionian theory bears a strong resemblance to the Baconian theory. Casual remarks by Cicero (Letters to Atticus 7, 3, 10), Quintilian (10, 1, 99), and Suetonius (De Viris Illustribus) scrambled together help to explain Camões' notion.

7-8. Plutarch (Life of Alexander) and Strabo (XIII, i, 27) between them have the story of "the casket copy" of Homer which was kept in the perfume chest of Darius. It was said to have been revised by Aristotle and annotated by Alexander himself. A collector's item of some interest!

97.   8. Suetonius (Twelve Caesars, Nero, Cap. XX) quotes Nero as "repeating a Greek proverb to this effect, that no one had any regard for music which he never heard."

99.   Burton says that there is a tradition in this connection. Some one quoted the Lusiads because the poem honored the great name of Gama. A descendant of the discoverer, evidently subnormal, replied: "We have the titles and don't want the praise."

BOOK VI

ARGUMENT

Vasco da Gama departs from Melinde and, while he sails prosperously on, Bacchus descends to the sea. Description of the palace of Neptune. Bacchus convokes the sea-gods and persuades them to destroy the voyagers. While this is taking place, Velloso, to amuse his companions, relates the history of the twelve champions of England. A horrible storm rises and is stilled by Venus and the nymphs. After the return of good weather the voyagers finally arrive at Calicut, the ultimate and much desired goal of their expedition.

THE LUSIADS

THE SIXTH BOOK

HOW best strong sailormen to entertain,
The pagan King but ill could understand,
Who had in mind the amity to gain
Of the Christian King and nations strong of hand.
Hard was the fate that ruled he must remain
Far from each bounteous European land,
And granted not some neighboring abode
Where Hercules to Ocean broke the road!

2

With dances, games, and such devices gay
As by Melindian courtesy are used,
With pleasant fishing in their wonted way,
Wherewith Lageia Antony abused,
Yet pleased him too, the great King every day
The Lusitanian company amused.
And there were feasts and many an unknown dish
And every sort of fruit, fowl, flesh, and fish.

3

But the Admiral, perceiving that they stayed
Here overlong and that the fresh wind bore,
Which urged departure, straight on board conveyed
The pilot and provisions from the shore.
No more he tarried, for, yet to be essayed,
Stretched a vast tract of silver salt before.
His leave of that good Pagan did he take,
Who steady friendship of them all bespake.

VI And he desired them that their squadrons should
Come to his harbor oft and oft again,
For he could never hope for greater good
Than to yield chiefs like these his state and reign,
And, while his soul lord of his body stood,
Would in perpetual readiness remain
To venture life and realm, entire and whole,
For such a King and men of lofty soul.

5

In other words of similar intent,
The Captain answered. Then with sails spread wide
On toward the countries of the Dawn he went,
In whose discovery he so long was tried.
Our pilot now was on no treason bent,
But one who faithfully the ships would guide
On a sure course. Ahead the Chief could steer
Not as before, with everything to fear.

6

Lifting across the Orient waves they came.
In India's seas already they perceived
The sun's bridechambers where he is born aflame.
And now were their desires almost achieved,
But fortunes destined for the Lusian name,
That well deserved them, so Thyoneus grieved
In his base soul that he, as if on fire,
Was fit to die, blasphemed, and burst for ire.

7

That it was Heaven's will, he knew aright,
Of this our Lisbon a new Rome to make,
That other Power of all-compelling might,
From what It purposed, he could never shake.
Desperate, he fled down the Olympian height,
On earth new remedy to seek and take.
He plunged in Ocean and to his court him got,
To whom the wet dominion fell by lot.

8

Within the innermost of caverns deep
And high, where the sea hides itself away,
There, in the place whence the fierce combers leap
When Ocean the winds' anger will repay,
Neptune and the Nereids bright their station keep.
More deep-sea deities beside him lay,
Where the waters for those cities leave a space,
In which the wet gods have their dwelling-place.

9

The Deep he sounded no man ever knew,
Where all the sands were of the silver fine.
In the open field tall towers came in view,
And all transparent, massive, crystalline.
The nearer to the wonder the eye drew
The less the sight was able to divine
If what it saw were glass or diamond stone,
That with a light so clear and radiant shone.

10

The gates were all pure gold and were inlaid
With richest pearl that's born within the shell,
Likewise with noble sculptor's work arrayed,
Where cruel Bacchus' eyes could feast them well.
There first he saw, in various hues displayed,
Old Chaos' face where all confusions dwell.
And the four Elements were seen beside,
Each with some different labor occupied.

11

There Fire uptowered in sublimest state,
That from no substance draws his nourishment,
Fire, made all living things to animate,
Since to purloin it first Prometheus went.
Behind him rose, ethereal, delicate,
Invisible Air, that seeks incontinent
His station and, though heat or cold oppress,
In this world never suffers emptiness.

VI   Nearby was mountainous Earth, with trees most fair
Of flower and with the green grass covered o'er,
That to whatever creatures she may bear
Gives life and all their diet's various store.
And the bright form was also sculptured there
Of Water spreading between shore and shore,
From whom all fishy beasts their birth derive—
And 'tis her liquor keeps all life alive.

13

That war was sculptured in another place,
Waged when the gods and giants fought the fight.
Typhéus launched his crackling flame apace,
Where he lay deep under vast Etna's height.
There he saw Neptune carved, who, for a race
That did not know the horse, the earth would smite,
That they might have the beast. And he could see
Pallas with her first peaceful olive tree.

14

Wrathful Lyaeus stood not long to stare
At all that sculpture, but his entrance made
In the palace of great Neptune, who, aware
Of his approach, to watch for him had stayed,
And at the gate now gave him greeting fair
Amid his nymphs, who strong surprise betrayed,
Seeing the wine-god come on such a road
Into the water's kingdom and abode.

15

"Neptune," he said, "I pray you, do not fear
To welcome Bacchus in your realm and state,
For unjust fortune showeth all too clear
Her power against the potent and the great.
Ere I speak more, if more you fain would hear,
Summon the gods of all the ocean straight.
They'll see strange modes of evil that befall.
So let all hear the ill that threatens all."

And since the circumstance in Neptune's sight   **VI**
Such threatening and strange appearance wore,
Triton he bade those deities invite,
Who in cold seas dwell between shore and shore.
Triton conceived his birth was glory's height,
Whom to the King divine Salatia bore.
The youth was huge, dark, and of aspect dire,
And trumpeter and courier to his sire.

17

His beard and likewise the long hair that fell
From his head downward, sweeping either spall,
Were soaking seaweed, which, as one could tell,
Had never known the gentle comb at all.
Nor lacked his elf-locks the black mussel-shell,
Which there had place of birth original.
No cap he had but wore upon his head
A heavy helm of crawfish bone instead.

18

Naked his body and parts genital,
That to his swimming might no hindrance be.
But he was covered o'er with creatures small,
Hundreds and hundreds, natives of the sea;
With prawn and crab and such-like animal
That get their growth of Phoebe's charity.
Oysters, foul cockles, in the weed that hide,
And snails with single shell swarmed on his side.

19

A monstrous twisted conch in hand he bore,
Upon the which with all his might he blew.
Afar was heard the musical loud roar,
That wide re-echoed all the ocean through.
Whereon, after such warning, all the corps
Of gods together toward the palace drew
Of him who the Dardanian rampart raised,
Thereafter ruined by the Grecians crazed.

VI   Thither came Father Ocean and he led,
     Of his begotten children, all the train.
     Came Nereus, unto whom was Doris wed,
     He who with nymphs had peopled all the main.
     And thither the prophetic Proteus sped,
     Leaving his sea-born flocks behind to gain
     Their forage in the bitter deep, though he
     Knew what Sire Bacchus quested in the sea.

21

Neptune's delicious bride was likewise there,
Coelus and Vesta's child. Her charming face
Was serious, yet so wonderfully fair
The marveling sea was ravished by her grace.
A tunic rich exceeding did she wear,
Made of a tissue of fine linen lace,
Which well her crystalline body could reveal,
For it was far too lovely to conceal.

22

And Amphitrite, as any flower sweet,
To fail at such a time was not the one,
With her dolphin, which, to the King's amorous heat,
Once counseled her obedience must be done.
The eyes of each possess such power complete
As make them seem fit to surpass the sun.
They came together, who as equals reign,
For true wives of one husband are the twain.

23

She who, from Athamas his fury wild,
Fled and was lifted to divinity,
Brought her son with her, a most beauteous child,
And also numbered with the gods is he.
Sporting before, the boy the time beguiled
With pretty shells, the fabric of the sea,
And very often Panope the fair
To her bosom took him on the beaches there.

And the god who once a human shape had worn   VI
And, by the virtue of an herb of might,
Was changed into a fish, which hurt forlorn
Thereafter won for him his godhead bright,
Came also, who for Scylla sweet must mourn,
And Circe's false abominable sleight.
Scylla he loved, and she in him delighted.
But yet the stronger proved love unrequited.

25

Now finally when all were seated there
In that great chamber splendid and divine,
Goddesses on rich couches past compare,
And gods upon the high seats crystalline,
The Father gave them all his greeting fair,
Throned with the Theban in equal place condign.
And smoke of ambergris filled all the room,
Sea-born, that passes Araby's perfume.

26

And when the tumult had been set at rest,
Which the gods welcoming each other made,
Then the Thyonean from his secret breast
The cause of his tormenting fears portrayed.
His countenance a weight of care expressed,
And terrible affliction he displayed,
So death by stranger steel might overtake
The Portuguese. Unto that end he spake:

27

"Prince, who hast sovranty, by right most sound,
Over the angry sea, from pole to pole,
And, that none pass his limitary bound,
Keepest all nations under thy control,
And Father Ocean, thou, who, circling round
This universal world, art wont to roll,
And whose decrees with equity ordain
That none shall live, save in his own domain;

VI   "And you, you sea-gods, who no insult sore
Suffer against your empire to be done,
Unless with equal pains you pay his score,
Who may desire your realm to overrun,
Did you then dwell in folly heretofore?
Who might he be who thus has worked upon
Your hearts, so justly hardened in intent
Against mankind, feeble but insolent?

29

"You saw with what audacity supreme
They came against high Heaven in days of yore,
And also have beheld their madman's dream
Of conquering the sea by sail and oar.
You have seen—each day such insolence extreme
Of pride we see that in a few years more
They will be gods of Earth and Sky, and then
We, as I fear, shall be no more than men.

30

"Look now upon this weakling progeny,
Named for a vassal of my retinue.
With courage proud and high, they mean to be
Lords of a world conquered from me, from you.
You may behold them, how they cleave your sea,
A greater thing than Rome's brave breed could do.
You see how they would trespass on your realm
And go about your laws to overwhelm.

31

"I myself saw, when Minyans, first to go
Into your kingdom, opened wide the way,
Wronged Boreas and his fellow Aquilo,
With other winds, the enterprise withstay.
Hence, if the winds felt the foul injury so,
Done them by that adventurous array,
Revenge should now concern you even more.
What hope is yours? What are you waiting for?

"That you should think, O gods, I left the sky   **VI**
For love of you, I never shall agree,
Nor for the pain you bear, and insult high,
But rather for the evil done to me.
The glories which I won in time gone by
In the world's sight, as you yourselves could see,
When India's Orient coasts I overthrew,
I now must watch this race wreck and undo.

33

"For our Great Lord and Fate, who still conduct
This base world as may please them, have decreed
Honors whose like never before were plucked
In the great deeps to be these heroes' meed.
You may behold, O gods, how some instruct
Even gods in ill, and know in very deed
That none is valued at a lower rate
Than he whom sense might nobly estimate.

34

"For this cause from Olympus did I fly,
Seeking a remedy for all my pain,
To see if my lost credit in the sky
Peradventure in your seas I might regain."
More had he said, but out of either eye
So fast the tears in double torrents rain
He can no more. Whereupon the entire
Host of the water-gods flamed up like fire.

35

The rage, which, in a moment, out of hand
In the gods' hearts had altered their intent,
To any other counsel better planned,
Delay, or further change, would not consent.
Great Eolus was given their command
By Neptune to unloose the vehement,
Unnumbered furies of the raging gale,
So sailor never more that sea might sail.

223

VI Proteus in vain the first sought to declare
What his decision in the case might be.
And all the same opinion seemed to share,
That what he said was very prophecy.
But such a tumult was engendered there
Of a sudden in the sacred company
That furious Tethys screamed out like a shrew:
"Neptune knows well the thing that he bade do."

And now already Hippotades the proud
Unloosed the fierce winds from his dungeon hold,
To stir whose spirits up, he cried aloud
Against those heroes, high of heart and bold.
Suddenly quiet skies began to cloud,
For wilder gales than ever blew of old
Into their hands began to take new power,
So to cast down mountain and house and tower.

But while in council there as yet they stay,
On the wet deep the stately, weary fleet,
Before a gentle wind, on the long way
Across a stretch of tranquil water beat.
Time came when furthest off the light of day
Doth from the Eastern Hemisphere retreat,
And men of the first watch their rest would take,
And their comrades of the second must awake.

Half dead for sleep and scarce awakened still,
Yawning each second, along the yards they lie
Or lean, the lot of them, covered but ill
Against the nipping airs that sough and sigh.
Their eyes are open, much against their will,
And a man would stretch the while he rubbed his eye.
A cure they seek o'er sleep that can prevail,
A thousand things relate, and many a tale.

And some one said: "What better thing could be   VI
To pass this time that weighs upon us sore
Than to narrate some pleasant history,
That sleep's dead load may trouble us no more."
Leonard gave answer, whose thought constantly
Upon the troubles of true lovers bore:
"And to that end what better stories may
Compete with love-tales to pass time away?"

41

"It is not right," Velloso made reply,
"To talk of softness in such harsh distress,
For labor of the sea, whose cost comes high,
Endures not love and shuns delightfulness.
Instead stark burning battle let us try
In this our tale, for hard things will oppress
The lives of all of us, as I foresee.
Hardships that are to come say this to me."

42

They bade Velloso, having well agreed,
To tell whatever he was minded to.
"Against my tale," said he, "let no man plead,
I told you something fabulous and new.
And since, my hearers, it is meant to lead
Your hearts great acts of noblest proof to do,
I'll speak of men born where we also dwell.
And of the Twelve of England I shall tell.

43

"When John, the son of Peter, with light rein,
Ruled in the land, who brought peace and repose
And liberty into the realm again,
Where neighboring power had worked us many woes,
Fiery Erinys discord sowed amain
In mighty England where the northern snows
Abound at all times. And that feud withal
Was to be glorious for Portugal.

225

44

VI   "Between the English Court's delightful dames
And certain noble courtiers chance debate
Rose on a day, and wrath broke forth in flames,
Whether from whim or passion obstinate.
The courtiers, to whom insulting names
Were matters that had very little weight,
Said, as for honor, and they would make it good,
Women had none because of womanhood.

45

"If men there were, who with the lance and blade
Desired the ladies' quarrel to maintain,
In the pitched field or tilting palisade
They should be shamed or cruelly be slain.
Their woman's weakness, nakedly displayed
And little used to such insulting strain,
Lacked the just strength and the appropriate force
And, hence, to friends and kindred had recourse.

46

"But since their strong foes had such pride of place,
In all the kingdom none dared buckle to,
Kinsmen or lover hot, that would embrace
The ladies' quarrel, as a man should do.
With sweet tears on each alabaster face,
Enough to rouse up the celestial crew
Of gods to succor them, with one consent,
To the Duke of Lancaster, the ladies went.

47

"This mighty English lord in time before
Against Castile with us had fought the fight.
And seen his friends' great powers proved in war
Under their planet of benignant light.
Of amorous affections, furthermore,
He, in our country, had experience right,
Who here had seen his daughter's beauty tame
Our strong King's heart, who took to wife the dame.

226

"The Duke, lest civil broils might come to be,   **VI**
Did not desire upon their part to stand,
But said: 'The kingdom's quarrel formerly
I championed yonder in the Iberian land.
And 'mid the Lusitanians did I see
Such fair address, such might of heart and hand,
That, unless I greatly err, they can afford
The timeliest succor with both fire and sword.

49

"'And if, wronged ladies, you will have it so,
For you to them ambassadors I'll send,
Who all your bitter wrong shall let them know
In courteous letters most discreetly penned.
Surely, to men like these, your tears of woe
Your quarrel will most heartily commend,
And sweet and honeyed words. And I should say,
There you will find your firm defence and stay.'

50

"Even so the wise Duke gave them counsel right
And named a dozen brave men on the spot.
And, that each dame might have her own true knight,
Commanded them to draw the names by lot,
For they were twelve. And when it came to light,
What champion each of the dames had got,
Each wrote her knight in terms as might befall,
And all to the King, and the Duke to one and all.

51

"To Portugal, when came the messenger,
The novelty filled all the Court with glee.
The noble King would first himself prefer,
But it stood not with regal majesty.
The courtiers would have played adventurer,
And with a fiery spirit certainly,
But no one to that fortune could lay claim,
Save only those whom the Duke chose by name.

227

VI "And he whose hand governed the helm of state,
In the loyal town, bade a swift ship prepare,
Where the name Portugal, for all time great,
Had its beginning, as the tales declare.
The Twelve to all things look, nor long they wait,
But modern arms and gear they gather there,
And helms with legend and device and crest,
And steeds, and all in myriad hues are dressed.

53
"Already those picked by arbitrament
Of the English Duke, in such affairs well tried,
Have from the King obtained his full consent
To sail from Douro's famous waterside.
In the company no difference evident
'Twixt brave and skillful knights could be descried,
But one Magriço (so they called the man)
To those great cavaliers his speech began:

54
"'Brave friends, this long while it has been my dream
To visit foreign countries and behold
More floods than Tagus or the Douro's stream,
And men and laws and customs manifold.
Now is a fair occasion, as I deem.
I wish (for this world's wonders are untold),
With your good leave, alone by land to fare,
And, as for England, I'll be with you there.

55
"'Should he prevent me, as might well prove true,
Who at the end of all things draws his line,
From meeting with you at the rendezvous,
Little you'll lack from such default of mine.
You'll do for me whatever may be due.
But if my spirit doth the truth divine,
Rivers, heights, Fortune, and her enmity
Shall never bar, but with you I shall be.'

56

"He spoke, embracing all the good friends by,   **VI**
And went, who could their fair permission gain;
He passed Leon, Castile, and cast his eye
On ancient towns our patriot arms had ta'en.
Navarre, the Pyrenees, perilous and high,
He saw, which are the bounds of France and Spain.
And, having viewed in France her wonders vast,
In Flanders' mighty mart he paused at last.

57

"Once come, as whim or fortune might decide,
He went no further but abode there long,
While o'er the cold waves of the North Sea plied
The eleven champions' illustrious throng.
And reaching England's stranger coast, they ride
To London city hastily along.
And the Duke, feasting, welcomed every guest,
The while the ladies served them and caressed.

58

"And lo! the appointed day and hour at hand
With the twelve English in the field to fight,
Under the warrant of the King's command.
With helms and greaves and harness are they dight.
The ladies know these will uphold their hand,
The battailous Portuguese in armor bright,
And silken gear of many hues they wear,
And gold and myriad jewels rich and fair.

59

"But she who had by lot Magriço won,
Who was not come, was dressed in mourning guise,
Since champion allotted she had none,
To back her quarrel in the enterprise.
But the Eleven said battle must be done
Before the Court of England in such wise,
And the ladies would achieve the victory,
Though on their side two fell, or even three.

VI   "There in a noble open theatre
Sat England's King with all his court beside.
In threes and fours his gentles round him were,
As fortune had their station qualified.
The sun, such courage, strength, and martial stir,
Sees not, from Bactros stream to Tagus' tide,
In any twelve men, as could match at all
England against the Eleven of Portugal.

61

"The horses champ the gold bits, foaming white,
And furiously enraged the beasts appear.
The sun upon the armour glitters bright,
As on hard diamond or crystal clear.
But certainly a most unequal fight
Men upon either hand discover here,
Twelve to eleven, and the people fell
A-murmuring and as one man would rebel.

62

"Every one turned to look where they saw flare
The main beginning of that mutiny,
When in the lists, lo! a knight riding there
On horseback, armed for battle cap-a-pie.
The King and every dame he greeted fair,
Then joined the Eleven, Magriço, even he.
The great knight clasped each friend in his embrace,
Nor did he fail them in the perilous place.

63

"Glad was the lady when the man she knew,
Who to defend her name and honor came.
Vesture of Helle's beast on her she threw,
Which dull mankind loves better than good fame.
They gave the signal and the trumpet blew,
The spirits of the valiant to inflame.
The spurs prick in, and all let loose the rein.
Down go the lances. Sparks fly on the plain.

64

"The thunder of the horses over all
Seems to compel the earth until it shakes.
Such sights the heart in a man's breast appall,
Who looking on them palpitates and quakes.
One hurtles from a horse that does not fall,
One, horse and man o'erthrown, his outcry makes.
One his white armor in vermilion dips,
One with his helm-plume the steed's quarters whips.

65

"Some in those lists their sleep eternal found,
Whose lives in a brief moment took their flight.
Here, riderless, a charger gallops round,
And there, without his charger, stands a knight.
Dethroned, the English pride falls to the ground,
For two or three have fled the field of fight.
And they, who with the sword come to assail,
Encounter more than harness, shield, and mail.

66

"To waste more words, at greater length to go
Into sad thrusts and buffets with the blade,
Best suits such spendthrift poets as we know,
And evil times in fabulous dreams portrayed.
It will suffice to say the case fell so:
Such noble skill in arms our men displayed
That the palm of conquest unto them remained,
And the ladies gloriously the triumph gained.

67

"The Duke welcomed the Twelve from victory
Home to his palace with festal pomp and gay,
The while the ladies' lovely company
Set cooks and hunters to their tasks straightway.
The champions who won their liberty,
They would feast thousand-fold each hour and day,
So long in England as they might sojourn,
Till to their own dear land they must return.

VI "Men say that brave Magriço, in despite
His will to see strange things, was wrought upon
To tarry where high duty as a knight
For Flanders' Countess he erewhile had done.
And since he was no simple acolyte
In hard affairs, where, Mars, thy writ doth run,
In the field he slew a Frank. His was to be
Torquatus and Corvinus' destiny.

69

"Another of the Twelve to Alamain
Departed, where he presently defied
A traitor German, who by treason plain
To put him to the sword most falsely tried."
And while Velloso spoke in such a strain,
The watch besought him not to lay aside
Magriço's legend, yet remember well
What things the man in Germany befell.

70

In the nick, as they were waiting for the tale,
The boatswain, watching with a weather eye,
Blew on his pipe, and straight at either rail
The mariners, thus quickly roused, stood by.
The boatswain bade them reef the foremast sail,
Because the freshening wind was rising high.
"Look alive! She's blowing up," he cried aloud,
"From over yonder, out of that black cloud."

71

But scarcely had they reefed the foresails well
When broke the sudden and tremendous squall.
"Strike," screamed the boatswain with a mighty yell,
"Get in the mainsail! Strike! Strike!" came his call.
But the winds, full of indignation fell,
For furling of the sail stayed not at all,
And, tearing at it, all to tatters rent,
With sounds as if the world to ruin went.

Therewith the crew with shouting smote the sky,　VI
Of a sudden in confusion terrified.
At the sail's rending, in the trough they lie,
Shipping a lot of water overside.
"Overboard with it! Every man stand by!
Overboard with it!" stoutly the boatswain cried.
"You soldiers, man the pumps and never shrink!
Go man the pumps, for we are like to sink."

73

Then forthwith hastened the stout soldiery
To man the pumps, but, just as they fell to,
The shocking roll which that appalling sea
Gave to the ship all men to leeward threw.
Three mariners as hardy as might be
Were not enough the helmsman's task to do.
The tackles fast on either side they triced,
But neither human skill nor strength sufficed.

74

So terrible the winds that none might blow
With a more cruel force than in that hour,
If they had come in hope to overthrow
The main strength of the Babylonian tower.
But as a cockboat did the great ship show
Amid enormous seas that grew in power,
Which moved the heart to fear and wonder strong,
To see it in such seas endure so long.

75

On the ship where Paul da Gama held the sway,
The mainmast had been broken quite in twain.
And the crew cried, while half awash she lay,
On Him Who man's salvation came to gain.
Coelho's carrack shouted in dismay
Shouts no less wild to empty air in vain,
For all her master with a careful mind
Had shortened sail when first burst forth the wind.

VI   And, now the waves, while Neptune rages so,
The ships above the very cloud-banks cast,
Or they behold, as down the trough they go,
The inmost entrails of the sea-deep vast.
For Boreas, Auster, Notus, Aquilo
The World Machine's whole fabric seek to blast.
And flame shoots through the black and ghastly night,
Till the whole Pole is burning with wild light.

77

The Halcyonean birds, their tragic song
Still crying, near the windward bulwarks stayed,
And memory of their ancient grief prolong,
Upon them by thy furious waters laid.
And meanwhile the enamored dolphin throng
The hollow caverns undersea invade,
Shunning the blasting wind and hurricane,
And yet no safety in the deeps attain.

78

Never were forged such fiery thunderbrands,
To quell the Titans' insolence of mind,
By the great soot-stained ironmaster's hands,
Who once his stepson's burnished arms designed.
And the huge Thunderer never o'er all lands
Shook lightnings forth that flamed after this kind
In the great flood, when those two 'scaped alone,
Who into human beings changed the stone.

79

What crags the while the combers overbore,
That battered with a violence so stern!
What age-old trees wild winds upwrenching tore,
Which with such furious indignation burn!
The firm-fixed roots had never thought before
That, haply, sometime they would skyward turn;
Nor had the deep sands dreamed the sea had might
In such wild sort to whirl them to the height.

Vasco da Gama, when he saw how near   **VI**
His heart's desire he now was like to die—
And the sea opening down to Hell Mouth clear,
Or with new fury heaving to the sky—
Of life despairing and confused by fear,
Where naught availed him any remedy,
For strong and sacred help his plea would make,
That can the impossible, and thus he spake!

81

"Divine angelic Guardian, heavenly bright,
Of Sky and Sea and Earth, Who art the Lord,
And Who good refuge to the Israelite,
In the midmost Red-Sea waters, didst accord;
Who Paul didst free, and then deliver quite
From sandy shoals and from the wave abhorred,
And with his sons didst save him, who should found
New peoples in a world empty and drowned;

82

"If such strange perils I have come through whole
As in new Scylla and Charybdis be,
Or other Syrtes of the sandy shoal
And fresh Acroceraunian infamy,
At the end of all such dangers hard to thole,
Why are we now forsaken thus by Thee,
If our labor in Thy sight be not to blame,
That was only undertaken in Thy Name?

83

"How noble was their fortune, who could die
'Mid Africa's sharp spears, who, true and bold,
In Mauretania came to testify
In battle, and the Holy Faith uphold,
Whose actions were illustrious and high,
Whose memory for sovereign is extolled!
And they yet have their lives, because they gave,
And kind death does them honor in the grave."

VI While thus he speaks, the winds in battle strain,
And like to tameless bulls they bellow proud.
Harder and harder drives the hurricane,
With whistling shriek, through slender stay and
The shocking lightnings flash and flash again, [shroud.
While the thunder tells in crashes long and loud
How Heaven to earth must from her axles fall,
And the elements do battle one and all.

85

But now, before the sun's clear-gleaming ray,
The amorous planet her bright radiance shed,
And the bright-browed ambassadress of day
The earth and the wide ocean visited.
In Heaven the goddess, the star that rules alway,
From which Orion the sword-bearer fled,
Looking on the sea and the fleet she held so dear,
Was in a moment filled with wrath and fear.

86

"For sure this must be Bacchus' work," said she.
"But he shall not have his will, who could prepare
Designs so damnable. Discovery
I still shall make of evil he may dare."
So saying, down she flew to the wide sea,
Nor time she wasted on her journey there.
To the amorous nymphs was her commandment
Their heads with wreaths of roses to adorn. [borne,

87

Garlands she bade them wear of various hue,
On golden hair, that a sweet contrast made.
Who would not say that rosy flowers grew
On native gold which love is skilled to braid?
By love she had determined to subdue
The stormwinds' whole outrageous cavalcade,
Showing her nymphs, who in their beauty are
Unmatched for loveliness by any star.

So it befell. No sooner were they there
Than at the sight the fury died away,
That made the stormy winds such battle bear.
Like unto soldiers yielded, they obey.
Their hands and feet seem fettered by the hair
That has made dark the very light of day.
To Boreas, in whose breast desire awoke,
Thus the delicious Orithyia spoke!

89

"Think not, fierce Boreas, I would confess
That constant love to me you always bore.
The surest sign of love is tenderness.
Rage suits him not, who truly would adore.
Unless this madness you shall quite suppress,
From me henceforward look for nothing more,
Who yet might love you, but must fear instead,
For love with you transforms itself to dread."

90

And even so spake Galatea bright
To savage Notus, for she saw too plain
How long the lad was quickened by mere sight,
And him to everything she could constrain.
He knew not if he read his fortune right,
Who heart in breast no longer could contain.
Content to know what she would have him do,
Little enough he cared how tame he grew.

91

The other nymphs in like sort overbore
Swiftly the rage in every lover's mind.
The winds to Venus sweet themselves gave o'er,
Softened their fury and their wrath unkind.
And seeing they were all so fond, she swore
In love her favor they should always find.
In her white hands she took their homage due,
Who promised with the voyage to deal true.

VI Over the heights the shining morning spread,
    Yonder where Ganges runs with murmurous sound,
    And the sailors stationed at the topmast-head,
    Before the bows, discovered rising ground.
    And the vain terror from the spirit fled,
    Free of the storms and oceans earliest found.
    Cheerily the Melindian pilot spake:
    "That land is Calicut, or I mistake.

93

    "This is the country you are seeking for.
    The veritable India is there.
    And if in this world you desire no more,
    Then here's an end of your long toil and care."
    To find known country was a joy so sore
    That Gama could that joy no longer bear.
    Kneeling on deck, hands lifted to the sky,
    Thanks unto God he gave for mercy high.

94

    Thanks unto God he gave, and reason too,
    Not only that 'twas granted him to see
    Lands, which to find, he lived all terror through,
    Enduring every labor that might be,
    But also that deliverance he knew
    From death, the grim winds, full of cruelty,
    On the high seas prepared in rage extreme.
    So a man wakes out of a fearful dream.

95

    Such men as are Fate's favorites, by grace
    Of hateful danger, fear, and labor dire,
    Often attain to greatest pride of place
    And everlasting dignities acquire,
    But never by relying on the race
    And lineage of some great ancestral sire.
    Nor upon golden couches may they lie,
    Lapped in fine ermine furs of Muscovy;

96

Nor eat strange dishes exquisitely dight,
Nor junket soft abroad in laziest state,
Nor dally with such infinite delight
As makes a noble heart effeminate,
Nor yield to the unconquered appetite,
Which fortune ever keeps so delicate,
It suffers not a man his way to change
And find out action of heroic range;

97

He with strong arm must go to seek his share
Of honor, and thereto his just claim press.
On watch, the forged steel on his back he'll bear,
Enduring storm and the rough waves' distress.
In the South's lap, vile chills he must outwear,
Sailing in desperate regions harborless,
And of corrupted food must eat his fill,
Whose only spice is hard enduring ill;

98

He forces his blanched face so to appear,
As he were gay, resolved, and safe from harm,
Amid the burning bolts which whistle near
And shear away some comrade's leg or arm.
Thus the heart hardens into honor clear,
For which gold and promotion have no charm,
Promotion, gold, which Fortune may bestow,
Though just and rigid Virtue does not so.

99

The light breaks in upon the intellect,
By experience to serenity inclined,
Which can, as from a towering throne, inspect
The base, bewildered actions of mankind.
Such a one, whom the laws of right direct,
Not mere imaginations of the mind,
Shall rise to highest honor, as he ought,
Unwilling, who such honor never sought.

NOTES

BOOK VI

2.   4. Lageia is Cleopatra. She is so-called after her ancestor Ptolemy son of Lagus. The lady, it is alleged, at a fishing party on the Nile, had a huge salted fish attached to Antony's line by a diver. (Plutarch, Antony.)

3.   Perhaps Camões is imitating "the wondrous space of brine" in Odyssey, V, 100–101.

7–8. The episode at Melinde, in reality, seems to have been less harmonious than the poem represents. Gama practically blackmailed the King, who was frightened to death by the new arrivals, into giving him pilots.

4.   Burton notes that a species of good will was maintained. The King of Melinde became a sort of client of the Portuguese, who protected him against neighboring Mombassa and Quiloa.

5.   Lencastre observes that the fleet left Melinde on April 24, 1498, and that the pilot's name was Malem Cana (Barros, I, iv, 5). De Goes calls him Malemo Canaqua. One may guess that he was a Mahometan. Barros alleges that he had a chart of the East Coast of Africa on which he indicated the course to Gama. Ravenstein (The First Voyage of Vasco da Gama, p. 18) says the pilot was a Guzrati and that his name means "Teacher of Pilots."

6.   6. Bacchus is called Thyoneus after his mother Semele, whose other name is Thyone. This name (the Raging One) was given after her son brought her up from Hell. It symbolizes Bacchic fury. Horace knows all about this (Odes, I, xvii).

7.   8. When the young gods divided their father Saturn's patrimony by lot, Jupiter won Heaven and Earth, Pluto the Underworld, and Neptune the Sea (Ovid, Met., II, 201–292). But Homer is the origin of the myth (Iliad, XV, 187–193).

8.   Burton thinks the palace of Neptune is modeled on the temple of Apollo erected by Daedalus at Cumae and described in Aeneid, VI, 14–41. I see no particular connection.

10.   6. Chaos, the unformed out of which all form comes.

7. The four elements are fire, air, earth and water. Burton traces details to Ovid, Met., I.

11.   1–4. The sense seems to be that fire in its essence is independent of fuel. Pliny (II, 111) asks a queer question: "What is the natural principle that pastures a most voracious appetite on the whole world while itself unimpaired?" Later on (XXXVI, 68) he wonders if fire does not create more than it destroys. These notions and several others may have been in Camões' mind.

   5–8. These four lines appear to indicate that Camões had not read his Lucretius, and in any case either did not understand or else did not agree with the system of Epicurus. The notion of atoms and the void is implicitly denied in the last verse. Epicurus is mentioned in the Lusiads (VII, 75), but, in the best manner of his adversaries, as a mere votary of sensual pleasure.

12.   8. . . . . . . Vapor umidus omnes
         Res creat (Ovid, Met., I, 432–3).

13.   3. Typheus shared the fate of Enceladus apparently.

       5. Camões' favorite myth of the creation of the horse again.

       8. Athena, it will be remembered, won the competition for Athenian favor by producing the first olive (Ovid, Met., VI, 80). See also Georgics, I, 12–13 and 18–19. Pliny says that this tree was still living in his time.

16.   2. Triton, son of Neptune and Amphitrite sometimes called Salatia. Many of the descriptive touches are derived from Ovid's account of Triton (Met., I, 330–342). Mr. H. M. Landon's remark that Triton resembles a figure on a Renaissance fountain is suggestive.

18.   6. Phoebe, the moon. The idea that the moon affects the edibility of shellfish is wide spread.

       Burton quotes Faria y Sousa (who has much to say on the subject, as I learn from Mr. Glaser) but only for a Roman street cry:

              Ecco li granci cotti in buon vena!
              Son buoni adesso que la luna e piena.

But Pliny (II,.41) is perhaps Camões' source. Pliny says that the bodies of oysters, mussels, cockles, and all shellfish grow and waste by the power of the moon. He repeats this in at least three other places. Ptolemy has the same notion (Tetrabiblos, I, 3).

19.   7. Neptune built the Dardanian wall for Laomedon, King of Troy, whose failure to reward the god properly was one of the diplomatic errors that led to the Trojan War. Laomedon cuts a poor figure in Valerius Flaccus.

20.   1. Father Ocean, the god of the Ocean Sea which surrounded the world of Antiquity, as opposed to the Mediterranean which lay within it.

       3. Nereus, the son of Ocean. Doris, his wife and sister.

       4. Proteus, Master of the Seals in the Court of Neptune, and

endowed with the gift of prophecy. Touches that might be derived from Claudian (De Nuptiis) are all over these stanzas. I could easily specify, but spare the reader.

21. 1. Neptune's delicious bride, Tethys, a lady whose ancestry has been confused by Camões. Professor Ford is right when he says her mother was Gaea (Earth). Vesta could have had nothing to do with it.

22. 3. Amphitrite's dolphin is a fixture in marine mythology, but his role is anything but edifying.

23. 1. Ino, the second wife of Athamas, King of Thebes. Athamas went mad and killed one of his children, but Ino escaped with the younger, Melicertes. Mother and child became sea deities. The Athamas episode is one tributary of the vast river system of the Golden Fleece myth, but it is connected with other legends. See Ovid, Fasti, VI, 487 ff.

7. Panope, one of the Nereids and helpful to sailors in storms.
. . . . on the level brine
Sleek Panope with all her sisters played.
Lycidas, 98–99.

24. 1. Glaucus, a fisherman, became a sea-god after eating an herb. He loved Scylla who was changed into a sea monster by jealous Circe (Ovid, Met., XIII, 900 ff., and XIV, 1–75). Camões' account is a good abridgment of Ovid.

27–34. This tirade of Bacchus is a sort of anthology of various speeches by Juno in the Aeneid. It is all in her best manner.

29. 7–8. In Statius (Thebais, IX, 445) the river-god Ismenus says that his threats against Hippomedon who has slain his grandson will be made good, "unless I am mortal and thy blood is derived from heaven."

31. 1. The Argonauts were called Minyae because some of them belonged to that Boeotian tribe.

3. Boreas and Aquilo are both northerly winds. The fury of the winds rises high in Valerius Flaccus (Argonauticon, I, 597 ff.).

34. 5–7. Sonnet XXIV has a similar neo-classical cliché.

35 ff. It is unnecessary to point out Virgilian reminiscences that crowd these stanzas. But for the curious, Aeneid, I, 50–64, may prove suggestive. Needless to say, Virgil often borrows from Homer. This editor does not think Camões does so directly except very rarely.

37. 1. Hippotades, Eolus. He frees or locks up the winds.
Clauserat Hippotades aeterno carcere ventos.
Ovid, Met., IV, 663.

38. 2. Tibullus has the phrase "fessas puppes" (weary ships) in Book II, V, 45. This sort of thing can be pushed too far. But the expression may have been in Camões' mind.

5–8. Professor S. E. Morison, in his remarkable Admiral of the Ocean Sea, raises the question as to what time the watch was changed at night during the Age of Exploration. Camões apparently means midnight, as Professor Morison correctly infers. At all events, this is perhaps the first account of changing watch in literature.

40.   5. Leonard, a soldier on the voyage named Lionardo Ribeiro, according to Professor Ford. He is the hero of an episode in IX, 75–82. Is it fanciful to imagine that Ribeiro is a foil for Velloso?

41.   1. Velloso, the hero of the affair with the savages in V, 30 ff., and the discoverer of the nymphs in IX, 69.

42.   8. This story may have some faint historic foundation. But it looks as if it had been much improved from the standpoint of Portugal. Lencastre quotes from a chivalrous romance, Memorial das Proezas de Segunda Tavola Redonda by Jorge Ferreira de Vasconselos (printed 1567), which tells of thirteen Portuguese in the reign of John I, who fought for the ladies of the Duke of Lancaster in England. It may be mentioned that Chaucer, when Clerk of the Works, erected the scaffolds for two such tournaments. Lencastre quotes a list of the heroes from Faria y Sousa.

1. Antão Vaz (or Vasques) de Almada, commander of the left wing at Aljubarrota, for whom Ford substitutes Rui Mendes Cerveira.

2. Alvaro Vaz de Almada, later Count of Avranches, nephew of the former, and confused with Antão by Camões.

3. Lopo Fernandes Pacheco.

4. João Fernandes Pacheco.

5. Pedro Homem da Costa.

6. João Pereira Agostinho, son of Gil Vaz da Cunha, lord of Basto, and nephew of Nuno Álvares Pereira "the holy Constable."

7. Luis Goncalves Malafaia.

8. Alvaro Mendes Cerveira.

9. Rui Gomes da Silva.

10. Soeiro da Costa.

11. Martim Lopes da Azevedo.

12. Alvaro Gonçalves Coutinho (Magriço, "the lanky one"), brother of the Count of Marialva.

Ford quotes Bruno (Rev. litt. sc. e artistica do Seculo, No. 195, June 3, 1906), as follows: "The battle in the lists of the Twelve of England is a simple and imaginative Portuguese adaptation of the historical reality of the jousts of Richard of England carried out in association with his uncle, the Duke of Lancaster."

43.   1. John I (1357–1433), the victor of Aljubarrota.

5. Erinys, a Fury who drives the guilty mad.

46.   8. John of Gaunt, father-in-law of John I of Portugal.

47.   7. Philippa, daughter of John of Gaunt.

52.   3. The Eternal Name of Portugal is probably derived from Portus Cale, a small harbor town at the mouth of the Douro, now part of Oporto.

53.   7. Magriço (the lanky, according to Professor Ford), the nickname of Alvaro Gonçalves Coutinho, who was the son of the Marshal of Portugal.

55.   1. Burton notes the Horatian echo (Epistles, I, xvi, 79), Mors ultima linea rerum est.

60.   5. Bactros, the river that gave its name to Bactria, a country at the eastern end of nowhere for classic writers, but actually in Northern Afghanistan.

61.   1. It is a pity that Virgil's horses champ so many bits, for Camões is in duty bound to follow suit (Aeneid, IV, 135). Claudian's horses champ with the same monotony (De Quarto Consulatu Honorii, 549–550).

    5–8. This account of the crowd's protest is not without interest. It must be one of the earliest statements by an outsider to the effect that the English like fair play.

63.   3. Helle's beast was the golden ram. This is a long way of saying that the lady put on a dress of cloth of gold (Ford).

64.   Though no connection seems possible, it may be observed that this passage reminds one of the tournament in Chaucer's The Knight's Tale. But there is no consonance in the sequel, for in Stanza 66 Camões is at some pains to deprecate the elaboration of such narratives. Tastes had altered in two hundred years.

66.   Camões really should have known better than to try to write Ariosto down.

68.   4. According to Burton, Magriço defended the Countess of Flanders in an ordeal by battle and killed the French representative. But he notes Musgrave's chronological objections. Evidently the matter is not cleared up yet.

    8. Torquatus and Corvinus, ancient Romans who slew Gauls in single combat.

69.   1. Álvaro Vaz de Almada, who agreed to fight a German, the condition being that neither champion should wear armor on his right side. The German was left-handed. Perceiving this, Almada dropped his sword, grappled the man, and crushed him to death (Burton). This is the Almada who actually was Count of Avranches. He is not the commander of the left wing at Aljubarrota.

70 ff. It is perhaps a pity that Camões, the first great poet to write about a typhoon, did not rely more on his actual experience in his description. He himself had been in at least two such storms, off Good

Hope (Elegy III) and at the mouth of the Mekong (X, 128). But, although there are details which are drawn from what he had himself seen, the whole episode is based on Ovid (Met., XI, 475–543) with Virgilian variations.

72.   7. It was the duty of landlubber soldiers to man the pumps.

76.   1–4. Virgil's hand seems evident here (Aeneid, I, 106–108).

5. As noted before, Aquilo and Boreas are northerly winds. Auster and Notus are stormy south winds.

6. The world machine. A similar cliché appears in Elegy III (Juromenha, III, 174).

77.   1. Alcyone, daughter of Eolus, threw herself into the sea when her husband Ceyx was drowned. They were both changed into king-fishers. They were believed to build floating nests, and their nesting time brought calm weather. They perished in the Ovidian storm which Camões is imitating. See Stanza 70, note.

78.   3. Vulcan, who made the arms of Aeneas, the son of his wife Venus by Anchises (Aeneid, VIII, 608 ff.).

4. Deucalion and Pyrrha, Greek pendants of the Biblical Noah and his wife. After the flood they obeyed the oracle which ordered them to throw behind them the bones of their grandmother. They reasoned that this must mean stones. Deucalion's stones were trans-formed into men, Pyrrha's into women, and thus Earth was repopu-lated (Georgics, I, 61–63).

82.   3. Syrtes, sandbanks on the south shore of the Mediterranean—one near Tunis, one in the Gulf of Sidra. Strabo (XVII, iii, 17) goes into the subject.

4. Acroceraunian infamy, Acroceraunium, the Cape of Light-nings, on the Coast of Epirus. Camões is remembering Horace's "Infames scopulos, Acroceraunia" (Odes, I, iii), which is certainly more to the point than Lucan (De Bello Civili, II, 625–627) cited by Burton.

83.   1–4. Camões had fought in Mauretania, had lost an eye there, and did not like it at all, which lends some personal point to Vasco da Gama's pious ejaculation. The rhetorical pattern is evidently Homeric, whether Camões knew it or not (Odyssey, V, 305–307): "How blessed those Danaans, etc."

84.   7. The image of the earth shaken from her axle may be found in Elegy XXIX, Juromenha, II, 258. If this elegy is by Camões, it must be one of his earliest compositions.

85.   1. The amorous planet is of course Venus. The phrase is in Petrarch's Triumphs and, naturally, in the Portuguese translation, by some believed to be by Camões (Juromenha, V, 51). But the expression is ultimately Homeric (Iliad, XXIII, 226–228).

6. Orion is setting as Venus rises. Lucan (De Bello Civili, I, 665) calls Orion "the sword-bearer."

86.   1–4. This is imitated from the description of Neptune's discovery of Juno's proceedings against the fleet of Aeneas (Aeneid, I, 129–130).

88.   7. Boreas carried off Orithyia, daughter of Erectheus, sixth of the mythical kings of Athens (Ovid, Met., VI, 681–721).

90.   1. Galatea's amour with Notus the south wind appears to be Camões' own invention.

92.   2. The Ganges was at least a thousand miles from Gama's landfall.

4. The rising ground is, according to Damião de Goes (I, 149), Mount Delli near Cananor. De Goes is perhaps following Gaspar Correa. See Stanley, The Three Voyages of Vasco da Gama, p. 145. But the line of the Western Ghats lay before, and there is perhaps a choice of peaks.

99.   1–4. Perhaps these lines are a reminiscent of Statius (Thebais, II, 131–132). But the thought is a commonplace. Lucretius at the beginning of Book II has some remarks about true wisdom as she contemplates the futility of mankind. And it was impossible for Claudian (De Consulatu Flavii Mallii Theodori, Panegyris, opening lines) to miss a trick like that.

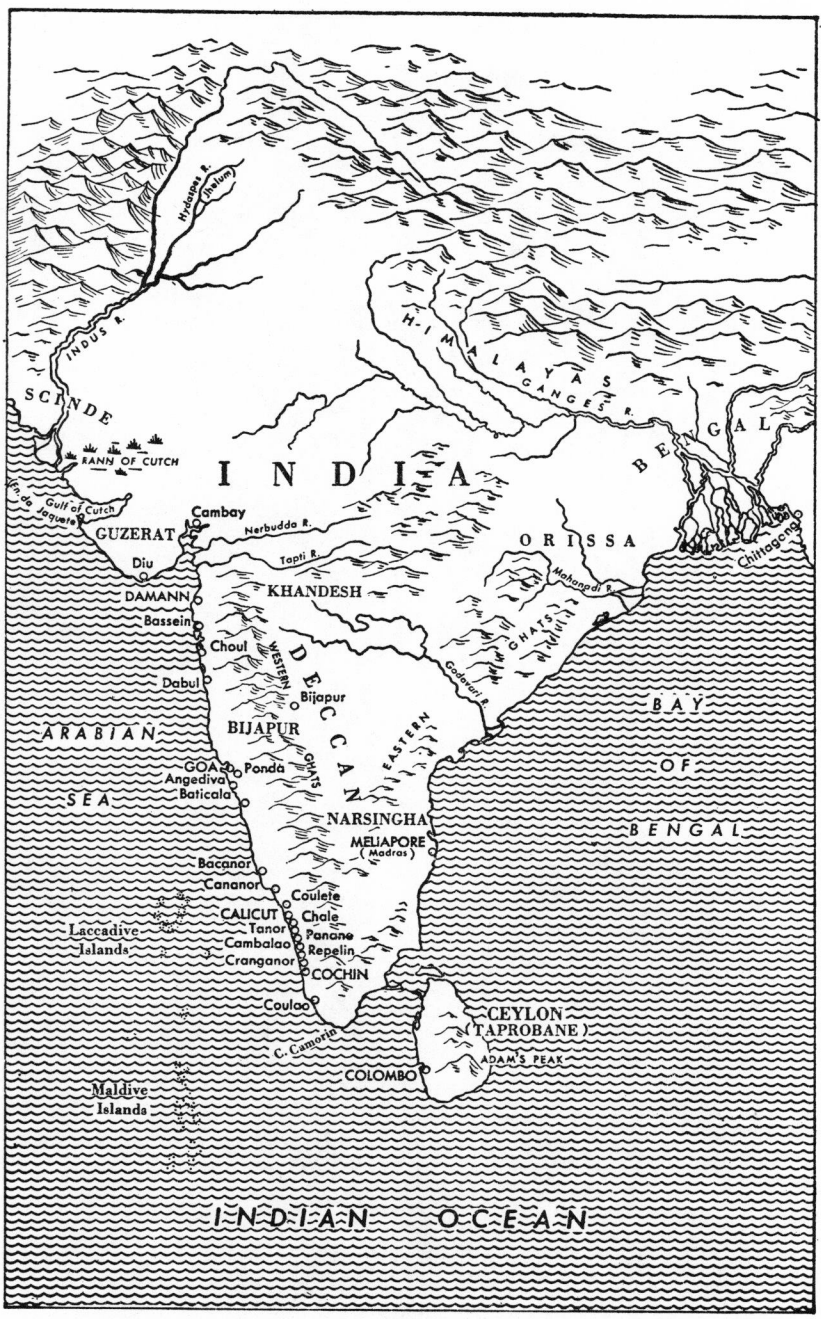

BOOK VII

ARGUMENT

This famous discovery of India is occasion for a notable and poetic exhortation to the Princes of Christendom, exciting them to undertake similar enterprises. Description of the Kingdom of Malabar, in which lies the realm of Calicut, the port where the fleet anchors. The Emperor, or Zamorin, receives Gama honorably. The Moor Monçaide appears and gives Gama information, at the same time informing the natives. The Catual, or Governor of Calicut, goes out to see the fleet.

THE LUSIADS

THE SEVENTH BOOK

ALREADY they were come hard by that ground,
So long and by so many much desired,
Which by the Indus stream is girded round
And Ganges in his earthly Heaven retired.
Up! Up! Strong race! To seize the palms renowned
For triumph, still in war you have aspired.
You are arrived and have the land before,
Which with abundance of all wealth flows o'er.

2

I say to you, O Lusian generation,
Yours in this world is but a little place,
Not in this world, but in His congregation.
Whose rule doth the round firmament embrace;
You, in whom risk quelled not determination
Wholly to subjugate a loathesome race,
Or greed, or an allegiance incomplete
To Her Whose Essence hath in Heaven Her seat;

3

You Portuguese, so strong, though you are few,
Who your weak powers never stop to weigh,
Who, though you pay the price of death, ensue
The law of life that shall endure for aye,
Such was the die which Heaven cast for you,
That, be your numbers little as they may,
For Christendom you act a mighty part.
So dost Thou, Christ, exalt the meek in heart!

VII   Look on the proud herd of the Germans there,
Who in their vast plains find their nourishment,
And, in rebellion against Peter's heir,
Seek a new shepherd, a new sect invent.
Look on the hideous wars to which they fare
(For with blind error they are not content),
Not against the Ottoman full up of pride,
But the Pope's sovereign power to set aside.

5

See the hard Englishman, who King by right
Of the divine old city claims to be,
Which town is ruled by the vile Ishmaelite.
How far vain honor is from verity!
Amid his northern snows he seeks delight
And Christian in a novel sense is he,
Against Christ's men drawing the naked brand.
But not for the reconquest of Christ's land.

6

A king unrightful has to him the sway
Of this Jerusalem on earth denied,
The while the English King will not obey
Law sacred of Jerusalem enskied.
And now of thee, vile Gaul, what shall I say,
Who as "Most Christian" would be magnified,
Not to defend the Faith, or to protect,
But wholly to abhor it and reject?

7

Your claim to Christian lordships you have laid,
Though you have huge possessions of your own,
But Nile and Cinyphus have not withstayed,
Of the ancient Holy name the foemen known
So men must prove the edges of the blade
On him who balks at Peter's corner-stone.
Charles! Louis! Are you their inheritor?
Their lands, their names, yet no just cause for war?

8

And what of them, who, in their luxury,
Which with vile ease must still as comrade go,
Waste all their lives, heap wealth continually,
Nor ancient courage any longer know?
Tyranny has begotten enmity,
Which makes a strong folk its own proper foe.
Italy! I speak to you, now drowning quite
In countless crimes done in your own despite.

9

Unhappy Christians, are you, as it were,
The teeth Cadméan, who are sown like seed,
While each becomes his brother's murderer,
Though of a single womb you are the breed?
Do you not see the Holy Sepulchre
Governed by hounds, who, being well agreed,
Still come to take your ancient lands outright,
Thus earning excellent repute in fight?

10

You see how they by custom and decree,
Which they observe with all their faith entire,
Gather their hosts stirring uneasily
Against the folk who their dear Christ desire.
But fell Alecto will not let you be,
Sowing among you seeds of quarrels dire.
See if secure from danger you repose,
For they, and you yourselves, are now your foes.

11

And if the passion for a great domain
Urges you forth to conquer alien lands,
Have you not looked upon the rivers twain,
Pactolus, Hermus, rolling golden sands?
Africa yet conceals the shining vein.
Assyria, Lydia, weave the aureate strands.
Such riches may perhaps your spirits spur,
Whose hearts the Holy Temple cannot stir.

VII   Of those inventions terrible and new,
The mortal enginery of ordinance,
We now should make our trial stern and true
Against the walls of Turkey and Byzance.
To woodland caves drive back the Turkish crew,
To Caspian heights, to Scythia's cold expanse.
Their progeny are waxing and grow great
Upon your wealthy Europe's pomp and state.

13

Armenia and Georgia, Greece and Thrace,
Are calling to you, for a bestial folk
Compels their dearest children to embrace
The Koran's vileness, to hard tribute broke.
Glory in this: At acts that shame the race,
Bravely and wisely, strike the avenging stroke!
Nor, proud ones, for great honors clamor longer,
Because against your friends you proved the stronger,

14

But while you are so blind and thirst so hot
For life-blood of your brothers, men insane,
Adventurous Christian courage falters not
Within our Lusitania's small domain.
Africa's ports have fallen to her lot;
In Asia more than sovereign is her reign;
In the world's new fourth part she plows the field
And there will go, where more shall be revealed.

15

Now for the moment let our glance be bent
On those great sailors' fortunes once again,
After sweet Venus calmed the impotent
Opposing fury of the hurricane,
And when to them appeared the continent,
The end of all their constant strife and pain,
Whither they came Christ's law like seed to strew,
And, with a new King, brought their customs new.

Scarce on the coast of the strange land were they   **VII**
When the light barks of fishers they beheld,
Who thereupon before them led the way
To Calicut, the city where they dwelled.
And to the place the ships their courses lay,
Because it was the city that excelled
The best in Malabar, where the King reigned,
Who chief dominion in the land maintained.

17

Beyond the Indus, on Ganges' hither side,
Lies an enormous region, much renowned,
Bordered upon the south by Ocean's tide,
Caverned Emodius its northern bound.
There various kings impose diversified
Shapes of strange faith. Some worship vile Mahound,
And some, adoring, to their idols cleave.
Others, in beasts that dwell with them, believe.

18

And in the ranges huge that cut in twain
This vast land and across all Asia lie,
Which have as various appellations ta'en
As different nations choose to call them by,
The springs are found from which the rivers drain,
Whose large floods in the Indian Ocean die,
And, circling round the cantle and the piece
Of the terra firma, form the Chersonese.

19

Between the courses where the rivers stray,
A long cape thrusts afar from the main shore,
Wedge-shaped, in the sea's bosom, and alway
Looks on the island of Ceylon before.
And near huge Ganges' springs, they used to say,
In keeping with old legendary lore,
That people in the neighboring regions dwelling
Lived upon odors of the flowers sweet-smelling.

VII   But in customs, as in names, the populace
Of new sort and most various now is found;
It is the Delis and the Pathan race,
In numbers, as in lands, that most abound,
Deccanis, Orias, they who look for grace
Where waters of the Ganges stream resound.
There also is the country of Bengal,
So fertile that it quite outranks them all.

21

There is Cambaya's kingdom tried in fight,
They say the strong King Porus held of old,
And there Narsingha's realm that founds her might
Not on brave men but on her gems and gold.
And from the heaving sea the vasty height
Of a very lengthy range one may behold.
For Malabar these hills are bulwark sure,
Whereby from Canará they live secure.

22

They are called Ghats by natives of the land,
And at their feet there lies, though it be strait,
Like a fringe along the coast, a stretch of strand,
Which strives against the ocean's native hate.
And here, 'mid others, no one may withstand
That Calicut enjoys such princely state
As may a fair, rich capital behove,
And Zamorin they call the lord thereof.

23

Scarce did the fleet that lordly coast attain
When a Portuguese went forth ambassador,
Unto the heathen monarch to make plain
Their new arrival on so far a shore.
And up a river, where it met the main,
The envoy went. The novel garb he wore,
His foreign look and color and strange air,
Brought all the people hurrying to stare.

Among the folk who thronged that sight to see,   **VII**
There came a follower of Mahomet's law,
Who had been born in the land of Barbary
Where once Antaeus had been held in awe.
Either he learned from such propinquity
Or from our steel might clearer knowledge draw,
But Portugal he knew at all events,
Though fate had banished him this long way thence.

25

When he saw the envoy, then with gracious cheer,
As one who well could Spanish speech construe,
He asked him: "And what was it brought you here
From Portugal to worlds so far from you?"
He answered: "We came forth the road to clear
Through the Great Deep that no man ever knew,
And find where Indus' giant stream may flow,
For thus the Faith of God will wax and grow."

26

The Moor (Monçaide called) with wonderment
Was stricken, for the voyage was so great.
He harked what woes at sea they underwent
And all the Lusitanian might narrate.
But, seeing that the message's intent
Only to the country's ruler could relate,
He told the Portuguese that the King lay
Outside the city but a little way.

27

And till the King this advent strange should know,
The Moor would well the Portuguese entreat
To rest in his own house, though it were low,
The victual of the country there to eat.
And after resting, he himself would go,
Together with the envoy, to the fleet,
For nothing is more pleasing to the mind
Than in a strange land neighbor folk to find.

VII The Portuguese well to accept was fain
The blithe Moor's offer, and with good will too.
As if old friendship were between the twain,
He ate and drank and did as bid to do.
Then from the city they went forth again
Unto such ships as well Monçaide knew.
They climbed aboard the flagship. All men there
Gave to the visitor a welcome fair.

29
The Chief embraced him, for his joy was great
When he heard him speak clear language of Castile.
He set him near, and, eager yet sedate,
Begged him the country's nature to reveal.
As trees in Rhodope might congregate
When the lover of Eurydice made peal
The lyre of gold, if only they might hear,
So, but to hark the Moor, the crew drew near.

30
He spake: "All you, whom Nature has created
Near neighbors where my father's dwelling lay,
What challenge, what large destiny, has fated
That such a perilous road you should essay?
Not without cause, dark and uncontemplated,
You left hid Minho, Tagus faraway,
Sailing, where no other bark has plowed the seas,
To regions as remote and lone as these.

31
"God brought you certainly, Who must intend
That you his cause should forward and maintain.
And therefore doth he guide you and defend
Against the foe, the sea, the hurricane.
You are in India, where afar extend
All sorts of peoples, who great profit gain
From shining gold, from gems of richest price,
From odorous perfume, and from burning spice.

"The province, in whose port you came ashore   **VII**
This short while since, as Malabar is known.
Idols of an old cult, the folk adore,
And round about this faith is widely sown.
Many kings rule, though one in times before
Reigned sole, or so the ancient legends own.
Under his hand Sarama Perimal
Held last the united rule imperial.

33

"However, when there came into the land
Men from beyond the Gulf of Araby,
Who brought Mahomet's precept and command,
In which belief my parents nourished me,
Then, it befell, the wise and eloquent band
By prayer converted Perimal, and he
Forthwith turned Moslem, with belief so high
That in the faith he chose, a saint, to die.

34

"Ships he prepared, wherein he stowed with care
His offerings of richest merchandise,
That he might sail to take religion where
The prophet who first preached the doctrine lies.
But ere he left, because he had no heir,
The kingdom to his men he let devise,
And dealt so with the worthiest, indeed,
That the poor were wealthy and the subject freed.

35

"Cochin to one, to another Cananor,
Chalè to one, Pimenta's isle to one,
This man, Coulão, that other, Cranganor,
And most to him who had best service done.
But one young man to whom much love he bore
Came after all was given, whereupon
The gift of Calicut to him he made,
A noble town, grown wealthy by its trade.

257

VII   "To him he gave the town and high estate
Of Emperor who over all holds sway.
And this done, thither he departed straight,
Where as a saint he might live out his day.
Hence the high Zamorin's style sublime and great,
Prouder than all, unto this very day
Remains unto that youth and to his heirs,
Of whom is he, the sovranty that bears.

37

"The faith of all, though rich or poor they be,
Is made of myth, so fancy must decide.
Naked they go, save that in some degree
They hide with clouts what nature bids us hide.
Two sorts there are. For the nobility
Are called the Nairs, and those less dignified,
The Poleas, and their law forbids these last
Ever to marry with the ancient caste.

38

"And those who always the same crafts pursue
With those outside their guild can never wed,
Nor will the sons consent a task to do
Unlike their sires' until themselves are dead.
The Nairs as horrible debasement view
A Polea's very touch, and be it said
That, if such touch unto a Nair betide,
With many rites he must be purified.

39

"The ancient Jewish stock in the same way
Would touch no person of Samaria's race,
But matters even stranger than I say
You'll note in various customs of the place.
The Nairs alone in perils of the fray
Engage and for their King a foe will face,
In the left hand still bearing in the fight
The buckler, and the good sword in the right.

"The Brahmins are their priests, which would appear   VII
An ancient title of peculiar fame.
And in his famous rule they persevere,
Who, first of men, to science gave a name.
They slay no living thing, such is their fear
Of all flesh, and they quite eschew the same.
And only in the sexes' intercourse
They claim more licence and less rule enforce.

41

"Women are held in common, but they are
In this restricted to the husband's kin.
Happy that race, under a kindly star,
Who feel no pang of jealousy within.
Such practices, the men of Malabar,
Like others odder yet, esteem no sin.
And the land fattens on all trade the while,
Which the seas fetch from China to the Nile."

42

Thus spake the Moor. But now, on every hand,
Tales of the coming of a stranger race
Ran through the town, till the King gave command
That he might know the substance of the case,
While, thronging, either sex, all ages, stand
Around the princes, down the streets who pace,
And who at the King's bidding go to meet
The Captain who commands the new-come fleet.

43

He, who already had the King's consent
To disembark, with many a noble knight
Of Portugal, did not delay but went,
In his rich robes adornèd. And the bright
Contrasting colors filled with high content
The people, all enchanted at the sight.
The oar-blades, beating their due measure, thresh
First the cold sea, then river water fresh.

VII On the beach stood an officer of state,
Whom in their language Catual they call.
He, 'mid his Nairs, high Gama doth await,
With pomp of unfamiliar festival.
And Gama in his arms he lifted straight,
And a rich cushioned palanquin withal
He gave the Captain ('tis their custom tried)
For thence, upon men's shoulders, he must ride.

45

The Portuguese, with him of Malabar,
Thus, where the King was waiting, would repair.
His men march in formation regular
Of a foot squadron, with defiant air.
In wild confusion all the people are,
Who throng to look upon the strangers there,
And fain would question. But, in time long fled,
At Babel's tower this was prohibited.

46

Gama and the Catual, while on they went,
Spake of things, as occasion might provide.
Monçaide then translated their intent,
Who understood the speech on either side.
They cross the town. A pile magnificent
Towers up before them in its sumptuous pride,
A temple, namely. So those gates they gain,
And through the portal entered in the twain.

47

Images of gods were all about the place,
Sculptured in frozen stone or else in wood,
Various of hue and various of face,
As the demonic fancy found it good.
Those statues were abominations base,
Chimera limbs in divers fashions hewed.
And Christians, used to see their God portrayed
In human form, were baffled and dismayed.

48

One has upon his head horns carven fair;   VII
Ammonian Jove in Libya seemed e'en so.
Or a single body many a face may wear,
As once they painted Janus long ago.
Another shape such myriad arms doth bear
As if he would like to Briareus show.
Another a dog's countenance displays,
Such as brought Memphian Anubis praise.

49

After the heathen barbarous had prayed
Unto his gods in superstitious strain,
Then, without other turn, their way they made
Where was the King of all those pagans vain.
Small knots of people swelled to a parade,
Who the strange admiral to behold were fain.
At windows and on housetops all along,
Old men and boys and maids and matrons throng.

50

Now they draw near, but at no easy pace,
To the fair gardens filled with scent of flowers,
Where hidden lies the royal dwelling-place,
Sumptuous, although it has no lofty towers.
There stands his palace in its stately grace,
The which the wood delightfully embowers.
It likes the rulers of that people well,
In the country and the town at once to dwell.

51

Upon the gates of the encircling wall
Was subtle art of Daedalus to see,
That showed in images majestical
India's most faraway antiquity.
And tales of old time immemorial
Were sculptured on the walls so vividly
That he who looked on them and took good heed
Could truth essential from the shadow read.

VII There a great host trampled the Orient land
O'er which the waters of Hydaspes pour.
The brow of him who governed them was bland,
And with the leafy thyrsus he waged war.
Nysa had been erected by his hand
There where the river watered the low shore.
Were Semele near, so well the work was done,
For certain, she had said it was her son.

53

And further on, drinking a river dry,
Appeared the vast Assyrian multitude,
Subjected to that woman's sovranty,
Who was as beautiful as she was lewd.
And the great rutting stallion stood hard by
Her burning flank, with whom in contest shrewd
Her own son must the rivalry endure,
Brute lust and love unspeakably impure.

54

And further on, whipping in air, there flew
The Grecian gonfalons whose fame waxed great.
The third of monarchies, India they o'erthrew,
To where the streams of Ganges undulate.
A youthful captain they submitted to,
By palms surrounded in triumphant state,
Who Philip's son no longer claimed to be,
But bragged he was Jove's rightful progeny.

55

While at these records gazed the Portuguese,
The Catual to the Captain put the case:
"Time comes when triumphs far surpassing these,
Which you behold, such victories will abase.
And here they will inscribe new histories
For aftercomers of a stranger race.
Thus did out wisest mages testify,
When they stared deep into futurity.

56

"Their magic science told them even more,
That to resist such overwhelming might
Poor man's resistance could not pay the score.
Against the Skies avails no human sleight.
'So great,' they said, 'the strangers' skill in war,
Who shall be apt in peace and apt in fight,
That the victor shall throughout the world be known
For glory that was of the overthrown."

57

Conversing thus, a room they entered there,
Wherein that powerful emperor reclined
Upon a couch, which was past all compare
Whether for cost or workmanship refined.
Good fortune and great majesty, his air,
As he lay at ease, suggested to the mind.
He wore a robe woven of golden thread,
And many a precious jewel crowned his head.

58

An old man reverent, at his sovereign's side,
Kneeled and, whene'er he found occasion good,
The green leaf of the burning herb supplied,
Which, as his custom was, the monarch chewed.
A Brahmin eminently dignified
To Gama came with grave solicitude,
That he might lead him the high Prince to greet,
Who signed to him to take hard by his seat.

59

Gama being seated that rich couch a-near,
His troop more distant, then, intent and keen,
The Zamorin studied the guise and gear
Of men whose like he never yet had seen.
From his wise breast, in a grave voice severe,
Which lent compelling grandeur to his mien
In the King's sight and also 'mid the folk,
The Admiral after this manner spoke:

VII   "A mighty King, beyond the regions where
The circling sky, in its perpetual round,
With earth itself conceals the solar glare
From parts it leaves darkling in gloom profound,
Has heard the rumor that resoundeth there,
Echoing thou art the ruler most renowned
In India, and the most in majesty,
And would in friendship bind himself with thee.

61

"By far-flung ways he sent us with command
To let thee know whatever riches ply
Across the ocean, and from every land
That beyond Tagus to the Nile may lie,
And all the way from Zealand's freezing strand
To where the sun in Ethopia's sky
Changes the quality of day no more,
All these his realm has in abundant store.

62

"And if thou wilt with treaty and with pact
Of peace and friendship, open and divine,
Trade out of superfluity enact
Between his country's merchandise and thine,
Thus greater gain and plenty to attract
(For which in toil and sweat men chiefly pine);
Unto thy realms, then there will surely be
For him great glory, and great wealth for thee.

63

"And that the knot of friendship 'twixt you tied
May with the greater permanence remain,
He will stand instantly upon thy side,
Should war's adversity afflict thy reign,
With ships and men and weapons, fortified,
And for brother he will know thee and maintain.
And on the point speak out thy whole desire,
But give an answer certain and entire."

Such message did our Chief deliver o'er,   **VII**
To whom the heathen ruler made reply
That to see envoys from so far a shore
Could only his own honor magnify.
But in such case behoved him all the more
With his advisers to take counsel high,
So that a clear inquiry they might make
As to King, race, and realm of which he spake.

65

Now let him rest after laborious days,
But the King himself would in brief space prepare
His resolution, couched in justest phrase,
That to his Lord fair answer he might bear.
Then came the night, her barrier to raise,
As is her wont, against man's weary care,
Who would heal worn-out limbs with soft repose,
And eyes delivered unto quiet close.

66

Gama and all his Lusitanian corps
Thither, where they found ready welcome, went,
At the house of the great Indian governor,
With festival and general content.
The Catual felt a duty to explore,
In the service of his sovereign, diligent,
Out of what region this strange people came,
What laws, what lands, what customs they might
67   [claim.
When he saw the fiery chariot of the fair
Young Delian who creates the light anew,
Monçaide eagerly he summoned there,
To get of the newcomers tidings true,
And, keen and curious, urged him to declare
If he had knowledge, and well proven too,
About these strangers, for it had reached his ear,
Their country and the Moor's were neighbors near.

VII   And in particular he was to show
Such matters forth at large, for so he might
Do the King service good, who thus might know
What in the present business would be right.
Monçaide answered: "Though my will be so
To tell thee more, more I cannot recite.
I know they come from the far side of Spain,
Where is my home, and the sun sets in the main.

69

"They keep a Prophet's law, whose Mother bore
No carnal blemish when she gave Him birth,
God's very soul, according to their lore,
Who holds the government of all the Earth.
And rumor ran among my sires of yore
That these men proved their sanguinary worth,
When they used the weapons in their hand that gleamed,
Which clear enough to my forefathers seemed.

70

"For with a superhuman spirit bold
They flung us forth from all the fertile leas
By Tagus rich and Guadiana cold,
Whose famous acts wake mighty memories.
And not content, to Africa they hold
The course, and plow across the windy seas.
Nor will they let us live in peace at all,
But storm the city and the towering wall.

71

"No less of soldier skill and courage main
In other wars they hap on, they display,
Whether against the gallant men of Spain,
Or who came down the Pyrenéan way.
So never yet, to spear of outland strain,
Have they acknowledged that they lost the fray.
And this I swear: No memory recalls
Any Marcellus for such Hannibals.

"And if my story less sufficient be VII
Than you desire, from their own lips, do you
Inform yourself. For they love honesty,
And naught offends them like a thing untrue.
Their fleet and weapons likewise go to see,
Their well-cast metal that can all subdue.
For it may give you pleasure to con o'er
The ways of Portugal in peace and war."

With passion now the heathen was on fire,
To see the things described in the Moor's tale.
He bade launch boats, so great was his desire
To gaze at ships that Gama wont to sail.
They left the beach. After them the entire
Nair nation choked the waters on their trail.
They came aboard the flagship high and fair,
And Paul da Gama made them welcome there.

Awnings and flags were all of purple hue,
Sewn with rich thread which the poor worm has spun,
Whereon were painted deeds of derring-do,
That the strong hand in time gone by had done.
Pitched battles desperate were there to view,
High challenge. Grim those pictures, every one,
Which when the heathen first beheld, straightway
He feasted well his eyes on the display.

He asked about that sight, but Gama prayed
That first he would be seated there and try
Those pleasures of which such account is made
By those who dwell in Epicurus' sty.
Out of the beakers flowed in a cascade
Liquor that Noah gave humanity.
But such a feast the heathen must reject,
As counter to the teaching of his sect.

VII   The trumpet, which in peace is to the mind
Symbol of battle, now the welkin tore.
Flaming, that engine by the Fiend designed
Compelled the ocean depths to hark the roar.
The heathen noted all, though more inclined
To dwell on deeds that such high aspect wore,
Done by these men, which, rapidly conveyed,
Painting in silent poetry portrayed.

77

He rose, and with him Gama rose as well,
And on their side Coelho and the Moor.
His glance on a white, noble ancient fell,
Depicted in a warlike portraiture,
Whose name undying in the world shall dwell
While human intercourse shall still endure.
Dressed in the true Greek manner did he stand,
A branch for ensign held in his right hand.

78

He held a branch in hand—But I, O blind!
Who thus launch forth, a madman desperate,
Mondego's nymphs and Tagus' left behind,
On paths so various and rough and great.
Nymphs, I invoke your grace, for I must find
My course through high seas where such gales frustrate
That, if you help me not, my fear is strong,
My fragile cockboat will go down ere long.

79

Lo! What long years since fate first made me sing
Songs of your Tagus and your Portuguese,
The fate that still has kept me wandering,
Seeing new labors and new pains increase,
Now seaward gone, now suffering everything
'Mid perilous battle's inhumanities.
Like Canacé, resolved herself to kill,
One hand still holds the sword and one the quill.

Now by abhorrent proverty bestead,   **VII**
By others' charity degraded quite,
And now from hope that just had raised the head,
Cast down anew, and in yet sorrier plight;
Now snatching back bare life, that on a thread
Must needs depend, so delicate and slight,
Miracle 'twas not less to 'scape alive
Than for the King of Israel to thrive.

81

And yet, my nymphs, it does not yet suffice
That such vast miseries should gird me round,
But they will not pay my poetry the price,
Whose glory on my way I made resound.
Instead of rest to which my hopes entice,
Or the head with honorable laurel crowned,
Labors undreamed did they devise for me,
And cast me down into this agony.

82

Look, nymphs, upon the great and splendid lords,
Your Tagus breeds, with wit in overplus.
Too well they know how to prepare rewards
For him whose poem made them glorious.
To future poets, example this affords,
Whose rising genius shall be quickened thus,
Who would those things in memory renew,
Of which eternal honor is the due.

83

And though so many evils overbore,
Your favor may I have, if yours alone,
And with more cause, for now I stand before
Ventures diverse, whose glory must be shown.
Give but yourselves. A solemn oath I swore
Never to use you but for merit known,
Nor to one, however great, will flatterer play,
For so ingratitude were my just pay.

269

VII   Nor think me, nymphs, his fame's promotioner,
Who, before good of Country and of King,
His own advantage ever will prefer,
And still God's law and Man's to naught will bring.
Nor for the proud, who would administer
The mightiest enterprises, will I sing,
Who for this seeks power only, that he may
With wicked acts give his vice freer play;

85

Nor who, having authority so great,
Employs it but to serve his passion base,
And, the foolish vulgar to propitiate,
More than did ever Proteus, changes face.
Nor, Muses, think that I will celebrate
One I have seen, though he seem full of grace
To please the King, who once in the new job
The unhappy people still will strip and rob;

86

Nor one who finds that it is right and fair
The King's law harshly to enforce alway,
But never sees a just cause anywhere
The wretched people for their sweat to pay;
Nor one who, though his thought be thin and bare,
Seeks reasons, thinking the wise man to play,
And mulcts, with hands to meanness well inured,
The toils of others, which he ne'er endured.

87

Those only who sweet life adventured free
For God and for their King, will I proclaim,
Who, losing life, gave it eternity
Of honor by deeds worthy of such fame.
Phoebus and the Muses in my company
Will double power, who granted me the flame,
While I draw breath and for a little rest,
Ere to my task I turn with greater zest.

NOTES

BOOK VII

1.   4. The Ganges was supposed to rise in the Earthly Paradise.

4.   As Burton notices, the Lusiads was being composed in the very heat of the Reformation. With the possible exception of Damião de Goes and Gil Vicente, that motion of the mind seems to have had few important sympathizers in Portugal.

5.   1. "The hard Englishman" may afford us a slight clue as to the date when this particular passage was written. Henry VIII is represented as still functioning. It would have been absurd to allude to Edward VI as a hard Englishman, still more so to speak of Mary or Elizabeth in such terms. It would seem then that the stanza was written before 1547 when Henry died. If so, Camões wrote these verses when he was twenty-three at latest.

The claim of the English kings to Jerusalem, according to Lencastre, derives from Richard I. Burton notices an allusion to Henry VIII in Ariosto (O. F., XXVI, 35). Ariosto also takes Henry VIII for a ride in O. F., XXXIII, 54.

Professor Ford thinks there is no evidence in favor of Camões' notion that Henry VIII took the style of King Jerusalem.

5. The same reasoning which applies to Henry VIII applies to the vile Gaul, Francis I, who also died in 1547.

Burton notes the curious fact that the first quatrain of this octave became a piece of prophecy for the Sebastianists. See Camões and the History of Portugal.

7.   3. Cinyphus, now a wadi in Tripolitania but symbolic of Moorish power.

7. Charles, Charlemagne. Louis, Louis IX, otherwise St. Louis (Ford).

9.   2. Cadmus, like Jason, sowed the dragon's teeth, which sprang up as armed men and killed each other, except for five survivors who helped him build Boeotian Thebes.

10.   5. Alecto, one of the Furies.

11.   Pactolus and Hermus, two rivers in Lydia, famous for gold-bearing sands. See Herodotus, History V, 101. Burton notes that they were no longer productive in Strabo's time, i.e., the first years of our era.

12.   1–4. Burton's omniscient note on the invention of artillery must be seen to be appreciated, but it's not dull.

13.   1–4. This is an allusion to the Turkish custom of forcibly enlisting Christian children into the Corps of Janizaries.

14.   8. Lencastre (unquestionably quoting Faria y Sousa, as pointed out by Mr. E. Glaser) notes that the first European to see the shores of Australia was the Portuguese Pedro Fernandes de Queiroz in 1606, twenty-six years after the death of Camões. The line is accordingly one of those successful flights of prophecy, which poets occasionally make.

16.   1. The landfall, according to Lencastre, May 24, 1498.

17.   4. Emodius, the Himalayas.

The description of India which begins in this stanza is a salmagundi of ingredients from Pomponius Mela (I, 15), Strabo (XI, viii, 1), Pliny (V, 27), and Barros (I, iv, 7), who himself is clearly relying on Ptolemy.

19.   5–8. Burton notes that this legend is found in Pliny (VII, 2). Strabo (XV, i, 57) has a practically identical account of these odd creatures. They had no mouths, according to Pliny (VII, 2) and Strabo (XV, i, 57), both of whom independently, are copying Megasthenes, who pretends he saw them in the camp of Sandracottus. Camões mentions them in his Carta a huma Dama (Juromenha, IV, 19), where he says that, if these persons could live on odors, he can live on the mere sight of the lady in question. The mouthless men have been accounted for. They were a vegetarian Hindu sect, who covered the mouth with a veil so as not to breathe in, and so kill, gnats, etc. India is familiar with similar customs to this day.

20.   3. Delis, supposed to be inhabitants of the Punjab (Lencastre).

Pathans, Afghans, of whom there are many colonies in India proper.

5. Deccanis, inhabitants of the Deccan, roughly the huge triangle of India, south of the Nerbudda.

Orias, presumably inhabitants of the province of Orissa, not far from Calcutta and the delta of the Ganges.

21.   1. Cambaya, on the western coast, at least 1000 miles from Bengal. The distances of Asia were terrifying to Europeans.

2. Porus, who fought Alexander with extreme gallantry (Plutarch, Alexander).

3. Narsingha (Land of the Trumpet), Visnagar (Ford). "Narsingha lieth between the Mountain Gate (Ghat) and the Gulf of Bengala" (O. E. D., s.v. Ghat).

5. The vasty height describes the Western Ghats.

6. Canara, the northern half of the Malabar Coast.

22. 1. Ghats, the name in several native tongues for the passes between the mountains rather than for the mountains proper. Barros (II, v, 1) speaks of the Ghats as a wall against the fury of the sea.

23. 2. A Portuguese, said to be a certain João Martins. The Moorish pilot went with him (Lencastre).

26. Monçaide is historic (Barros, I, iv, 8). Damião de Goes (I, 82) calls him "mercador de Tunez." But the Roteiro, cited by Burton, has a more picturesque story. Several Moors of Barbary exclaimed, "What the devil are you doing here?" when they saw the hated Portuguese. Gaspar Correa has a good deal about the embassy. See Stanley, The Three Voyages of Vasco da Gama, p. 160. Camões could have known Correa and might have seen his book in manuscript.

29. 5. Rhodope, in Thrace where Orpheus made the trees follow his music. Camões was fond of the legend and uses it to magnificent purpose in "By the Rivers of Babylon." Horace (Odes, I, xii) describes the streams staying their currents and the trees in confusion following Orpheus to hear his music.

30. Monçaide's speech has a family resemblance to that of the Jew of Angediva (Barros I, iv, 11).

32. 7. Apparently Camões has got hold of more or less authentic history here. Lencastre places Sarama Perimal in the 9th Century. He further states that Barros (I, ix, 3) and Castanheda (I, 13) are the authorities whence Camões derived his details. Sarama Perimal died on his voyage to Mecca (Lencastre) and was buried at Dofar (Yule, Marco Polo, III, 38, note 2), evidently in the odor of sanctity. The King of Coulão became the chief ecclesiastical dignitary of the Malabar Empire, but was in due course succeeded by the King of Cochin. The King reigning at the time of the Portuguese conquest, fortunately for the newcomers, took their side. Camões himself fought in defense of a King of Cochin in 1553.

35. 3. Coulão, Kayan Kulam in Travancore (Burton).

7. Burton's note, quoted by Ford, to the effect that Calicut was not built at the time of the division is apparently in error, for the town was already great in the 7th Century.

37. 6. Nair, a name for the military noble caste of the Malabar Coast (first appearance in English in the first translation of Castanheda, 1582, O. E. D.).

7. Polea is probably a transmogrification of the word we now write "pariah" (Burton).

38. Camões' account of the effect of the caste system is reasonably good, though he has nothing to say of the four principal castes. As far back as Arrian (Indica, 12), the custom of not marrying outside the

273

caste was familiar knowledge in the West, and Strabo knew about it even before.

39.   2. The parable of the good Samaritan gains its force from the fact that he was a heretic.

Then saith the woman of Samaria unto him, How is it that thou being a Jew, askest drink of me, which am a woman of Samaria? for the Jews have no dealings with the Samaritans. John, IV, 9.

40.   1. The priestly caste.

3–4. Mr. Edward Glaser has pointed out that Faria y Sousa's note explained this line more than three centuries ago. The thinker who first to Science gave a name is Pythagoras. Faria y Sousa quotes Diogenes Laertius (VIII, 8) and Petrarch's Triumph of Fame (III, 10–11) in support of this. Some have thought that the 16th Century Portuguese translation of this last poem was the work of Camões. It may be remarked that Cicero (Tusculan Disputations, V, 3–4) also attributes the invention of the term philosphy to Pythagoras.

41.   Although Camões might have noticed conditions on the Malabar Coast for himself, Lencastre refers us to Barros, I, ix, 3, and do Couto, VIII, ii, 10. Be that as it may, Camões is in surprising agreement with Dr. D. G. Mandelbaum's brilliant paper, Polyandry in Kota Society (American Anthropologist, Vol. 40, No. 4, October–December, 1938). The Kotas live on the Nilghiri Plateau, almost in sight of Calicut, to this day. And this passage is a locus classicus for contemporary anthropologists.

Lines 3 and 4 of the stanza waken memories of a chorus from "The Gondoliers":

> And jealousy yellow,
> Unfortunate fellow,
> Is drowned in the fathomless blue.

Burton, quite unnecessarily, drags in the polyandrous Agathyrsi in north central Europe (Herodotus, IV, 104), but such an omnivore is entitled to his fun now and then.

44.   2. Catual, a police officer, magistrate, castellan. The word which appears in the English translation of Castanheda's Conquest of the East Indies (1582, O. E. D.) is usually written Kotwal.

47.   7–8. Damião de Goes (I, 84) is explicit and interesting on the arrival at Calicut. The Portuguese, contrary to Camões' statement, thought they were in a Christian church when they entered the temple. They kneeled accordingly, thus creating an excellent impression by accident. Lencastre quotes a passage from Barros to much the same purpose.

48.   2. Jupiter Ammon had ram's horns. Lucan (De Bello Civili, 513–514).

My investigations of the Hindu Pantheon have revealed no deity with ram's horns, but the Brahmany Bull is sacred to Shiva. And some image of that god might conceivably bear the attributes of his sacred animal.

4. Janus, a Roman god with two faces, which looked to the future and the past. For Pliny he was the god of peace, of war, and of time. The many-headed god could be the six-headed war-god Skanda, otherwise known as Subrahmanya, Kumara, and Karttikeya. He is the son of Shiva the destroyer and Parvati, "who also is Kali."

5. Briareus, the hundred-handed giant. The many-armed God could be either Vishnu or Shiva, who are often represented with many arms. So was Brahma, who, though many-armed and four-headed, is unlikely, for there is only one temple to him in all India.

8. Anubis, "the dog Anubis" of the Egyptians and Milton. Professor Franklin Edgerton has pointed out in a letter to the translator that Camões must be in error here. There is no dog-headed god in the Hindu Pantheon. What Camões saw was either Vishnu in his lion-headed aspect, or Hanuman the monkey-god. Ovid (Met., IX, 690) calls Anubis "latrator," the barker. Professor C. W. Mendell adds, so do Virgil (Aeneid, VIII, 698) and Propertius (IV, ii, 41), both favorites of Camões.

50. 1. At no easy pace. Damião de Goes (I, 83) says that litters were carried at the run.

7–8. Pliny (XIX, 19) observes that up to the time of Epicurus it had never been thought of, to dwell in the country in the middle of the town. Epicurus made the first garden in Athens.

51–54. These stanzas are perhaps indebted to Virgil, who describes Caesar's triumphs sculptured on the gates of a temple (Georgics, III, 27–35). The temple of Juno in Carthage may also have affected Camões (Aeneid, I, 446–458). And Burton (quoted by Ford) suggests the palace of Latinus (Aeneid, VII, 170 ff.).

52. 2. The Hydaspes is the Jhelum—quae loca fabulosus lambit Hydaspes. Lucan (De Bello Civili, VIII, 227) speaks of Nysean Hydaspes, implying that Nysa, Bacchus' town, is on its banks.

5. Nysa, see I, 31, 8.

7. Semele, the unfortunate mother of Bacchus, who was blasted and consumed at the sight of her lover Jupiter.

53. 1. Drinking rivers dry is Herodotéan. Herodotus gives many instances of streams that were insufficient for the army of Xerxes. One will serve, History, VII, 58. But Juvenal (Satire, X, 176–177) and Claudian (De Laudibus Stilichonis, I, 170–171) have also embalmed the cliché.

275

3. Semiramis, whose private habits are here sufficiently explained. Arrian alludes to her Indian expedition (Indica, 5). So does Strabo (XV, ii, 5). Pliny (VIII, 64) displays her singular habits on the authority of the lost history of King Juba.

8. After his visit to the Temple of Jupiter Ammon, Alexander, doubtless for political purposes, proclaimed himself a god, the son of Ammon (Arrian, Anabasis of Alexander, IV, 9). The legends about his birth are curious. Plutarch thinks Alexander had no illusions on the point, but found his divine origin useful.

56. 7–8. That the victor, etc. In the Octaves to Antonio de Noronha, the same thought is repeated in almost the same words (Juromenha, II, 307).

58. 3. The Zamorin was chewing betel-leaf, as is still the custom in India. Damião de Goes (I, 86) has a full account of this old man with the betel-box and supplies him with a golden cuspidor.

60. In this stanza the point seems to be that Portugal is a northern country, where in winter the days are short. This species of periphrasis has happily been given up.

67. 2. Delian, Apollo. He and his twin sister Diana were born at Delos.

Lencastre notes, I do not know on what authority, that the interview between the Catual and Monçaide took place not in Calicut but in Angediva.

69. 1–4. Burton, quoting a fellow enthusiast, Stanley (The Three Voyages of Vasco da Gama, p. 201), makes the point that Monçaide's remarks are orthodox Mahometan doctrine and that Camões understood Islam better "than most Anglo-Indians of the present day" (1880). As Christ was begotten by the breath of God he could not suffer death.

71. 8. Marcellus, as Burton points out, hardly makes the antithesis good. For Marcellus died in an ambush set by Hannibal. Plutarch (Lives of Fabius and Marcellus).

76. Plutarch (The Glory of Athens, quoted in Life of Simonides, Lyra Graeca, Loeb Edition, Vol. II, p. 259) reports Simonides of Ceos as saying that painting is silent poetry and poetry painting that speaks.

78. 1. He held a branch in hand—Lusus, of course, the eponymous hero of Lusitania.

Burton thinks that Camões indulges too much in self-pity, beginning the evil practice here. He also thinks the poet is leaning on Juvenal's Satire VII.

79. 7. Canace, a daughter of Eolus, who killed herself at the command of her father. One can understand the old gentleman's

irritation if one investigates the episode (Ovid, Heroides, XI, 3). See V, 96, note.

80. 8. Faria y Sousa (as I learn from Mr. E. Glaser) refers this to the episode when King Hezekiah's life was extended for fifteen years after what should have been a mortal illness.

85. 4. Proteus, like Nereus and several other sea divinities, had the gift of changing himself into anything he desired. See Georgics, IV, 387–414.

BOOK VIII

ARGUMENT

The Governor of Calicut sees the various pictures on the ensigns of the fleet and listens to Paul da Gama's discourse; origin of the name Lusitania; glorious deeds of the Kings of Portugal and their vassals till the times of Afonso V. The Zamorin commands the seers to study the future concerning the fleet. They reply unfavorably as to the voyagers. Gama clears himself of the charges of piracy. But after receiving the Zamorin's leave to trade he is prevented from returning to the Fleet by the Catual. Gama escapes from the man's clutches by appealing successfully to his greed.

THE LUSIADS

THE EIGHTH BOOK

B Y THE first image would the Catual stay
To view the figure he saw painted there,
That branch in hand for ensign did display.
The beard was white and long and combed with care.
"Who may the old man be? And in what way
Is the symbol fitting, he in hand doth bear?"
Paul made him answer, whose intent discreet
The wise Moor in translation would repeat.

2

"All of the pictures that are shown you here,
Fierce in aspéct and gallant to behold,
Fiercer, more gallant still, in fame appear
Because of great works done and action bold.
Ancients they are, whose splendor still shines clear,
For 'mid great spirits are their names enrolled.
He, whom you see, is Lusus, from whose fame
Our Kingdom Lusitania takes its name.

3

"He was the Theban's son and comrade good,
That once such various realms could overthrow.
It seems he reached our Spanish neighborhood,
While on some raid, who used in arms to go.
Proud plains, once called Elysium, twixt the flood
Douro and Guadiana, pleased him so
That there he sought for his worn limbs a grave
Eternal, and to us our name he gave.

VIII "The branch you see for emblem in his hands
Is the green thyrsus Bacchus often bore,
Which to our time for a memorial stands,
That he was the god's son and friend of yore.
Dost see one marching through the Tagus lands
After long plowing all the ocean o'er,
Who battlements perpetual doth raise
And Pallas' fane that still in memory stays?

5

"Ulysses there erects the sacred shrine
To her who made his speech so nobly sound.
In Asia, if he burned down Troy divine,
In Europe giant Lisbon he could found."
"Who's he who, raging in his phrensy fine,
With the dead corpses covers all the ground?
He has thrown into rout their monstrous bands,
Upon whose flags the painted eagle stands."

6

So spake the heathen. Gama made reply:
"He was a shepherd in a bygone year.
Viriathus is the name we know him by,
Less skillful with the crook than with the spear.
From him Rome's fame has suffered injury,
Unconquered conqueror, of fame most clear.
That chivalry to him they did not show,
Nor could, as once to Pyrrhus long ago.

7

"For, not by force but by dishonest guile,
They murdered him, who so had made them quake.
What a great grief it is when on a while
Those who were noble their fair custom break.
By his fierce fatherland entreated vile,
With us this other would rebellion make.
His fellows in revolt he justly chose,
For with eternal light his memory glows.

"And lo! with us the flags he overbore,   **VIII**
On which Jove's birds are blazoned in their might.
For in that time the nation best in war
Learned at our hands how they could lose a fight.
See how his arts are subtle furthermore,
And conquer peoples with deceitful sleight,
Which she imparts, the prophetic deer divine.
He is Sertorius, she his mark and sign.

9

"Look on that banner. From the painting know
The great sire of the kings who first held sway.
He was Hungarian, or we take it so,
Though a Lorrainer born, as strangers say.
Having beat the Moor in battle and brought low
León's knights, and Galicia's, in the fray,
To Holy Land our sainted Henry went,
So to bring blessing on his whole descent."

10

"Say who he is, at whom I wonder sore"
(So the astonished Malabari prayed),
"Who with so few has overthrown in war
Such armaments, and myriad men dismayed.
Tireless, he fights his battles evermore,
And strongest ramparts has in ruin laid,
While in a hundred countries many a crown
And many a flag are at his feet cast down."

11

"The first Afonso," e'en so Gama spake,
"Who wrenched the whole land from the Moorish
For him Fame vowed it by the Stygian Lake   [grip.
To praise no more the Roman fellowship.
And his God loved him well for his zeal's sake,
Whose Arm helped get the Moslem on the hip,
Till the Moor in his own land rased every wall
And left his sons no heritage at all.

VIII   "If Philip's son and Caesar had relied
On men-at-arms so few and power so slight,
And must the stress of foes so numerous bide
As this excelling soldier beat in fight,
Perhaps their names would not have ranged so wide,
Which now are with undying glory bright.
But turn from the King's deeds not to be told,
And his vassals' actions notable, behold.

13

"Mark him there, glaring, furious of face,
At his beaten ward, and with what haughty air
He bids him rally his broke force apace
And back into the foughten field repair.
With the ancient, see the youth his steps retrace,
Who turned the vanquished to a victor there.
Egas Moniz, that good old man, men call,
The very mirror of true vassals all.

14

"With noose on neck, to yield him, see him now
Leading his sons, stripped of his silken gear,
For the boy would not in submission bow,
As Egas to Castile pledged honor dear.
He raised the siege with argument and vow,
Where the foe's coming triumph was too clear.
Children and wife he forced to pay the price
And for his lord's life would be sacrifice.

15

"That consul never wrought a work so high,
In the Caudine Forks, blockaded unbeknown,
What time the yoke of Samnite victory
To bow the neck compelled the overthrown.
He, for his host struck by calamity,
Constant and firm, yielded himself alone.
This other self and sons alike gave o'er,
And guiltless wife, which hurts our nature more.

16

"Lo! one from ambush sallying to fall
On a king beleaguering that strong walled town.
He takes the king and lifts the siege withal,
A martial action worthy all renown.
And yonder, in that fleet pictorial,
At sea the Moors to death he hurleth down,
Seizes their ships, and raises to the height
The glory of our earliest naval fight.

17

"Fuas Roupinho, he it is, whose name
With splendor gleams alike by land or sea,
Who by Mount Ábyla once lit the flame
On galleys of the Moorish progeny.
In wars that had a just and holy name,
Behold how well content to die is he,
Whose happy soul from the Moor's grasp could rise,
With palms well-won, in triumph to the skies.

18

"Do you see yon host that foreign armor wear,
Landing from their armada huge and new,
Who to the first King aid in battle bear
At Lisbon, sacred proof that they are true?
Lo, Henry, the good knight whose fame is fair!
Behold the palm hard by his tomb that grew!
A miracle for them, God showed it plain.
Christ's martyrs they, those men of Alamain.

19

"Against Arronches, lo, a priest on high
Lifts sword. He takes it. So is vengeance found
For Leiria stormed by them in days gone by,
Who lay in rest their lances for Mahound.
'Tis Prior Teotonio. Cast your eye
On leaguered Santarem. What courage sound
Is seen in him, who first swarms up the wall
To hoist the five-shield flag of Portugal.

VIII   "And look on him, where Sancho makes alway
Vandalia's Moors in the dread battle reel.
He breaks their ranks and doth the ensign slay,
Hurling to earth the banner of Seville.
Mem Moniz! Who such courage could portray
As, with his father's bones, the tomb could seal?
Well were those banners earned, for without fail
He made his foeman's fall, his own prevail.

21

"Lo! one with the spear's help descending there,
Who grasps the heads of the two sentries slain,
Where lurks the ambush, whence with crafty care
And courage high the city he will gain.
Yet the armorials of that city bear
The knight who holds the cold heads of the twain.
A deed impossible it must appear.
That gallant heart is Gerald-without-Fear.

22

"Do you see how the Castilian mortified
By the ninth Alfonso of Castile, and long
Hated by Lara, with the Moors allied,
Becomes of Portugal the foeman strong?
He takes Abrantès city. At his side
The cruel armies of the faithless throng.
But look! A Portuguese with men but few
Beats him and takes him with right derring-do.

23

"Martim Lopes they call that cavalier,
Who on those palms and laurels could lay hold.
But look once more! A warrior priest is here,
Who to a steel lance turns his ring of gold.
'Mid doubters he is confident and clear,
Nor shuns the battle with the Paynim bold.
And look what sign appeared to him on high,
Who roused our handful's courage up thereby.

286

"Do you see the Kings, Cordova and Seville,   **VIII**
Presently routed, with another pair?
Routed? Dead first. In marvels God doth deal,
For no man's hand was raised against them there.
Lo! Naught avails courage or wall of steel,
For, humbled, lies the city Alcacer,
What time Matthias, Bishop of Lisbon town,
Could put upon his head the palm-leaf crown.

25

"Look! The Grand Master, sprung from a Lusian line,
Comes from Castile. Behold the man prevail
Against the Algarve lands, that give no sign
Of any that in arms dare him assail.
With skill and courage, 'neath a star benign,
The cities and the castles, see him scale.
Canst mark Tavila from its people won,
And vengeance for the seven hunters done?

26

"Dost see how Silves from the Moor is ta'en
By warlike wit, which Moorish might o'erthrew?
Paio Correia thus, by courage main
And skill, the envy of his rivals grew.
Nor pass those three, who through all France and
Reputation could perpetually renew   [Spain
By challenge, tourney, joustings with the lance,
And public trophies left in Spain and France.

27

"Look! Known for brave adventurers they came
Into Castile. Alone they had the prize
And guerdon of Bellona's honest game,
Which some have found a costly exercise.
Behold the proud knights dead, even those same
Who sent the foremost of our three defies.
Gonçalo Ribeiro, so the man they call,
Whom Law of Lethe never could appall.

VIII   "Look on the man whose glory Fame hath spread
Till she prefers no hero known of old,
Who, when the land's fate hung on one weak thread,
On two strong shoulders could the realm uphold.
Do you see him rage, his face for anger red,
Against the base suspicion, chill and cold,
Of folk on whom he forced the gentle rein,
Their own King's and no other's, once again.

29

"See how by courage and by counsel clear,
With only God and his good star to guide,
Alone he does what hopeless must appear,
Crushing Castile's huge army in its pride.
Behold how toil, courage, and virtue sheer,
In havoc new, fair victory decide,
'Gainst folk as fierce as numberless past telling,
'Twixt Guadiana and Tartessus dwelling?

30

"Dost thou see Lusitania to rout
Almost delivered, for, so far away
Absenting him, the general devout
To the High Essence, Three in One, would pray?
Dost see him swiftly by his men sought out,
Who tell him they are like to lose the day
Against such odds, unless he come with speed
To give the weaklings courage in their need?

31

"But lo! with what divinest confidence,
'It is not time,' he answers them again,
Like one who has from God the certain sense
Of triumph he is shortly to attain.
So Pompilius, when foes in force immense
Burst through the boundaries of his domain,
To him who brought him that forlorn advice,
Gave answer, 'Therefore I make sacrifice.'

"If, of the man who dared adventure so, **VIII**
Trusting in God, you list the name to hear,
He might be called Portugal's Scipio,
But 'Nuno Álvares' keeps his fame more clear.
Lucky the land that such a son can show,
Or, better, father. While in his career
The sun round Ceres' globe and Neptune's runs,
The land will yearn for ever for such sons.

"In the same war see yonder captain make
Huge fortune with his little retinue.
He beats the chieftains and the herds doth take,
That erst were lifted by the desperate crew.
See him once more in blood the spear-point slake,
To free, because of strong affection true,
His captive friend, for loyalty in thrall.
'Tis Per' Rodrigues, he of Landroal.

"Look on the traitor, and what pay he found
For perjury and plot of vile intent.
But Elvas' Gil Fernandez beat him sound
And sent him to his final punishment.
Gil ravaged Xeres' fields, and half-way drowned
Castile, with blood of her own lords besprent.
And lo! There Rui Pereira forward sallies,
Whose face is as a shield to guard his galleys.

"See those bold Portuguese, but seventeen strong,
Who fend themselves high upon yonder height.
Four hundred of Castile around them throng
To take them prisoners when encircled quite.
But they will learn, from injury and wrong,
These do not only ward but also smite,
An action fit for ever to be known,
In old time noble, noble in our own!

VIII "We know how the three hundred long ago
Against a thousand Romans did engage,
When Viriathus' acts that manly show
Cast such a glorious light upon the age.
And many a memorable overthrow
Has handed down to us this heritage:
Though few, of numbers we are not afraid.
And this a thousand times has been displayed.

37

"Lo! Peter, with him Henry, princes twain,
Who were John's noble-hearted progeny.
One did such deeds that still in Alamain
His praises sound, which cheat mortality.
The other's glory Fame has published plain,
For he was the Discoverer of the Sea,
Who the Moor's swollen vanity put down
And entered first the gate of Ceuta town.

38

"Dost thou behold Count Peter, who could stand
Two sieges laid by Barbary entire?
And lo! that other Count, who in the land
Seems Mars himself for strength and warlike fire?
Alcacer town to hold, with the strong hand,
Against long odds, sufficed not his desire.
But there his King's dear life he warded well,
And made his own the wall thereof and fell.

39

"There are many others whom the men who drew
Might have depicted here, the truth to say,
But they lacked the pencil and the colors too,
And what must nourish art, fame, favor, pay.
Fault of successors who their vice ensue!
For they degenerate and fall away
From the ancestral gallantry and gust,
Wallowing in mire of folly and of lust.

"Those great old sires, who in the times gone by   **VIII**
Founded the races which from them derive,
Established them by their own virtue high,
But to leave houses that will never thrive.
Blind men! For though afar their fame may fly,
And though at heavy labors they may strive,
Always they leave a progeny obscure,
Heirs to what makes them idle and impure.

"And there are others high and arrogant,
Although they spring from no great-hearted strain,
For oft to favorites kings in error grant
More than a thousand wits or heroes gain.
No pictures of their stock these worthies want,
Who take no pleasure in the color vain,
Which they conceive their natural foeman still,
For if a painting speaks, they take it ill.

"There are withal, as I do not deny,
Sons of rich houses and of great descent,
Who noble mind innate exemplify
Because of manners high and excellent;
And if the glory of their ancestry
They brighten with no brave accomplishment,
At least they fall not off, nor hide away.
But painting finds too few of them today."

Thus Gama could the mighty deeds declare,
Which thus were bodied forth in various hue
By the hand instructed of the artist rare,
Who such fine acts in full perfection drew.
The Catual stood with eager eyes a-stare
Before those histories distinct and true,
And often questioned and as often stayed
To hear of noble fights he saw displayed.

VIII Now came the time when doubtful showed the light,
For the great lamp had hid itself away
Below the horizon line and, shining bright,
Carried to the antipodes the day.
The heathen with those generous men of might,
The Nairs, no more on the strong ship would stay,
But sought that rest which gives her sweet release
To weary creatures in the night-time peace.

45

Meanwhile the famous prophets, falsely deeming
By sacrifice the future to foresee
In whatsoever case of dubious seeming,
From diabolic sign and augury,
At the King's order, studiously scheming,
Practiced their art's whole ritual ministry,
As to the advent of the stranger strain,
New come upon their coasts from unknown Spain.

46

A sign to them the truthful demon sent,
That the new nation on the land would bring
Perpetual yoke, endless imprisonment,
And as for men and wealth wreck everything.
Forthwith in fear the astonished augur went
With his interpretation to the King
And told of signs of terrifying awe
Within the victims' entrails that he saw;

47

This too befell. Unto a priest sincere
Who to Mahomet's law did well incline,
And still the hatreds, thus conceived, held dear,
Against the all-excelling Faith Divine,
Bacchus the baleful did in dream appear,
In the famed false prophet's shape who from his line
Was come, that erewhile the slave Hagar bore,
For Bacchus did not give his hatred o'er.

"Look to yourselves, my people," thus he spake,   **VIII**
"Because of ills your foes are plotting here,
They who across wet seas the highroad take,
Ere to the danger you are come too near."
He said. The Moor was suddenly awake,
For the vision had oppressed his soul with fear,
Then thought 'twas but such custom as dreams keep,
And, soothed in mind, went quietly to sleep.

49

But Bacchus came again and said his say:
"Is not the great law-giver recognized,
Who taught your sires the rule which you obey,
Without which, hosts of you had been baptized?
Knave, must I wake for you who sleep alway?
For these newcomers, you are well advised,
A scourge most horrible will prove to be
For laws I gave to dull humanity.

50

"However weak may be this people's might,
Resistance to the uttermost ordain,
For, when the sun first rises, the sharp sight
Can look him in the face with little pain.
But, after he has risen, hot and bright,
If triumph o'er keen eyes he shall attain,
They stay as blinded, just as you will stay,
Unless you cut their roots of growth away."

51

He spake. At once he and the vision fled,
Leaving the wondering Hagarene afraid.
Yelling to his men for lights, he sprang from bed.
Wild work within him the hot poison made.
When the new light that ever comes ahead
Of Dawn her still, angelic face displayed,
He called his sect's chief rulers unredeemed,
And strict account he gave of all he dreamed.

VIII   Opinions most diverse and opposite
      Might then be heard, according as each thought;
      Treason ingenious, foul play infinite,
      Perfidies, they discovered or they wrought.
      But, shunning counsels of too rash a wit,
      They undertook to bring our race to naught,
      With subtle art and better planned device,
      By purchasing their rulers at a price.

53

With bribes, with gold, with secret gifts, they fain
The country's princes would conciliate,
With reason sound and notable, maintain
These men will bring perdition on the state.
They hold the strangers are a restless strain,
Who, as the western seas they navigate,
Their living get as only pirates can,
Without a king or law of God or Man.

54

How must a king, that well would rule his own,
Watch that his counselors and favorites be
Persons of conscience and of truth ingrown,
Dowered with affectionate sincerity!
For he who sits upon the towering throne,
Of things accomplished in dern privacy,
Is likely to have notice less complete
Than counselor tongues may unto him repeat.

55

Nor should he take, I say, without due care,
That conscience as all clear and sanctified,
That doth a poor and humble mantle wear
Where masked ambition may at hazard hide;
Nor trust a saint, though he be true and fair,
Who the world's business hath no skill to guide;
For quiet innocence takes count but ill
Of such affairs, to Heaven constant still.

The Catuals, ever greedy to the core,

Who in the heathen empire held the sway,
By the infernal wretches quite won o'er,
Their answer to the Portuguese delay.
Gama, who for his part desired no more,
Whatever plots the Moors had under way,
Than to his King to carry proof most sound,
Concerning the new world which he had found,

57

For this worked only; for he well might ken
That, if such proof once came to Manuel's hand,
Forthwith the King would send ships, arms, and men,
Since it was he who held the great command.
And 'neath his yoke must be subjected then
The whole vast rondure of the sea and land,
For Gama in himself could be no more
Than keen discoverer of the Orient shore.

58

To the heathen King to speak was his intent,
That with the letter he might leave straightway,
For he perceived that those malevolent
All his desire would hinder and gainsay.
No wonder, if from their bedevilment
The King was full of trouble and dismay,
For in his seers his faith was fixed and sure,
Confirmed too by the judgment of the Moor.

59

Though chilly fear made his base heart afraid,
Yet still the power of covetous desire,
By which his nature was at all times swayed,
Lighted and kindled hope's immortal fire;
For well he saw huge profit to be made,
If he, with justice and with truth entire,
The treaty struck, thus given to his hand,
With the King of Portugal long years to stand.

VIII Whenever he conferred on the affair,
Of contrary beliefs he found his fill.
For upon all who might his counsel share
Money its constant power exerted still.
Then he bade summon the great Admiral there,
To whom he said at once: "You, if you will,
May now the pure and naked truth confess,
And so find pardon for your wickedness.

"This embassy I have good knowledge of,
Which your King sends me. It is but a cheat.
You have no king, no country which you love,
But vagabond through life the highways beat.
Who, from Hesperia at such far remove,
Or king or lord, would send his ships and fleet
On voyages so doubtful and remote,
Unless in madness without bound he dote?

"For, if from kingdoms powerful and great
Your King doth his high majesty receive,
What presents do you bring commensurate,
Proof that your unknown truth we may believe?
With metal coined, high gifts of sumptuous state,
Great kings their amity are wont to weave.
And sign and warrant are required, beyond
The mere word of an ocean vagabond.

"If haply exiles from your land you be,
As may to fortunes of great men belong,
My realm shall show you hospitality.
The whole world is a country for the strong.
If you are pirates wedded to the sea,
Tell me, not fearing death or shameful wrong;
For at all times the need to live constrains
All men to seek whatever life sustains."

Thus he spake. Gama, who had guessed what game   VIII
Had been devised against him by the hate
Of those same Moslems, whence the act of shame
Which the King wickedly did meditate,
With such high confidence as him became
And could but make his reputation great,
These words then uttered from his prudent heart,
As Acidalian Venus might impart:

65

"If ancient crime, which human infamy
Erewhile committed in the days of old,
Caused not those vessels of iniquity
(Sharp scourge of them who with Christ's teaching
To stir the quarrel up eternally   [hold)
'Gainst Adam's breed, with many falsehoods told,
O mighty King, by this same hateful sect,
You would not now thus wickedly suspect.

66

"But, since no great thing ever can be done
Without great hardships, and in the whole quest
Fear at the heels of Hope comes hurrying on
(Hope living but by sweat of a man's breast),
Scant is the confidence that you have shown
In my good faith, nor have you thought to test
My counter-reasons, which you would perceive,
If you believed not men none should believe.

67

"If, a sea-rover and denied my home,
I got my livelihood as pirates do,
Why do you think I should so widely roam,
Seeking out lands remote I never knew?
With what a hope, what purpose, should I come,
Who wrathful oceans still must struggle through,
And cold Antarctic and such heats as well
As they must suffer, 'neath the Ram who dwell?

VIII   "If, with some mighty offering sublime,
You bid me credit of my tale maintain,
I only came to find this stranger clime
Where nature planted once your ancient reign.
But if fair fortune hold until the time
I reach dear land and friendly realm again,
Then you shall know with what rich gifts and high
My second journey here I'll justify.

69

"And if you think it an unheard-of thing
That far Hesperia's Lord sent me to you,
The noble heart and courage of the King
Thinks nothing hard that man can rise untó.
To the superb and high imagining
Of Lusitania's soul more trust is due,
A firmer credit, faith of nobler flight,
Fit to believe actions of such a height.

70

"And you should know that it is centuries
Since it seemed good in our old rulers' eyes
To vanquish labors vast and jeopardies,
Which threaten every valiant enterprise;
And deeps discovering, the enemies
Of quiet peace, they felt the craving rise
To know the sea's frontiers, and where are found
The ultimate beaches Ocean washes round.

71

"His thought was worthy of the lineage clear
Of that brave King, the first to plow the sea
That he might banish from his homeland dear
The last man who in Ábyla might be.
His heir, by genius and by toil severe,
Sent ship on ship to make discovery.
And they found out the regions which the light
Of Argo, Hydra, Hare, and Plow makes bright.

"And, growing with first good success apace,   **VIII**
Within the breast adventurous hope rose high.
Little by little the strange paths they trace.
The one succeeds another. On they ply.
The last and southernmost of Afric's race,
That never on the Seven Stars set eye,
Were seen of us, we who left far astern
Infinite numbers whom both Tropics burn.

73
"Thus, with stout hearts and these great ends in view,
At length we have the upper hand of fate,
And now in your strange land we visit you,
Here to set up our column ultimate.
The terror of the dead calms breaking through,
Or tempests awful and importunate,
We come to you, and this is all our care,
Letters from you to our own King to bear.

74
"King, this is truth, for I would never say,
For such uncertain good, such trifling gain,
Instead of simple truth, as hope I may,
A prologue long and falsified and vain.
Before that I would yield to rest straightway
On the wild bosom, evermore a-strain,
Of Mother Thetis, a buccaneer unblest,
From others' labors feathering my nest.

75
"And if, O King, you take my honor clear
For what it is, faithful, and not two-faced,
Then with all swiftness give me letters here,
Of my return deferring not the taste.
But if to you falsehood it still appear,
Think well of reason that on proof is based.
For one may see, if the clear mind attend,
Truth is an easy thing apprehend."

VIII   That good assurance the King heard intent,
As Gama proved the truth of all he said,
And thence he drew reliance confident
And firm belief, his cause while Gama pled.
He pondered the sufficient argument.
In the authority great worth he read.
That the Catuals were dupes, he now believed,
Corrupted, prone to judgment ill-conceived.

77

Likewise the burning itch he had for gain,
Which from the Lusian pact he might expect,
To do the Captain honor might constrain,
Eschewing treason with the Moorish sect.
At length, exempt from penalty or pain,
Gama he bade go to the fleet direct,
Whence certain merchandise he was to send
Ashore, for spice, to barter and to vend.

78

The King commanded to bring merchandise,
Of which the Ganges kingdoms have small store,
Goods of right kind, fetched from the coast that lies
Where sea begins and there is land no more.
From the royal presence, sacred in men's eyes,
The Captain went and sought upon the shore
A vessel from the Catual, for he
Had charge of Gama, whose own boat was at sea.

79

He sought a boat, unto his ships to speed,
But the bad governor, a novel snare
Now meditating, nothing would concede,
And balked him and held back in the affair.
To the quay he took him. Gama he would lead
Far from the royal palaces, and there,
The while the King thereof no knowledge had,
He might accomplish what his malice bade.

Oh! he would give him—after long delay—
A well-found craft in which he might depart,
Or urge upon him, till the light of day
Should come next morning, to defer his start.
Gama from these devices saw straightway
That the heathen had consented in his heart
To vile plots of the bad mad Moorish crew,
Something he had not guessed at hitherto.

VIII

81

The governor was one of their cabal
The Moorish sect did by corruption win,
And he it was who, as chief principal,
Ruled in the towns of the great Zamorin.
On him alone the Moors had rested all
Their hope of carrying out their deed of sin.
He, who in concert vile with them conspired,
Babbled not of the thing his heart desired.

82

Gama required him with insistency
To get him to the ships. No help was there,
Though, as he said, it was by the decree
Of the good Perimal's imperial heir.
Why was he balked and checked in such degree,
Who here the goods of Portugal must bear?
For no man is permitted to withstand
One to whom kings have given their command.

83

The Catual corrupted small worth set
Upon such words. Nay, rather he designed
In fancy an ingenious subtle net,
A fearful trap of diabolic kind.
And means whereby cold iron might be wet
In our abhorrent blood possessed his mind,
So too some scheme the fleet with fire to burn
That not a ship should ever home return.

VIII For the Moors' hellish council thus had planned
That not a ship should ever home return,
So that the limits of the Orient land
Portugal's King in vain would seek to learn.
There Gama stayed. For he who held command
O'er those brute beasts gave prohibition stern,
Nor could he go without the man's consent,
Who could all use of watercraft prevent.

85

To the Chief's reasons and complaining high,
The heathen answered he might well ordain
That his ships afar nearer the coast should lie,
The better to go forth and come again.
"It were but sign of thief or enemy
If they at such a distance should remain,"
He said, "for from a true and faithful friend
There is no danger one need apprehend."

86

From such words uttered, Gama the discreet
Saw that the Catual would have them near,
That he with fire and steel might storm the fleet.
So openly did burning hate appear!
In thought perplexed he stood, at loss complete,
In his mind seeking some deliverance clear,
Which, if he gave command, would check the ill.
All things he feared, yet thought of all things still.

87

As, from the mirror smooth, reflected light,
Whether it be of steel or crystal fair,
When rays of the strong sun upon it smite,
Strikes with a sudden brilliance otherwhere;
But if the hand of some small curious wight
Tilt the glass idly, through the house the glare
Darts on, across the roof or up the wall,
Here and there trembling, never still at all;

88

Even so the wandering judgment fluctuated
In captive Gama, as his mind mulled o'er
Coelho's plight, who haply for him waited,
As he was bid, with boats beside the shore.
His thought he secretly communicated
And bade him to the fleet return once more,
On guard lest he be taken in the net
He feared that savage Moslem crew had set.

89

Such must he be, who, having Mars his gift,
Would imitate the great and equal meet them.
Everywhere soaring thought that man must lift,
And he must guess all dangers and defeat them.
With soldier genius and with artful shift,
He must perceive his foes' intents and cheat them,
And watch all things. I praise him not a whit,
Some chief who says: "I never thought of it."

90

The Malabari meant to keep him there,
Till to the shore his squadron he should call.
Constant in mind, with noble rage aflare,
He heeded not such menaces at all.
Nay! the whole weight vile malice might prepare
He fain would have on his own shoulders fall,
Or ever he would put in jeopardy
His Master's fleet where it rode safe at sea.

91

And there the whole night long he was detained,
And part of the next day, when he thought right
To go unto the King, though sore constrained
By the multitude of guards, which was not slight.
The heathen other tricks against him trained,
Fearing the King's wrath on himself might light,
If once he knew the plot, which he would know
In season, if he let not Gama go.

VIII He bade him for goods vendible to send,
Whate'er he had, and bring them to the shore,
At leisure there to barter and to vend,
For who desires not trade is seeking war.
Though Gama understood the wicked end
The man locked in his breast's accursèd core,
He gave consent, for, as he rightly thought,
With those same goods, his liberty he bought.

93

That the black should send his boats, they well agree,
Fit for the task, to bring the stuff again.
But as for risking his own craft, not he,
Where foes might seize or their return restrain.
Forthwith the pinnaces put out to sea
To fetch appropriate merchandise of Spain.
He wrote his brother to send him with all speed
The trading goods, whereby he should be freed.

94

At length the goods came to the beach, and there
The Catual base put all of it in store.
Álvaro and Diogo for the stuff must care
And set such price as they might sell it for.
More than his duty or command or prayer,
Greed ruled the bosom of the governor,
Which the Hindu to observing minds made clear,
Since he loosed Gama for that merchant-gear.

95

For that he loosed him, thinking he had withal
A pawn sufficient, whence he might attain
To larger profit than to him would fall,
If he forced the Chief yet longer to remain.
It seemed unwisdom to the Admiral
To land anew, for to be trapped again
He must not risk. So he, once come on board,
Stayed with the fleet to rest and be restored.

Aboard he rested, still and leisurely,
Till time had made for him discovery sure
That in the covetous heart no trust could be
Of the governor ignoble and impure.
Let curious judgment to the question see,
How in the rich as also in the poor
Vile interest rules, and the thirst horrible
For gold, that men to all things can compel.

VIII

97

The Thracian King Prince Polydorus slew,
So that he might possess his splendid hoard;
And golden rain that pierced the stronghold through
Upon the daughter of Acrisius poured;
And with Tarpeia greed such work could do
That, for bright yellow metal's rich reward,
To foes she would her lofty tower betray,
And perished suffocated in her pay.

98

For gold can take the well-defended place;
Gold, of true friends, has knaves and traitors made,
Gold oft compels great lords to actions base;
And captains to their foes are thus betrayed.
Gold can corrupt the virgin's purest grace,
Of peril to her honor not afraid.
And gold foul things on sciences has wrought,
Blinding the conscience and impartial thought.

99

Gold text expounds with too much subtlety,
Gold makes the law and can unmake in turn.
Gold, 'mid the people, breedeth perjury,
And often changes kings to tyrants stern.
Even those dedicated utterly
To God Almighty, you not rarely learn,
The enchanter can corrupt and well delude,
With color of some virtue still endued.

NOTES

2. 6. Lusus has been duly dealt with, I, 24, note.

3. The queer mistake about the imaginary Lusus and his kinship with Bacchus is due to a mistranslation of Pliny. But a great deal of the odd lore in Stanzas 3, 4, and 5 is the result of an intellectual foible of Strabo's, who, persuaded that Homer was not only the greatest of poets but the greatest of geographers, came to the conclusion that Tartessus (the region of Cadiz) must be Tartarus where Ulysses visited the shades. The adjoining plains between the Douro and the Guadiana, that is to say Portugal, thus became the Elysian Fields (Strabo, III, ii, 12–13). Though there is almost certainly no connection between Ulysses and the town Olissipo (Lisbon), the etymology was too tempting for Strabo and Pliny (IV, 21 and 22).

4. 2. Bacchus habitually carried the green stave called the thyrsus.

5. 1. Ulysses has been mentioned as a founder of Lisbon twice already. Pallas (Odyssey, XXII, 230) reminds him that by his device Troy was taken, of which Line 3 is a reminiscence. Strabo (III, iv, 3) vouches for the temple of Minerva.

6. 8. Pyrrhus and the Romans were uncommonly civil to each other during their wars. Probably Camões alludes to the occasion when the Consuls Fabricius and Aemilius Papius warned Pyrrhus that there was treason in his household (Cicero, De Finibus, V, xxii, 64, Plutarch, Life of Pyrrhus, and Claudian, De Bello Gildonico, 270–273). Camões had in all probability read these writers and very likely Florus, who is severe on Roman treachery with respect to Viriathus (II, xvii).

7. 5. Sertorius.

8. The account of Sertorius in this stanza is practically a paraphrase of a passage in Plutarch's life of that hero. Pliny also speaks of the white hind (VIII, 50).

9. 2. Henry of Burgundy. See III, 25, and note.

10. 1. Afonso I. See III, 30 ff.

13. 1. Egas Moniz at the Battle of Guimarães, 1128 (Ford). See III, 31.

15. 1. Spurius Postumius Albinus, captured by the Samnites, 321 B. C. See Livy, IX, 1–10 (Burton) and Florus, I, xvi.

16.   1. Fuas Roupinho, admiral under Afonso I (reigned 1140–1185). Camões mentions him in I, 12. His victories were mainly interesting as early specimens of Portuguese naval prowess.

2. According to Lencastre, the place was Gomi.

3. Fuas Foupinho fought several actions by land and sea. Lencastre specifies the defence of Porto de Mõs, and at least two naval fights. Judging by Stanza 17, the battle in question was fought near Gibraltar.

18.   5. Henry Bon, one of the German crusaders (Lencastre). Burton says his tomb is in the monastery of St. Vincent, minus the palm.

19.   5. Teotonio, an heroic priest in the time of Afonso I, and Prior of Santa Cruz de Coimbra (Lencastre).

20.   1. This hero is Mem Moniz, the son of Egas, who fought valiantly under Sancho I (reigned 1185–1211). See Lencastre.

21.   8. Gerald-without-Fear captured Evora in 1166. He climbed an outpost watch-tower, on the shaft of a lance, and put to death a Moor and his daughter who were the sentinels. The arms of Evora commemorate this unpleasant feat (Lencastre).

22.   1. Pedro Fernandez de Castro, exiled by Alfonso IX of Castile and persecuted by the House of Lara, went over to the Moors, and attacked Castile and Portugal with complete impartiality (Ford).

23.   1. Nothing beside this seems to be known about Martim Lopes.

3. Don Suero, a militant prelate under Afonso III, Bishop of Lisbon under the name Matthias. He won a battle at Alcacer do Sal. Lencastre states that the battle was really won by another bishop, Soeiro Viegas, and that Camões fell into error by following the chronicler Rui Pina.

7. The sign was the appearance in the sky of an old man wearing a red cross on his breast (Lencastre).

24.   2. The other pair, the kings of Badajoz and Jaen (Burton).

25.   1. Paio Peres Correia was a Portuguese but Grand Master of the Spanish Order of Santiago. He fought for Afonso III in the Algarve war.

8. The seven hunters were Portuguese who were killed by the Moors near Tavira. Correia avenged them (Lencastre).

27.   7. Ribeiro in the reign of Afonso IV (1325–56) was a distinguished knight errant. His two companions were Vasco Anes, foster brother of the Queen of Castile (the beautiful Maria, daughter of Afonso IV, the victor of the Salado, III, 101) and Fernando Martins of Santarem (Lencastre).

8. The phrase "law of Lethe" is also found in Ode VII, where

Camões recommends himself and his epic to the attention of Dom Manuel de Portugal (Juromenha, II, 274).

28. 1. Nuno Alvares Pereira. See IV, 14.

29. 4. The battle of Aljubarrota, August 14, 1385.

5–6. The battle of Valverde (Ford).

7–8. The reference is to Andalusia (Ford).

Burton, with his usual industry, has got up the antiquities of Tartessus, according to him, 270 years older than Carthage.

31. 5. Numa Pompilius, one of the mythical kings of Rome. Plutarch (Life of Numa Pompilius) tells the story. Ford believes that the allusion is to Pereira's victory at Valverde. Burton compares Pereira to the Collingwoods and Hardys left over from the Napoleonic wars, whose memoirs were appearing in Burton's time (1880).

33. 1. Pedro Rodrigues, governor of Landroal, defeated a Spanish raid on Evora (Ford).

3–8. He also rescued Álvaro (Manuel, according to Lencastre) Gonçalves, an adherent of John I (Ford), from a Portuguese named Vasco Porcallo who was working for Castile.

34. 1. Gil Fernandes was captured by Paio Rodrigues Marinho, a pro-Spanish Portuguese. Fernandes ransomed himself at a cost of 1000 doubloons and later killed Marinho. He subsequently led a raid into Castile. (Ford and Lencastre.)

7. Rui Pereira defended the mouth of the Tagus for John I against a Spanish fleet. Professor Ford thinks that this is an allusion to the defence of Almada near Lisbon. Mr. Glaser has sent me Faria y Sousa's long note on the subject. Pereira attacked the Castilian flagship, so that his galleys were able to cross the Tagus in safety. Pereira, however, was killed.

35. Martim Vaz and seventeen squires went to get water during John I's siege of Vilalobos and defeated 400 Castilians with considerable slaughter (Lencastre).

36. Viriathus. See I, 26, III, 22, and notes.

The usual pun on Viriathus appears in the Portuguese.

37. 1. Pedro, Duke of Coimbra, one of John I's extraordinary sons. Burton, who got his facts from Faria y Sousa, as Mr. Glaser points out, says he fought for Sigismund (Super Grammaticam) against the Turks and otherwise distinguished himself. See Camões and the History of Portugal, for his tragic end. It is said that he introduced the guitar. Soldier, lawmaker, musician, he did not inherit his father's good fortune.

Henry the Navigator (1394–1460), perhaps the most attractive and interesting figure of his time. He was at Ceuta in 1415. And he was the organizer of the continual voyages of discovery, to which he gave such an impulse that the Portuguese became the greatest maritime nation in the world.

38.   1. Pedro de Meneses, Count of Viana (Vila Rial, says Lencastre), Governor of Ceuta after its capture (Ford).

3. Pedro's son Duarte. He saved Afonso V, in an ambush but perished himself (1464). He was literally cut in pieces by the victorious Moors so that "not a finger could be found for burial" (Juromenha, III, 489 and Ford). Lencastre calls him Count of Viana and Tarouca.

39, 40, 41, 42.   Ford quotes a quaint comment of the French Editor Lamarre, who is of the opinion that these last remarks are not of a sort to give the Catual a high opinion of the Portuguese, and that Camões has forgotten Paul da Gama is speaking. The translator thinks that "What of it?" is the appropriate reply.

46.   Lencastre says that this consultation of the seers is historic and refers to Barros. The circumstance was natural enough. Correa (Stanley, The Three Voyages of Vasco da Gama, pp. 146–147) might account for the seer and the prophecies. Burton points out that a Hindu seer would have consulted not the entrails of animals but the stars in their courses. He thinks that the globe in which Proteus saw the future (X, 7) is connected with Hindu crystal-gazing.

50.   1–4. Burton, well qualified to speak on the point, is sure that these lines have "the true Eastern touch."

51.   This stanza provides a species of contrast with Manuel's dream in IV, 75 ff. Such correspondences are common in the Lusiads, as for instance the lament for Afonso Henriques in III, 84, and for St. Thomas in X, 118, not to mention the barbed criticism of the Italian poets in I, 11, and of Homer and Virgil in V, 87–89.

52.   The Mahometan traders of the Malabar Coast were naturally and immediately alarmed by the arrival of the Portuguese, which was visibly a threat to their control of the commerce of the Orient, on the Red Sea trade route. The fear was justified. In a very few years the Portuguese entirely destroyed the profitable monopoly hitherto enjoyed by the Red Sea traders and their Christian partners, the Merchants of Venice.

55.   5–8. At a guess, this might be an esoteric gibe at the Cardinal Henry, who, although regent for a great part of the reign of Dom Sebastião, showed no trace of the ability of his ancestors.

57.   The naiveté of the sentiments in this stanza is not without interest. The natives had every reason to fear the Portuguese.

61.   The Zamorin's speech is much like what Barros says (I, iv, 9), the catual had reported to the Zamorin about the Portuguese.

62.   5. The King of Calicut's remarks have a historic basis. The presents of the Portuguese were a source of innocent merriment to the persons they were meant to impress. Damiaõ de Goes (I, 91) speaks of this. And Mr. E. Glaser has sent me a long passage from Faria y Sousa on the subject of the anticlimactic effect, when the Portuguese gave gifts which would have been appropriate enough on the west coast of Africa to cultivated Asiatics.

63.   4. Perhaps Camões is remembering Valerius Flaccus (Argonauticon, VII, 227): Omnibus hunc potius communem animantibus orbem.

64.   8. Acidalian Venus. The fountain of Acidalia in Boeotia was sacred to Venus, who has many similar epithets. It has nothing to do with the Idalian Mount in Cyprus, also sacred to the Cyprian.

66.   1. Camões can hardly have failed to recollect his Horace (Satires, I, ix, 59–60):

> . . . . nil sine magno
> Vita labore dedit mortalibus.

68.   7. Gama was made Admiral of India in January 1502.

"On reaching Calicut da Gama [his second voyage] immediately bombarded the town, treating the inhabitants with a savagery too horrible to describe." (Encyclopaedia Britannica, s.v. Gama). He had been provoked by the murder of Cabral's men. But as usual unhappy Asia was no match for Europe in barbarity.

70.   Damião de Goes (I, 87) perhaps provided some of the elements in this speech of Gama's, although in the Chronicle Gama delivers his account of the seventy-year effort to reach the Orient during his first encounter with the Zamorin.

71.   1. Henry the Navigator, son of John I.
2. John I.
8. All these are southern constellations.

72.   6. The Seven Stars are the Great Bear.

73.   4. The Portuguese explorers set up cairns or columns to mark their progress. Camões makes Gama report finding Dias' monument beyond the Cape. Gama's own in India marks the termination of seventy years of Portuguese discovery. Pliny (VI, 18) notes that all conquerors of India, Hercules, Bacchus, Cyrus, Semiramis, and Alexander, erected altars. So does Strabo with respect to Hercules and Bacchus (III, v, 5).

78.   2. The coast is of course the coast of Spain or Portugal.

79.   Damião de Goes (I, 93) has a full account of the Catual's operations.

80.   Lencastre, pathetically and with justice, laments that in this stanza and several that follow the Poet is writing straight historic

narrative divested of imaginative adornment. Nothing can be done about it.

85.   5–6. Another of the places where Oriental aphorism is set down in much the way a modern student of the East might try to reproduce the speech of actual Hindus.

87.   The simile of the mirror goes back to Virgil's simile of light reflected from the surface of bowls of water (Aeneid, VIII, 17–25), as Faria y Sousa (E. Glaser) noted long ago. Burton observed that Ariosto had employed the image (O. F., VIII, 71). Silius Italicus borrowed the idea still earlier in Punica, VII, 143–145. But William Stewart Rose pointed out that Virgil derived it from Apollonius of Rhodes. And as usual Homer is lying at the bottom of the pile (Iliad, XV, 80–83). Camões, characteristically, has given it his own special twist.

89.   This picture of the good soldier should have been studied by "o gram Sebastião." I am indebted to Mr. Edward Glaser for his observations on Faria y Sousa's note on this passage. The gist of it is that Camões very likely had a couple of not very convincing remarks from Cicero in mind. Faria y Sousa also cites Valerius Maximus (VII, 2), who quotes Scipio as opining that it is a bad sign when a soldier says that he had not thought of something. Finally the same useful old commentator brings in Ariosto (O. F., XXXVIII, 38):

> . . . . mal convegna
> A un Capitano dir, "non me'l pensai."

Obviously, the soldier who does not think must be as old as soldiering. The commonplace comes pat enough.

94.   3. Alvaro de Braga and Diogo Dias were their real names, according to Barros (I, iv, 10), who adds that Fernão Martins and four sailors were with them.

97.   Camões could not have avoided knowing Horace's Ode to Contentment (Odes, III, xvi), which begins with Danaë in her brazen tower and develops the power of gold. Camões does not bring his treatment of the subject to so edifying a conclusion.

1. Polydorus, a son of Priam, who was sent for safekeeping to the Thracian King Polymnestor with a huge treasure at the outbreak of the Trojan War. Polymnestor killed him and seized the treasure (Ovid, Met., XIII, 429 ff.; Virgil, Aeneid, III, 21 ff.). It may be observed that Camões ignores the Homeric account of the death of Polydorus, who was slain by Achilles in Hector's presence (Iliad, XX, 407–408).

2. Danaë, the daughter of King Acrisius of Argos, was under a curse that her son should kill her father. Acrisius shut her up in a brazen tower, where Jupiter visited her in the form of a shower of gold. She

bore Perseus, who in due course killed Acrisius by accident (Ovid, Met., IV, 604 ff.).

5. Tarpeia let the Sabines into Rome. As payment for her treason she demanded what they wore on their arms, meaning their golden bracelets. They gave her those but buried her under the weight of their shields. The Tarpeian Rock is named for her (Ovid, Met., XIV, 772 ff., Plutarch, Life of Romulus).

BOOK IX

ARGUMENT

Delivered at last from treason and danger which threatened him, Vasco da Gama departs from Calicut with the glad tidings of the discovery of India. Venus guides him to a delicious island. Description of the island. Festive demonstrations with which the soldiers are welcomed by the Nereids and Gama by Tethys.

THE LUSIADS

THE NINTH BOOK

THEIR goods within the city a long while
Remained unpurchased with the factor pair,
For the infidels, by falsehood and by guile,
The merchants caused from commerce to forbear,
It being end and purpose of their wile
To keep the Indian discoverers there,
Until the ships from Mecca came anew,
Which should our squadron utterly undo.

2

In the Red Gulf, where Egypt's Ptolemy
Could once Arsinoë's foundations lay,
So named after his sister formerly,
Though it be changed to Suez in our day,
There lies the port, removed in some degree
From famous Mecca, which grows fat alway
On the profane and superstitious lies
That from Mahound's religious waters rise.

3

Jiddah they call that harbor, where the trade
Of all the Red Sea flourishes apace,
And vast and grateful gain is thence conveyed
To the Sultan who is master of the place.
Thence, too, according to a compact made
With the people of the unbelieving race,
O'er India's sea fair fleets of tall ships steer
To Malabar for spices every year.

315

IX   And with those ships the Moors had hope alway,
For tall and very mighty were the same,
Our own, which to their commerce put a stay,
Utterly to burn up in crackling flame.
And in this succor such a trust had they
That nothing further from us would they claim
Than that we still should linger in that ground,
Till their ships came from Mecca the renowned.

5

But the Ruler of the Heavens and mankind,
Who, to attain His purpose ultimate,
Means to accomplish it afar can find,
Whereby determined are the ends of Fate,
Made pious accidents work on the mind
Of the Moor Monçaide, with effects so great
That he was saved but to give such advice
To Gama as should merit Paradise.

6

He, whom the Moors in some sort might ignore,
For he too was a Moor, and also had
A part in their intrigue some time before,
Discovered their intention base and bad.
Oft to the ships at anchor far off shore
He went, considering with pity sad
The lawless outrage, which was the design
Of the nation of the Saracen malign.

7

Of the ships he told wise Gama all the tale,
That yearly from Arabian Mecca tracked,
The which his friends so eagerly would hail
As perfect instruments for such an act.
He said with large crews they were wont to sail
And were with Vulcan's dreadful thunders packed.
Gama, by fortune, they might overbear,
If so it were they caught him unaware.

8

Gama considered in himself likewise
The time had come which told him to depart,
Nor hoped for letters of a better guise
From a king who cherished Moslems in his heart.
The factors on the shore he let advise
To seek the ships. And lest a rumor start
Which might prevent their leaving suddenly,
He gave them orders secretly to flee.

9

Nor is it long before the rumors fly
Sounding the tidings, which are all too true,
That in captivity the factors lie,
Being seen as from the city they withdrew.
To the wise Captain's ear when came the cry,
He made reprisal then without ado
On those who to the ships were wont to throng
To sell the jewels they had brought along.

10

These men were ancient merchants, well-renowned
In Calicut and wealthy as might be.
Being missed, among the noblemen resound
Stories that they are prisoners on the sea.
Now on the ships strong sailormen spin round
The capstan and divide their company
For toil. And some by hand the cables start,
While others at the bars heave, strong of heart.

11

And some that stretch along the yards begin
To shake out sail, shouting their chanteys high.
About the King, with even fiercer din,
They yell the fleet is just at point to fly.
The women and the little ones, whose kin
Are captives, in their grief are like to die,
And, screeching, round the Zamorin lament
Husband or father to perdition sent.

IX   The Lusitanian factors he forthright
Sent forth with all their goods in happy case,
And in their Moslem enemies' despite,
That we might free our captives of his race.
And large excuse he made for trick and sleight.
The Captain welcomed with much better grace
Our men set free than the excuses stale.
He loosed a black or two and then made sail.

13

Southward he sailed, for strong conviction grew,
He labored with the heathen King in vain,
Seeking the peace his hope was to ensure,
That he his chance to traffic might obtain.
But since the land in some degree he knew,
Where it bears east, he turned away again,
Leaving the coast, for the dear homeland bound,
With tokens sure of all that he had found.

14

Some men of Malabar with him he bore,
The Zamorin's, whom by the heels he laid,
What time they gave the captive factors o'er.
And he brought burning pepper got by trade.
Banda's sere flower lingers at home no more,
Or the nut, or the black clove that famous made
Molucca's new-found isle, or cinnamon,
The wealth, the fame, the beauty of Ceylon.

15

All this was his because of diligence
In one he took with him, Monçaide true,
Who, breathing in angelic influence,
Would in the book of Christ be written too.
O happy African, whom Providence
In mercy out of dark eternal drew
And, far a-field, showed you the way to come
On high unto your veritable home!

318

16

Thus at length from that burning coast they steer,   **IX**
Turning the prows of the adventurous fleet
Unto the realms where nature hath let rear
In far Good Hope her southern bound and mete.
With the glad tidings and an answer clear,
Lisbon-bound, from the Orient they beat,
And once again with fear and peril cope
On seas unsure, full of their dread and hope.

17

What pleasure the dear land to reach once more,
And the dear kinsmen and dear dwelling place,
Strange tales of the far voyage telling o'er,
And every various sky and various race;
There to enjoy the prize, by travail sore
Well-earned 'mid effort and in bitter case;
Men think, when they feel bliss so infinite,
That the heart's chalice is too slight for it.

18

But the Cyprian goddess, who as ever stood,
By the Sire Eterne commanded, on the side
Of Lusitania, as their genius good,
And for long years had always been their guide,
Already, honor due their labor rude
And prize for grief borne nobly, would provide,
For unto them she had in mind to measure
Amid the dreary waves their fill of pleasure.

19

Venus, who had considered for a space
How they had sailed through that tremendous sea,
And labors, which the god whose native place
Is Amphionian Thebes had brought to be,
Had long while pondered what in such a case
Might best reward them for their misery,
And for them sweet delight and comfort find
In the liquid kingdom, crystalline and kind;

IX Some little rest for them at last, whereby
She might worn manhood with new courage fill
Among her voyagers, with guerdon high
For toils that shorten our brief lifetime still.
And she resolved the thing to notify
Unto her son, whose overwhelming will
Makes gods descend to the vile dust obscene
And raises mortals to the Skies serene.

21

This well considered, it was her design
For the wanderers, in the center of the Sea,
Well to prepare a certain isle divine,
Enamelled bright and green eternally.
Many her isles in the kingdom whose confine
Still the First Mother's earthly breast must be,
Apart from those, subject to her decrees,
That lie within the Gates of Hercules.

22

The sea-nymphs she desired to tarry there,
Those doughtiest of heroes to await
(No one of them but must be called most fair
The eye's delight, heart's grief inveterate),
With jig and dance, for it was all her care
Secret affection thus to animate,
So that a greater zeal the maids might move
To please the men with whom they fell in love.

23

Such a device aforetime she had tried,
That the son she bore Anchises thus might find
Welcome in meadows which the bullock's hide
Girdled about by trick of subtle kind.
She sought her son, in whom alone reside
Her powers, young Cupid of the cruel mind,
Who, as he helped her in old enterprise,
In this would aid her and abet likewise.

24

To her car she yoked the birds that their life through IX
Continually death's exequies do sing.
And those whose form Peristera must indue,
What time the daisies she was harvesting,
Around the goddess as she journeyed, flew,
Bartering lascivious kisses on the wing.
She, whereso'er she wandered, everywhere
To gentler motion stilled the windy air.

25

O'er the Idalian mountain did she bend
Where, as it chanced, her bow-boy bode the while,
With many henchmen, for he doth intend
An expedition in the noblest style
Against the rebel earth, so to amend
Great errors that so long the world beguile,
Which loves too much gifts granted from above,
Designed for use alone and not for love.

26

He saw Actaeon in the hunt, austere
And in mad brutal pastime ever blind,
Who, to chase furious brutes of aspect drear,
Fled from fair human bodies and mankind.
To show him Dian's beauty, a severe
But pleasant penalty, Love had in mind.
On guard, Actaeon, lest in this very hour
The dogs you love consume you and devour.

27

He looks upon the princes the world o'er,
Whose thought to public good can never reach,
And sees what love they have is nothing more
Than of themselves and what self-love can teach.
He sees the throngs through courts of kings that pour,
Instead of doctrine sound and truthful speech,
Sell adulation, which but ill indeed
Consents from springing wheat to pluck the weed.

IX He sees that they to poverty who owe
Divine love, and pure pity to the folk,
Only the love of wealth and places know,
Under integrity and virtue's cloak.
As tyrants hard, as cruel men, they show,
Who frame our laws and harshness feigned invoke.
For laws which favor kings are stablished high,
But those in favor of the people die.

29

And last, he sees that none loves what he should
But only his own covetous intent.
Nor any longer does Love think it good
Thus to remit his just hard punishment.
His chiefs he gathers, that a multitude
He may raise up, fit for that war's event,
Which he would wage against the wicked sway
Of those who all his precepts disobey.

30

Many of the little loves so light on wing
All busy at their various labors slave,
For some their piercing barbs are sharpening;
Others the while the shafts of arrows shave,
And, as they work, the uncertain chance they sing
That love still suffers, in the sweet-cadenced stave,
Sonorous melody with parts well found.
Smooth is the verse, angelic is the sound.

31

In the deathless smithies, where the arrowhead
They hammer out, so well that pierces through,
Hearts all in flame they use in firewood's stead,
And entrails live and throbbing add thereto.
The waters that should temper weapons dread
From miserable lovers' tears they drew.
The living flame, the immortal gleam, desire,
Is the one burning unconsuming fire.

322

To keep their hands in, some among them fare   **IX**
To smite hard hearts of peasants rough-beseen.
And thick the sighs come breathing through the air
From all those stricken by the arrows keen.
And lovely are the nymphs who have in care
Wounds so received, whose ministry may mean
Not only life to broken hearts forlorn
But also bring to life the yet unborn.

33

Most beautiful are some, others again
Are foul, as suits with the wounds' quality,
For venom that has run through every vein
Sometimes requires a bitter remedy.
And there are victims bound as with a chain
By subtle words of witches' wizardry.
This haps at times when secret herbs have shed
Their dangerous poison on the arrowhead.

34

From shots so random and immoderate,
That awkward cherubs oft and oft let go,
Arise a thousand loves inordinate
Amid the stricken people in their woe.
Also 'mid heroes of the noblest state
Cases of love forbidden we may show,
As with the maids Biblis and Cinyréa,
The Assyrian lad, the stripling of Judea.

35

And you, you great men, for some shepherdess,
See well enough the cruel wounds you get.
You ladies, too, lured by low men's address,
Not seldom stumble into Vulcan's net.
Some through the dark hours yearn in bitterness,
And others scale the roof or parapet.
But I believe that such a love defiled
Is fault more of the Mother than her Child.

IX But now the light car in the meadow green
The bright swans brought to rest with gentle care.
Venus, on whose sweet face the rose is seen
Among the snows, swiftly descended there.
And, to receive her, with a jocund mien,
Approached the archer who high Heaven would dare.
And thither all the attendant cupids move
To kiss her hand, who goddess is of love.

37
But she, that time she might not waste in vain,
Embraced her son and said with confidence:
"O my belovèd son, whose hands contain
The very source of my omnipotence,
My son, in whom my forces still remain,
Holding as naught Typhéan armaments,
I am compelled by hard necessity
To beg thee in thy power to succor me.

38
"Thou seest the Lusitanians' troubled state,
A people of whom long I much have made;
From Fate I learned, since I am friend to Fate,
That these adored me and due honor paid.
And since with such good will they imitate
Old splendors of my Romans, to their aid
I have addressed me with all arts I know,
As far as our two powers conjoined can go.

39
"Since Bacchus by his hateful treachery
In India this people could molest,
And since, by damage of the heaving sea,
Dead men they were, rather than men distressed,
In that same ocean that is wont to be
Their terror I desire that they may rest
And take their pleasure and find guerdon meet
For labors, which their memories shall keep sweet.

"This I would ask, that thou with love wilt smite   IX
The Nereids, where in the vast deeps they bide.
Let passion for the Portuguese burn bright,
Who have but now a new-found world descried.
Those nymphs together on an isle shall light,
Which, in the center of the deepest tide
Of Ocean, I shall presently prepare,
With Flora's gifts, and Zephyr's, painted fair.

41

"There, with a thousand cates and odorous wine,
Refreshment meet and blossoms roseate,
In palaces superb and crystalline,
On delicate beds, themselves more delicate,
'Mid all delights, save those not sweet and fine,
Let the nymphs enamored for the wanderers wait,
Wounded by love, prompt to yield out of hand
Whatever eyes that covet them demand.

42

"I will that Neptune's realm imperial,
Where I was born, get noble progeny,
And the vile world malign may learn withal,
That has rebelled from thy authority.
So let it find that adamantine wall
Avails not, nor does sad hypocrisy.
He who shuns love on land but ill will fare,
If thy immortal fires on Ocean flare."

43

Thus Venus. And her child malevolent
At once made haste to do as he was told.
For the rich ivory bow forthwith he sent
And chose the shafts whose points are dipped in gold.
And in her car the Cyprian, content,
Took up her son, with an arch look and bold,
Giving free rein unto the birds whose song
The death of Phaëthon lamented long.

IX   But Cupid spake of the necessity
Of using a most famous go-between,
Who, though a thousand times his enemy,
Had quite as oft his coadjutress been—
The goddess huge and rash eternally
Brags on, and truth may mean or lie may mean,
And, where she flies, sees with a hundred eyes
What with a thousand tongues she magnifies.

45

They sought her out and bade her run before
And, as she went, on her clear trump to sound
The praises of the sailors o'er and o'er,
More than for any ever yet renowned.
Already Fame the caves of Ocean's floor
Had pierced, and, murmuring, sowed the tale around.
And truth she tells, or what is held to be,
For the goddess brings with her Credulity.

46

The splendid praise, the noble rumor heard,
In the gods' spirits, who had thought so ill
Of brave men, moved by Bacchus' evil word,
Aroused some little feeling of good will.
And woman's bosom, which is lightly stirred,
Whatever course is chosen altering still,
Now thought it cruelty and wicked zeal
Unkindness for such bravery to feel.

47

The furious boy now one by one let fly
His shafts. At each shot Ocean gave a groan.
Straight through the waves heaving unquietly,
Some lanced, where others in long curves had flown.
The nymphs fall and aloud their sorrows cry
From their most secret hearts, with burning moan,
Before the faces of their loves they scan,
For Fame can do as much as seeing can.

48

The tameless lad now bent the moon-horns twain IX
Of the bow of ivory with excelling might,
For to wound Tethys he was very fain,
Who more than any held him in despite.
Within his quiver no more shafts remain,
Nor on the waters living nymph in sight.
Or if the wounded there still living lie,
'Tis with the knowledge they must shortly die.

49

Give place, cerulean combers, huge of height,
For, look you, Venus brings a remedy
Where she displays the sails, swelling and white,
That ride across the crests of Neptune's sea.
Hot Love, that you may make your answer right
Unto the fires of femininity,
This is of honest modesty required,
That she do all that Venus has desired.

50

The nymphs' bright choir now deck themselves with
And presently in company are gone.   [care.
Dancing sweet ancient dances, they repair
Unto the isle, and Venus leads them on.
The beauteous goddess gave them counsel there
To do what she in love had often done.
And they, whom Love had conquered one and all,
Forthwith the victims of her counsel fall.

51

But now the ships go plowing the broad way
Toward the dear homeland, over Ocean vast,
And fain to take sweet water in were they,
For voyage that so long was like to last,
When, rapturous, as they closed up their array,
Upon the Isle of Love, their eye they cast,
While Memnon's lovely mother, through the sphere,
Of Heaven, calm and beautiful, dawned clear.

327

IX Afar they saw the isle loom, cool and fair,
Which Venus through the waters toward them bore
(Just as the wind a milk-white sail might bear),
Wherever the strong ships were seen before.
For, lest the armada should pass by her there,
Nor, as she hoped, find harbor on her shore,
Acidalia, sure o'er all things to prevail,
Her island steered wherever they might sail.

53

But fixed and motionless she made it stay,
Seeing that the sailors saw and sought the place,
Like Delos when Latona laboring lay,
Who Phoebus bore and the goddess of the chase.
And thither, where the coastline formed a bay,
Forthwith the prow cut through the sea apace.
The beach was curved and still, and the white sand
Strewn with red shells by Cytherea's hand.

54

And there, uptowering in their graceful pride,
Three mountains exquisite for shape appear,
Painted with grassy greens diversified,
Deep in the sweet isle of such pleasant cheer.
Freshening the verdure, from the summits slide
Transparent rills out of the fountains clear,
For still they bubble up through pebbles white,
Sonorous waters in perpetual flight.

55

In the sweet vale, between the hills that wends,
At length together run the limpid streams,
And form a mirror that afar extends,
Lovely as any that the fancy dreams.
And over it a gracious grove impends,
That like to one who dons fine raiment seems,
Viewing himself in crystal-bright reflection,
Which paints his every feature to perfection.

56

Skyward a thousand fruit-trees tower tall,
Laden with apples odorous and fair.
The orange bears its fruit ambrosial,
Which has the very hue of Daphne's hair.
The citron totters as about to fall
Under the yellow burdens he must bear;
And beauteous lemons breathe out perfume here,
And as they were the breasts of maids appear.

57

The forest kind, which on declivities,
With leafy mane, make such a splendid show,
Alcides' poplars are, and laurel trees,
The golden god loved and lamented so,
Cytherea's myrtles and Queen Cybele's
Dark pines, whom faithless love could overthrow.
And also there doth the sharp cypress rise,
Still pointing to ethereal Paradise.

58

Pomona's offerings, Nature here is fain,
With various sorts of savor, to contrive.
Nor is there need at husbandry to strain.
Without such toil, better the harvests thrive.
There are the cherries with the purple stain,
And mulberries, which their name from love derive.
That apple which once came from Persia's field,
On alien shores, now gives a better yield.

59

And crimson-colored the pomegranates gape,
The which, O ruby, make your price more mean.
In the elm branches hangs the lusty grape,
With here a rosy cluster, there a green.
You pears, like to the pyramid in shape,
If your rich boughs you still would live between,
Submit to any vengeance, which the beak
Of cruel sparrow may upon you wreak.

IX   There is a tapestry most fair and fine
That covers over all the rustic place,
And Achemenian weave makes less divine,
Lending to the dark vale a sweeter grace.
And here Cephisian flowers the head incline
Above the pool's serene and shining face.
Cinyras' son and grandson blooms hard by,
For whom, O Paphian goddess, yet you sigh.

61

It were a thing not easy to declare,
In earth and heaven beholding dyes the same,
If flowers their color drew from morning fair
Or morning's color from fair flowers came.
Zephyr and Flora's self had painted there
The violets with the hue that lovers claim,
The crimson lily, and the rose new-blown
That in the cheeks of girlhood still has shone,

62

And white flags, on which dawn her dewy tear
Has dropped, with the sweet marjoram beside.
The letters on the hyacinth appear,
For whom Latona's son, lamenting, cried.
Between the flowers and fruits, one saw it clear,
How sharply Chloris with Pomona vied.
And birds in flight utter melodious sound,
While happy beasts inhabit all that ground.

63

On the waters the white swan repeats his air,
While from the bough gives answer Philomel.
The shadow of his horns no more can scare
Acteon, seen in the bright crystal well.
And lightly here leaps up the flying hare
From the dense brush, or timorous gazelle.
Swift to his nest the swallow homes once more,
In his bill carrying his little store.

Those second Argonauts their landing made IX
In that delicious weather from the fleet,
Where fairest nymphs throughout the forest strayed,
As if they felt a confidence complete.
And some upon their pleasant zithers played,
Others on harps or flutes resounding sweet.
And some with golden bows made feint untrue
Of hunting beasts which they did not pursue.

65

For thus had counselled them their mistress wise,
To wander through the forest, scattered wide,
That the heroes in a moment of surprise
Might fall in love with those whom they espied.
Some, who upon the grace without disguise
Of their fair bodies hopefully relied,
Their artificial beauties put away
And, in the pure stream bathing, naked lay.

66

But the brave lads, who on the beaches there
Set foot, all yearning for the land that came
(For every man of them ashore would fare),
And with the passion of the chase a-flame,
Thought little that, without a gin or snare,
They, in those lovely hills, would come on game
So gentle, so well-tamed, and so benign,
And ere now stricken by the Erycine.

67

Some lads, who in the cross-bow or the gun
Have put their trust, in hope to strike the deer,
Through sombre thickets and the forest run,
And on with resolution persevere.
Others through shades, which, from the fierce noon sun,
Protect the greenness, rove, now there, now here,
Along the waters that so gently pour
Over white pebbles to the pleasant shore.

IX   But they began to notice suddenly
Colors most various where green boughs embower,
Colors which, at a glance, the eye might see
Were never of the rose or other flower,
But fine wool or shot silk's variety,
Which upon love exert exciting power,
In which when vestured, many a human rose
By artifice to greater beauty grows.

69

Velloso gave a great shout as in fright.
"My lords," he said, "strange quarry have we here.
This wood, if yet holds the old pagan rite,
Sacred to goddesses might well appear.
More we discover than the human sprite
Could ever wish. 'Tis manifestly clear
That there are matters great and excellent
The world conceals from the improvident.

70

"Follow these goddesses, and let us find
Whether they be fantastical or true."
He spoke, and forthwith swifter than the hind
The heroes rushed the water-meadows through.
And the nymphs fled through branches intertwined,
But with less speed than purposeful ado,
Smiling the while, yet raising many a cry,
Till, bit by bit, they let the hounds draw nigh.

71

The wind blows wide one runner's golden hair,
Of another whips up high the dainty dress.
Desire is kindled, fattening on such fare
As white skin seen in sudden nakedness.
One rises, that had fallen with much care,
With greater show of kindness than distress,
For, tangled with her, he had fallen too,
Who would the nymph along the sands pursue.

72

And others on that other quarter light
Where naked goddesses a-bathing lie,
Who sudden cry aloud in their affright,
As not expecting violence so high.
Some, feigning shame a less thing in their sight
Than force can be, all mother-naked fly
Into the thicket, yielding to the eyes
What virtue to the lusting hand denies.

73

Another, as to guard the modesty
Of the huntress-goddess, with what haste she may,
Hides in the flood. Another hurriedly
Would don the garments that she put away.
One of the lads, though clad and shod was he,
Plunged boldly in (he feared that to delay
And strip might prove that over late he came),
In water to put out his inward flame.

74

As the hunter's dog that crafty is, and tried,
Used with hurt fowl from water to return,
Sees the gun raised, his master's cheek beside,
Against the long familiar duck or herne,
And, ere the shot crack, scarcely can abide,
But straight leaps in, nor doubts his prize to earn,
Swimming and yelping; that youth so darted he
Towards her, not Phoebus' sister certainly.

75

Leonard, a soldier in his art complete,
Skilful withal, and a most amorous knight,
To whom love dealt not merely one defeat,
But treated with continual despite,
Had held it the presupposition meet,
His love affairs would never end aright,
Though yet of hope not wholly desperate,
As to some alteration in his fate.

IX He tried his luck, and in pursuit he pressed
Of Éphyre, beauty's type, for he was fain
To give to her, more than to all the rest,
What Nature gave us to be given again.
Weary from running, thus did he protest:
"Beauty, not made to show such fierce disdain,
Since o'er this life I grant you victory whole,
Wait for the body whence you take the soul!

77

"O purest nymph, of flight the others tire.
At their foe's will they make surrender due.
You only flee me only through the briar.
How did you learn 'tis I who follow you?
If it were told you by misfortune dire,
Which everywhere my footsteps must pursue,
Never believe it, for, when I believed,
My luck each hour a thousand times deceived.

78

"Weariless, you weary me. And, if you will,
Flee from me, for to touch you cannot be.
My fate is such as must your hope fulfill,
And so make winning you too hard for me.
Wait, if it please you. I am curious still
To know the arts by which you shall go free.
At last you'll see what vantage I shall get.
'Twixt hand and wheat-ear, what a wall is set!

79

"Oh! flee me not! So may the little day
Of this your beauty never take its flight
For, only if your fleeting foot you stay,
Shall you subdue my fate's outrageous might.
What emperor, what army in array,
Has power to shake my fortune's hateful spite?
Which on my heart's desire still follows sure,
And, if you flee not, you alone can cure.

IX

"Will you then take the part of my ill fate?
To aid the stronger is a weakling's deed.
My heart, once free, will you thus subjugate?
Release it, and the swifter you will speed.
Is not this soul of mine too mean a weight,
Which bound in threads of gleaming gold you lead
Your slave? Or have you changed my lucklessness?
And does my captive spirit now weigh less?

81

"For you in this one hope I still will chase,
Since either you such weight will not endure,
Or, by the virtue of your lovely face,
My star shall change his harsh distemperature.
This altered, you no more will flee apace,
For Love will smite you, gentle and demure,
And you will stay for me, if Love should smite.
And if you stay, my hope will reach its height."

82

Less swift the fair nymph fled, her body dear
Being fain to yield to him who followed sad.
Also she longed his sweetest song to hear
And the tale of all the amorous wounds he had.
She turned to him a face gentle and clear,
And yet all full of gaiety and glad,
And let herself fall at the victor's feet,
Who melted utterly in love's pure heat.

83

What famished kisses were there in the wood!
What gentle sound of pretty lamentation!
What sweet caress! What angry modest mood
That into bright mirth knew sweet transformation!
From dawn till noon such pleasures they pursued
As Venus kindled to a conflagration,
Which men would rather taste of than condemn.
Rather condemn who cannot taste of them.

IX All the fair nymphs, in this conforming quite,
At peace with sailor-lovers all around,
Adorned the men with garlands of delight,
With laurel, gold, and flowers in foison found.
As loving wives, they gave their hands milk-white.
With words in form and stipulation bound,
They promised their eternal company,
In life and death, with mirth and honesty.

85

One greater than the rest, unto whom bend
All the nymph choir who yield obedience true
(Coelus and Vesta's child, as they pretend,
Which from her lovely face is clear to view),
Who land and sea makes marvel without end,
Gave the illustrious Chief the welcome due
Such high desert, frankly and queenly done,
Like a great lady without paragon.

86

Thereafter, who she was the dame made clear,
And, in high speech of loftiest style ornate,
Let Gama know that she had met him here
By the strong influence of changeless Fate,
To show the secrets of the united sphere
Of the vast earth and seas none navigate,
But by profoundest prophecy made known.
And this his nation had deserved alone.

87

She bade him rise and by the hand him led
To the tall summit of a mount divine,
Whereon a splendid palace raised its head,
Wrought all of crystal and pure gold and fine,
And there the greater part of day they sped
In joy continual and jest benign.
She in her palace revels in love's powers,
But her sisters in the shadows 'mid the flowers

88

And thus the brave and charming company
Linger out the best portion of the day,
While in the soul sweet unknown gaiety
Knows how such heavy labor to repay.
Of the guerdon of great deeds and bravery
Famous and fierce, the world takes count alway,
The prize at length well earned, gigantic fame,
And the glory of the high exalted name.

89

For Tethys, the sea-nymphs with such beauty bright,
And the painted Island of angelic kind
Are nothing more than honors which delight,
Whereby life is exalted and refined.
And all pre-eminence at glory's height,
The triumphs, brows that palms or laurels bind,
The splendor and the wonder of it all,
These are the joys that in the Isle befall.

90

The immortalities, which men of old,
Loving the great, poetically might frame,
On starred Olympus he might have and hold,
Who rose to them on the bright wings of fame,
For high things that he did, by conduct bold
And toils enormous. And such course men name
The road of virtue, rock-set, huge of height,
But at last sweetness, pleasure, and delight.

91

Those immortalities naught else they were
Than prize for deathless action without stain,
Which the world used on heroes to confer,
Made gods by courage, though of human strain.
For Phoebus, Mercury, Mars, and Jupiter,
Romulus, Aeneas, and the Theban twain,
Dian, Ceres, Pallas, Juno, even they
Were all of them but feeble human clay.

IX But Fame, the trumpet of such action high,
Strangely in the world doth them denominate
As gods or demigods that never die,
As patron sires, as heroes, as the great.
Therefore all you who glory magnify,
If in this world you seek such noble state,
Must wake from idle sleep deserving scorn,
Which makes a slave out of the soul free-born,

93

And curb with the stern bit all impulse lewd,
Ambitions sought too oft unworthily,
And the obscene and sombre turpitude
Of infamous oppressing tyranny.
Vain honors, purest gold, have ne'er endued
One man with veritable dignity.
To merit, not possess them, seems the best,
But worst, unmeriting, to stand possessed.

94

Either in peace just laws unchanging frame,
That give the great naught from the poor's distress,
Or else take up the arms that shine like flame,
The Moslem foe's false doctrine to suppress.
Thus you will found strong realms of potent name,
And all men will have more and no man less.
This to your hand riches deserved will bring,
And honor which makes life a noble thing.

95

Keep the King famous for your high love's sake.
Now, it may be, with counsel wisely planned,
Now with the sword that shall immortal make
Your names, like all your forebears in the land.
The impossible you do not undertake.
Where will is there's a way, and you shall stand
With splendid figures of heroic kind
And in the isle of Venus welcome find.

NOTES

BOOK IX

2. 2. For Arsinoë, see X, 98, 3, note.

3. 1. Jiddah, the Port of Mecca. Soares' fantastic operations there have their amusing side. See X, 50, note.

4. 3. Lencastre rightly points out that the arrival of the Portuguese ships was an immediate threat to the Red Sea spice trade. In a very few years Lisbon superseded Venice as the great Emporium for the trade of the Orient.

7. The plot to destroy Gama's fleet seems to be historical if we can trust Barros (I, iv, 9). Camões has practically paraphrased a considerable part of this chapter of The Decades of India.

8. In his Encyclopedia account (Eleventh Edition) of Camões and the Lusiads, Professor Prestage, the most accurate of men, states that Gama came back from India with a letter from the Zamorin. And the Encyclopedia elsewhere (s. v. India, History) quotes the following letter purporting to be from the Zamorin to Manuel: "Vasco da Gama, a nobleman of your household, has visited my kingdom and has given me great pleasure. In my kingdom there is abundance of cinnamon, cloves, ginger, pepper, and precious stones. What I seek from thy country is gold, silver, coral, and scarlet."

In this stanza Camões appears to imply that Gama had no letter from the Zamorin, which seems likely in view of the violent circumstances of his departure. The letter quoted above has in my sight a factitious air, as if it had been composed on the principles of Pooh-Bah. Except as an emporium, the Malabar Coast would have had no great supply of cloves. Cinnamon flourishes in Ceylon. But pepper they would have had and possibly ginger. Barros states that such a letter was sent (I, iv, 10), and so does de Goes (I, 94). I still think the letter was concocted on the way home "to corroborate a bald and unconvincing narrative." The Roteiro is the original source for the letter (Ravenstein, The First Voyage of Vasco da Gama).

10. According to Barros, the men whom Gama seized were fishermen, not merchants, but de Goes (I, 93) says they were persons of distinction.

339

13.　　1. Gama left Calicut August 29, 1498 after a stay of seventy-four days (Barros, quoted by Lencastre).

　　4. But since the land in some degree he knew—Correa (Stanley, The Three Voyages of Vasco da Gama, p. 225) says Gama visited Cananor, in which he differs from the other sources. Perhaps this line is based on Correa.

14.　　1. For once Burton agrees with Macedo. Carrying off the unhappy men of Calicut was thoroughly dishonorable. Barros (I, iv, 10) tries to excuse Gama on the ground that some of the goods had not been surrendered. The real motive appears in Barros, I, iv, 11. The captives on their return were to report on the power of Portugal. De Goes (I, 95) says Gama sent reassuring messages to the families of his victims.

　　5. Banda. There are several small islands of this name in the southeastern quadrant of the Molucca group. Banda's sere flower is mace, which is really the dried pulp of the fruit of which nutmeg is the kernel. Botanists call the nutmeg tree Myristica fragrans.

　　7. Molucca. The nut is the nutmeg.

　　The clove's scientific name is Caryophyllus aromaticus. It is a variety of pink.

17.　　8. There is a line that plays with this conceit about the chalice in Ode V (Juromenha, II, 269), and another in Canzone XI (Juromenha, II, 217).

　　The whole stanza seems to owe something to Catullus, XXXI, 7-11.

18.　　1-3. With what is certainly a leer, Burton says: "The joint mention of the Cyprian Goddess and the Padre Eterno has been justly blamed." But, as has been often noticed, Milton scrambles Scripture and Myth in Lycidas.

19.　　4. Amphionean Thebes, so-called because Amphion, the inventor of music, raised the walls by playing on his lyre. Bacchus is the god in question.

　　8. The crystalline kingdom is a phrase which may be found elsewhere in Camões, for instance Elegy XX (Juromenha, III, 233).

20.　　De Goes (I, 96) says thirty men died on the way back to Melinde. The ships made the African coast at Mogadiscio in Somaliland.

21.　　6. I will not go into "the battle royal" (Burton) about this line. I follow Professor Ford, who adopts the reading of Senhora de Vasconcelos.

　　Burton was never more eloquent than on the episode of the Isle of Venus. I should like to quote him entire, as Professor Ford has done, for no man was better qualified to understand "the revenge of success, and the 'rapture of repose' following a successful exploit full of difficulty, hardship, pain, and danger. Every explorer knows it right well." Straight from the horse's mouth!

23. 1. When Aeneas came to Carthage, Venus prepared the way for him by causing Cupid to inflame Dido.

3. Dido had tricked the natives of Tunisia by asking for as much land as a bullock's hide would enclose. She cut the hide in strips and thus got enough territory to start her settlement.

24. 1. Where the idea that swans sing arose, and why, is left to the ingenious reader. Pliny is skeptical (X, 33), but see Rackham's note on the whooping swan, Loeb Edition). Camões doesn't forget his Horace (III, xxviii) or Venus, who rules Cnidus and the gleaming Cyclades, and driving her yoke of swans visits Paphos.

2. Peristera was changed into a dove by Cupid in a moment of unjustified irritation.

25. 1. The Idalian mountain is Idalium in Cyprus.

4. Some commentators profess (as my betters have noticed) to find many specific allusions in the account of Cupid's preparations which begins at this point. Is it likely, in view of the invocation at the beginning of the Epic and the valedictory at the end, that Camões meant to satirize King Sebastian as Actaeon in Stanza 26? Burton is, I think, at his very worst here.

26. The history of Actaeon is related with great detail in Ovid, Met., III, 138–252, and with less in Heroides, XX, 103–5.

28. This stanza is probably an attack on corrupt clergymen, not unlike the outburst in X, 119. Ford's point that it is not specific with respect to the Jesuits or the Holy Office is probably correct. The Holy Office was established in Portugal in 1536, and did not command the entire admiration of the people. There were various schools of thought with respect to the Jesuits also.

30. 6. Burton sees a resemblance to Sonnet I.

34. 7. Biblis, a lady who died of guilty love for her brother (Ovid, Met., IX, 454 ff.).

Cinyrea, Myrrha, daughter of Cinyras, King of Cyprus. Her tragic passion for her father resulted in the birth of Adonis. Myrrha herself was transformed into the shrub whence the perfume myrrh is extracted (Ovid, Met., X, 312 ff.).

8. The Assyrian lad is probably Ninyas, the son of Semiramis, who had an affair with his mother.

The stripling of Judea is Amnon who violated his sister Tamar. Absalom killed him (II Samuel, 13).

Burton has two other candidates as well. Antiochus, the son of Seleucus, who fell in love with his stepmother, and Reuben who got involved with his father's concubine. But these last seem improbable, although Camões wrote a play on Seleucus.

35. 4. Camões could have found the net of Vulcan in Statius (Thebais, II, 271) and Valerius Flaccus (Argonauticon, II, 87–106), as well as in a dozen other poets, for instance Odyssey, VIII, 266–366 and Ovid (Ars Amatoria, II, 561). The net was used to trap Mars and Venus. Camões speaks of the net in Canzone XV (Juromenha, II, 227). The stanza resembles the speech of Dionysa in Camões' play Filodemo, Act II, Scene VI (Juromenha, IV, 367).

37. 6. Typheus was confined under Mt. Aetna. There the thunderbolts of Jupiter were by some believed to be manufactured. The meaning of the passage is that Cupid can defy Jupiter himself. The whole speech is imitated from Ovid, Met., V, 365 ff., and Virgil, Aeneid, I, 663–666.

40. 8. Flora, the goddess of flowers, is the wife of Zephyr, the west wind.

43. 3. It is to be noted that Cupid on this occasion used only the gold-pointed arrows. Ovid describes the two kinds of arrows in Met., I, 468–71.

7. Swans draw the chariot of Venus. Cycnus (Swan) was a friend of Phaëthon and was changed into a swan while he was lamenting the death of the unsuccessful charioteer.

44. 2. Fame. "Enter Rumor painted full of tongues."

The whole passage has touches from the account of Fame in Ovid (Met., XII, 39–63). In the octaves on Saint Ursula, a parallel stanza appears. But these octaves are under suspicion.

See also Ovid, Met., IX, 134–140, Virgil, Aeneid, IV, 173–183, and Persius, V, 1–4, whose editor in the Loeb Edition has many other parallels.

46. 5–6. These lines about feminine changeability are of course drawn from Virgil (Aeneid, IV, 569–70).

Camões plays with the same idea in the famous sonnet XIV (Juromenha, II, 8), Todo animal da calma repousava.

48. 3. Tethys, one of Neptune's consorts and a goddess of the sea.

49. Horace again (Odes, II, x):
contrahes vento, nimium secundo
turgida vela.

51. 7. Memnon's mother, Aurora, the Dawn (Memnonis alma parens, Martial, VIII, xxi).

53. 3. The island of Delos was believed to have floated to its present position where it was fixed at the time that Latona gave birth to Apollo and Diana. Strabo (X, v, 2) quotes Pindar for floating Delos. Pliny (XII, 89) tells the story.

54.   The Portuguese find this landscape beautiful past description. Claudian's account of the Vale of Henna (De Raptu Proserpinae, II, 101 ff.) may have something to do with Stanzas 54–57.

57.   3. The poplar is sacred to Hercules (Alcides).

4. The golden god is Apollo. He lamented for Daphne, who became a laurel tree.

5. Cybele's lover Atys was transformed into a fir as a penalty for breaking his vow of chastity. Sonnet CXC, as pointed out by Burton, relates the legend. It is just possible, as Burton suggests that there is a pun on the word "Pinheiro" in the sonnet, which implied a compliment to a Bishop of that name. Catullus' terribly moving verses on Atys (Catullus, LXIII) must have been known to Camões.

Lamarre's note (quoted by Ford) is to the effect that Ovid's catalogue of trees (Met., X, 99 ff.) is the original.

A sort of sketch of this stanza may be found in the Octaves on Echo and Narcissus (Juromenha, II, 356).

6. Ovid (Met., X, 140) says of the cypress into which Cyparissus was changed:

sidereum gracili spectare cacumine caelum.

58.   1. Pomona is the goddess to whom fruits are sacred.

3–4. Horace (Epodes, XVI, 41 ff.) describes that most convenient type of agriculture which is practised in the Islands of the Blest. And Strabo quotes Odyssey, IX, 109, to the effect that all things grow there without sowing and without the plow.

6. The Portuguese word for mulberry is "amora" which has no etymological connection with "amor."

7–8. The Persian apple is the peach (Pliny, XV, 12). Hamilton and Falconer in a note to Strabo (XVII, ii, 2) quote Diodorus Siculus (I, 34), who says the peach was brought from Ethiopia by the Persian Cambyses.

60.   3. Achemenian, Persian, from Achemenes, ancestor of Cyrus.

5. The narcissus is called Cephisian because Narcissus was the son of the Boeotian (not the Attic) river Cephisus (Ovid, Met., III, 343). Camões has a long poem on the story of Echo and Narcissus (Juromenha, II, 345), and Narcissus comes into Canzone XVI (Juromenha, II, 232) in some particularly musical lines.

7. Cinyras' son and grandson is Adonis. The flower that sprang from his blood is thought to be the anemone (windflower). See Ovid, Met., X, 503. The phrase, son and grandson of Cinyras, occurs in Elegy X (Juromenha, III, 201).

8. Venus is the Paphian goddess.

61.   1–4. This pretty antithesis is apparently derived from Ausonius, De Rosis Nascentibus, 15–16.

> Ambigeris, raperetne rosis Aurora ruborem
> An daret et flores tingueret orta dies—

But Burton found it in Ariosto (O. F., XXXIV, 49).

5. Burton says that Camões means the white violet. Two other passages in Camões (Eclogue I, Juromenha, III, 12, and Eclogue VII, Juromenha, III, 84) seem to bear this out. Burton runs it down in Horace (Odes, III, 10), Ovid (Ars Amatoria, I, 729), Petrarch, and Mary Stuart.

62.   3. The hyacinth is so-called in memory of Hyacinthus, a friend whom Apollo accidentally killed with a quoit. The letters AI (Alas) are supposed to be inscribed on the petals (Ovid, Met., X, 209–215, Virgil, Eclogue III, 106–107). I like to think that the flower intended by the poet is the Turk's-cap Lily.

In Canzone XVI the groans engraved on the flower are described. Claudian (De Raptu Proserpinae, II, 131–132) is specific:

> Te quoque flebilibus moerens, Hyacinthe, figuris
> Narcissumque metunt.

63.   1. Burton notes that this is not a dying swan and says he has heard "their curious piping."

2. Philomel, the nightingale. The myth is summarized in a note on III, 32, 1.

66.   8. Mount Eryx in Sicily is rich in legend and sacred to Venus and her son, whence the adjective Erycine.

> . . . . Erycina ridens
> quam Iocus circum volat et Cupido.
> Horace, Odes, I, ii.

71.   A great part of this stanza seems derived from Ovid's description of the flight of Daphne (Met., I, 527–529).

75.   1. Leonard. See VI, 40, 5, and note.

76.   2. Ephyre is the name of many nymphs, not to mention one of the names of the city Corinth. It does not appear that it has any special connection. The description of her flight has a close resemblance to the account of Daphne in Met., I, 452 ff. It is probably absurd to point out the numberless variations on Ovidian themes in this episode.

77.   4. "Good old Fanshawe" (Burton's just phrase) has the perfect translation of this line:

> Who told thee, I am I, that follow thee?

7–8. Martial (II, xxv) has the same idea: "You never grant my prayer, Galla, but are always refusing. If you are always false, my prayer is now: Galla, refuse!"

78.   8. The last line of the stanza is a direct quotation from Petrarch, and in the text appears in the original Italian. Burton refers to some

older edition. The sonnet from which Camões quotes is No. LVI in Bartoli's edition of Sonetti e Canzoni.

81.   7–8. In the Portuguese there is a play on the two senses of esperar which means to hope and to wait.

83.   This stanza at least looks as if Camões had not forgotten Ovid (Ars Amatoria, II, 724):

Et dulces gemitus aptaque verba ioco.

85.   3. Camões' confusion of Vesta with Terra, who, Lemprière supposes, is Tethys' mother, may arise from the fact that Vesta has some affinity with Rhea and Cybele.

90.   Burton derives this stanza from Cicero, De Natura Deorum, II, 24, as Professor Ford notes.

7–8. It is possible that the teachings of Pythagoras are alluded to here, as in Persius (III, 57).

91.   6. The Thebans must be Bacchus and Hercules, as Professor Ford notices. Claudian (De Quarto Consulatu, Honorii, 132) says the glory of Bacchus and Hercules is the living principle of Thebes.

In this stanza, written, as it is thought, at the behest of the Censor, Camões expresses the ideas of the Sicilian philosopher, Euhemerus, who believed "that the gods of mythology were but deified mortals."

93.   7–8. Professor Ford notices Burton's observation that a very similar couplet occurs in Erçilla's Araucana, the first part of which was published three years before the Lusiads. But he adds that Erçilla's couplet is in the second part of his poem, which was not published till after the Lusiads was in print.

BOOK X

ARGUMENT

The feast of Tethys for the voyagers. Sirena's prophetic
song, in which she touches on the actions and conquests
of the Portuguese viceroys, governors, and captains in
India, down to the days of Dom João de Castro. Tethys
and Gama ascend a mountain whence she shows him the
Celestial Sphere. Description of the World, particularly
of Asia. The voyagers leave the island and, continuing
their journey, come safe to Lisbon.

THE LUSIADS

THE TENTH BOOK

NOW the bright lover of the adulterous bride
Larissa-born, to drive his steeds, began,
Toward the vast ocean gulf that, circling wide,
Far in the west girdles Tenochtitlan.
Favonius restrained the sun's hot pride
With his cool breath, across wild pools that ran,
Ruffling still waters, and awoke from rest
Lily and jasmine which the heats oppressed;

2

When every lovely nymph, leading her swain,
Well-willing and contented, by the hand,
Came to the Courts that flashed and flashed again
With glittering metal. At the Queen's command,
For a high feast assemble all the train.
Abundant cates upon the tables stand,
Diet that can to its full strength restore
Enfeebled nature, weary to the core.

3

And there, upon the rich chairs crystalline,
Lover and lady sat them, pair by pair.
At the head, on other thrones gold-wrought and fine,
Were splendid Gama and the goddess fair.
And noble meats delicious and divine,
From matching which old Egypt must forbear,
Are heaped upon the plates of yellow gold,
Which had been brought from Atlas' treasure-hold.

349

X The odorous wines, which excellence attain
With which no Italy Falernian vies,
Or that ambrosia whereof Jove was fain,
Like all his deathless crew of deities,
In cups whereon the file will rasp in vain,
Run over, as the swollen bubbles rise,
And the heart's core with sudden pleasure thrill,
While liquor mingles with the water chill.

5

Many soft counsels, each with each, they share,
And subtle banter sharp and laughter light
Are heard 'twixt courses of the pleasant fare,
Which waken every merry appetite.
And music's instruments they lack not there
(Such as permit to every naked sprite
Rest from eternal pain in Hell profound),
Nor Siren voice of an angelic sound.

6

The fair nymph sang, and her clear accents went,
Re-echoing, the towering palace through,
Concerted with each several instrument,
Softly in time keeping the measure due.
And silence checked the winds, incontinent,
And made the waters murmur gently too,
And every wild beast in its native bower
Compelled to quiet slumber by its power.

7

With her sweet voice she lifted to the skies
Tall heroes, on this planet yet to be,
Whose great ideas Proteus had seen rise
In his hollow globe of clear transparency,
The gift which Jupiter could once devise,
That he might see his visions. Thenceforth he
In the deeps prophesied. And without fail
The nymph from memory told the famous tale.

8

Matter of the buskin, not the sock, she spoke,   **X**
Knowledge whereof from the great deep she drew,
Which Demodocus amid Phaeacian folk,
Or Iopas in his Carthage, never knew.
You, my Calliope, I now invoke
In this last labor, that you pay my due:
Grant to my writing what I crave in vain,
Gust in my writing, half-way lost, again.

9

The years descend, and of my summertide
Little is left, for Autumn comes anon.
Fortune makes cold my genius in its pride,
Which I no longer boast or count upon.
My sorrows lead me to the waterside
Of endless sleep and black oblivion.
Great Queen of Muses, grant what shall fulfill,
As for my nation, what I greatly will!

10

From Tagus, sang the goddess, fleets would wend
Over the seas that Gama opened wide,
And as the conquerors on all coasts descend,
Where sobs the oceanic Indian tide,
Also that Hindu kings who would not bend
Neck under yoke would see well verified
What angry iron hard strong arms can wield,
Till to those arms, or till to death, they yield.

11

She sang of one of the Malabarese,
Who 'mid their priesthood was chief personage,
Nor with our mighty men would break the peace,
For which in a firm bond he gave his gage
But chose to see his towns and villages,
With fire and steel, barbarity and rage,
Ravaged by the great Zamorin, who bore
Such hatred to the stranger on his shore.

351

X From Belem, so she sang the history,
One would embark the evil to abate,
Not knowing in himself he took to sea
Lusia's Achilles, Pacheco, called the Great.
The curved ship and hot Ocean, verily,
When he is once aboard, will feel the weight.
The hulls that bear him, 'gainst their natural law,
Groan loud and greater depth of water draw.

13

When to the Orient's bound he shall repair,
To succor Cochin's heathen King he'll go.
And with a native handful shall o'erbear,
Where branches of the curved salt river flow,
The host entire of the accusèd Nair
By the Strait of Cambalão, and make them know
Such terror as their Eastern heat shall chill,
Seeing so few so vast a task fulfill.

14

"The Zamorin will call fresh hosts anew.
Bipúr's king with Tanór's shall thither ride,
Who proof shall offer they are liegemen true,
In their kingdoms on Narsingha's mountain-side.
And he shall force all Nairs the like to do,
'Twixt Calicut and Cananor that bide.
And both the foeman sects are for the war,
The Moors at sea, the Hindus on the shore.

15

"By sea and shore he'll shatter them again,
Our great Pacheco ever prompt to dare,
And with the mighty army of the slain
Strike Malabar with wonder and despair.
The Hindu, other battles to deraign,
In hottest haste will zealously prepare,
Cursing his people, vowing his devotion
In vain to vain gods, deaf and without motion.

16

"He will not merely hold the double strait,
But fire to town and house and temple lay.
The Dog, enraged that they who desolate
His cities never weary of the play,
Will force his men, that life but cheaply rate,
Against Pacheco, who will wing away
Through either pass at once, but in retreat
His foes in both the straits will soundly beat.

17

"Himself, to see the battle and incite
His men to war, shall march the Zamorin,
But one sole salvo, whistling in its flight,
With blood shall purple the great palanquin.
He'll find no remedy or skillful sleight
Or force Pacheco values at a pin,
Though treason he will try, and poison vain,
But, Heaven so willing, will less and less attain.

18

"A seventh time, she sang, he shall renew,
With the unconquered Portuguese, the fray,
Whom toil shall ne'er o'erburden or subdue,
But who shall always rout him in dismay.
In the rough battle, hideous to view,
His strange machines of wood he will array,
The caravels therewith to grapple tight,
With which before it were but vain to fight.

19

"Mountains of flame he'll raise upon the sea,
And thus with fire would burn the fleet amain.
But soldier art and ingenuity
Will make the courage of his onset vain.
No hero, great in warplay though he be,
Though wings of Fame aloft his worth sustain,
Can match him, who from all the palm takes home.
Forgive me this, illustrious Greece or Rome.

X   "Because so many battles he shall fight,
With a scant hundred or a little more,
And by stratagem and art throw into flight
So many hounds, not ignorant of war,
His deeds seem but as dreams and fables slight;
Or the celestial choir, invoked therefor,
Might then descend to aid him and impart
Courage, strength, craft, and steadfastness of heart.

21

"For he who once, in the field Marathonian,
Darius' power could to destruction send,
Or who with thousands four Lacedemonian,
Would for Thermopylae's strait pass contend,
Or even the youth Cocles, the Ausonian,
When against all Tuscany he must defend
The bridge, or Quintus Fabius, was no more
Than was this soldier strong and wise in war."

22

But now the nymph, the melody of song
Abating, hoarse and grievous music made,
And in low voice, with lamentation long,
She sang great courage very ill repaid.
"Belisarius," she cried, "whom all the throng
Of Muses still in grandeur have displayed,
Great Mars quelled in yourself you could behold,
And here may have wherewith to be consoled.

23

"You have a comrade in achievements high—
His prize, like harsh injustice to endure!
In both we look on magnanimity
In wretched case and humble and obscure,
Doomed in poor beds in hospital to die,
Who for the king and law were bulwarks sure.
Such is the wont of kings, whose whim and will
Can overmaster truth and justice still.

"Such is the wont of kings when, counting on   X
Appearance smooth that gives them much content,
They grant the prize which Ajax' merit won
For vain words of Ulysses fraudulent.
But vengeance! When division is ill done,
On his advice who fair show can present,
Then kings who give not gifts to captains wise
Their tribute pay to avarice full of lies.

25

"But you who could so evilly repay
Such vassal, O my King, wear this sole stain:
Though ne'er to him you gave fair lands away,
He added a rich kingdom to your reign.
For, while around the world Apollo's ray
Shall circle, in your teeth I will maintain
That he among the bright and great shall stand
And you shall bear for this the miser's brand.

26

"But see!" she sang, "one who the royal name,
As of a king, doth for his title bear,
With him his son, who shall by sea get fame
As great as ever fell to Roman's share.
With weight of arms and heavy hand, those same
For rich Quilóa shall harsh doom prepare.
Forth the perfidious tyrant they shall fling
And there set up a true and loyal king.

27

"So will they serve Mombassa, rich arrayed
With palaces and houses builded high;
Wrecked by their fire and steel, at length repaid
In full for evil done in time gone by.
To India's coast their course shall then be laid,
Where hostile plots and navies multiply
Against the Portuguese. With sail and oar,
Laurence the youth shall yet do wonders more.

X   "The giant ships of the great Zamorin,
Which choke the whole sea, with his iron hail
That leaps from red-hot brass with thundering din,
He'll shred to pieces, helm and mast and sail.
And then the gallant, his grapnels heaving in
The flagship, will thereof the bulwarks scale
To make there, with the lance and with the sword,
Good riddance of four hundred Moors on board.

29

"But God in secret Providence Who knows
Alone what is His servants' greatest good,
Will set him where no wisdom can oppose
Destruction, and no more can hardihood.
And in Chaúl, where all the ocean glows,
With fire and steel, with battle and with blood,
The fleets conjoined of Egypt and Cambay
Will see he carries not his life away.

30

"There thronging powers of many an enemy
His courage, only by main force, could break.
The winds that fail, the perils of the sea,
Which come in myriads, all for his ruin make.
Let every spirit of Antiquity,
To look upon such fire as this, awake.
They'll see a second Scaeva, rent and maimed,
Who knows no yielding and will not be tamed.

31

"When into pieces shattered is his thigh
By a chance shot fired at adventure blind,
Still on his stalwart arm he shall rely,
And strength that dwells in the heroic mind,
Till another shot break every cord whereby
Body and soul themselves together bind,
And the free soul flies from her pinfold's bound
Whither her final victory shall be found.

     X

"Go in peace, spirit, from the turbulent war,
Where such sweet peace by merit you could gain.
For the broken body that was rended sore,
He who begat you vengeance shall ordain.
For I can hear rebellow the huge roar
Which is to bring dire and eternal pain,
By force of bombard, basilisk, mangonel,
On Mameluke and the Cambayan fell.

33

"For lo! with his soul sickened comes the sire,
While grieving wrath through all his fancy flies.
His father love moves all the man entire,
Fire in his heart, though tears be in his eyes.
And promise sure is made by noble ire,
That right up to the knee the blood shall rise
In the foe's ships. This shall to Nile be clear.
Indus shall see it, and the Ganges hear.

34

"As a jealous bull, his strength that will essay,
Makes trial of his horns for brutal fight,
And butts tall beech or oak tree in his way,
Or wounds the air, and thus gives proof of might,
So, ere he enters the Cambayan bay,
Francis in fury shall the sword whet bright,
And in Dabul, the rich and splendid town,
Shall utterly their swelling pride put down.

35

"And the gulf entering in raging heat
At Diu, famed for siege and feats of war,
He'll put to flight the vast but feeble fleet
Of Calicut, whose armor is the oar.
And the armament of Malik-Yaz discreet,
With bombshells which you, Vulcan, broadcast pour,
He'll send to find a rest profound and cold,
Where Ocean's secret bed it shall behold.

X   "Mir-Hocem's fleet, together grappled fast,
     To wait the avenger's fury there will stay,
     Watching on the waters legs and arms drift past,
     From the bodies of their masters torn away.
     And fiery blast follows on fiery blast,
     Which well brave conquest in blind wrath portray.
     And naught is there, whether for ear or eye,
     Save smoke and steel and flame and battle cry.

37

     "But oh! What sequel to brave wars I see!
     When he to his own Tagus would repair,
     He dies in darkness and in tragedy,
     Half way despoiled of reputation fair.
     The Cape of Storms, his bones, his memory,
     Shall still preserve, yet, unashamed, shall tear
     His life forth from this world, which all in vain
     Egypt with India yoked strove to attain.

38

     "But savage Kaffirs have sufficient might
     To do what balked skilled foemen one and all.
     With rough stakes hardened in the fire they fight
     And quite outdo the bow and musket-ball.
     Judgments of God are hidden from our sight,
     And those men understand not, who miscall
     That which they term mischance and fate malign,
     Which is pure Providence of the Divine.

39

     "But what a dawn do I see break again,"
     Exclaimed the nymph, and louder rose her cry,
     "That scarlet all Melindè's sea can stain,
     Where the towns, Lamo, Oya, Brava, lie?
     'Tis Cunha, whose name lives where the wide main
     Washes the Southern Isles and coasts hard by,
     Which now from sainted Laurence take their name,
     And over all the south has flown their fame.

"Yon gleam from weapons and from fires burns   X
Where Albuquerque comes to pacify   [bright,
The Ormuz Parsees, brave in their despite,
His mild and honest yoke who would deny.
But they will see the whistling arrow flight
Wheel right around, recurving in the sky
On him who shot. God fights upon his side,
Who faith of Mother Church spreads far and wide.

41

"Nor can the mounts of salt within the land
Keep from corruption corpses in that war,
Far spread, or on the sea, or on the strand,
By Gerum, Muscat, or by Cálayat's shore,
Till from his mere arm's strength they understand
That necks must bow, under compulsion sore
Which shall for ever bind a shameful nation
To yield the Bahrein pearls in rich oblation.

42

"And lo! what glorious palms are woven here,
Whereby his brows with victory are crowned,
When, without shadow of fear, or worse than fear,
He'll seize the isle of Goa the renowned.
Then, yielding to necessity severe,
He leaves it, till a fair occasion's found,
And comes once more. Art and heroic will
Compel the Fates and Mars incarnate still.

43

"For look! Unto the town he comes anew.
Despite walls, fire, spear, shot, he breaks a path,
Where with the sword, their hateful squadrons through,
Or Moor or Hindoo ranks, he cuts his swathe.
His famous soldiers greater deeds will do
Than bulls or lions in their hungry wrath,
When dawns that morning, memorable alway,
Saint Catherine the Egyptian's holy day.

359

X   "Nor you, Malacca, shall like fate evade,
For all your treasure, yonder on your throne,
Where you were born in Morning's lap, arrayed
In splendid opulence and famous grown!
The arrows dipped in poison that you made,
Curved knives you use in war, as I have known,
Brave Javanese and amorous Malay,
Alike must Lusitania's will obey."

45

The Siren would have sung a longer strain
In praise of Albuquerque, proud and high,
But thought of his wild rage, which is his stain,
Though his fame circling round the world shall fly.
The great chief, by whose toils the Fates ordain
That he should his eternal glory buy,
Might rather to his men be comrade kind
Than a just judge so merciless of mind.

46

But in a time when famine and harsh need,
Arrows and thunderous fire and ail and pain,
Season and place, in soldiers roughness breed,
Though discipline they otherwise maintain,
Then mere brutality it seems, indeed,
Of a spirit insolent and inhumane,
Extremest vengeance on that crime to wreak,
Which love forgives, and human nature weak.

47

For hateful incest that crime will not be,
Nor on pure virgin a rape violent.
Still less is it unchaste adultery.
'Tis but for a vile slave incontinent.
Whether was it modesty or jealousy,
Or his heart upon mere cruelty was bent,
Wild wrath against his men he held not back,
And his white glory's smirch is foul and black.

Alexander, seeing how Apelles loved   X
His own Campaspe, freely gave her o'er,
Although the man was not his soldier proved,
Nor had he been beleaguered hard and sore.
Cyrus knew through what fires Araspas moved
For Panthea, o'er whose person watch he bore,
Burning for her, after his promise made
Into no ill desire to be betrayed.

49

When the great Persian saw him in the fight
Of love o'ercome, for no defence was there,
Lightly he pardoned him, and guerdon right
He had from service in a great affair.
Hard Baldwin married Judith by mere might,
But Charles, the lady's father, could forbear,
And let him live, nay, raised him to be great
And to be founder of the Flemish state.

50

But the nymph, following her song's long flow,
Now sang Soáres' banners waving high,
When he should come to scatter grief and woe
The length of the red coasts of Araby:
"Shameful Medina fears, and even so
Mecca and Jiddah, and coasts that farthest lie
Of Abyssinia. Barbora will shake
For fear whereat proud Zeila's mart shall quake.

51

"So too the noble isle Tapróbané,
Once by the ancient name so nobly known,
As now its pride is highest in degree
For the hot bark of odorous cinnamon,
Shall pay her tithe of it for tribute fee
To Portugal's great banner, when 'tis flown,
Triumphant on Colombo's high-built tower,
Where every native trembles at its power.

X   "Sequeira shall the Red Sea waves divide,
    And therewithal new highroads shall prepare
    To you, vast Empire, who yet vaunt your pride,
    As Cándace's and Saba's home whilere.
    Massaua's cisterns full shall be descried,
    Also Arquico's port that neighbors there.
    Of far isles he shall make discovery,
    That yield fresh marvels for the world to see.

53
    "Meneses comes, who, for the most part, tries
    His steel in Afric countries far away,
    But Ormuz proud, for crime, he shall chastise
    And double tribute he will make her pay.
    You, Gama, for this exile shall this prize
    Obtain, hither returning on a day,
    With a count's title and great honors crowned,
    To govern all the region that you found.

54
    "But that same hard necessity of fate,
    From which no human creature can retreat,
    Though wearing dignity of royal state,
    Will take you from the world and its deceit.
    A new Meneses, not in years so great
    As in his high intelligence discreet,
    Shall rule. And well-starred Henry shall perform
    Deeds that shall always keep his memory warm.

55
    "Not only Malabar shall he o'erbear,
    Laying Pananè and Couletè low
    And fronting guns whose volleys in the air
    Take vengeance but on who dares front them so;
    But he, with virtue singular and rare,
    The spirit's seven foemen shall o'erthrow
    And conquer envy and incontinence,
    In youth the very top of excellence.

"When he is summoned 'mid the stars to stay,   X
You, stalwart Mascarenhas, shall succeed.
And, though the scoundrels strip your power away,
I swear eternal fame shall be your meed.
As for your foes, they will confess one day
Your lofty courage, which your fate would lead
Up to command. Palm wreaths were granted you,
Not Fortune's comradeship, your proper due.

"In Bintang's kingdom, which Malacca's reign
So long with outrage used to violate,
You will avenge a thousand years of pain
In one day with the gallant and the great.
All dangers and all labors inhumane,
Steel caltrops by the thousand, narrow strait,
Palisades, bulwarks, lances, arrow-squall,
You'll beat or break. For I foresee it all.

"But in India envy and ambition base,
That are wont openly in manner clear
'Gainst God and Justice still to set the face,
Will sicken him no slander can besmear.
He who, unreasoning, when in power and place,
Does a vile injury gets no victory here.
For veritable victory is won
By seeing naked justice wholly done.

"And yet Sampaio, I will not deny,
A courage splendid and illustrious shows.
He's wild-fire on the sea, and shall descry
The waters choking with a thousand foes.
At Bacanor the cruel test he'll try
On Malabar. And Cutialè goes
In terror of him after that defeat,
However powerful had been his fleet.

X   "Diu's wild squadrons that Chaúl dismay,
Though huge and daring, he shall also smite,
Thrown wholly into rout and cast away
When Hector of Silveira they but sight—
Portuguese Hector, concerning whom they say
That, by armed coasts of the Cambayan bight,
On Guzerat such a vengeance he could wreak
As once the Trojan wrought upon the Greek.

61

"Cunha the fierce Sampaio's charge will take,
Whose hand will guide the helm for many a year.
While splendid Diu at his name shall quake,
The lofty towers of Chalè he shall rear.
And strong Basséin a captive he shall make,
But not without much blood, for which we hear
Their captain groan, when her proud palisade,
He shall see taken by the naked blade.

62

"Follows Noronha, who by conduct wise
From Diu drives the Rumis' savage train,
Diu, which strength and martial exercise
Of Antony de Silveira well maintain.
When in the common way Noronha dies,
Then, Gama, shall an offspring of thy strain
The empire's rule attempt, whose passion stern
Shall the Red Sea for fear to yellow turn.

63

"Your Stephen's troubles will yield presently
The reins to one whose glory shall prevail,
Who in Brazil shall scourge and conqueror be
Where the French pirates used the seas to sail.
Then, Captain-general of the Indian Sea,
Damann's insulting fortress he will scale,
The first of all to force the gate unbarred
That flame and arrows by the thousand guard.

"To him the arrogant monarch of Cambay   X
Will in rich Diu give a castle o'er,
If he will be the kingdom's prop and stay,
And with the Great Mogul maintain the war.
Calicut's heathen King upon his way
His courage suffers not to pass before,
And, for all the press of men that with him come,
Choking in his own blood, will drive him home.

65

"He shall destroy the town of Repelin,
Whose king with all his thousands he shall rout,
And later on, hard by Cape Comorin,
His glorious enterprise will carry out.
For the chief squadron of the Zamorin,
Which thinks to wreck the universe past doubt,
With fury, fire, and steel he will o'erthrow,
And Beadala's self the yoke shall know.

66

"India thus being wholly cleared of foes,
At length the rod of empire he shall bear,
Nor battle finds, nor danger undergoes.
All tremble, and to speak no man will dare.
Baticala only would essay the woes
That erewhile fell to Beadala's share.
With corpses filled, the place with blood will run,
By flame and bombshells fouled and all undone.

67

"Such is that Martin, who from Mars his name
Derives, together with his actions high.
No less for arms shall he have lasting fame
Than for wise thought and perspicacity.
Castro will follow, who the oriflame
Of Portugal shall make for ever fly,
Of his forerunner the successor fit,
For one built Diu, one defended it.

68

X   "Abyssinians, Persians fierce, the Rumi race,
Who that their name comes down from Rome's
As various in habit as in face   [profess,
(For many wild breeds to the leaguer press),
Because a handful bar them from the place,
From earth to heaven howl in vain distress.
In blood of Portugal the miscreants swear
To wet the curled mustachios which they wear.

69

"Dread basilisk, the fearful trebuchet,
The falconet, and subterranean mine,
Mascarenhas and his heroes face, but they
Confront sure death with spirit proud and fine.
And then, when heaviest the hardships weigh,
Castro the liberator shall resign
His sons' lives, who desires the youths to give
Their all to God and still in fame to live.

70

"Ferdinand, branch of a tree that is so tall,
Where violent flames mid rolling thunder rise,
Hurling in air the fragments of the wall,
Shall be snatched up and carried to the skies.
Álvaro, when Winter, descending to appall
Mankind, the use of wet sea-roads denies,
Shall break his way and wind and wave o'erthrow,
And every peril, and at length the foe.

71

"Now the sea cleaving, the sire follows straight.
Of Lusitania's host, he heads the rest.
With strength and craft (which last is most of weight)
He'll offer battle, in its outcome blest.
Some storming o'er the wall avoid the gate,
Some burst it in, a raving mob close-pressed.
Deeds they will do for memory to rehearse,
No history large has told, nor any verse.

72

"In the field presently he will appear,
A strong and fearless conqueror, before
Cambay's great King, who at the sight, for fear,
With all his trampling horde, is troubled sore.
Hydalcham ill will cover his frontier
Against the arm triumphant still in war.
He smites Dabul upon the coast that stands,
Nor shall Pondá far inland 'scape his hands.

73

"These and other heroes, for their quality
Fit 'mid the famed and wondrous to be placed,
Who upon earth as Mars himself shall be,
Will come the pleasures of this isle to taste,
With flags triumphant sweeping all the sea,   [haste.
Through which the cleaving keels shall make good
Such nymphs and such repasts, they here shall find,
Glorious rewards for deeds of gallant kind."

74

So sang the nymph and, with sonorous peal,
Calling, her sisters give their voice aright,
And then in joy their wedding vows they seal,
The which they celebrate in pure delight.
"For longer time than turneth fortune's wheel"
(In one melodious sound their songs unite),
"You shall not lack, O men of noble name,
Honor and valor and eternal fame."

75

But after their requirements bodily
Were satisfied upon that noble fare,
And they, in sweet and gentle harmony,
Had heard great acts set forth by Tethys' care,
She then, in all her grace and dignity,
Desired to add to them in double-share
Yet nobler joys of that delicious day,
And thus to happy Gama did she say:

X   "Wisdom supreme, O hero, shows you grace,
In that you shall behold with corporal eye
What the vain science of the erring race
Of wretched mortal men cannot descry.
Firm, strong, and prudent, follow me apace
Up this wild crag, with all your fellows by."
Even so she spoke and through a thicket led,
Rough, difficult, and hard for man to tread.

Not far they went, ere on the towering height
Within a field themselves they shortly found,
With ruby and emerald so thick sown the sight
Conceived that they were treading holy ground.
There, high in air, they saw a globe, for light,
Piercing right through it, shed such glory round
That to the eye the center was as clear
As ever was the surface of the sphere.

Whereof it had been made there was no sign,
But one could see that it was wholly wrought
Of various orbs, shaped by the rod divine,
Which all had to a common center brought.
Whirling, though it make rise or make decline,
Itself nor rises nor declines in aught.
One face it turns to all, and in each part
Begins and ends at last by sacred art.

Uniform, perfect, by itself upheld,
And like unto the Archetype Who made!
Gama, when he saw it, felt his spirit quelled,
And half-way was desirous, half afraid.
Said the goddess: "Into little space compelled,
This transcript of the world I have conveyed
Hither before your eyes, that you may know
Your heart's desire, and where you come and go.

80

"This universal vast machine you see,   X
Ethereal, elemental, He could found
By deep, high wisdom of infinity,
Who no beginning has, or mete or bound.
He, in His circle set eternally,
The whole sphere's well-smoothed surface, hedging
Is God, Whose nature none can comprehend, [round,
For human wit cannot so far extend.

81

"This orb, which, circling, doth the rest enclose,
Containing in itself all lesser light,
And such a clear transplendent radiance throws,
It blinds the poor intelligence and sight,
Is the Empyréan where pure souls repose,
Rejoicing in that Goodness Infinite,
Which Its own mystery understands alone,
Nor upon earth is Its resemblance known.

82

"Here only gods of truth and glory dwell,
For Saturn, Janus, Juno, Jove, and I,
From the beginning, were but tales to tell,
Feigned by blind, mortal ingenuity.
We are mere themes for verses that please well,
And if man's wit to grant us more should try,
'Tis only that the genius of your race
Has art among the stars our names to place.

83

"Moreover, because Sacred Providence
Here, under Jupiter's appearance, reigns,
By means of spirits of intelligence
In thousands, o'er this whole World It sustains—
Prophetic Science brings as evidence
Many examples and this truth explains—
Good spirits guide and favor men alway.
The evil seek to harm them if they may.

X   "I would, by painting with variety,
That to delight or teach will seldom fail,
Give spirits names, which ancient poetry
Once gave the gods in many a fabled tale.
Angels of the celestial company,
As gods, the sacred verse is wont to hail.
True it is that this name beyond compare
Evil spirits often take, but falsely bear.

85

"While highest God doth in this world secure
His will by second cause, and all commands,
Elsewhere I turn to give you knowledge sure
Of works profound done by His holy hands.
Below this Heaven, where sacred spirits pure
Dwell in their bliss (which without motion stands),
This other, so light and swift that none can see,
Speeds on. It is the Primum Mobile,

86

"Compelled by speed thus vehement, whatsoe'er
Dwells in its bosom drives along with it,
Wherefore the sun, moving with anxious care,
Makes day and night, whose course is opposite.
Below the second slowlier doth fare
A third sphere, subject to the obdurate bit.
Phoebus, not niggard of his light, his race
Ten score times runs, while this strides but a pace.

87

"Lo, the next sphere that doth enamelled go
With shining points of radiant light far-beaming,
Which nonetheless keep their strict course alsó,
Turning for ever on their axles gleaming.
See how it vested is, and fair of show,
With its great belt of gold, where the star-streaming
Twelve beasts are figured forth; those effigies
Are the sun's limitary hostelries.

88

"Otherwhere look upon the portraiture,

The shining stars have painted overhead.

Yonder is the Wain. Behold the Cynosure,

Andromeda and her sire, the Dragon dread.

Gaze on Cassiopéa's beauty pure,

Orion's face by turbulent wrath o'erspread,

And lo! the Swan that, dying, must suspire,

The Hare, the Dogs, the Ship, and the sweet Lyre.

X

89

"And underneath this spacious firmament,

The Heaven of Saturn, that old god, you see.

Near circles Jove. Below armipotent

Mars hath his seat, the common enemy.

And fourth, the eye of Heaven, magnificent,

Comes Venus leading the loves' company.

And Mercury sweet-spoken hath his place

This side Diana of the three-fold face.

90

"Each of these orbs sweeps through a different gyre,

As you may see, for one is swift, one slow.

From the center now they distantly retire,

Again from Earth but a brief journey go,

Even as God Almighty may desire,

Who fashioned fire and air and wind and snow.

Those, as you see, still farther inward stand

And, for their center, have the sea and land.

91

"This is the hostel of humanity,

Who, not content in overweening pride

Only to bear the hard ground's injury,

The perils of the unstable deeps have tried.

You will mark various regions which the sea,

Raging, dissevers, in which parts reside

The various nations, whose several kings their reign

With different customs, different laws, maintain.

X "Lo! Christian Europe, fair exalted state,
Excelling all in might and manners meet,
Afric, for worldly wealth insatiate,
Incult, and all brutality complete.
Her Cape has barred your passage till of late,
Where Nature in the South set up her seat.
Look well! The country and the people view,
Infinite numbers, law that never knew.

93

"Benomotapa's vast realm see appear,
Where the black savages all naked go.
Gonçalo death and hateful insult here
For the glory of his Holy Faith must know.
And all about the unknown hemisphere
The ore is born that nations sweat for so.
Lo! From that lake, whence the Nile river flows,
Likewise descending, the Zambesi goes.

94

"Look on the negro huts. With confidence
They dwell in houses that no door possess,
Trusting in the king's justice for defence,
And in their neighbors' honesty no less.
Look, for the brutal crowd of them immense,
Like a black cloud of starlings, thickly press
Against Sofála's fort, which Naia's skill
Duly contrives to hold against them still.

95

"Yonder are the lakes, the birth-place of the Nile,
Which none among the Ancients ever kenned,
Wide watering, where it bears the crocodile,
The Abyssinian race, who Christ befriend.
Watch them, without a wall, in novel style,
So well against the foe their lands defend.
And look on Meroë's isle of ancient fame,
Which in these times the natives Noba name.

"In that far country, reputation fair   **X**
In arms against the Turks thy child will gain.
Christopher is the name he is to bear,
But against death all safeguards are in vain.
Look to the Coast. Once in Melindè there
Yourself they royally would entertain.
And mark the Rapto river racing down
(In their speech, Obi) through Quilmancè's town.

97
"On the Cape, once styled the Aromatic, gaze,
Which now the inhabitants call Guardafu,
Where first the mouth of the Red Sea embays,
The sea that from its bottom takes its hue.
Like a frontier those waters part the ways,
'Twixt Africa and Asia cutting through.
These towns are best along the Afric rim,
Massaua and Arquico and Suakim.

98
"Look on far Suez, which was anciently
A town that heroes founded, as some say,
Though others think it was Arsinoë.
O'er the Egyptian fleets it rules today.
Those are the waters where across the sea
Great Moses in old time made wide the way.
For here beginneth Asia. There she stands,
With her rich realms and stretch of far-flung lands.

99
"There is Mount Sinai, which they celebrate
As sepulchre of Catherine the Divine,
There Toro and Jiddah, where the lack is great
Of water sweet from fountains crystalline.
And there are found the portals of the strait
In Aden's arid kingdom, whose confine
Is the Arzira height of living stone,
Where never yet was rain from Heaven known.

X   "Look where the three Arabias are displayed,
Huge countries full of wanderers swart of face,
Whence come those horses but for battle made,
Swift steeds, high-spirited, of noble race.
See how the coast runs on to barricade
That other Persian strait. A cape doth trace
The road, and they have named it from the town
Fartak, which thereabouts has much renown.

101

"There proud Dofar sends forth her fragrant store
Of incense, which for altars they prepare.
But stay where Rocalgatè lies before,
This side the sea. On niggard beaches there
Ormuz his realm begins, all down that shore
Extending, which will get a name most fair
When the Turk's fleet of galleys, keen in fight,
Of Castel Branco's naked sword catch sight.

102

"There is Cape Asaborus, which today
Sailors call Mosandan, and here is found
The passage leading to the land-locked bay
'Twixt Araby and Persia's plenteous ground.
Lo! Bahrein's isles, whose deeps with rich array
Of pearls that match the morning sky abound.
And yonder Tigris and Euphrates glide
Through one sole channel into the salt tide.

103

"Look on great Persia's empire, rich in fame,
For ever in the field and on the steed,
Who deem the use of smelted bronze is shame,
And hands by swords uncalloused shame indeed.
Lo! Gerum's isle which doth abroad proclaim
To what the intervals of time may lead,
For in the place where once stood Ormuz town,
She stole the name and likewise the renown.

374

"And Philip de Meneses very clear

X

His brilliant soldier qualities will show,
When, with a Lusitanian handful, here
Lara's huge Parsee horde he shall o'erthrow.
Pedro de Sousa likewise will appear,
Whose cut and thrust they bitterly will know,
Who proved him at Ampaza, which he laid
Utterly waste by mere force of the blade.

105

"But now beyond those narrows let us fare,
And known Cape Jask, Carpella named of old,
And lands for which Nature hath little care,
Nor grants her wonted plenty manifold.
Carmania is the name it used to bear.
Now Indus the magnificent behold,
Which is born in yonder mountains, where likewise,
On a near crest, doth rolling Ganges rise.

106

"Look on the Land of Scinde so richly sown!
Behold where enters in Jaqueta's bight,
With the flood-tide suddenly gigantic grown,
Whose ebb retreateth with so swift a flight!
There the Cambayan region, treasure-strown,
Where the gulf thrusts in deep, lies full in sight.
And I pass by a thousand cities there,
That only wait to be your lot and share.

107

"Southward to Comorin (Cori anciently)
You may behold all India's famous shore,
Which the island that was called Tapróbané,
But now Ceylon, hath still in sight before.
The Portuguese will pass across that sea,
After your time is done, to levy war.
And victories and lands and towns they'll win,
And for long ages they will dwell therein.

X "The provinces, 'twixt stream and stream that lie,
Are full of various folk and infinite.
One realm is Moslem, heathen that hard by,
For whom the Devil did their scriptures write.
Narsingha's lordship, as you may espy,
Has holy relics of most blessèd might
From Thomas' body, hero sanctified,
Who thrust his hand into our Savior's side.

109

"There was a city here called Meliapore,
A great and beautiful and wealthy place,
Which used the ancient idols to adore,
As yet is done by the same miscreant race.
Far from the sea it stood in days of yore,
When to the world was published Faith of grace,
Which Thomas preached. And the Saint travelled
A thousand lands, teaching the Gospel true. [through

110

"And being come, he preached and equally
Gave health to sick men, life unto the dead.
But it befell one day, the wandering sea
Unto that coast a monstrous timber sped.
The king would fain cut lumber from that tree,
For he was building and had little dread
But he could haul the giant trunk ashore
With gins and elephants and men good store.

111

"So heavy was the tree that naught sufficed
Even to budge that fearful weight a jot.
But the true ambassador of Jesus Christ
Labor on such a business wasted not.
The cord he wore about the trunk he triced
And lightly raised and dragged it to the spot
Where a most splendid temple he let rear,
Example high for many a future year.

376

"If one of perfect faith, as well he knew,   X
Shall give command that a deaf mountain move,
The sacred voice shall have obedience due,
And what his Christ had taught the Saint could prove.
Hence a great rapture mid the people grew.
The Brahmins, marveling, thought much thereof,
Who miracle and holiness could see,
And greatly feared for their authority.

113

"These were the priests among the heathen there,
Whom envy did most deeply mortify.
They cast about for subterfuge and snare
To stop his mouth, or cause the Saint to die.
Their chief, who on his breast the threads did wear,
Did a deed horrible in the world's eye,
For never can such fearful hatred be
As a false virtue bears to honesty.

114

"He killed his own son and forthwith accused
Thomas of murder foul, all innocent,
And by false witness, in the manner used,
They sentenced him to die incontinent.
The Saint, no better way to be excused,
Perceived, than to pray God Omnipotent.
Before the King and all his lords in state,
He prayed God for a miracle most great.

115

"He gave commandment the dead corpse to bring,
Which he made live and then with question plied,
As to his slayer, and we believe a thing
The dead attest is not to be denied.
All saw the youth to his feet living spring
In the name of Jesus Who was crucified.
Thomas he blessed, who gave him life again,
And his sire-murderer discovered plain.

116

X   "The miracle so great a terror woke,
The King was straight baptized, and many more.
Some kissed his mantle. Many of the folk
The Deity of Thomas did adore.
And with such hatred did the Brahmins choke,
And their own envy poisoned them so sore,
That the rough mob to their purpose they would bend,
And on his death decided in the end.

117

"For as he preached one day a tumult feigned
They caused among the people to arise,
Since Christ already in that hour ordained
His martyr should be carried to the skies.
The multitude of flying stones they rained
Smote down the Saint, a willing sacrifice.
And, to end quickly, one of the unblest,
With the cruel spear, pierced the Apostle's breast.

118

"Ganges and Indus made their loud lament.
Lamented every land your footsteps knew.
Yet more lamented souls of those who went
Clothed in the Holy Faith you taught them true.
But Heaven's angels, with song and sweet content,
To glory earned thus nobly welcomed you.
We pray that you with God will intercede
And help your Lusitanians in their need.

119

"And for you others who usurp the name,
Envoy of God, which Thomas was, now say
If you are called, how can you make such claim,
Who go not forth to preach the Faith straightway?
For if you be the salt and fall to shame
At home, where not one prophet stands today,
Wherewithal shall we salt in times like these
(Forget the heathen!) swarms of heresies?

378

"But now such perilous matter I pass o'er,
And to that painted seacoast turn your eyes.
For at that famous city Meliapore
Curves of the Gulf of Ganges first arise.
Go by rich powerful Narsingha's shore,
And where, with weaves endowed, Orissa lies.
At the Gulf's head the river of renown,
Ganges, to the empire of the salt goes down;

121

"Ganges, whose peoples, as sure truth, protest
That if therein they bathe them when they die,
Though they be sinners great and manifest,
The sacred stream will cleanse and purify.
Yonder lies Chittagong among the best
In all Bengal, a province boasting high
Her plenty. Mark the town which has its seat
Where the coast south commences its retreat.

122

"Lo! the realm Arakan, and yonder there,
Once full of monsters, standeth Pegu's throne.
These were engendered by a loathesome pair,
A dog and woman cast away alone.
On generation's instrument they wear
The sounding brass, a custom that was shown
This people by the cunning of their queen,
Who thus put down their practices obscene.

123

"There is Tavai, and there begins alsó
Siam's vast empire stretching far and wide,
Tenassarí, Queda, chief of all who grow
The pepper harvest in that countryside.
You must go further still, if you would know
Malacca and her noble market's pride,
Where every land in the great sea that lies
Delivers all its richest merchandise.

X   "They have a saying that the sea erewhile
With huge waves clove the land and overbore
And thus cut off Sumatra's splendid isle,
For the Ancients saw the two conjoined of yore,
Which "Chersonesus" they were wont to style,
And, from its many veins of aureate ore,
"Golden" they further gave it for a name.
Some deem this land and Ophir are the same.

125

"But on that cape you will see Singapore,
There where the track for ships so narrow grows.
Hence toward the Cynosure the coast once more
Curves round, yet also toward the morning goes.
Lo! Pam's and Patan's realms! Siam's long shore
Which holds these two and others at dispose!
Yonder is the Menam river flowing by
From the gigantic lake they call Chiamai.

126

"In that huge tract you see a countless throng
Of tribes whose names a man can scarcely tell,
The Laos in their lands and numbers strong,
And on vast hills Burmese and Avas dwell.
Look! Those far heights to other clans belong,
Where self-styled Gueos live grim lives and fell.
Man's flesh they eat and with hot iron brand
Their own, a cruel custom of the land.

127

"See through Cambodia the great Mekong go,
Captain of streams, his name interpreted.
In summer time so many to him flow
That, perilous, o'er wide fields his waters spread.
He has such risings as chill Nile can show.
His people think (unwisely, be it said)
That all brute beasts of every sort and strain
After death live in glory or in pain.

"In his bosom, gentle and compassionate,
He shall receive the sea-drenched Epic Song
That fled the wreck, in sad and piteous state,
Upon the shoaling reefs where the gusts throng.
Hunger shall be, and danger grim and great,
Till they at length shall do that shameful wrong
To him whose lyre, with its sonorous sound,
Shall make him far less happy than renowned.

129
"The coast beyond Tsiampa has to name,
Whose forests with the odorous tree are fair.
There's Cochin-China, hardly known to fame.
Hainan's hid roadstead also lieth there.
China's proud empire that hath such acclaim,
With wealth and lands that thought cannot declare,
Onward extends, whose lordship all must own
From the burning Tropic to the Frozen Zone.

130
"Lo! the Great Wall that all belief defies,
Builded between two empires, and a plain
And certain proof, easy to recognize,
Of her superb and strong and wealthy reign.
When they choose kings, born princes do not rise
To power, nor sons their fathers' rank attain,
But they elect a person wise and good
And famous for his knightly fortitude.

131
"Yet greater stretch of land is hid from thee,
Till the time come her mystery to show.
But do not shun the islands of the sea,
For Nature wills that hence her fame should grow.
This that fronts China, though half-hid it be
And first found out this little while ago,
Is called Japan, whence comes the silver fine.
It shall be lighted by the Law Divine.

X   "Look where the oceans of the Orient lie,
With their infinity of islands sown,
Tidorè and Ternatè, whence on high
From his hot crest the waves of fire are thrown.
There trees of burning cloves you may descry,
Portuguese blood has purchased for our own,
And there the golden birds that ne'er descend
To earth, hence never seen till their lives end.

133
"Look on the Banda Isles, enamelled fair
With changing hue which the red fruit bestows.
The many-colored birds that flutter there
Their tribute on the emerald nuts impose.
There's Borneo, whose trees lack not their share
Of tears from juice, dry-curdling, as it flows
Out of the trunks. This is the camphor tree
Whence the isle has its vast celebrity.

134
"And further on you may behold Timor
That yields the healthful sendal odorous.
There Sunda great, so huge it hides one shore
From the aspect of the sun calamitous.
Men of the inland, who the land explore,
Say there's a stream, they think miraculous,
For where, unfed by brooks, it runs alone,
It changes logs that fall in it to stone.

135
"The land that Time an island made, now see,
In vapor still her tremulous fires dispelling,
The spring oil-spouting, and the marvellous tree,
Out of whose bark the odorous tears come welling.
For Cinyras' girl still lodged in Araby
Cannot distill a liquor so sweet-smelling.
This land has whatsoever have the rest,
And soft silk too and fine gold of the best.

"Behold Ceylon, where the crag soars so high   X
It tops the clouds, or cheats the vision quite.
A human footprint in the rock hard by
Is a thing holy in the people's sight.
In the Maldive Isles hath its nativity,
Deep in the sea, that plant of sovran might,
Whose fruit, against all poison vehement,
Is thought the antidote pre-eminent.

137
"Socotra stands the Red Sea strait before,
Whose fame for her tart aloes wide is blown,
With other isles off Afric's sandy shore,
Which you have made true subjects of your own.
Thence of that perfect perfume comes great store,
The precious stuff of origin unknown.
There is Saint Laurence's far famous isle,
Which certain others Madagascar style.

138
"Thus the new Orient is made manifest,
A gift for all the world which you bestow,
You who so bravely o'er the waters pressed,
Open the gates of the great Sea to throw.
But 'tis but reason now that in the West
A Lusitanian's action you should know,
Who, that his King has injured him, shall deem,
And make a voyage none could ever dream.

139
"See from the Bear to the Pole opposite
Vast countries stretching on without a let,
Which shining mines with metal shall make bright.
Such ores their hue from yellow Phoebus get.
Castile, your friend, may well assert his right
The slave-ring on the savage neck to set,
Where in those regions various tribes abide,
With rites and customs much diversified.

X "But where the continent bulks largest, lo,
A part for barwood famed shall be your own.
'Tis Santa Cruz, for you will name it so,
When your first squadron shall have made it known.
Magellan down that coast of yours will go,
Seeking the lands, of all lands, farthest thrown
And by that action prove himself to be
Right Portuguese, but not in loyalty.

"For, after sailing more than half the way
That to the Antarctic Pole runs from the Line,
He'll see huge men, better, true giants, say,
In the lands seated by the Pole's confine.
Through straits that shall grow splendid on that day
And bear his name, his course he will incline
To a new sea and unto those dominions
The South yet hides under her frozen pinions.

"O Portuguese, it has been granted you
To know the great deeds of futurity,
Which on the sea brave men one day will do,
Because you taught them wisdom of the sea.
But now, since you have heard the history through
Of acts, whereby the darlings you shall be
Of those immortal ladies delicate,
Who your bright coronets of honor plait,

"You may embark, for now the wind stands right
And the sea is calm, for your loved native shore."
Even so she spoke. From the sweet island, bright
And lovely, presently to sea they wore.
Provision fit for noble appetite
And the dear troop of nymphs with them they bore,
Who with them to eternity shall live
Longer than the sun his heat to earth shall give.

144

Across calm waters, where the winds alway   X
Were soft and never angry, did they steer
Till they beheld their country where it lay,
Land of their birth, and so far ever dear.
And entering delicious Tagus Bay,
To the homeland and the King men love and fear,
They gave all praise, for he had bid them sail,
Whose honor with new titles should prevail.

145

Alas! my Muse, alas! because my lyre
Is wholly out of tune and my voice hoarse,
Not from my song, but knowing I must quire
Always for a people who are deaf and coarse.
The favor which sets genius all on fire
My land grants not to song, but runs perforce
After its envious lusts and brutishness,
Sunken in harsh, depraved, and gross distress.

146

I know not by what influence of fate
There is no general gust, no happy pride,
Which might our souls at all times animate,
That we might toil with constancy glad-eyed.
Therefore, O King, whom Heaven did elevate
Upon this throne, by counsel sanctified,
Look that you be (scan other nations well)
Lord only of such subjects as excel.

147

Look by what different roads with what good will,
Like rampant lions or brave bulls, they fall
To work, outfacing watch and hunger still,
And fire and steel and bolt and musket-ball,
And either clime, the burning or the chill,
The Moor's stroke and the idolater's withal,
The nameless perils in the world that be,
Shipwrecks and sharks and great deeps of the sea.

X They are prepared all service to ensue
Obeying still, though ne'er so far away,
Whatever your stern order bids them do,
Content, without debate, without delay.
If they but know that they are seen by you,
Black fiends infernal, flaming, in the fray
They'll face for you, and, never doubt the thing,
Make you their victor, not their vanquished, King.

149

Honor them, then. Give them their heart's delight
With your presence and your sweet humanity.
From action of harsh laws absolve them quite,
For thus to virtue is the road made free.
And raise up those who have experience right,
If virtue to experience equal be,
To sit in council. These are men who know
The how and when and whither things will go.

150

And in their calling honor men alway
According to the merit they attain.
And let religious persons fast and pray
And discipline their spirits for your reign.
For thus the common vices they withstay,
And but as wind they count ambition vain.
The only veritable priest is he
Who seeks not wealth or this world's vanity.

151

And hold your cavaliers in high esteem,
For, with their burning blood that knows not dread,
Not only they exalt the Faith supreme
But far abroad your splendid empire spread.
For they who go to the world's end extreme,
And in your service diligently tread,
Two enemies must vanquish in their war,
Live foes, and heavy labor which is more.

386

So do, my Lord, that never German, Gaul,   **X**
Italian, Briton, though admired, can say
That the Portuguese take orders from them all.
Rather 'tis Portugal they must obey.
To counsel only the experienced call,
Who saw hard months and hard years in their day.
For though of knowledge many can dispose,
In things particular the expert knows.

Elegant philosophic Phormio,
Hannibal, as you may behold, mocked sore,
Who would, discoursing in a loud voice, show
The inner meaning of the art of war.
Good soldier discipline is not learned so,
My Lord, by such as fantasy explore,
In studies, visions, and strange thought delighting,
But by seeing and by practising and fighting.

What shall I say, who am humble, rough, and low,
Nor known, not even in a dream, to you?
Out of the mouths of babes, as well I know,
At times may come the perfect praise and true.
I lack not what hard study can bestow,
And much experience can add thereto,
And genius, which, as you may see, is here,
Things which together not too oft appear.

To serve you, here's an arm for battle wrought,
To sing you, here's a mind, the Muses' own.
Only I need to have your kindly thought,
To whom true virtue's value should be known.
If Heaven grant and your great heart is fraught
With brave adventure which I may intone,
As my prophetic soul may well divine,
Seeing what way your heavenly thoughts incline;

X   And if mere sight of you Mount Atlas shake
     With terrors no Medusa could implant,
     If in the Ampelusa fields you break
     Moors of Morocco and of Tarudant,
     My glad triumphant Muse will undertake
     So on your world-wide glory to descant,
     Alexander shall himself in you discern,
     Nor longer for Achilles' honors burn.

NOTES

BOOK X

1.   1. Coronis, the mother of Aesculapius (the first physician) by Apollo, jilted the god in favor of Ischys. Various stories are told of Apollo's revenge upon her infidelity. See Ovid, Met., II, 542 (Burton).

2. Tenochtitlan, Mexico (the Aztec name for the valley in which Mexico City stands). Camões' visible pleasure in the barbaric name (Temistitão in the Portuguese) has in it something of Milton's pleasure in place names for their own strange sake.

2–4. The account of Tethys' banquet reminds one of Cleopatra's feast in Lucan (De Bello Civili, X, 155–171). Burton throws in Homer and Virgil for luck.

3.   8. Atlas lived in northwest Africa, which was an imaginary Eldorado for the Greeks (like all Eldorados for everybody).

4.   2. Falernian, a wine much admired by Horace, and accordingly symbolic of a perfect vintage. Horace (Odes, I, xx) implies that it is too expensive for him.

3. Ambrosia, the food of immortality.

5. Cups of glass, or, as Professor R. T. Hill suggests, of diamond.

7.   4. Burton is persuaded that this globe is the ball of the Oriental crystal-gazer. It may be worth pointing out that what Proteus sees in the globe are Platonic Ideas. Some modern scholars think Camões disliked Platonism, but there are whiffs of it here and there in his poems.

8.   1. The buskin was the high-heeled footgear that ancient tragic actors wore to increase their height. The sock was worn by comedians. This line is perhaps imitated from Petrarch in the Trionfo d'Amore, Capitolo IV:

Materia da coturni, e non da socchi,

But Camões may have gone straight to Horace (Ars Poetica, 80):

Hunc socchi cepere pedem, grandesque cothurni.

6. Demodocus, the blind poet who sang before Ulysses at the court of Alcinoüs, Odyssey, VIII, 62, XIII, 27.

7. Iopas sang before Dido and Aeneas, Aeneid I, 740 ff.

11.   1. The King of Cochin, in whose city (1500) the Portuguese under Cabral established a station, after failing in their negotiations with the Zamorin at Calicut. Late in 1553, Camões, almost immediately

after his arrival in India, sailed on an expedition undertaken in support of a Rajah of Cochin. This is described in the Third Elegy.

12.   4. Pacheco. See I, 14.

The classic hyperbole may provoke a smile, but the fault is Ovid's (Met., XV, 693-694):

numinis illa
sensit onus, pressa estque dei gravitate carina,

in which passage the weight of the god Aesculapius pressed the ship down in the water. Mr. Duff in the Loeb Library Lucan points out that "weight is a regular attribute of divinity in ancient mythology." We might add that the burden of Christ is heavy in the legend of St. Christopher.

13.   Pacheco, according to de Goes (I, 180), had two ships at Cambalão, rather less than a hundred Portuguese, and some extremely unreliable native allies. Pacheco almost literally gave a preview of Clive's later activities. And Cambalão, although an amphibious operation, resembles Plassey.

14.   1–4. Camões is almost as pedantically meticulous as a German Ph. D. Both Barros (I, vii, 7) and de Goes (I, 182) list the Kings of Tanor and Bipur among the allies of the Zamorin, and de Goes adds the detail that they are from a region "near the mountains of Narsingha."

17.   1. Burton, without giving a source, says that a bombard killed two men close to the litter of the Zamorin.

18.   Barros (I, vii, 8) describes the devices which the Zamorin invented to cope with the caravels.

21.   1. Miltiades defeated the Persians at Marathon in 490 B. C.

3. Leonidas at Thermopylae in 480 B. C.

5. Horatius Cocles, the defender of the Bridge at Rome against Lars Porsena (507 B. C.?). Livy (II, 10) tells the story first. Horatius can turn up anywhere from Plutarch to Claudian.

7. Fabius Cunctator, the delayer, who, by avoiding battle, slowly wore Hannibal down.

22.   5. The poverty of Belisarius (floruit, first half of the 6th Century, A. D.), probably a Slav and certainly a great soldier, is doubtless mythical. It is said to be a mediaeval invention.

23.   King Manuel treated the great men who served him with conspicuous meanness.

24.   3. Ajax was cheated of the armor of Achilles by the sophistry of Ulysses. Camões' favorite Ovid has a long debate between the two heroes at the beginning of Book XIII of the Metamorphoses.

Burton believes that special persons are under fire, the King's two Jesuit counsellors and certain courtly poets like Sa de Miranda and Bernardes. It could be, but——!!

26. 1. Almeida, the first viceroy (1505-1509), and his son Laurence who have already been noticed (I, 14, 6).

28. Lourenço de Almeida won his victory, May 18, 1506 (Barros, I, x, 4).

29. 5. Camões may have felt some special interest in Chaúl, for, late in his seventeen-year residence in the East, he was granted the reversion of the collectorship of the port. The salary, when the reversion fell in, would have been enormous, 129,000 reis, more than eight times the pension which he ultimately received from King Sebastian.

7. Cambay, in northwest India.

30. 7. Scaeva, the heroic centurion in Lucan (De Bello Civili, VI, 140-260), who provides a lot of fighting and rhetoric at Dyrrachium. In Book X of Lucan's poem he appears again, as a sort of good omen for Caesar, when the fighting on the mole begins at Alexandria (ad finem). Suetonius also mentions him (Twelve Caesars, Julius Caesar, LXVIII), and he shows up in Plutarch (Caesar).

31. 1-4. The pattern of heroism is the same for all the nations of men, however little be thought of it in these times.

> For Withrington my heart was woe
> That ever he slain should be,
> For when both his legs were hewn in two
> Yet he kneeled and fought on his knee.

The account of young Almeida's death seems to be modeled on the account of the death of Camilla (Aeneid, XI, 828-837).

32. 1. In the Portuguese translation of Petrarch's Triumph of Death (Juromenha, V, 41), by some attributed to Camões, a very similar line occurs.

8. Mameluke, meaning Egyptian.

34. 7. Dabul, in the general region of Bombay.

Virgil has several jealous bulls (Georgics, III, 229-236 and Aeneid, XII, 101-106). Lucan has another (De Bello Civili, II, 601-607). Statius obliges with two more, point for point, e. g., Thebais, II, 323-332 and XII, 601-605. Very likely the lot were in Camões' mind.

35. 2. Diu on the northern shore of the Gulf of Cambay is still part of the Portuguese Empire.

5. Malique-Yaz, strangely enough, a Russian adventurer who made himself Lord of Diu (Barros, II, viii, 4). He wrote the Viceroy a letter of condolence on his son's death.

36. 1. Mir-Hocem (Mir Husain), an Egyptian admiral sent by the Sultan to assist the Zamorin. He was in command of twelve ships (Lencastre).

2–4. Perhaps Camões remembers the Ismenus full of disjecta membra. See Statius, Thebais, IX, 259–262.

37.   Barros gives the gory details of the death of Francisco de Almeida at the Cape (II, iii, 9).

39.   4. Lamo, Oya, Brava, all on the east coast of Africa, close to the Equator. Barros (II, i, 2) mentions all three.

5. Tristan da Cunha discovered the islands called after him, 2000 miles southwest of Good Hope, in 1506 (Lencastre), and landed in Madagascar (Saint Laurence).

40.   2. Albuquerque (governor 1509–1515), the model of faithful and honorable heroes. See I, 14 and II, 49.

3. Ormuz, in the Persian Gulf. The Parsees are Persians who are still Zoroastrian fire worshippers, but Camões must be referring to genuine Persians, and not to a small unwarlike sect. See Lencastre. At the battle of Ormuz the Portuguese used no bows, but a number of bodies of the enemy were found pierced by arrows. This was supposed to be a miracle. The phenomenon, of course, was due to the confusion of battle. In the Octaves to King Sebastian, the fifth stanza is on Albuquerque and narrates the circumstance of the reversed arrows.

5. These arrows, already mentioned in II, 49, have an odd parallel in the arrow of Adrastus (Statius, Thebais VI, 938–941) which hit the mark and returned to the mouth of the king's quiver.

41.   1. There are natural mounds of salt in the vicinity of Ormuz.

4. Gerum (Ormuz), Muscat, Cálayat, on the shores of the Persian Gulf.

8. The Bahrein Islands in the Persian Gulf now produce another form of wealth, petroleum.

42.   4. Albuquerque seized Goa permanently in 1510. Accordingly, it must be the oldest European colony in Asia.

43.   8. Saint Catherine the Egyptian's holy day, November 25th O. S., 1510 (Lencastre). Her martyrdom (she was broken on the wheel in one of the last persecutions) is said to have taken place in 307 A. D.

44.   1. Malacca, in the Straits Settlements, northwest of Singapore.

45.   2. Albuquerque appears to have been ahead of his time, like Alexander. He wished the natives to be justly treated, and there were teeth in his laws. When his orders about proper treatment of native women were disobeyed, he hanged an officer, to the shocked astonishment of the army. Lencastre, without citing his authority, says that the Indian woman who was thus avenged was a slave of Albuquerque himself. The name of the officer was Roy Dias. And Sonnet C is by some supposed to be to his address. It may be, but Dias was hanged before Camões was born, and Sonnet C, "that epic in fourteen lines,"

as it has been well called, makes me believe that Camões is lamenting the loss of a dear friend.

48.   1. The story of Alexander, who gave up Campaspe to Apelles the painter, has its pleasing side (Pliny, XXXV, 36 and Aelian, Various History, 12, 34). I owe these references to Professor C. W. Mendell.

2. The story of Cyrus, Araspas, and Panthea requires no learned comment (Xenophon, Cyropaedia, V and VI, noted by Ford).

49.   5. Baldwin (Bras de Fer), according to Professor Ford, eloped with Judith the daughter of Charles the Bald (9th Century). He is said to have founded Bruges (Lencastre).

50.   2. Soares succeeded Albuquerque in 1515. He was the great governor's mortal enemy, and many believed that the appointment killed Albuquerque, who died almost at once. If Miss Sanceau's account of him is based on reliable sources, Soares was incompetent and perhaps a coward. How Camões could write this stanza with a straight face is difficult to explain. Soares sailed into the harbor of Jiddah and failed to fight the enemy fleet anchored there. De Goes (IV, 34) speaks well of him.

5. Medina, the city to which Mahomet fled from Mecca, and almost as holy as Mecca itself. Mahomet's tomb is there.

6. Jiddah, the port of Mecca.

7. Barbora, modern Berbera in British Somaliland.

8. Zeila. The conqueror of Gama's son in the war in Abyssinia was Granye of Zeila, in Somaliland.

51.   1. Tapróbané, Ceylon. See I, i, 4, note.

7. Soares is said to have built this tower (Lencastre).

52.   1. Sequeira succeeded Soares in 1518.

4. Saba, Sheba. Candace is mentioned in Acts of the Apostles, VIII, 27. The word is probably the title and not the name of the queen whose eunuch the apostle Philip baptized. Pliny (VI, 35) speaks of the Candaces of Meroë in Ethiopia.

5. Massaua, in Eritrea. De Goes (IV, 111–112) speaks of these cisterns.

6. Arquico, Milton's Ercoco.

53.   1. Duarte de Meneses, governor (1521–24). He had been successful against the Moors in Tangier.

5. Vasco da Gama died while viceroy of the region he discovered late in 1524, the year of Camões' birth. He only held the post a few months. His character, as stated before, has been softened in the Lusiads. He appears to have been a savage brute, even by 16th Century standards. But the abilities which brought off the astonishing voyage ought not to be undervalued on that account. His courage, presence of mind, resolution, and craft remind one of Cortez. The exile of

Gama, Burton thinks, is the period when the discoverer was in disgrace with King Manuel.

54.   5. Henrique de Meneses, at the age of twenty-eight, succeeded Gama and made a great reputation (1525–1526).

Camões' Sonnet LXXXVIII is addressed to the memory of a remarkable governor, and I suspect that Henrique de Meneses is the man. Lencastre reports a legend to the effect that this governor died possessed of thirteen reis, one of the few Portuguese officials in those times who thought more about governing well than amassing the customary fortune.

56.   2. Mascarenhas, a good soldier and an honest man, was the victim of a junto and abominably treated by Sampaio, who intrigued against him, while he was fighting in Malacca. The story is that on his return to Portugal he was well received and properly rewarded.

57.   1. Bintang, an island near Malacca.

59.   1. Sampaio, governor 1526–1529.

        7. Cutiale, a Mahometan admiral, defeated by Sampaio.

60.   4. Heitor de Silveira, under Sampaio's command, worsted an Egyptian or Native admiral, whose name was Halixa (Ford). One of Camões' versified dinner invitations is addressed to a Heitor de Silveira (Juromenha, IV, 32). The Poet wrote some lines for him (Juromenha, IV, 84), which were sent to Francisco Coutinho, Count of Redondo and Viceroy, who apparently quashed the charges brought against Camões at Macão. In these verses Silveira is called a Lusitanian Hector. The man who won the battle is said to have died in 1531. The younger Hector was probably his son or nephew. Camões' friend, together with Diogo de Couto and others, paid the Poet's debts in Mozambique, and Camões sailed to Lisbon with his deliverers. Silveira died as they crossed the bar at the mouth of the Tagus.

61.   1. Nuno da Cunha (governor 1529–1538), the son of Tristan, succeeded Sampaio (1529) and ruled for ten years (Lencastre). He was a great governor and very badly treated. His father, the famous old sailor, is said to have sent John III the price of the irons that fettered his son.

        6. I have translated Melique here as captain. In Arabic it means king, chief, etc.

62.   1. Garcia de Noronha (Viceroy 1538–1540).

        2. Rumi, a name for an inhabitant of Asia Minor, therefore a Turk. It is derived from Rum, meaning Rome, i. e., Constantinople.

        3. Antonio da Silveira, governor of Diu during this siege, the first, 1538 (Lencastre).

        6. Estevão da Gama (governor 1540–1542) failed in a naval

expedition up the Red Sea, which was an unhappy region for the House of Gama. Cristovão, his brother, was killed in Abyssinia.

There was another ruler of India of the House of Gama, who almost a hundred years after the discovery saw the Goa mob tear down his ancestor's statue in the great square of the city.

63.   2. Martim Afonso de Sousa was next governor (1542–1545). As stated in the preceding stanzas, he had been a naval commander on the Brazilian Coast, and later served under the viceroy da Cunha (Burton).

6. Damann, on the northeast coast of India. In the Octaves to Constantino da Braganza (Juromenha, II, 307) Damann becomes a new Byzantium which should be called New Constantinople.

64.   1. Bahadur, King of Guzerat, granted to Cunha the right to build a fort at Diu in return for support against Humayun (1508–1556), the Great Mogul and father of Akbar. Bahadur was killed later in a brawl on one of Cunha's ships (1537).

It is odd that Camões has so little to say about the Mogul Empire. The most powerful ruler in India is mentioned only twice, in the Lusiads, in this stanza and in I, 8.

65.   3. Comorin, the extreme southern tip of India.

5. 1537 was a year of active expansion. The naval defeat of the Zamorin and the capture of Beadala took place at the time.

67.   1. Martin is Martim de Sousa.

5. João de Castro, governor 1545–1548, but viceroy for two weeks. The account of him in the text is historic. Camões might have put in the picturesque detail that the hero pawned his beard and the ashes of his son with the business men of Goa, to raise funds to carry on the war—as strange security as was ever put up.

68.   1. This miscellaneous force was led by the Sultan of Cambay (1546), who wished to expel the Portuguese from Diu (Lencastre).

3. João de Mascarenhas, not the luckless victor of Malacca.

72.   3. Camões' word "quadrupedante," a Virgilian borrowing, means "going on four feet." Professor Ford thinks it refers to elephants, but in Virgil (Aeneid, VIII, 596) it is applied to horses:

Quadrupedante putrem sonitu quatit ungula campum.

The King of Cambay, Bahadur Shah, doubtless had both elephants and horses (Lencastre).

4. The ruler of Goa before its capture was called Hydalcham by the Portuguese, perhaps a corruption of Adil Khan. Adil Shah of Bijapur might be the person meant. His reign (1535–1557) would fit nicely with Castro's term of office (Elphinstone, History of India, 756). Burton says he is the man (Camões and his Lusiads, I, 282), no doubt relying on Barros (II, v, 2).

8. The Portuguese seldom went far inland. The capture of Pondá thus has the effect of a rather special triumph.

77.   Luciano Pereira da Silva, in his "A Astronomia dos Lusiadas" (quoted by Lencastre), wonders if Camões had ever seen the armillary sphere which amused the last days of Charles V at Yuste. It had been made by the mathematician Leonelo, and showed the motions of the planets, the precession of the equinoxes, etc. We may also wonder if the glass armillary sphere of Archimedes, described by Cicero (De Republica, I, xiv), Ovid (Fasti, VI, 277-280), and Claudian (Epigrams XVIII and XXV), may not have had something to do with Camões' strange vision of the transparent model of the universe which Tethys exhibits to Gama. De Lambre (Histoire de l'Astronomie Ancienne, 1817, pp. 101-103) goes into the subject of the ancient spheres and quotes freely from the classic writers. And E. L. Stephenson (Terrestrial and Celestial Globes, 1921, pp. 15-17) quotes Cicero. I owe this reference to Dr. J. K. Wright and his secretary, Miss Alice Taylor, whose kindness saved me many laborious days. One sentence from Cicero's dissertation seems to the purpose: "And more especially was that invention of Archimedes to be admired, for he had so contrived that one revolution of the machine served somehow to produce unequal and varied movements through their different paths." Camões knew Cicero very well, it would appear. He had Ovid by heart. And some of the notes in this volume would suggest that he was not unfamiliar with Claudian. There is perhaps a certain charm in the notion that Camões' great fantasy may have had its origin in the strange device of Archimedes.

A lot of good learning has been expended on Camões' exposition of the Ptolemaic system. It would be easy to quote or to abridge. The Poet is really clearer in his explanations than professional astronomers. But the ideas are not wholly familiar, and accordingly a summary of the Ptolemaic system, a system which has always appealed to poets for its beauty, is presented here.

The earth, according to this theory in its final form, lies at the center of eleven concentric spheres. The seven planets, including sun and moon, have each a sphere whose motion, irregular or otherwise, accounts for the motion of the "planets" as seen against the background of the eighth sphere, which belongs to the fixed stars. Outside the fixed stars lies the Crystalline Sphere which accounts for the precession of the equinoxes. Beyond lies the Primum Mobile, which actuates the whole, and beyond that empyreal Heaven. The miraculous model which is shown to Gama exhibits the system of concentric spheres. Tethys guides him inward till he comes to Earth at the center, when she delivers her geographical discourse.

79.   1. A sentence from Pliny (II, 1) may be noticed: "Sacred it is, everlasting, infinite, all in all, or rather itself all and absolute."

2. As recent scholars have observed, Camões seems to have had no particular interest in the neo-Platonism of his time. But here he employs a Platonic term in a Platonic sense. The Archetype is the divine model from which all earthly things are imperfectly copied.

80.   Lencastre notes Pereira da Silva's opinion that Camões had Pedro Nunes (Tratado da Sphera) in mind, which means ultimately the famous work of Sacrobosco. It may well be.

5–8. Strabo (XVI, ii, 35) quotes Moses (odd, but a fact) on "this one thing which encompasses us, all, land and sea, which we call Heaven, or the universe or the nature of things."

81.   1. This orb, the Empyrean, or Sphere of Fire, is inhabited by the Blest. Professor Ford makes the natural comparison with Dante. But Milton's brilliant brevity helps to explain. In the passage quoted below, the word "trepidation" means precession of the equinoxes.

> They pass the planets seven, and pass the fixed,
> And that crystalline sphere whose balance weighs
> The trepidation talked, and that first moved.

Milton understood the heliocentric system of Copernicus, but seems at all times undecided as to which school of thought he should join. Camões, if he had heard of Copernicus, evidently rejected the new ideas.

82.   1. The critics have displayed variously their general ineptitude on Camões' inconsistency, if any, in this connection. Some have supposed that the stanza was written at the insistence of the Censor of the Inquisition, as a guarantee of orthodoxy. Cicero, Pliny, and any quantity of Stoics are lurking in the background.

84.   It may be that Camões, while defending his past practice of introducing the gods of Antiquity into his poem, is defending it for the future as well. There is nothing improbable in the tradition that he was at work on a continuation of The Lusiads after he got home.

85.   8. Inside the Empyrean is the Primum Mobile, which gives motion to all the interior spheres.

This whole passage on the celestial motions may perhaps be illustrated by a passage from Ovid, Met. II, 70–75.

86.   5–8. According to Pereira da Silva, quoted by Lencastre, this passage describes the Crystalline Sphere whose motion provides for precession of the equinoxes.

7. Phoebus, the sun, is the next sphere. Perhaps Camões is a little involved here. The sun should be inside the sphere of the fixed stars, and in the fourth sphere, if the editor understands his Ptolemy. Camões knows this undoubtedly, but does not say so, and makes it

unclear by not putting the sun in fourth position in 89. Claudian (De Tertio Consulatu Honorii, 161–168) gives the orthodox order of the planets.

87.   1. The fixed stars, naturally including the belt of the Zodiac with its twelve signs (7), in each of which the sun appears in the course of a solar year.

88.   1. The constellations outside the Zodiac.

3. The Wain, Charles' Wain, or the Great Bear. The Cynosure, the Little Bear.

4. Andromeda, rescued by Perseus, is a northern constellation. Her sire was Cepheus, King of Ethiopia, also a constellation. The Dragon was the sea-beast from which Perseus rescued Andromeda by showing the creature Medusa's head.

5. Cassiopea, the mother of Andromeda, and also a constellation:

> . . . . That starred Ethiop Queen that strove
> To set her beauty's praise above
> The Sea-Nymphs, and their powers offended.

The Myth of Andromeda covers a great part of the Northern Heavens.

7–8. Constellations in the south.

89.   2. Saturn, father of the young gods, and outermost of the planets known to the Greeks and to the 16th Century.

3. Jupiter.

4. Mars.

6. Venus.

7. Mercury.

8. The moon's phases are thus alluded to of course, but Diana has three important aspects. She is goddess of the Moon, of the Chase, and of Hell. She has other aspects. The epithet is Virgilian, Aeneid, IV, 511. With respect to Diana, Catullus' ode to her (XXXIV) could hardly fail to be in Camões' mind, not to mention Horace (Odes, III, xxii).

90.   1. The apparent motion of the planets was ingeniously explained under the Ptolemaic system. By means of so-called "epicycles," they were made to circle upon the surface of their spheres. By virtue of this wholly fallacious device, the position of any planet at any time could be predicted with considerable accuracy.

8. The phenomena of the atmosphere were regarded as "meteors," which obey laws not unlike those which govern the stars in their courses, but these meteors lie inside the spheres proper, close to the surface of the earth.

92.   5. Her cape, Good Hope, of course.

93.   1. Benomotapa, properly, Monomotapa, and the title of a ruler, not the name of a region, on the east coast of South Africa.

2. Gonçalo de Silveira was at Coimbra in Camões' time, and in India for the first year or two of Camões' residence there. He was a Jesuit and was martyred in East Africa in 1561 (Ford). Sonnet XXXVII may well be to his address. Perhaps Silveira was a relation of the redoubtable Heitor. The martyrdom of Silveira is one of the few events Camões notices after his own arrival in the Orient.

3. The Nile and the Zambesi do not rise in the same lake. Barros (I, x, 1) had heard about the equatorial lakes, and identified the Cuama with the Zambesi.

94. 1-4. Strabo (XV, 1, 53) speaks of the unguarded houses of India.

6. Camões' flock of starlings probably owes nothing to Homer's flock of the same birds in Iliad, XVII, 755.

8. Sofala, (See I, 54, note). Naia held a fort here early in the Portuguese Drang nach Osten. Gama had visited the place in 1502. Naia was sent out in 1505 to exploit the Sofala gold. Barros (I, x, 1-3) tells Naia's story.

95. 1. The Nile actually does rise in Victoria Nyanza. This was not ascertained till the 60's of the last century. The Portuguese evidently had fairly accurate information.

7. Meroë, on the Nile above its junction with the Atbara. There was some sort of an oasis here. Lencastre has found a passage in Barros (III, 4, 2) from which the detail about the name Noba seems to be drawn. But Strabo (XVII, i, 2) notices the Nubae on the Nile's left bank near Meroë, and Ptolemy (IV, 6) has them near Lake Chad and on the upper Nile. Nubians, one supposes.

8. Camões would doubtless remember Pomponius Mela's brief notice of Meroë and the river full of crocodiles.

96. 3. Cristovão da Gama was slain (August, 1542) in a luckless expedition against the Arabs in Abyssinia. This expedition was as brilliant as Cortez' in Mexico. The young commander died heroically after two astonishing victories. What was left of his army subsequently avenged him with the aid of the Negus Claudius (February 21, 1543).

7. Rapto, a river which runs through Quilmance in the vicinity of Melinde.

97. 1. The Aromatic Cape, so-called as early as Ptolemy Phila-delphus (Third Century B. C.), according to Gosselin (Commentary on Strabo, XVI, iv, 14, quoted in Bohn edition). The region south of Guardafui (part of Somaliland) was called the Cinnamon Country. Evidently it produced some spicy or odorous plant, but not what we call cinnamon.

2. Properly Guardafui, but I have kept Camões' spelling, because it helped me to a rhyme.

4. Pliny (VI, 28) has this comment: "Others say that the name comes from the sand and the soil."

Camões had landed at Guardafui, as Sonnet C and Canzone X testify. In Canzone X he uses almost the same expressions to explain the change of name.

98.   2. Professor Ford notes that the original name was Heroöpolis. It was so known to Pliny (V, 12 and X, 6) and Ptolemy (IV, 5, 13). Ariosto (O. F., XV, 39) calls Egypt the land of heroes, to the astonishment of his great translator, William Stewart Rose.

3. Arsinoë, wife and sister of Ptolemy Philadelphus, and one of the most interesting women of Antiquity. She played an enormous rôle in the beginning of the Third Century before Christ, and in spite of her singular morals seems to have been one of the few civilizing influences of the times.

99.   2. Saint Catherine of Alexandria, a third-century martyr, nominally buried on Mt. Sinai. Professor Ford observes tartly that there was another far-off divine event that Camões might have mentioned to better purpose in connection with Mt. Sinai.

7-8. Barros (II, vii, 7) might help the poet a little here, but Camões knew the region.

100.   1. The classic division of Arabia, Arabia Petraea (stony) in the north, Arabia Deserta, south of Arabia Petraea on the shores of the Persian Gulf, separated from Arabia Felix (Araby the Blest) on the west and south.

3. Strabo (XVI, iv, 2) could be mistaken, but it is matter for astonishment when he states that in his time there were no horses in Arabia.

6. The Persian strait. Ormuz is situated here.

101.   1. Dofar, on the Arabian Coast.

4. Rocalgatè, easternmost point of Arabia (now Ras-el-Hadd, Burton). Barros (I, ix, 1) says that Ormuz' kingdom begins here.

5. Ormuz, one of Milton's magic names.

8. Castel Branco stood a siege at Ormuz in 1541 (Ford).

102.   1. Asaborus (the Promontorium Asabôn of Ptolemy, VI, 7, 12), northern point of the Arabian shore of the Strait. It is called Mosandan today, as in Camões' time. See Barros (I, ix, 1).

5. The Bahrein Islands are mentioned in X, 41, 7-8. Pliny (IX, 54) has this to say: "for it is certain that it (the pearl) was conceived from the sky and that pearls have more connection with the sky than with the sea and derive from it a cloudy hue or a clear one corresponding with a brilliant morning."

103.   5. Gerum is New Ormuz. The original city was some miles away on the mainland.

6. Both Lucretius (V, 1276) and Claudian (In Eutropium, II, 244–245) have this commonplace.

104. 1. Philip de Meneses fought at Ormuz in 1566 (Ford). This is another of the episodes which took place during Camões' time in India. Perhaps Sonnet VI is to this hero's address, but Juromenha thinks it is to another scion of the house, Fernão Meneses.

2. Lara, perhaps Laristan, a province of Persia. Lencastre suggests Larak, an island in the Persian Gulf, but this seems unlikely, as it is too small to support a vast Parsee, or rather Persian, army (Ford).

3. Pedro de Sousa provides another instance of a man whose exploits took place during Camões' sojourn in the East. Gonçalo de Silveira, Philip de Meneses, and Pedro de Sousa were evidently his friends. We know the Poet was on one expedition to Ormuz in 1554 or 1555, under the command of a Meneses. His almost finicking detail about the region suggests that he may have been on more. He may, however, be drawing on Barros to help out his own memory.

7. Ampaza, near Melinde.

105. 1. Cape Jask, so-called today. It is Ptolemy's Carpelas Akra (VI, 8, 5).

5. Carmania, Kerman.

6. Indus and Ganges. See IV, 74.

106. 1. Scinde, westernmost province of India proper, bordering on Southern Baluchistan.

2. Jaqueta, now called the Rann of Cutch. The tides there astonished Alexander. There is nowhere in the Mediterranean a tide of more than eighteen inches. The Rann of Cutch was like Fundy to a Greek, a Roman, or a Portuguese.

107. 1. Comorin. See Stanza 65.

Anciently Cori (Kori), Coliaci, according to Strabo (XV, i, 11). Ptolemy calls this cape Cori (VII, 1, 11).

Ariosto (O. F., XV, 17) evidently derives the same information from the same sources.

108. 4. Burton says these writings are the Vedas and Puranas, the Zoroastrian Books, and the Koran.

5. Narsingha (Land of the Trumpet), according to Lencastre, seems to be in part what used to be called the Carnatic. Its frontiers are pretty vague, but apparently stretched across southern India so as to include the Madras Presidency. See VII, 21, note.

7. St. Thomas' martyrdom in India is a tradition that goes back as far as the 6th Century and perhaps earlier. Burton, after summing up the evidence on "the Christians of St. Thomas," quite evidently relishes the satisfactory conclusion that Christianity was more

powerful in China in the 16th Century than in the 19th, and that the same was probably true in India.

109. 1. Meliapore, now Mylapur, a suburb of Madras. There is a Portuguese shrine, erected in 1547, on Mount St. Thomas (São Tomé). Lencastre says the name means Peacock Town. But there is some confusion here. Lencastre places Pulicat, which he thinks is Meliapore to the south of Madras, whereas it is at least 25 miles to the north. Mount St. Thomas is to the south. Lencastre believes that Camões derives his information on the Martyrdom of St. Thomas from Barros (III, xxi, 1).

113. 5. The threads are a symbolic triply-woven strand worn by Brahmins. The strand stands for the Trimurti or Triad, which consists of Brahma the Creator, Vishnu the Preserver, and Siva the Destroyer. The number Three (see any handbook) is rich in significance for men of many religions. De Goes (I, 88) describes the Trimurti.

115. Lencastre, after citing Barros, who relates this miracle, goes on to state that Constantino de Braganza, while viceroy, translated the relics of St. Thomas to Goa. Braganza is supposed to have been Camões' friend, though he does not seem to have done much for him during his difficulties in 1560. Braganza assumed the government in 1558 (Lencastre), and the episode would necessarily have made a great impression at the time in Goa.

118. This stanza is a sort of parallel to the lament for Afonso I in III, 84. To the translator it is less powerful. Is it fanciful to see a resemblance between the prayer for the intercession of Thomas and Aeneas' prayer to Venus in Aeneid, X, 252–256?

120. 6. Orissa, a province in Eastern India and a powerful center of Hinduism.

8. Perhaps Claudian (De Consulatu Mallii Theodori 236–237) was in Camões' mind:

. . . . eadem clementia sani
Gurgitis immensum deducit in ostia Gangen.

122. 1. Arakan, a province on the eastern shore of the Bay of Bengal.

5. The anthropologist can provide examples of such bizarre customs from other lands. Lencastre says Barros (III, iii, 4) is the source. But Camões could have heard it from a hundred traders. The custom was meant to discourage the practices of the Cities of the Plain. Pliny (XXXIII, 54) mentions a not dissimilar custom in Rome in his time, and his Bohn editors have a note that the queer business is mentioned by Celsus (VII, 25).

123. 1. Tavai, now Tavoy, in Burma (Ford). Tenassari, now Tenasserim, appears to have been Strabo's furthest east (I, i, 8, Bohn Edition).

3. Queda is probably Penang, the Island of Areca Nuts (H. M.

Landon). Barros (I, x, 1) calls Queda "the flower of all this coast for pepper."

124. 1. The legend of a union between Sumatra and the Malay Peninsula in historic times looks particularly unwashable (Barros, I, ix, 1; III, 51, 1, quoted by Lencastre). The Romans thought such a cleft had been made between Italy and Sicily (Aeneid, III, 414–419). Strabo (I, iii, 10) thinks that Italy and Sicily were separated by a convulsion. Valerius Flaccus (Argonauticon, I, 587 ff.) and Claudian (De Raptu Proserpinae, I, 143 ff.) tell the same tale.

3. Sumatra is separated from the Malay Peninsula by the famous Strait.

4. Chersonesus, the Greek word for peninsula.

8. Ophir, the Biblical El Dorado whence Solomon derived his treasures. Milton considered that Sofala was Ophir. Josephus (Antiquities of the Jews, VIII, 6) was the first to say that Malaya was Ophir.

125. 1. Singapore, unknown to Marco Polo and Ibn Batuta, appears to have been founded about their time, 13th Century. It is big enough, about 1560, to attract Camões' attention. But when the English acquired it in 1819, there were only "a few fishermen's huts" where the great city now stands. Dampier mentions no town here except Johore on the mainland, where he traded. Singapore means the Town of the Lion.

5. Pam (Pahung) and Patan, kingdoms on the peninsula, subject to Thai (Siam).

7. No map reveals any lake called Chiamai or otherwise, which is the source of the Menam, a great river in Siam. Camões has misread his Barros (I, ix, 1), who says that the river of Pegu comes from a lake called Chiamai. Barros further states that Menam means "Mother of the Waters." Cf. Camões' etymology of the name Mekong in Stanza 127.

126. 3. As Professor Ford remarks, "the word 'lao' means men and is not ethnically distinctive." Avas and Bramas are Burmese. Burton, says that the Gueons or Karens practise a particularly nasty variety of tattooing, which involves fire.

127. 1. The Mekong, the river of Cambodia, enormous for length and volume. Cambodia is a province of French Indo-China.

2. Sir Henry Clifford (In Kambodia, I, Blackwood's Magazine, June, 1910) notes that Linschoten called the Mekong "the Captain of all the Rivers." Linschoten reached the Indies in 1583, eleven years after the publication of The Lusiads. This is another instance of Camões' odd accuracy.

5. Pomponius Mela (I, 9) might inform Camões about the Nilotic inundations.

403

6. Professor Ford believes that this is a reference to the Oriental belief in transmigration of souls. If so, Camões does not explain it well. But he did know the Pythagorean notions on the subject, as appears from Elegy III (Juromenha, III, 171).

128. This account of Camões' wreck on his way to Goa from Macão in 1560 is apparently veracious. Some have believed that he wrote one of his most famous short poems, "By the Rivers of Babylon," while he was detained in Indo-China, but as explained in the introduction this seems improbable.

129. 1. Tsiampa, otherwise Champa, Cochin-China.

2. According to Lencastre, who is quoting Ficalho, Aquilaria Agallochum, Royle Agalloch or Eaglewood in English, once supposed to be the Biblical aloes. Barros alludes to this odorous tree (I, ix, 1).

4. Hainan, an island off the southwest coast of China.

5. China, at the empire's greatest extent, actually ran from the tropic to fifty-five degrees north, which is some twelve degrees south of the Arctic Circle. Professor Ford is a little severe on this exaggeration.

130. 1. We should hardly reason that the Great Wall was a proof of power. Such defences are usually built by nations in decline.

4. The system of electing emperors in China was not at all as described by Camões. Where he got such misinformation would be interesting to know, but his statement, which is vague in the original, might be taken as applying to the Mongols and not to the Chinese (Lencastre).

131. 4. Japan was accidentally discovered by Europeans early in the fifth decade of the 16th Century, and Camões would have heard the news when he was about twenty.

7. The silver mines of Japan were exhausted long ago. But Major C. R. Boxer informs me that in the last fifty years of the 16th Century the production of silver was very large and that the Portuguese were getting the metal to the value of "a million in gold" annually from the islands. The Omori mines were the chief source, but Sado and Izu Islands were also worked. The Portuguese carried silk from China, which they exchanged for the silver. A curious by-product of the silk and silver trade was a fancy portrait of Camões, which was painted by a Japanese artist at Goa for some friends of the Poet, apparently not from life but from their description.

8. St. Francis Xavier arrived in Japan as early as 1549, four years before Camões reached India.

Burton thinks that there is a break in the narrative here, and that the prophecy of Tethys is based on two different journeys of the Poet, the last of which was to Indonesia.

132. 3. Tidore and Ternate, in the spice islands.
      4. The volcano is on Ternate.

> As when far off at sea a fleet descried
> Hangs in the clouds, by equinoctial gales
> Close sailing from Bengala or the isles
> Of Ternate or Tidore, whence merchants bring
> Their spicy drugs; they on the trading flood
> Through the wide Ethiopian to the Cape
> Ply stemming nightly toward the Pole. So seemed
> Far off the flying fiend.
>
> Paradise Lost, II, 636-643.

5. Cloves—the bud of Caryophyllus aromaticus (Lencastre). It was only second to pepper in importance in the Oriental trade.

7. The perpetual flight of the Bird of Paradise is as mythical as the song of the swan. Dr. Robert Cushman Murphy of the American Museum of Natural History observed in a note to the translator that the first specimens of Birds of Paradise which reached Europe had had their legs carefully removed by the natives who prepared the skins. "Linnaeus, who, of course, knew better, named the type-form Paradisaea apoda (footless)." It is believed that Camões visited Tidore and Ternate. If so, this is a singular departure from his usual accuracy, for he must have seen the creatures at rest. The facts may be discovered in Alfred Newton's article in the Encyclopaedia Britannica. Toynbee notes that the Bird of Paradise plumes were imported into Turkey to be the crests of the Janizaries.

Many have thought that Camões spent some time at Ternate. The evidence is ambivalent, but if he ever did reside there, a diverting contrast may be drawn. He would have been there in the latter fifties of the 16th Century. Almost exactly three centuries later Alfred Wallace studied the Bird of Paradise in the Island and during a bout of fever independently arrived at Darwin's hypothesis.

133. 1. The Banda Isles, Spice Islands, in the Moluccas.

2. The nutmeg (Myristica fragrans) is a drupe whose fleshy or membranous part turns scarlet "when the fruit splits at maturity." I owe this information to the courtesy of Professor T. Harper Goodspeed. Ficalho (Lencastre) cites Barros in this connection.

3. Burton says this bird is the nutmeg pigeon (Ducula spilorrhoa). Dr. Robert Cushman Murphy kindly identified the creature, but properly suggested that many varieties of fruit pigeon might feed on the fruit of the nutmeg tree.

4. Camphor is still a Borneo export.

405

134. 1. Timor, an island at the extreme eastern end of Indonesia. Half of it is still Portuguese at this writing.

2. Sandalum album.

3. Sunda, Java. The petrifying stream is otherwise unknown. But the phenomenon is well explained by Professor A. G. Lawson. Fossils formed in silted-up lakes are washed by the current of a stream that cuts through the silt. And thus the story arises. Oddly enough Ovid (Met., XV, 313–314) mentions a stream with similar qualities:

flumen habent Cicones, quod potum saxea reddit
viscera, quod tactis inducit marmora rebus.

Camões again alludes to this strange stream in the Redondilhas, Carta a huma Dama (Juromenha, IV, 22).

Through the courtesy of Dr. J. K. Wright of the American Geographical Society and his able colleague Dr. Anastasia Van Burkalow, I am able to report that something like the phenomenon described by Camões actually occurs in Yellowstone Park. I quote: "Microscopic study proved that silica had not merely coated the surface but had actually penetrated the structure of the wood to a depth of three or four millimeters, precipitating in the form of delicate linings inside the separate cells and ducts, and completely filling them in many cases, thus faithfully preserving all the minutiae of structure."

In Kashmir, Megasthenes learned of a river called the Silas, "in which all substances go to the bottom like stone" (Cambridge History of India, Vol. I, 404). Pliny (XXXI, 20) has a chapter on such streams. Silius Italicus (Punica, VIII, 580–581) provides another petrifying stream, this time in Italy. It was called the Silarus, now the Sele, and was known to Pliny (II, 106) and Strabo (V, iv, 13). For Dante, The Elsa petrified objects (Purgatorio, XXXIII, 67–78).

135. 1. Sumatra. The point about its former connection with the Malay Peninsula has been raised in Stanza 124, note.

2. Volcanoes.

3. Petroleum is found in Sumatra.

4. Styrax benzoin. This aromatic resin, according to Webster, takes the form of "tears," apparently the commercial term.

5. Myrrha, already described in V, 34, 7 (Balsamodendron Myrrha).

136. 1. The Crag is unquestionably Adam's Peak.

2. Perhaps Camões remembered Statius' account of Taenarum on Cape Malea (Matapan) in southern Greece, "which suffers no vision to reach its summit" (Thebais, II, 32–34). But the commonplace is all over classic literature.

3. The footprint is sacred in the sight of three religions,

Hindu, Mahometan, Buddhist (Ford). Colonel Yule (Marco Polo, III, 15) has gathered everything about the miraculous footprint.

4. Burton traces this to Barros, who talks about a submarine palm whose fruit neutralizes poison. Ficalho clears it up. Sea cocoanuts (the fruit of Lodoicea seychellarum) are carried by currents from the Seychelles Islands and washed ashore in India and Ceylon. Hence the legend of a submarine origin. The superstition that the mere presence of one of these enormous nuts in a room was a sufficient antidote against all poison is hard to account for, but was so prevalent that the heirs of a Dutch admiral in the first decade of the 17th Century refused the Emperor Rudolph II's offer of four thousand florins for their specimen (quoted by Lencastre).

137. 1. Socotra, an island at the mouth of the Red Sea.

2. Aloes, Aloe socotrina Lamarck, the most famous species of aloe (Ficalho, quoted by Lencastre).

5. Ambergris, still the most precious of the ingredients of perfumes. It is found chiefly in the Indian Ocean, and appears to be a substance secreted in the alimentary tract of dyspeptic whales. Milton mentions it in Paradise Regained, II, 344, as a condiment.

138. 6. The Lusitanian is, of course, Magellan. Magellan (1480–1521) had fought in India under Almeida and Albuquerque and had visited some of the Spice Islands. On his return he went to North Africa with King Manuel, but fell into disfavor. He thereupon offered his services to the King of Aragon and Castile and commanded the great expedition around the world, from which one ship out of the original five returned safely to Spain.

139. 2. Callisto, the Great Bear.

140. 1. Brazil, first called Terra de Santa Cruz, officially discovered by Cabral, when blown westward by a storm, on his way to India in 1500. It is odd that Camões never mentions his name among the Portuguese worthies. A Cabral commanded the ship on which the Poet sailed for India. I cannot account for the omission except by supposing that some personal prejudice was in Camões' mind.

2. Barwood, better, logwood, used in dyeing. Lencastre, quoting Ficalho, notes that a species of this wood was called brasil in Italy as early as 1193. The Brazilian species is related to the Asiatic and African trees which are used to make dye.

3. The European sailors were impressed by the tall Patagonians.

142–143. "Straight out into that fragrant night, ever-noble Jack Chase . . . pointing shoreward, cries: 'For the last time hear Camoens, boys!'" Herman Melville, White-Jacket, first edition, 462. Jack Chase, captain of the main-top of the U. S. S. "Neversink," is one of the most enthusiastic and discriminating of Camonian critics. He quotes

Camões at all times, calls him "Commodore Camoens," and sums his poem up in the fine aphorism: "The Lusiads . . . It's the man-of-war epic of the world!" (White-Jacket, 318.) Mr. Ferris Greenslet drew my attention to Melville's novel.

144. 8. The new titles were approximately those used with bitter irony by the Old Man of Belem, IV, 101, 8. Barros (I, iv, 11) has them all.

153. 1. Phormio, a philosopher whose theoretic discourse bored Hannibal extremely. Cicero relates the anecdote (De Oratore, II, XVIII, 75, as Professor Ford has noted). Hannibal said he had seen many old madmen but never one madder than Phormio.

156. 2. The giant Atlas was turned to stone when Perseus showed him Medusa's head.

3. Ampelusa, used for North Africa generally, but specifically Cape Espartel.

4. Tarudant, as late as the 19th Century, a holy city in Morocco, where no Christian could be admitted, as in Mecca, or Bokhara. See G. B. Shaw, Notes to Captain Brassbound's Conversion, in Three Plays for Puritans.

If Sonnet CCCLVI in Juromenha's Edition is by Camões, it is a singular footnote to the Lusiads. Recent editors are not sure it is. In any case it is a piece of irony of a sort dear to the cheating gods. A translation is appended.

Sonnet CCCLVI

His noble face was trenched by the sharp blade,
His royal brows were black with dust and blood,
When, to the dreary ship on Acheron's flood,
At length drew near the Great Sebastian's shade.
The hateful boatman, when perforce he prayed
To be borne over, up before him stood,
Saying: "Here none e'er made his passage good
Before his body in the earth was laid."

To him the valiant King spoke in reply,
Much angered: "False old man, is it then sure
That with gold only one may cross this wave?
And do you ask your guerdon for the grave
From a King drenched in life blood of the Moor?
Ask it of one less nobly hacked than I."

A NOTE
ON
BY THE RIVERS OF BABYLON

Camões' lyrical poetry is at least as splendid as his epic, and of many noble poems "By the Rivers of Babylon" is perhaps the noblest. The translator is not alone in this opinion. Prestage, with visible approbation, quotes Lope de Vega who called it "the pearl of all poetry." And comparisons with Milton and Dante are inevitable, however obvious. One thinks at once of "Lycidas" and the "Ode on the Morning of Christ's Nativity." And it would hardly be too much to say that the poem's intranslatable beauty suggests a "Divine Comedy" compressed into 365 lines.

Little is known about its composition. The notion that it was written when Camões was wrecked at the mouth of the Mekong is not susceptible of proof. I should think it more likely that it got on paper while he was in prison in Goa, or that at least part of it did. The protagonist in chains in Babylonian Hell would seem to be a captive in a great city rather than a shipwrecked sailor on a tropic beach. But no argument can lead to certainty in such a connection.

The poem is written in the form which the Portuguese call Redondilha, about equivalent to our word roundel. The translation preserves the rhyme-scheme of the original, which varies slightly here and there. Metre and rhythm are approximations of the Portuguese. No man wishes more than the translator that the language of his version resembled the original splendor.

The poem is, of course, an expansion of the 137th Psalm, every verse of which, with one exception, is quoted in it. That Camões left out the conclusion of the psalm has its interest. One is apt to believe that his mind and heart were revolted by the barbaric savagery of the 6th Century before Christ, but in any case such a piece of sadism would not have harmonized with the Poet's visionary ecstasy.

For such readers as may wish to make the comparison the 137th Psalm is printed here in full.

PSALM 137

1. By the rivers of Babylon, there we sat down, yea, we wept, when we remembered Zion.

2. We hanged our harps upon the willows in the midst thereof.

3. For there they that carried us away captive required of us a song; and they that wasted us required of us mirth, saying, Sing us one of the songs of Zion.

4. How shall we sing the LORD'S song in a strange land?

5. If I forget thee, O Jerusalem, let my right hand forget her cunning.

6. If I do not remember thee, let my tongue cleave to the roof of my mouth; if I prefer not Jerusalem above my chief joy.

7. Remember, O LORD, the children of Edom in the days of Jerusalem; who said, Rase it, rase it, even to the foundation thereof.

8. O daughter of Babylon, who art to be destroyed; happy shall he be, that rewardeth thee as thou hast served us.

9. Happy shall he be, that taketh and dasheth thy little ones against the stones.

BY THE RIVERS OF BABYLON

By the rivers of Babylon,
I found me.* And on that shore
I sat me down and wept sore,
Remembering all that was done
In Sion long years before.
And the river of tears flowed on,
That from my eyes was fed,
For, when all has been rightly read,
Present evil is Babylon.
Sion is time that is dead.

2

Remembrance of what is good
The soul made shift to portray,
And things that were far away
Right in my presence stood,
As before the end of their day.
And when, in tears, at last
I woke from the dream again,
And the spell which the vision had cast,
I saw that the good which was past
Had not been pleasure but pain.

* mi ritrovai per una selva oscura. Dante, Inferno, I, 2.

3

And I saw how my griefs and fears
Arose from the changes of things,
And that changes come with the years,
Whence I saw what deception appears,
Which Time to the fair hope brings.
Our trust in the bright and great
But a little space can endure.
Swift marches evil fate.
And he is in perilous state,
Who thinks his fortune is sure.

4

I saw what men most praise
First comprehended well
When harsh disaster befell.
After good came the evil days.
And a worse thing was yet to tell.
And I saw with what travail vast
I bought repentance, but there
Fortune could never turn fair.
And I see how I sow broadcast
Poor words in the empty air.

5

On this page the sad tears rain,
That into a stream have grown.
And how cruelly have I known
Every condition of pain,
And confusion in Babylon!
As for great memorial
Of labor heavy and sore,
Some man at the end of his war
Hangs on the temple wall
The weapons that once he bore;

6

Even so do I decree,
Since Time all waste has laid,
And high on the willow tree,
Because of this agony,
I have hanged the harp I played.
The harp that pleased my mood
I left with my years forespent.
Sweet music excellent,
I leave you here in the wood
For a sacred monument.

7

My flute, whenever I played,*
Great mountains you could force
To come where you delayed.
And river and cascade
Turned back upon their course,
No tiger his wrath will curb
When he hears that melody strong,
And the sheep that feed in a throng
Will not leave uncropped the herb
Only to hear that song.

8

You will change the thorn no more
To the rose's gentler guise
On the flowering river shore,
Or turn back torrents that pour,
Or dry the tears in my eyes.
The forest you cannot lure
Your pathway to pursue,
Or compel the well-spring pure,
Since you cannot change or undo
Fate's sharp discomfiture.

* Virgil, Georgics, IV, 507 ff.

9

My well-belovèd flute,*
To Fame I offer you,
Whose watch is absolute.
All things in life transmute,
And love for them alters too.
Youth and innocence find
Pleasure commensurate,
And then the older mind
As trifles will estimate
The joys it has left behind.

10

Pleasure today that rose
Tomorrow will see retire,
So change of our lives must dispose.
After hope new hope grows,
And after desire, desire.
But what hope is so strong as to stay
In life as niggard as this?
Weakness in man it is,
Who, as life passes away,
Must sing death's litanies.

11

But now, where these thickets weave,
Farewell youth's rhythm and rhyme.
Nor let the future believe
It will be the work of Time,
Which only Fate can achieve.
Age, Time, and the terror strong
Of seeing how swift they remove
Never could do me such wrong
That, though I give up the song,
I give up the cause thereof.

* Hic arguta sacro pendebit fistula pinu. Virgil, Eclogue VII, 24.

But in grief and sad surmise,
Or in contentment high,
Sun, snow, or windy sky,
I shall have her before mine eyes,*
For whose sake I desire to die.
The harp and the flute also,
Though they were dear to me,
I left where the willows grow,
Trophies hung there to show
What power has conquered me.

13

But how the memories spring
Of passion that captured me there,
Pleading and questioning:
Where is my music, where,
That in Sion I used to sing?
What of the noble air
That won the people's praise?
That song no longer I raise,
Though it helped a man to bear
Hard labor in bygone days.

14

Blithe travellers, chanting clear.†
On the hard highway tread,
Though the wood looms thick and drear.
And they sing in the night for dread,
For singing can conquer fear.
Cheerly, despite the chain,
The voices of prisoners ring.
Gay reapers lift their strain,
And laborers, as they sing,
Make less their toil and their pain.

* This line and the next are from Boscan, as the commentators notice. Camões
wove them into his poem in the original Spanish.
† Virgil, Eclogue X, 63-65.

15

I, who these things have known
In the spirit choked with despair,
Reply: Who is lost to his own
Dear life, how shall he intone
In an alien land the sweet air?
What music can possess
When his breast is wet from his grief?
For, although when labors oppress,
Song conquers weariness,
I can reject relief.

16

For it were not an honest thing,
Or well and wisely done,
If, to draw this agony's sting,
I sang in Babylon
What in Sion I once could sing.
For, when the terrible weight
Of my sadness shatters these strong
Forces that animate,
Better die desolate
Than quench desolation with song.

17

If thought's nobility
In grief hath foundation sure,
I shall fear no agony.
If I die of sadness pure
What greater joy could be?
My flute shall utter no strain
For sorrow I bore and bear.
Still less will I write it plain,
For my pen would grow weary there,
And I never shall rest again.

18

If life, so brief and so small,
In this strange land long shall last,
And if love shall order all,
Then for weakness the pen must fall,
That writes of a grief so vast.
Though the pen that sought to indite
Sorrow the sad heart bore
Should be too weary to write,
Memory tires not of flight
But homes to Sion once more.

19

Land of desire, I pray,
If some spiritual stress
From my heart should take you away,
May my pen be given that day
To endless forgetfulness.
And this pain of exile long,
Which I would see etched clear
On rock or on iron strong,
May no man ever hear.
So may be punished that wrong.

20

If I sing thy harmony,
In Babylon, oppressed,
Nor, Jerusalem, look on Thee,
Why then may my voice be
Frozen within my breast.
Let my tongue cleave, say I,
To the roof of my mouth, when to me
Thou art lost, if presently
A time comes when I deny
Nor keep remembrance of Thee.

417

21

O glorious Land of Light,
If I saw not your essence plain,
How remember the absent again?
You blot me from memory quite,
Though at best some trace may remain.
For the soul is a page all clean,
Whereon great doctrine penned
Helps her to apprehend,
Who, leaving the common scene,
To Holy Land can ascend.

22

There sadness of the lands,
Whence the flesh came, comes not nigh
For that land belongs to the Sky
Where the Holy City stands,
And the soul came down from on high.
Think not of the human face
That once could trouble me sore.
That I need seek no more,
But rather that radiant grace
Which alone I ought to adore.

23

For the eyes with their radiance fine,
That kindle and conquer my soul.
Are not sun or candle-shine
But the shadow of thought divine,
Which in God is perfect and whole.
And the eyes which have made me their prey
Are but fancies passionate,
Men's hearts which subjugate,
Sophists, who taught me to stray
Into crooked paths from the straight.

24

Their tyrannous powers constrain
And the frenzied spirit incline
To sing, though I cry for pain.
Songs of the love profane,
Not songs of the love divine.
But bathed in the sacred light
In this land of sorrow abhorred
And confusion and fear and despite,
What psalm can I sing aright
That should only be sung to the Lord?

25

So high can mercy exalt,
Which brings salvation apace
And change with change can replace,
That what I took for a fault
Became my stairway to grace.
For natural love in the mind,
Which men so yearn to possess,
From the shadow the truth divined,
And in special loveliness
Found out the eternal kind.

26

This flute hang up and resign,
Whence I made melody.
O Jerusalem divine,
Let the golden lyre be mine,
That only shall sound for Thee.
Not chained in captivity,
In the Hell of Babel I stand,
But from my sin set free
And lifted up hence to Thee,
To my own native land.

27

If this neck I ever submit
To things of this world again,
Hard, urgent, tyrannous, then,
My name, erase Thou it
From the book of living men.
Rather this hand shall try
The blest lyre fit to prolong
Other invention high.
Let the time of confusion go by
And the vision of peace be the song.

28

Let the shepherd hear and the king,
And the echo divine rebound.
Let wonder the world astound.
Not the evil I wont to sing
But my palinode shall sound.
Captain and Lord in thy power,
I would come only to Thee.
For surely it cannot be
That I should climb Sion's tower
If thou reach not thy hand to me.

29

In the last and strangest of days,
When on the lyre I rehearse
Nobly Jerusalem's praise,
Forget not to chasten the ways
Of the children of Edom perverse.
All those abroad that go,
On whom blood of the innocent cries,
Whose pride is but empty show,
Do thou root them out likewise.
That they are but men, let them know.

And the strength tyrannical
Of my passions, consuming whole
Both my genius and soul,
Which already have broken the wall
Of the Will which is in my control;
Lusts that come shouting loud
To storm me, so fierce have they grown,
The damned and demoniac crowd,
Who would drive me with insolence proud
From my sure foundation stone;

31

Uproot them, and let them remain
Feeble, unfit for war.
This, alone, we cannot attain,
Nor, with them, find Thee again,
Nor, without Thee, 'scape from them more.
For infirmity supine
Never could hold the fort,
If Thou, great Captain Divine,
Into this fastness of mine
Lead not some strong support.

32

Thou daughter of Babel abhorred,
Vile flesh who canst work such charms,
Full of uncountable harms,
Who against thy King and thy Lord
So often hast taken up arms,
A blessed man shall he be,
With heavenly comfort strong,
Who shall prevail against thee,
And who shall presently
Avenge upon thee his wrong;

Who himself smites o'er and o'er,
To cruel discipline used,
Whose spirit that sins no more
Bruises his own flesh sore
That the spirit aforetime bruised.
And blessed is he who shall quell
His fugitive thoughts within
And stifle them ere they begin,
That they may not come to dwell
With error and deadly sin;

34

Who can conquer them utterly,
Undone and overthrown,
On that rock's wild sanctity,
That Rock which has come to be
The head and the corner-stone;
Who, when lust of the flesh malign
In his fancy has prevailed,
His wayward thought can incline
To look on the Flesh Divine
That once on the cross was nailed.

35

The luxury vile and high
Of the world that stands in our sight,
As far as lies in his might,
He shall wholly deny and put by
For the world of living light.
All content shall he find,
Made perfect and full of clear
Music of sweetest kind.
Nor for any want shall he fear,
And excess shall not sicken his mind.

36

To him in the High Place
Great mystery shall be shown,
For when nature is overthrown
This world's most delicate grace
For lowly and gross is known.
And Thou, my Paradise,
Dear Country beyond compare,
If to dream of Thee be so fair
That the spirit seeks the skies,
What then, when I find me there?

Envoy

What noble fortune has he
Who goes to Thee, Land of the Blest,
Justified and confessed,
And when he has risen to Thee
May take his eternal rest.

CAMÕES AND THE HISTORY OF PORTUGAL

The history of Portugal plays such a part in the Lusiads that the skeleton of a sketch seems not inappropriate. What I have tried to do is to illustrate the epic with a few relevant facts and remarks based on what is now believed. Naturally, a mere layman, I have ravaged encyclopedias. But my chief reliance has been Dr. H. V. Livermore's noble book, A History of Portugal (Cambridge University Press, 1947), from whose fascinating pages I have drawn and abridged what I thought might throw light on Camões' narrative. My obligation to this work cannot be overstressed. I am grateful to Dr. Livermore for permission to pillage. But he is not responsible for any wrong I may have done history.

It must not be forgotten that Portugal is a very small country with an area about four-fifths that of the State of New York, and a population of 7,200,000, which is probably seven times larger than when she held Brazil, a great deal of Africa, a lot of India, and most of Indonesia. The land is mountainous, with few peaks over 6,000 feet, but there are fertile plains intersected by famous and beautiful rivers, the Minho, the Douro, the Mondego, the Tagus, and the Guadiana. Save for the Mondego, all these rise in Spain, a point of some importance with respect to an incredible number of wars. The climate is mild enough for the vine and the olive.

About 200 B. C. the Romans brought Portugal into history, under the name Lusitania, which is derived from a tribe, one of several they found when they entered the region. These people proved hard to subdue. But in spite of the heroism of Viriathus, who beat the invaders in many battles over a period of ten years, and whom the Romans shamefully assassinated in 139 B. C., the country in due course was brought under the rod. A lifetime after Viriathus, Sertorius, a Roman general with a touch of Caesar in him, led a revolt in Lusitania against the dictator Sulla and set up a republic at Evora. He was so able that he too had to be assassinated in 72 B. C. Camões speaks of these heroes with enthusiasm, but has little to say of the Roman period in Portugal, as is natural. The region was absorbed by degrees into the provincial system. Christianity lifted its head, apparently, about 200 A. D., and there were saints, martyrdoms, and heresies which may profitably be ignored.

Before the official fall of the Western Empire the whole Peninsula was taken over by Barbarians. And Swabian kings ruled part of Lusitania from

410 A. D. to 585. It was in their time that a town then called Portucale, on the site of Oporto, began to lend its name to adjoining regions. Camões knows that "the eternal name" of his country originated at Oporto, whether or no he ever heard of Swabians. He had some knowledge of their conquerors, the Visigoths, who now ruled the whole of Iberia, and whose empire was disturbed by dynastic and religious turmoil, till Islam crossed over from Africa in 711 and swamped the Peninsula except for a few centers of resistance in the North. Camões alludes to the legendary Julian who betrayed Spain to the Moors.

Little is known of Portugal in those times. But what is called the Reconquest began in the Asturias only a few years after the fall of the Visigoths. And it extended swiftly to Northern Portugal, where Spanish kinglets and local resistance against the pervasive Moors gnawed at the fringes of the country between the Minho and the Douro. A sort of climax was reached when Ferdinand the Great of Castile, whom Camões barely mentions, captured Coimbra in 1064 after many campaigns, and the nucleus of the future Kingdom may be said to have formed.

Ferdinand's successor, Alfonso VI of Castile, gave the reconquered territory as a fief to some noble French adventurers, who had aided him against the Moors, in 1087. And about 1095, Henry of Burgundy, a member of the French family, and not a Hungarian as Camões calls him ("though admitting that Henry might be a Lorrainer"), seems to be ruling the "County of Portugal." Henry, certainly, not the obscure soldier that Camões represents him to have been, married the King's bastard daughter, Teresa, at which point Camões launches into his narrative. The Count governed the embryo kingdom till 1112. No abbreviation can possibly give a succinct account of his wars and dynastic ambitions with respect to Leon and Castile. But Teresa and he wanted something more than a "county." And if Teresa made war against her sister, it is not surprising that in due course her son made war on her.

It is not certain when Henry's son Afonso Henriques was born, but he was still a child when Henry died. And his mother and her lover Fernando Peres ruled the County, apparently badly, during his minority and perhaps longer. They quarreled most of the time, with neighboring powers. If their rule was usurpation, as Camões implies, Afonso Henriques ended that in 1128, when he defeated his mother in battle near Guimarães. She and Peres vanish. But Camões' story that he put Teresa in chains, like the story of the self-sacrifice of Egas Moniz, seems legendary. In fact, the legendary is endemic, yet here and there the actual looks timidly out. In 1139 Afonso Henriques won some sort of victory at "Ourique," probably near Santarem, and took the title of king. Devastating as Camões represents this triumph to have been, it does not seem to have troubled the Moors a great deal. But thenceforward Afonso warred perpetually to enlarge his "kingdom" at the expense of Moor or Christian impartially. In 1147 he fought his way into Santarem on the Tagus, and in the same year took Lisbon from the Moors with the help of a crusading fleet. Camões sticks very closely to his chronicles in the account of the conquest. The advance was tremendous and permanent. But Afonso's success continued, and at one time he, or such commanders as Gerald-without-fear, dominated a region as large as modern Portugal, though they did not get to the sea in the South. However, good luck forsook him in 1169 when he was defeated and captured at Badajoz by his son-in-law, Ferdinand II of Leon. And the Poet makes his elaborate comparison between Pompey and Afonso I. Camões does not mention the Moorish squabbles which had helped Afonso on his way. But he notices the Almohad invasion from Morocco in particular the last (1184), when the Miramoline died and the King and his son had at least the appearance of victory. The reaction was so fierce that Afonso, in spite of his son's raids into Andalusia, was really on the defensive all through his later years, except for a truce, during which the King translated the relics of St. Vincent from the Cape to Lisbon. Cape St. Vincent was still in Moorish control. Camões touches most of these points, with some pardonable exaggeration perhaps, nor is he in the wrong to dwell on what must have been greatness. In a reign of fifty-seven years the King had won his crown (acknowledged by the Pope, at least, in 1178) and doubled the size of his inheritance. Of course Camões does not note that the Portuguese Church became independent of any Spanish See in Afonso's time, or that the Templars, important throughout the Reconquest, were established, or that, best of all, the royal charters to towns and districts began to eliminate serfdom. And it would be too much to expect that he should report Afonso I's relation with the Papacy as a feudatory of the Church. But Camões pays him the noblest of compliments, when he quotes the pretty proverb that in Portugal the echoes still cry: "Afonso! Afonso!" however vainly. The great King was more than a soldier.

Afonso I's son and successor, Sancho I, though able and energetic, was hardly the battler Camões makes him out to be. As Camões says, he took Silves in the extreme South with the help of another crusading fleet. But it was soon lost. And his wars against his Christian neighbors, of which Camões speaks, were not spectacularly successful, in spite of the Poet. Some of the military orders came in under Sancho I, but his true glory appears to be best expressed by his nickname, the Town-maker. Camões, in the nature of things, knows nothing about Sancho I's difficulties with the Church, whose claims to temporalities and privileges he resisted with pertinacity, though he had to knuckle under on his deathbed in 1211.

His son, Afonso II, the Fat, was apparently sickly at all times, but a man of resolution, who, like his father, opposed the pretensions of the Church with heroic persistence. His military campaigns, though it appears he could not take personal part in them, were not unsuccessful. Camões mentions the permanent capture of Alcacer do Sal, which had been won and lost. It was a step forward in the Reconquest. But why Camões ignores the great fight at Las Navas de Tolosa in 1212, where Afonso II's Portuguese contingent played a brilliant part, is not clear to me. The momentarily united Christians of the Peninsula really turned the corner in the seven-century war against the Moors, and Camões is silent. Be that as it may, Afonso II fought the Church to the bitter end, and, though about to be reconciled, died under an excommunication, probably quite as painful to a man of his time as the leprosy which killed him in 1223.

Camões is curiously unjust to his son and successor, Sancho II, called the Cowl because of the monk's hood he wore in the field. This reign is said to be uncommonly murky from the historian's standpoint, but it has been clearly demonstrated that Sancho II was a valiant soldier, the victim of clerical and baronial propaganda, and not at all the tool and wastrel described by the Poet. By the time his brother, the Count of Boulogne, in ignoble conspiracy with the Church, succeeded in deposing him in 1245, Sancho had practically completed the Reconquest and given Portugal approximately her present frontiers. Afonso, the treacherous brother, wrote the Church a blank cheque, took the reins when Sancho fell, and succeeded to the throne when the brave and unfortunate King died in 1248.

For a man capable of such an act, Afonso III did uncommonly well. Camões, as the commentators notice, mistakenly calls him the Brave, an epithet which belongs to his savage grandson, Afonso IV. But the new king perhaps deserved it. He put the final touches on the Reconquest, for which Camões possibly gives him too much credit. And almost at once he began to break the promises he had made the Church in order to dethrone his brother. If he was to do this, he had to have popular support. And the Cortes held at Leiria in 1254, where the towns were first represented, was a first-rate device to obtain it. His resistance to the bishops, circuitous, ingenious, and dragged out for years, is regarded as a turning-point in the struggle with the Church, even if the King, pro forma, repented on his deathbed. Quite as important, serfdom was waning fast in his time. Nor is it without interest that his court was highly cultivated and that he had his son magnificently educated. Camões talks of his wars, but not of these things, any more than of a subject no poet is apt to mention—a debased currency which was to become a nightmare.

Afonso III's son, Denis the Ploughhand, so-called, it is said, because of his interest in agriculture, succeeded in 1279, and is perhaps the most attractive of Portuguese kings. A poet of parts, a soldier, a diplomat, the founder of the University of Coimbra, interested in everything, he is all Camões says of him and more. His reign was not a golden age of peace, as implied by the Poet, for he had plenty of civil wars, but he was powerful as well as charming. Naturally, Camões does not go into his capacity to outmaneuver Popes or his suppression, or rather absorption, of the Templars, without the brutality then fashionable against the hapless order. Nor does he allude to the Queen, St. Isabel, whose forte was peace-making. But Camões might well have mentioned the pine forest which Denis, who was building up his navy, planted at Leiria, from whose timber Henry the Navigator is said to have built ships four generations later. A bit of proverbial doggerel, which perhaps reflects his multifariousness, may be thus translated:

> King Denis who still
> Did all he might will.

In 1325 his son Afonso IV, the Brave, came to the throne. He had revolted several times against his brilliant father toward the end of his reign, as Camões hints obliquely. A good soldier, and perhaps not much more, he was certainly cruel. Naturally he became embroiled at length with Castile, whose King Afonso XI had married Afonso IV's daughter Maria and treated her badly, which, as Burton noticed, Camões does not mention. The inconclusive war ended in 1340. And in that same year Afonso IV went to the aid of his imperfect son-in-law against the allied Moors of Morocco and Granada. Perhaps the much-wronged Maria may have pleaded her husband's cause with her father as the Poet says she did. At any rate, the great battle of the Salado near Tarifa was a complete success for the Christian allies, though hardly so huge as Camões represents. But the victory was a big nail in the coffin of waning Moorish power.

The tragedy of Ignes de Castro was played to the end, some fifteen years after the Salado. Ignes de Castro came of a noble Galician family and had been lady-in-waiting to the Princess Costanza, the wife of Pedro the heir apparent. The Prince's infatuation for Ignes was a source of anxiety, for her two brothers were powerful borderers who aimed at thrones. She bore the Prince four children, and it was feared that her influence might be dangerous. In any case, after Costanza's death she was an obstacle in the way of any second royal marriage. National prejudice came into play. And the Chief Justice Alvaro Gonçalves, Diogo Lopes Pacheco, and Pedro Coelho conspired against the Prince's mistress (or wife?). Camões is certainly following the chronicler (quoted by Livermore), who says the King shrank from doing what he had determined, but was finally persuaded. The wretches killed her with their own hands—as nasty a business as history records. Pedro, naturally, revolted against a father who had not acted like the son of a saint, but peace was made somehow. And, unbelievably, the Prince swore assent to "a general pardon."

Pedro the Doer of Justice succeeded in 1357 and by 1360 was in a position to break his promise when he got two of the murderers into his clutches, by treaty with Pedro the Cruel of Castile. They were tortured to death with a barbarity as great as their own. The story goes that Pedro exhumed the corpse of Ignes and that there was an actual coronation. Camões' thumbnail sketch of Pedro fits the facts, some of which are entertaining. The King appears to have been able. But his passion for sadistic punishment, which he loved to inflict himself, combined with other personal oddities, leads this abridger to believe that he was no saner than the rest of us. Yet Portugal throve under that powerful eccentric, and he left his heir a huge treasure when he died in 1367.

Pedro's successor was Fernando the Fair, his son by the Princess Costanza. The new ruler was the last and most incompetent of the Burgundian line. He failed conspicuously at everything, war, diplomacy, finance. Camões lays his troubles to his union with Leonor Teles, one of the most hateful women in history, whom the King took from her husband, in spite of the rage of Lisbon and in spite of the fact that he had promised to marry a Castilian princess, which last led to war. The Queen's acts are hardly credible. Thus, she persuaded one of the sons of Ignes de Castro to murder his wife, actually her sister. She thought the girl was too near the throne and promised Castro the hand of her daughter, the Infanta Beatriz, as the price of blood. That Camões overlooks this ghastly sequel to the story of Ignes seems curious. Leonor further played the King false with her lover the Count of Ourem, and Camões repeats the scandal about the birth of Beatriz, which, however, may be false. But Leonor cannot bear the whole burden of Fernando's folly. He lost a great part of his fortune by breaking his word, a habit of his. He provoked the footless wars against Henry of Trastamara, the King of Castile, who was too much for him. And toward the end of his reign (persuaded by Leonor and Ourem) he lent himself to what was worse. If he had meant to sell Portugal to Castile, he could have found no better way. Beatriz was married to John I of Castile under conditions that meant subjugation. And John of Castile backed his Queen's claim at once when Fernando died in 1383.

Two remarkable men, still in their twenties, headed the resistance which broke out savagely. They were John, Master of the Knights of Avis, a bastard son of King Pedro (the enemy of adultery, according to Camões), and Nuno Alvares Pereira, an heroic soldier. John was thoughtful, and Nuno was impetuous. But it was John who started the avalanche going by killing Ourem with his own hands, though apparently not in the Queen's presence as Camões says. Leonor Teles fled. And the Lisbon mob murdered as many of the Castilian faction as possible. John of Castile besieged the city but had to draw off because of an epidemic, besides which he suffered two slight defeats. And the patriotic party profited by his retreat. Camões does not waste time on the first Castilian invasion, but goes straight to the

Cortes of Coimbra, where the friends of the Master of Avis, after a good deal of skullduggery (which was not to Camões' purpose), outmaneuvered the adherents of Beatriz and the Castro family, whose claims were not worse than the young patriot's. John of Avis was chosen king by the Cortes, which made him into something like a constitutional ruler. And the Constable of the Kingdom was Nuno Alvares Pereira, a very good one. They were none too soon, for John of Castile was back again. Camões does not tell us that Nuno literally bullyragged John into fighting at long odds. But fight he did, and at Aljubarrota, about sixty miles north of Lisbon, on August 14th, 1385, the war was really decided in a day. A force of 8,000, who used a few crossbowmen and English archers cleverly, totally defeated nearly four times their number. Camões mentions the storm of shot but not its provenience. It is hard to see how the two heroes who saved Portugal could have done better. They really represented the People's will. And John I, and his sons after him, henceforth governed with the aid of the Cortes.

In 1386 John I gave new force to the English alliance, which had been initiated thirteen years earlier by Fernando in a lucid interval. It continues to this day and, except during Portugal's subjection to Spain (1580–1640), has been troublesome to several Great Powers. John sealed the alliance by marrying Philippa, the daughter of John of Gaunt, and a little later her half-sister married Henry the Infante of Castile. An uneasy peace between Portugal and Castile came in sight and finally became a reality. Camões does not mention the alliance, but he does notice the English marriages and the peace.

In spite of Camões' odd remark that John I was not granted to Portugal for long, he reigned forty-eight years, and they were not all good ones. The problems of inflation in "a time of troubles" seem to have been too much for a hero. And his ideas about conquering Northwest Africa obsessed succeeding kings and resulted in tremendous disaster two centuries later. Henry the Navigator, one of John's wonderful five legitimate sons, was in the easy storm of Ceuta in 1415, the year that his first cousin, Henry V, won Agincourt. John may not have coined the precept "Fear to misrule!" but the five lived up to it. Their bastard half-brother, Afonso, who married a daughter of the "Holy Constable," the great Pereira, it would seem, did not. And the greedy ambition of the House of Braganza (Camões ignores the family in the Lusiads) which sprang from that union, was a thorn in the flesh of Portugal for most of the 15th Century. Nevertheless, the unified Kingdom looked as if no Nemesis were near when the great King died in 1433, it is said, on the very day of Aljubarrota.

Henry the Navigator, sometime after the storm of Ceuta, began to interest himself in the development of the Atlantic islands and the coast of Africa, whether or no he envisaged India. And his enterprise, which, for duration, difficulty, and unpredictable results, may be compared with the sixty-year scientific effort which split the atom, fired Portuguese imagination, and in due course made an empire. Camões, though brief on the Prince, seems fully to recognize greatness which had its part in forming a poem more enduring than dominion. But while Henry labored things began to go badly in Portugal. Duarte (Edward, out of compliment to the English connection), who succeeded John I, was a cultivated and high-minded king, but his brilliance did not help him much. He sent out a new African expedition, which came to grief when his brother Ferdinand, called the Constant, was cut off and captured by the Moors near Tangier in 1437. Duarte refused to give up Ceuta for his brother, who was to die a prisoner, a bad decision, for Ceuta cost too much to hold. Duarte died the next year, and the troubles of a regency were at once apparent. The competitors for control of the little King, Afonso V, later called the African, were the Queen-mother, Pedro, oldest surviving son of John I, and the House of Braganza. Though Camões does mention Pedro's knight errantry in Germany, he doesn't notice Pedro's tragedy. Pedro, as noble a figure as Henry the Navigator, and a firm believer in constitutional government, became regent, but the Braganza faction gradually undermined him and finally, with the help of the young King, did a great man to death in 1449 at Alfarrobeira. Pedro had brought out the code of laws that goes by Afonso's name, but, except for the Navigator's operations, it was almost the only good thing in a reign full of miserable intrigues and almost as pointless as Fernando's. The King's three African expeditions, a pageant of victory for Camões, probably did little more than commit Portugal too deeply to a bad gamble. And his bid for the throne of Castile got a bloody check at Toro in 1476, where he was beaten by Ferdinand of Aragon. There was something ludicrous in his failure to make Louis XI of France and Charles the Bold of Burgundy his allies, and one is not surprised that his remarkable son became co-king in a Portugal of which the Braganzas are said at this time to have controlled almost a third.

Afonso V died in 1481, and John II, the Perfect, ruled in his stead. He was the right man to set a country on its feet, resolute, ruthless, intelligent, and subtle, and his tendency was toward absolutism. He did not like the internal situation, and he dealt with the Braganzas, who had milked his father dry. He had the Duke, the head of the family, beheaded in 1484 on a charge of conspiring with Castile. And he killed his own cousin, the Duke of Viseu, with his own hand because of untactful opposition. Camões, of course, does not go into these episodes or into such matters as the King's not too humane dealings with the Jews exiled by Ferdinand and Isabella after the fall of Granada in 1492. But Camões, without naming the men, tells at some length of the strange journeys of Covilham and Paiva, whom John sent out to discover the Orient by way of Egypt. And Covilham reached Calicut eleven years before Gama. He also got to

Sofala on the southern shore of East Africa and penetrated Abyssinia. And his letters are supposed to have reached John at the moment when Dias' discovery of the Cape was reported to the King. John did things with terrific thoroughness, whether murder or spying out new lands. He had other ideas too, for in 1494 his insistence on shifting westward Alexander VI's line of demarcation between Portuguese and Spanish discovery, added Brazil to the Portuguese Empire, after the remarkable King was dead. Some have thought he knew about the continent before Columbus sighted it. No stronger king ever ruled in Portugal, which he governed with stern ability. And though by this time such a voyage as Gama's was a logical necessity, the glory of initiating it belongs to John the Perfect. He died in 1495 without legitimate issue.

Manuel the Fortunate, his successor, was a son of Afonso V's younger brother, and brother to that Duke of Viseu whom John had slain ten years before. He was to reap the harvest and clearly knew it. He went on with the work of discovery, which came to a head when Vasco da Gama, a son of the officer John had picked, took the specially designed ships out of the Tagus on July 8, 1497. Camões gives Manuel most of the credit for what John had planned. Gama returned triumphant with a cargo of spice in September, 1499, and Manuel called himself Lord of the Conquest and Trade of Abyssinia, Arabia, Persia, and India. The phrase is bitterly ironic when Camões makes the Old Man of Belem utter it. But there was some point in the titles, for the King was the residuary legatee of Cairo, Alexandria, and Venice, whose monopoly of the spice trade was destroyed in ten years.

Manuel was active, if not so able as John II. He persisted in the Morocco business. And Brazil fell to the Empire (1500), as Camões notices. But really immense efforts were made in the East, where a succession of superlative chiefs did miracles. Cabral, Pacheco, Almeida, the great Albuquerque, and their numerous peers put Manuel's Empire together from the Cape of Good Hope to New Guinea, and northward to the Persian Gulf. But in general only coast-lines and islands were really held. Camões sings his paean on all of them, and not unjustly. Albuquerque seized Goa, which became the capital of the Portuguese Orient, in 1510. And his capture of Malacca in 1511 was a first-rate strategic move, for the town controlled the whole spice trade and was the jumping-off place for all Indonesia. His failure before Aden, which defeated the great plan of taking Mecca, may perhaps be laid at the King's door. At any rate, Manuel sent out Albuquerque's incompetent personal enemy Soares to supplant the greatest of Portuguese proconsuls, on whose severity Camões is uncommonly severe. Few kings have been better served, but, though Camões may exaggerate, gratitude does not seem to have been the King's strong point. Possibly he deserved to lose the services of Magellan.

Manuel is an ambivalent figure, inordinately successful, queerly unat-

433

tractive. He naturally was aiming at absolutism. And he was rigorous on occasion. Thus, he put down with savage severity some fearful anti-Semitic riots in Lisbon, of no interest to Camões. Few have acquired such vast possessions so swiftly, but the epithet Fortunate does not imply that he was an Alexander. Busy and stirring though he was, any Portuguese may well regret that John II did not live long enough to organize the new Empire.

Manuel's son, John III, the Peaceable, in 1521 succeeded to an emormous dominion whose roots, from the first, had been gnawed by the law of diminishing returns. And he was not the man to restore a declining business. He seems to have been a kindly, unintelligent bigot, who thought royal marriages would restore a damaged economy. But his sister's union with the Emperor Charles V and his own with the Emperor's sister did not have the desired effect. And the first marriage had a sinister result for Portugal in the shape of Philip II of Spain.

Valiant viceroys in the Orient maintained and even enlarged the Empire, while John brought in the Jesuits and the Inquisition at home. Energy had seeped away, and Camões is uncomfortably aware of national decay, which he mentions bitterly from time to time. One believes him. All through the sleepy reign things were building up for a storm. And the distant and occasionally spectacular conquests in the East, which Camões recounts with considerable accuracy, did not propitiate Nemesis.

The history which Camões relates properly closes in 1548 with the heroisms of João de Castro in India, though Camões mentions a few episodes after that date. But we must go a little further. Prince John, the son of John III, was an invalid and died in 1554, before his father. His wife was pregnant and bore a posthumous son, Dom Sebastião, who at the age of three succeeded John III in 1577. If the child had been still-born, Portugal would have been saved disaster and sixty years of slavery, for the boy was no new John of Avis. On the contrary he grew up through the long years of the regency into a strange, difficult, stupid young man, who was a religious fanatic and hopelessly ambitious of military renown. One might easily think him subnormal, and personal courage seems to have been his one virtue. He suffered from obscure diseases, perhaps could not beget children, and had a macabre taste for looking on the corpses of his predecessors, whose tombs he opened for the purpose. Flatterers, lay or ecclesiastic, led him by the nose. In short, he had quite enough incapacity to pull down Portugal. And the Morocco adventure begun by John of Avis was to reach a catastrophic conclusion under Dom Sebastião.

He went forth to conquer Morocco against the advice of the Duke of Alva who, urged by Philip II of Spain, tried to head off a desperate undertaking. The young King was now twenty-four and did not heed the words of the first soldier in Europe, or even the Pope's protest. And the folly which undertook the enterprise could only be equalled by the folly which conducted it. On August 4th, 1578, at Alcasar-Kebir about fifty miles south of Tangier, the greatness of Portugal was snuffed out in a few hours. Dom Sebastião was evidently bewildered at the first onset and showed symptoms of buck fever, but not of cowardice. The holocaust is often called the Battle of the Three Kings, because the Emperor of Morocco fell dead of heart failure as the carnage began, the pretender to his throne, on whose imaginary local support Dom Sebastião had vainly reckoned, was drowned in a wadi, and the King, who was incapable of being a general, at least died fighting. His whole army of 16,000 men was killed or captured. And his own death meant subjection to Spain, at whatever early hour the Cardinal Henry, the old man who succeeded Dom Sebastião, came to die. Catastrophe was never more complete.

Strangely enough the wrong-headed young creature became the hero of a cult. It was rumored that he was not dead, and several impostors made their appearance. In due course, rumor grew to legend. He is sleeping like Barbarossa, but will wake. To this day in rural Brazil, it is said, police officers are troubled when a bout of "Sebastianism" breaks out in a district. Men have never looked for the second coming of a more unpromising redeemer.

The prologue to the Lusiads is addressed to Dom Sebastião and so is the epilogue. The confident prophecies of conquest must have sickened the heart of the Great Poet, when the news of Alcasar-Kebir was shrieked down the streets of Lisbon. A sonnet on the disaster, to me impressive, may not be by Camões. If it is by him, then neither history nor poetry can provide an example of more poignant natural irony.

Nothing is claimed for this slight sketch, least of all originality. It could not, naturally, touch much except high points and has missed many of them. The rise of the Kingdom, the struggle with the Church, the Cortes slowly gaining strength from the time of Afonso III, and then losing it as the kings grew more absolute, the establishment of an empire are hard things to get on a thumbnail. But if this paper throws a little light on the Lusiads for those who have not dipped into Portuguese history, the purpose of this résumé will have been achieved.